Counseling and Psychotherapy of
WORK DYSFUNCTIONS

Also by the Author

The Clinical Practice of Career Assessment: Interests, Abilities, and Personality

Pre-Employment Screening for Psychopathology: A Guide to Professional Practice

Casebook on Ethics and Standards for the Practice of Psychology in Organizations (Ed.)

Counseling and Psychotherapy of
WORK DYSFUNCTIONS

Rodney L. Lowman

AMERICAN PSYCHOLOGICAL ASSOCIATION, WASHINGTON, DC

First printing July 1993
Second printing August 1994

Published by
American Psychological Association
750 First Street, NE
Washington, DC 20002

In the United States, copies may be ordered from
APA Order Department
P.O. Box 2710
Hyattsville, MD 20784

In the U.K. and Europe, copies may be ordered from
American Psychological Association
3 Henrietta Street
Covent Garden
London WC2E 8LU
England

Typeset in Palatino by Impressions, A Division of Edwards Brother, Inc., Madison, WI.

Printer: Braun-Brumfield, Inc., Ann Arbor, MI
Cover designer: Minker Design, Bethesda, MD
Illustrator: Margaret Scott, Washington, DC
Technical/production editor: Cynthia L. Fulton

Library of Congress Cataloging-in-Publication Data

Lowman, Rodney L.
    Counseling and psychotherapy of work dysfunctions /
    Rodney L. Lowman.
        p. cm.
    Includes bibliographical references and index.
    ISBN 1-55798-204-X (cloth : acid-free paper)
    ISBN 1-55798-2905-8 (paper : acid-free paper)
    1. Industrial psychiatry. 2. Job stress—Patients—Counseling of.
    I. Title
    [DNLM: 1. Psychotherapy—methods. 2. Counseling—methods.
    3. Work. 4. Mental Disorders—diagnosis. 5. Mental Disorders—therapy.   WM 420
L918c 1993]
    RC967.5.L68 1993
    616.89—dc20
    DNLM/DLC
    for Library of Congress   98-852
                                                                                  CIP

Printed in the United States of America

To Linda and Marissa
and to my clients,
past, present, and future,
with thanks and appreciation

WORK

for John Gardner, d. September 14, 1982

Love of work. The blood singing
in that. The fine high rise
of it into the work. A man says,
I'm working. Or, I worked today.
Or, I'm trying to make it work.
Him working seven days a week.
And being awakened in the morning
by his young wife, his head on the typewriter.
The fullness before work.
The amazed understanding after.
Fastening his helmet.
Climbing onto his motorcycle
and thinking about home.
And work. Yes, work. The going
to what lasts.

Contents

Preface

This book serves as a companion to *The Clinical Practice of Career Assessment: Interests, Abilities, and Personality* (Lowman, 1991b) and is intended to build on that foundation. It aims to provide first steps in creating an informed and systematic psychotherapy of work issues. However, unlike the other volume, which dealt with territory somewhat better charted (but poorly integrated) by an extensive research literature, this book covers somewhat less developed ground. Predictably, the interdomain model of career assessment (Lowman, 1991) has had its critics (see Lowman, 1993a, b). No doubt this book will have them as well, particularly among specialists in one or another aspect of this work.

Like *Career Assessment*, this book's primary intended audience is not those working *in absentia* from real-life occupational concerns but the practicing clinician seeking to help actual clients who present with psychologically relevant work issues. For this audience, the book provides a conceptual framework, a review of relevant literature, and plentiful case examples. If the book also proves useful to researchers and academics, so much the better. The astute reader will no doubt discover a number of topics needing further research attention.

Also like *Career Assessment*, this book focuses primarily on analysis at the individual level. As McMichael (1978) aptly noted,

> In the world of work, with rows of assembly line, blue collar workers and corridors of neatly pigeon holed white collar workers, it is easy to underestimate, even ignore the individuality of each worker. Workers of all shades of collar colour are, after all, people—not personnel. Given this ever present, marked human variability, it follows that an individual's response to his work environment will be idiosyncratic; tempered by . . . past experiences . . . current attitudes and aptitudes, and all the psychosocial subtleties of [the] life situation. Work environment stressors, therefore, induce different types and amounts of stress in different workers. (p. 143)

The purpose of this book is not as much the intensive *assessment* of individual career concerns and work dysfunctions as it is identifying appropriate strategies for *intervention*. Other approaches attempt to change the work organization or the job itself to be more accommodating to individual needs. Organization development, for example, generally attempts to manipulate the structural or procedural characteristics of the work environment rather than the psychological characteristics of individuals (e.g., Huse & Cummings, 1989). Personnel psychology, an increasingly sophisticated and statistical science, seeks to intervene at the entry or promotional phases of the organization's life cycle to choose employees who have the greatest likelihood of success in a particular job or work environment (Schneider & Schmitt, 1986) and who are therefore likely to be better matched with their work and less prone to work dysfunctions. Although such processes probably help decrease the number of work-related psychological problems that would otherwise exist, simply being in the "right" job from the perspective of interests, aptitudes, or personality is unfortunately no assurance of immunity from work dysfunctions.

It may seem a bit premature to write a book on the psychotherapy of work dysfunctions when the field is still in the process of being defined. Certainly, there is much more to be learned. However, a lot more is known about some of these conditions than one might imagine. To date, the relevant knowledge has appeared in disparate arenas and has lacked integration. If this book fails to provide final answers, it at least fulfills part of its purpose by focusing attention on how to begin the development of a systematic psychotherapy of the work dysfunctions. The practitioner is advised to use caution in proceeding and to monitor the literature carefully as emerging research and clinical guidance become available.

This book is directed primarily toward mental health practitioners (psychologists, psychiatrists, social workers, mental health counselors) and graduate students in these disciplines who seek to improve their competence in diagnosing and treating individual-level work concerns. I assume that the reader already has a basic knowledge of psychopathology, psychodynamics, and general psychotherapeutic principles and is interested in learning more about their specialized application to particular types of problems or populations.

What is *not* assumed, however, is that the reader has extensive knowledge of organizational settings in which the vast majority of work takes place. Mental health professionals can be markedly naive about the practical world. Many seem to have chosen a career in the helping professions at least partly because of limited aptitude for, or interest in, such settings. The book therefore begins with an overview of general issues in the psychotherapy of work and information about work settings and the work function itself. I have attempted to include both sound theoretical material and an abundance of case illustrations. I find much of the career and work counseling literature oddly unsatisfying because it offers too little case or other illustrative material that matches the complexity of the kinds of career and work issues that most clinicians encounter in day-to-day practice. I think that this is due to mental health professionals' own disinterest in understanding the role of work in the client's life situation. The result is that much of the existing work counseling literature appears sterile and unimaginative, forcing cases into simplistic illustrations of particular principles, variables, or tests rather than letting complex clinical case material create its own theory.

I hope that this book does a better job of helping the clinician and the researcher understand career and work counseling in more depth. Most of all, I hope that it helps mental health professionals become interested in, if not downright excited about, the possibilities of what often waits right in the consulting room for identification and assistance. Clinicians and researchers alike can make a difference in work performance if they open their minds to the possibilities and are prepared to address their own personal reactions that such explorations often generate.

And does work matter to our clients' lives? Ayn Rand (1943/1968), perhaps the world's greatest celebrator yet of the role and value of work, put it this way in *The Fountainhead*:

> "Look Gail." Roark got up, reached out, tore a thick branch off a
> tree, held it in both hands, one fist closed at each end; then, his

wrists and knuckles tensed against the resistance, he bent the branch slowly into an arc. "Now I can make what I want of it: a bow, a spear, a cane, a railing. That's the meaning of life."

"Your strength?"

"Your work." He tossed the branch aside. "The material the earth offers you and what you make of it." (p. 577)

Acknowledgments

When it comes to writing, I wish I could say that words flow effortlessly onto the page with the amazing speed and often grace of the late Isaac Asimov. Of my writing thus far in my career, the most descriptive statement I can make is that I enjoy having written. The process of writing itself, however, comes in fits and starts and always with periodic obstacles that for too long seem intractable. (I acknowledge with reluctance and embarrassment, for example, that it took me six months to get through the section on procrastination; little of *that* period was spent writing!) For me, it is not so much the matter of staring down a blank computer screen as it is the long lapses during which I simply cannot bear to look at a manuscript and so leave it for often overly extensive resting periods, sometimes forgetting that yeast only rises for a time before becoming flat.

And yet, try as I might to fill my time with activities as wide ranging as consulting to organizations, teaching, treating psychotherapy patients, doing volunteer work for professional associations, conducting research, creating and managing a professional practice, traveling incessantly, and even—when I am feeling particularly avoidant—cooking, working in the yard, and cleaning the house, it is to writing that I inevitably return. Since leaving academia as a primary place of employment, I have written more and, I think, better. No longer an activity forced to be done as a dutiful commitment to fulfill someone else's goals and the insatiable monster of institutional prestige, writing now provides the opportunity to explore personally chosen rather than institutionally dictated new directions. Still, writing on a schedule, whether internally or externally induced, is for me a tediously slow process.

If the end result is a reasonably readable text, then I can be satisfied with the result and thankful that the reader need not know the anguish and, in my mind, interminable trail it has taken to get there. Like any performing art, writing that appears effortless and just right comes at a price, and it is best not to see too often nor too closely the physical and emotional wreckage that may lie behind the stage.

My writing is also facilitated by having a patient spouse who, if not always fully understanding of the nooks and crannies between inception and final product, certainly helps keep me emotionally on track and reminds me of the importance of context (the broader world so often obscured when writing a book). She can also be a fine editor and constructive critic. Our daughter provides the comic relief and spiritual nurturance that sets for me the highest possible unobtainable goal: to create a product that can somehow approach the standard of excellence and well-being set by the beautiful, intelligent, and creative young woman she is and is becoming. If life forced a choice of my family or my creative work, it would be a simple, if frustrating, decision. A life that provides the opportunity both for personal and professional fulfillment is a special blessing.

As with any complicated enterprise, there are many people behind the scenes whose help and contribution I am happy to acknowledge. Thanks once again to Gary VandenBos and Julia Frank-McNeil for supporting the concept and making the arrangements for publishing this book. I am proud to be part of the fine and worthwhile enterprise that APA Books has become. Thank you Mary Lynn Skutley, Al Gabor, and Cynthia Fulton for your fine attention to editing that so improves the final product. Thank you Mark Savickas for serving as an outside reviewer of the completed manuscript. Thank you cartoonists and your publishers for granting permission to reprint your marvelous work that so often succinctly and humorously communicates the essence of a concept in a few lines and words. I admire your talent. Thank you, in advance, Ralph Eubanks and staff, for your professional efforts in letting people know this book is available—the gentle art of marketing.

Thanks also go to my administrative staff, especially Kirsten Blood, who have kept the wheels appearing to turn effortlessly at The Development Laboratories, my primary employer, while I have had the luxury and privilege of time away from (and in!) the office to write. I appreciate the fine art of invisible administration more with each passing year.

Thank you to my students, graduate students, and colleagues from all walks of psychology, among other professional disciplines, who continue to teach me what I need to know next. Thank you to my clinical supervisors and graduate school and internship mentors (Norm Abeles, Don Grummon, Gershen Kaufman, Walt deLange, Wendy Fisher House, and Carl Frost, among others) who helped me learn and mature as a clinician. Thank you to my adult mentors, including Doug Bray, Harrison Gough, and John Holland, activist scholars all. Thank you, most of all, to my counseling and psychotherapy clients, particularly those presenting with work-related problems, who have shared their concerns with me and my staff and from whom I have learned much more than I have taught.

And, finally, thanks to you, gentle readers, most of whom I will never meet or know (except in spirit), for acquiring and reading this book and, by your practice of its tenets and your own research and clinical writings, for helping to create a viable psychotherapy of work dysfunctions.

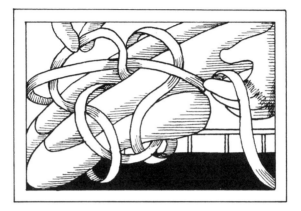

Introduction

No other technique for the conduct of life attaches the individual so firmly to reality as laying emphasis on work; for
his work at least gives him a secure place in a portion of
reality, in the human community. The possibility it offers of
displacing a large amount of libidinal components, whether
narcissistic, aggressive or even erotic, on to professional
work and on to the human relations connected with it lends
it a value by no means second to what it enjoys as something indispensable to the preservation and justification of
existence in society. (Freud, 1930/1961, p. 80)

T his book examines the psychological diagnosis and treatment of work-related problems. It is a topic for modern
times. Although work problems (here called *work dysfunctions*)
of psychological origin are certainly not new (see, e.g., R. V.
Davis & Lofquist, 1984; Halpern, 1964; Leader, 1990; Neff, 1968;
Savickas, 1991), concern for them as issues suitable for counseling and psychotherapy is of more recent vintage. Only a post-

industrial society can pause long enough from survival tasks to be concerned about whether work is meaningful, worthwhile, or a good match for an individual's needs and interests. Moreover, it is a later refinement in the development of psychotherapy to be concerned about such "pragmatic" matters as work.

Work, or productive accomplishment, has long been considered a critical component of an individual's positive mental health. As Thomas Edison said, "As a cure for worry, work is better than whiskey" (cited by Bohle, 1967, p. 453). Thomas Carlyle put it this way: "Work is a grand cure for all the maladies and miseries that ever beset mankind—honest work, which you intend getting done" (cited in Stevenson, 1964, p. 2233). Or again, as Robert Burton stated somewhat but not much less extremely, "There is no greater cause of melancholy than idleness; no better cure than business" (cited in Stevenson, 1964, p. 955).

Just as the therapist's own work constitutes an important, identity-defining aspect of self, so too does work constitute an im-

CALLAHAN

" I'd like to thank all those who made it possible for me to be here tonight."

Drawing by Callahan; April 23–29, 1992, *Houston Press*.

portant part of the client's personal identity. To ignore work issues as too pragmatic would be as limiting as pretending that a client's sex life was an irrelevancy. Moreover, work issues can be as interesting, complex, and challenging for clinicians as romantic or sexual ones. This book aims to illustrate how.

Like sex, work is a natural part of living, and the issues it raises are important parts of character. The mental health professional has only to listen to the emptiness and hollowness of the lives of many of those born to wealth (e.g., Coles, 1977; Wixen, 1973) to understand that the end products of work are vastly more extensive than money alone. A fulfilling life role achieved through productive work should be the legacy and expected birthright of each adult, given that life without purpose is generally life lived unhappily and not lived well. Whether that sense of purpose that justifies our existence in society is fulfilled in or out of the home, through paid or volunteer work, the individual who seeks personal happiness has an obligation to work through or around obstacles to achieve work effectiveness. Likewise, it is to employers' advantage that workers be well-suited and well-adjusted to their work and that people experiencing work-related difficulties receive relevant assessment and effective intervention.

Vaillant and Vaillant's (1982) important longitudinal study of the role of various psychological factors in predicting later career and life satisfaction suggests the importance of work in overall well-being. Using an inner-city, impoverished youth population (hardly the epitome of a work-oriented culture), these researchers demonstrated that, of all variables examined, capacity to work in the teens was among the most predictive of later career and life satisfaction and positive life adjustment. The study also illustrates the complex interactions that occur between work and nonwork activities, a theme also developed in the descriptive qualitative study of Piotrowski (1979), who examined the ways in which work and family life interacted for people in working-class occupations, and in the excellent book by Ulrich and Dunne (1986), who identified ways in which family and workplace dynamics interact clinically. Empirical researchers have reported more systematic studies (Barling, 1990; Brief & Nord, 1990b; Googins, 1991; Zedeck, 1992). Work does indeed play a role in positive mental health, and clinicians have a potentially important role to play in assisting clients experiencing work dysfunctions.

Work and Development

Symbolically, the capacity to work is similar in life importance to issues of mating and reproduction and constitutes one of the most significant developmental milestones in the transition to adulthood. Work represents the taking of one's rightful place in the productive adult world. In a real sense, work is a metaphor for adulthood and, by implication, an arena in which intrapsychic and interpersonal conflict may occur, be acted on, or be acted out (e.g., failure to achieve, the expression of displaced aggression, overvaluation of the work role). Moreover, abilities and goal-directed behavior mature on varying timetables among different individuals and within different types of occupations, so that personal readiness may interact with environmental demands to create early or later achievement and productivity. Work may therefore be a source of positive self-esteem or, for talents that bloom later in life, associated with a developmental delay or regression, serving in effect to create greater dependence on school, family, or friends for self-definition and identity.

Work Dysfunctions Defined

When work functions are impaired, dysfunctional consequences may ensue. Impairment of the capacity to work can result in serious personal difficulties, including threat to one's livelihood. *Work dysfunctions* is the term used in this book to refer to psychological conditions in which there is a significant impairment in the capacity to work caused either by characteristics of the person or by an interaction between personal characteristics and working conditions. In this definition, unemployment would not be classified as a work dysfunction because the condition is the result of an outside force (see Warr, 1987). The condition of a worker who is terminated because of depression would be. For purposes of this discussion, the defining condition is that psychological characteristics of the client have a demonstrated impairment of the work function or interact with aspects of the work or work setting to create personal difficulties. In later chapters, I explore patterns of dysfunction associated with undercommitment, overcommitment, work-related anxiety and depression, and personality disorders and the special challenges posed by many creative pursuits.

Although more research is needed before the parameters and epidemiology of work dysfunctions are well-charted (see chapter 3), there are ample clinical data to suggest that work pathology can affect even people who are well-suited to their jobs and organizations, such as an otherwise content and productive employee who has trouble dealing with a difficult supervisor or a person who is happily employed in a particular occupation but procrastinates at work (see, e.g., Burka & Yuen, 1983).

The following case illustrates an example of the work-related problems that lend themselves to psychotherapeutic intervention.

A Working Wounded

A tall, lanky graying man in his fifties at the time of referral, Paul had been placed off work by his referring managed mental health care group, which requested that he be seen in counseling twice a week to assist with what was viewed by the referral source as a serious depression. The client himself complained of persistent insomnia, chronic anxiety, and general malaise. He doubted his ability to return to work and wondered whether he might be forced to take a disability retirement.

Paul had not always been depressed. Owing to an unusual set of circumstances, he had become a public-sector employee after working in a similar capacity in the private sector for a number of years. Although he had taken a significant pay cut when joining the public sector, the alternative was not to practice at all in his chosen profession. In the government, he had worked his way up to become a manager and was well-respected in the system. Although the therapist's initial impression was that Paul had only recently made the transition to government service, in fact he had made the switch more than a decade ago; his extreme emotional reaction had begun less than a year before his referral.

Review of the client's current work situation and history indicated that he was in a truly difficult and, for him, new situation—almost a recipe for depression. In a step perhaps uniquely characteristic of the government, the client's agency had gone to a system in which each office was mandated at least to "break even" (cover its expenses) and return a "profit" to help cover the agency's expenses. Yet, the industry being regulated was in decline, and managers were given very little autonomy to make changes that could increase the system's revenues. Several layoffs had occurred, much to the distress of the client, who as chief of his office had to implement these externally made decisions.

Paul was significantly depressed at the time of referral, yet his depression was clearly associated with the problems at work. He had seen his family physician, who had prescribed a powerful antidepressant medication that was having no effect on even the psychophysiological symptoms of depression after several weeks of use. Concerning his personal life, the client was happily married, had several grown children, and voiced no major complaints about his life outside of work, except that he now had no energy or interest in partaking of it.

How should a therapist intervene in such a case? To what extent can the therapist, who almost inevitably will be unfamiliar with the client's specific work duties and organizational context, competently make recommendations that have any relevance for the workplace? How is the clinical diagnosis to be made in cases in which there are both work-related and nonwork-related symptoms? What treatment modalities have the most impact on different types of work-related problems? How much do we really know about ameliorating such conditions?

These are some of the questions addressed in this book. The discussion in chapter 5 (see pp. 137–140) of the case just presented shows that psychological intervention can be effective with clients suffering work dysfunctions, but there remains much to be learned about how and why to intervene in individual cases.

Primary Focus: Work Dysfunctions Versus Psychological Dysfunctions

Just as work can contribute positively to mental well-being, psychological dysfunction can impair the ability to work. Thus, clinicians may appropriately be called on to evaluate the work capacity of the psychically impaired. Successful mental health treatment can improve these conditions and therefore the ability to function well in the workplace. However, the secondary, symptomatic relief of work-related problems that are primarily reflective of psychopathology (e.g., Kramer, 1990)—an important and rather neglected issue—is not the primary concern of this book.[1]

Rather, the focus here is on the clinical treatment of psychological problems in which the major conflicts to be addressed by the therapy are work related. Such intervention constitutes the primary purpose of the treatment or is an identifiable phase of a more general treatment. This is not, of course, to suggest that work dysfunctions occur independently of the rest of the personality or that a need for more extensive therapy on nonwork issues will not occur before or after therapy directed toward the work dysfunctions. As this book demonstrates, different work issues call for varying therapeutic strategies. Many, however, are well-suited for goal-directed, brief intervention methods in which work can productively be the primary focus. Indeed, treatment of the work dysfunctions alone may often be sufficient to restore psychological health, contrary to Kleinberg's (1988) suggested use of career counseling as a precursor to "intensive psychotherapy" (as if successful treatment of work issues were neither intensive nor psychotherapy; see Blustein, 1987; D. Brown & Brooks, 1990).

---

[1] Note, however, that there is at least some indication that achievement in school or work may relieve the stress and feelings of low self-esteem in certain psychotic individuals.

Toward an Understanding of Work-Oriented Therapy

Only in the past few generations has psychotherapy moved from the generic ("grand") approaches (e.g., Freudian, Rogerian, Adlerian), believed by their proponents to be valid for a broad spectrum of psychological problems, to more modest and perhaps less exciting attempts to develop specific treatment-by-problem (and sometimes treatment-by-therapist) methodologies. As therapeutic goals of treatment have become more delimited, work problems have emerged as one area in which psychotherapists can make contributions to individual well-being. Often, such therapeutic goals can be accomplished without a major restructuring of personality and in a relatively time-efficient manner.

Today, practicing clinicians face complex environments in which to render assistance (see Lowman & Resnick, 1994). Too often, work-related concerns of clients are forced into the framework in which the clinician may have been trained, such as expressions of unresolved family-of-origin conflict, defenses against anxiety, and fear of success. Sometimes such dynamics are indeed operative, and the psychological model proves accurate. In other instances, the psychological approach is naive, overly individualized, and misguided. This book aims to expand the clinician's understanding of work issues, the interplay of personal and workplace dynamics, and alternative approaches to treatment so that what is already known or believed is not projected inappropriately onto the client presenting with work dysfunctions.

Examining Work Satisfaction and Work Dysfunction

Before embarking on an exploration of work dysfunctions, it is useful to keep in mind the "normal" course of development that intervention takes. For most individuals, work issues are resolved in a relatively nonconflictual way. People generally find a career or job that, if not optimizing of talents or rewards, is at least satisfying, and the work function proceeds more or less harmoniously. It is the failure to find, implement, or sustain a satisfactory work role or a change in the person or the work situation that creates psychological difficulties of the type discussed in this book. Mental health professionals are consulted by such individuals or by representatives of the work setting for the presumed minority of individuals for whom the natural development process has proved in some way dysfunctional. The therapist's charge is to assist such individuals in understanding and changing what is dysfunctional about their personality, work, or work environment.

This does not, of course, imply that work is of equal importance to everyone or of equal importance compared with nonwork factors in the achievement of a fulfilling life. The therapist's obligation is not to make each client into a junior-level professional but to assist the client within the client's own context in relieving work-related suffering and maximizing potential. The bright, ambitious, highly dedicated professional may suffer as much or more than the unemployed factory worker when work is not right, but the well-trained therapist can be prepared to handle both in an equally competent manner.

Clinically profound in its simplicity is the assertion attributed to Freud that the healthy personality is able to love and to work productively (see Freud, 1930/1961, p. 101). But to say that the healthy personality is able to work productively does not speak to the complexity that is associated with nonneurotic and nonfixated disruptions in that capacity. Assuredly, not all therapy clients (even some markedly neurotic ones) suffer from work difficulties or dysfunctions. For some, neuroticism is well-adapted to (if not prototypical of) their job duties (see Lowman, 1987). But those therapists who learn the territory, who learn to listen to their clients' perceptions about their work, and who attend to the differences in perceptions of work and nonwork issues will discover much that is relevant and clinically useful.

Like many problems treated by mental health clinicians, work dysfunctions can profitably be approached from a variety of theoretical disciplines or psychotherapeutic approaches. Still, the brief therapies (e.g., Budman, 1981; Malan, 1976) and those anchored in problem-solving approaches seem most promising, emphasizing as they do central themes and circumscribed foci. Whatever the theory of counseling embodied by the therapist, a careful juxtaposition of real-world dynamics and individual psychological characteristics is important (see chapter 3). Those clinicians with broad-brush, real-world experience in a diversity of work settings will most likely be able to separate reality from the distortions caused by an individual's psychological dynamics.

As an emerging area of clinical practice, work dysfunctions therapy offers many opportunities for the researcher and the practitioner alike. This book strives to base its recommendations on pertinent research studies and well-reasoned clinical judgment. In a rapidly developing field such as this, new knowledge will rapidly supersede what is currently known. Thus, the therapist should proceed with appropriate caution and clinical conservatism. Recommendations made in this book are based on general principles; they may not fit the specific cases with which the reader is confronted.

About the Cases

All cases in this book are based on actual client situations with which I or my associates have been involved over the years. Certain potentially identifying information has in each case been changed.[2] Although my professional practice concentrates on career and work issues and may therefore attract a clientele more concerned with work issues, the cases presented are largely typical of those encountered in general clinical practice. As a group, our clients are on average brighter and somewhat more complex than the general population, but the types of work concerns with which they present are hardly unusual. I have strived to include

---

[2] Because we conduct studies and also do professional writing, each of our clients is asked to sign a written consent form permitting use of disguised case data in our publications. Although the identity of the client is always carefully protected, the essence of the case has been faithfully reproduced.

a broad and representative sampling of cases, not just those that are highly dramatic or otherwise atypical.

Organization of the Book

In the next chapter, I discuss issues important in understanding how work environments affect individual behavior and suggest that the therapist must always consider nonpsychological explanations for reported problems in the work role. In chapter 3, I attempt to create a clinically useful taxonomy of work dysfunctions. In chapter 4, I use this taxonomy to focus on application of the generic diagnostic and treatment principles to specific types of work dysfunctions, with suggestions for assessment and treatment.

The remaining chapters address specific types of work dysfunctions that therapists may encounter. Patterns of undercommitment are discussed in chapter 3 and those of overcommitment in chapter 4. Chapter 5 addresses work-related anxiety and depression, two of the more commonly encountered work dysfunctions. The impact of personality disorders on the work role are reviewed in chapter 6, and the special problems of creative work are considered in chapter 7. In a final section, issues concerning the next directions of the field are identified and discussed.

Summary

Work is a natural part of living and therefore a life role with which all mental health professionals need to be familiar. Although much more has been written about the clinical psychology of love than of work, this book attempts to provide a conceptual framework for organizing a psychotherapy of work dysfunctions and to illustrate some of the assessment and treatment implications of a variety of types of work dysfunctions.

2

The Work Environment:
A Primer

Organizations are the social psychological environments in which most of the world's work gets accomplished.[1] Work organizations differ markedly from one another in characteristic style, purpose, structure, and control mechanisms and thereby assume a "culture" of their own (see, e.g., Denison, 1990; James & Jones, 1974; E. E. Lawler, Hall, & Oldham, 1974; Schneider, 1972).

In contrast to the occupations of many of their clients, psychotherapists and other mental health professionals often hold

---

[1] Exceptions include certain creative, artistic occupations such as writing or painting and the expanding world of freelance work, often accomplished in the home thanks to computer technology. It might be noted that such technology takes us full circle to the early, not always positive, merging of work and home (see C. A. Hamilton, 1987).

high-status positions and work relatively autonomously in organizations such as clinics, academic institutions, and hospitals. Because these organizations often differ in fundamental ways from those of their clients, these professionals may have limited appreciation of the nature and realities of other, perhaps more prototypical, workplaces. This chapter therefore provides a brief introduction to the nature of organizations as they are likely to affect the individual experiencing work-related problems.

Some Common Features of Work Environments

At least seven generic aspects of work and work organizations have implications for assessing and treating individual work-related problems in the mental health context. Labeled as *principles*, these general features of the work environment serve as a context against which individual presenting problems may need to be evaluated.

The Reality Principle

Except for a few professions (primarily the arts and creative occupations), productive work calls for a primary focus on reality external to oneself. Although individual needs are, of course, relevant in any work setting (or else employees would not remain, assuming they have a realistic choice not to do so), the fulfillment of personal needs is not the primary motive or purpose of the work institution.

Work emphasizes the here-and-now and those aspects of oneself that have real-world utility. One is employed by a work organization because of one's ability or presumed ability to accomplish some productive goals. Work therefore emphasizes the rational aspects of people and problem solving, even though the affective side may arise from time to time (more so in some occupations than in others) in the attempt to meet those goals.

Although this principle emphasizes reality-based interactions with the working environment, it must also be recognized that individual perceptions of the job or work environment will vary from one employee to another. Thus, how the individual perceives the working environment may be more highly correlated with individual outcomes than with formal specifications of the nature of the job (such as through job descriptions and the like) (Mehrabian, 1989–1990; Spector & Jex, 1991) or group perceptions of the working environment (Repetti, 1987).

The Subrogation Principle

Work organizations, by their nature, exist to serve some primary productive purpose: the provision of a service, the production of products or sales, or regulatory control. The component parts of the organization are in many ways subordinate to the primary goals, even though on a day-to-day basis there may be enormous competition among individual organizational members and among structural subunits of the organization about the specific means of implementing the organization's primary purpose or about defining that purpose.

Although subordinate goals can coexist with the primary purpose of an organization (e.g., providing employment, bettering the environment), these are generally secondary to the primary ones. Thus, although a currently popular, upscale ice cream producer touts its environmental conscientiousness and prints on its products that an unspecified portion of its profits are contributed to environmentally relevant causes, such charity can persist only as long as the product is successfully sold. Similarly, employees are valued by work organizations to the extent that they can help accomplish the primary objective of the organization at a particular point in time.

Employees who, through poor selection or unanticipated work dysfunctions, become marginal to the major or primary purposes of the organization, are removed, assisted to change, or kept on, although unproductive, in recognition of past accomplishments and contributions or in fulfillment of an actual or psychological contract that promises continuous employment. In general, however, employees are forced by the nature of work to subordinate personal needs to those of the employing organization if they are to remain employed. Networks of interpersonal relationships exist, of course, in a work organization to address socioemotional needs of employees, but such sets of relationships are tangential rather than primary and often survive outside the organization and after an employment relationship has ended.

The stereotypes of organizations that are "all business" or "heartless" corporations that are only secondarily if at all interested in the welfare of their employees may be exaggerations, although only mild ones. It is not that managers in work organizations do not or are not capable of caring for their employees or that work organizations cannot espouse humanistic values. Rather, it is simply that no matter what the rhetoric the employer states to the contrary, employees' needs are not the primary reason for the employment relationship. In Holland's (1985) occupational interests model, people with Enterprising vocational interests predominate in managerial roles of work institutions. Enterprising individuals are thought to be oriented to goal accomplishment and generally to be skilled and to take pleasure in exercising authority over others and coordinating the efforts of others to accomplish organizational goals. The goals, not the process, are the point (see Holland, 1985; Lowman, 1991b).

From an individual development perspective (see Lidz, 1976), one of the early lessons each employee must learn is how the organization's goals can be made compatible with personal needs and characteristics. The new employee must also discover viable strategies for getting nonwork needs met either while achieving required work goals or through nonwork outlets. The employee who, perhaps through psychological conflicts and complex family-of-origin motivations, conceptualizes the employer as a "bad parent" or who looks for the organization or job to fulfill more psychological needs than realistically it can will often end up in conflict with the organization's management. Alternatively, employees may grudgingly and unhappily acclimate to a relationship perceived to be unfair and remain, perhaps resentfully, only because no alternatives or options are thought possible. For most people, the process of making the transition from the self-centeredness of adolescence to the disciplined subordination of personal needs to the demands of the workplace is often difficult for short periods of time but then proceeds fairly smoothly, and the inevitable matching and accommodation process is resolved in a reasonably satisfactory, if not optimal, manner. Developmentally, the adolescent entering the workplace for the first time must learn what he or she has that is of value to the external world and that personal feelings and problems that are so often the center of prior attentions may be of little relevance in the workplace. Of course, this is not an altogether negative phenomenon. For many adolescents, learning from a source outside one's immediate world the tolerable limits of behavior and being appreciated and paid for some rational and productive aspects of oneself can be important psychological learning experiences. This is especially true if the employee has been fortunate enough to find work that makes use of important skills and abilities.

For others, however, the "partial inclusion" phenomenon (D. Katz & Kahn, 1979), in which only a fraction of the whole person is valued or made use of by the organization, is disruptive to psychological adjustment, and the transition may be poorly made. Unpleasant conflicts may arise in the work setting as the employee attempts, often from a relatively powerless position, to force the organization to change or to accommodate his or her perceived needs.

The mental health interventionist may fail to fully understand this subrogation principle. The personal predispositions and work preferences of people who choose helping professions may be encouraged by the norms of their occupation to make understanding and expression of personal feelings a central goal. Because a therapist is often in the business of assisting clients in blocking, at least temporarily, the reality principle in the service of working through psychic conflict, he or she may lose touch with the day-to-day realities of organizational life as experienced by the typical worker.

Indeed, some of those characteristics that may have caused the therapist to choose a helping profession (e.g., iconoclasm, nurturance, antiestablishment values) are generally ones that might not be appreciated in most work settings. Psychotherapists are the nurturers in an often rejecting and disinterested world of somewhat cold and distant producers. Thus, therapists may be poorly accepted by managers in work settings and, conversely, may at a fundamental level themselves be antagonistic to the organizational expression of issues of power and authority that inevitably arise in organizations.[2]

Such a situation may contribute to misunderstandings on the therapist's part of the nature of work organizations or to unrealistic efforts to attempt to have the employee make changes in the work setting to accommodate personal needs. Worse yet is the tendency of therapists to use psychodynamic concepts to explain all *work inhibitions* (the most common psychoanalytic term used to discuss what in this book are called *work dysfunctions*; Rohrlich, 1980; Ryan, 1980; Satow, 1988; Stark, 1989). Failure to make productive work adjustments in such models is due primarily or exclusively to neurotic dysfunctions such as narcissistic personality, success or failure phobias, or the neurotic conditions in which one was raised (e.g., daughters reared by depressive mothers; see K. G. Cole, 1983).

In reality, the work world is usually a complex interaction of characteristics of the person and the situation (e.g., Kinnuen, 1988), and it is the employee more often than the work setting that will be forced to make changes when there is a conflict between personal and professional requirements. What the naive therapist may view as the employee's perceptual distortions of the "real" external world of work may not in fact be distortion ridden at all. Thus, the therapist addressing work problems needs to become sufficiently familiar with "live" work settings to have an accurate understanding of the extent to which a client's description of a work situation is likely to be the result of parataxic distortion.

The Differential Influence Principle

By their nature, most work organizations are hierarchically organized collections of individual employees wherein members are ordered by their function and roles within the organization.

---

[2] This is not to suggest that counselors and psychotherapists are necessarily low in power needs or do not themselves experience conflicts over personal control. Often, they simply want control over their fiefdom but do not necessarily aspire to oversee others or to function in supervisory roles.

This is primarily a restatement of Tannenbaum's (1968, 1974) hierarchical principle, which holds that power differences are a defining and universal characteristic of organizations. Gottfredson (1984) added that hierarchical differences reflect intellectual and cognitive ability differences. Power differences influence the resources (including one's own) over which a person has control and potentially the degree to which an employee will experience stress on the job (Shirom, 1986). At higher levels of the organization, power is explicitly and formally defined, although it may be implicitly and informally wielded, such as by the force of key managers' personalities and even such subtleties as the tone of voice in which oral communications are made. The culture, tone, and messages may not be obvious to those outside the organization (see, e.g., Palazzoli, 1986).

In lower levels of the organization, individuals derive their control not typically from the power inherent in their positions (there is usually very little) but from their collective interaction,

"Don't make waves."

Drawing by M. Stevens; © 1991 The New Yorker Magazine, Inc.

such as through bargaining units. On an individual level, employees may exercise power by the extent to which they show up for work, actively participate in the organizational activities, and strive to advance within that system.

The implications of the hierarchical arrangements of organizations are significant. First, even though organizations inevitably give lip service to employees as being their most important resource, in reality, the lower the level of position within the organization, the more replaceable is the individual. Conversely, a high-status organizational member, usually defined as someone instrumental in helping to accomplish organizational goals (or who holds a position wielding high control over a significant number of employees), will more likely be afforded a greater latitude of behavioral deviance.

It also follows from this principle that members at higher levels of an organization who experience work dysfunctions are more likely to affect others in the organization when they have personal difficulties related to work. Furthermore, employees with such problems will more likely be tolerated in their behavioral and psychological problems because the power they wield protects them to some extent in their positions. Thus, managers with paranoid personality patterns (see chapter 7) may be tolerated longer than may rank-and-file employees with the same disorders simply because they can more easily protect themselves from others' control and because their skills may be less replaceable by the organization.

Employees with psychological dysfunctions that result in a failure to understand and/or respect the power differentials in organizations (e.g., passive–aggressive or narcissistic personalities; see chapter 7) are likely to be intrusively reminded of the power differential when they violate important organizational norms or expectations. Therapists need to keep such hierarchies in mind and use them as a standard against which to evaluate the likely versus the client-perceived reality when individual clients relay information about what has reportedly happened to them in an organizational context.

The Invisible Hand Principle

Work organizations differ significantly in their basic propensity to tolerate human differences, and there is increasing evidence that different personality types are attracted to different types of occupations and organizations (e.g., Holland, 1985; Lowman, 1991b, 1993a; Lowman & Schurman, 1982; Schneider, 1987). Furthermore, an "invisible hand" (Lowman, 1993a) operates in occupations and organizations to assure that people are reasonably well-matched with the demands of their occupations and the requirements and culture of their organizations (e.g., Holland, 1985; Smart, Elton, & McLaughlin, 1986). The greater the degree of screening and the longer the educational or apprenticeship program required before individuals become full-fledged members of a professional group, the more likely there is to be consistency among members of the occupation.

Thus, medicine, in contrast to, say, real estate, would be expected to have greater intragroup consistency simply because those who are ill-suited to the profession by virtue of their abilities, interests, or temperamental characteristics either are not chosen to study the field or are rejected or self-select out of training programs during their preparatory work prior to meeting the minimal entry requirements for practicing the profession.[3]

In any case, the invisible hand hypothesis, with its presumption that "like attracts like" (Lowman, 1993a), implies that occupations, and therefore organizations, systematically differ in certain aspects of ability, interest, and personality (see, among others, Gottfredson, 1986). Base rates for work dysfunctions and for psychological dysfunctions in the workplace therefore may

---

[3] Large, prestigious occupations that offer substantial financial rewards and that employ people with high general intelligence and high needs for achievement may encourage persistence in lengthy training programs regardless of whether candidates are mismatched with their position. Such "occupational misfits" may live out their careers unhappily or may make later, apparently radical, shifts in occupational choices as they understand the issues better, experience affective distress related to their job, or simply feel more able to assert their independence. If congruence between individual characteristics and those of an occupation and/or organization results in greater occupational satisfaction, then there should be greater job and occupational satisfaction for people in careers requiring longer apprenticeships or training. (Study of this issue is confounded, of course, by extrinsic factors because average income levels and societal rewards are generally higher with higher levels of pre-employment occupational training.)

well vary by type of occupation and organization (see Lowman, 1987). On the other hand, any finding of group differences does not assure on an individual level that a particular employee will be well-suited to the occupation or a good match with the modal employee in that job assignment.

The Environmental Influence Principle

Whereas there may be systematic differences in predisposing characteristics and in expected rates of psychopathology among members of different occupations and different organizations, work difficulties are not a function of individual difference characteristics alone. Aspects of the work and the workplace may, solely or additively, contribute to psychological distress experienced at the individual level. For example, Beutler, Nussbaum, and Meredith (1988) presented a small sample study of police officers who were judged asymptomatic at the time of hiring but who subsequently developed psychological distress, presumably at least partly due to their jobs. Gavin (1975) also illustrated aspects of working environments with presumably negative impact on individual mental health. Other relevant research is noted in chapter 3.

It is a surprisingly complex task to differentiate at the individual level sources of psychological distress in the work role attributable to characteristics of the person from those attributable to the work itself (Manning, Williams, & Wolfe, 1988), particularly if assessment takes place in a legal context (DeCarlo, 1987). It is common for employees in trouble on their job to ascribe blame to the organization rather than to themselves, just as organizational representatives tend to blame the individual employee rather than anything that might potentially make the organization legally culpable. M. P. Lerner (1982) argued that work stress is often based on power inadequacies and that work intervention methodologies often falsely assume that it is the individual rather than the organizational system that is to blame.

Determining who is at "fault" for an individual's experience of work difficulties can be a frustrating and fruitless task. Unless clinicians function as forensic evaluators of the work problems, they cannot assume that workplace issues will be described accurately by either the client or employer representatives. Thankfully, in nonforensic cases it is not the clinician's responsibility to apportion causality or shares of blame but rather to work to assist in remediating the current situation and hopefully assist in restoring worker productivity.

For the practicing clinician, particularly one who works only with individuals and not with organizations, it is important to appreciate that the workplace itself may be the source of the client's unhappiness and that the appropriate intervention may be changing not the individual's psychological dynamics but the organization's characteristics or dynamics. If such interventions are rarely within the mandate or competence of the practicing clinician, at least recognition can be made that the person appearing in the consulting room may be only one part of the identified problem. A practicing clinician need not be a job analyst or an organizational interventionist to understand or have an impact on a system, although recognizing the boundaries of one's competence is always an ethical imperative (e.g., American Psychological Association, 1992). If the therapist cannot personally change the work environment, he or she can certainly assist the client in identifying what might need to be changed for the system to be less stressful. Assisting the client to explore the dynamics of work and organizational issues can itself be a significant contribution to employee well-being provided that the therapist keeps in mind the limits of the approach.

The environmental influence principle extends more broadly than the interaction between individual employee and organization. The organization itself can be conceptualized as an open system that is constantly in flux with its environment (D. Katz & Kahn, 1979). As the organization's ability to interact effectively with its environment changes, it must itself adapt and modify its products and processes. Individual employees will themselves likely be affected as organizations change to accommodate new external realities. Personal dysfunctions that once were tolerated may no longer be accepted as external (and therefore internal) circumstances change. Individual employees, particularly those with psychological dysfunctions, may vary in their abilities to adapt their own behavior to such situations.

The Interactive Principle

The literature concerning organizational and occupational stress is too vast to review with any adequacy in this book (for reviews, see Beehr & Bhagat, 1985; Cooper & Payne, 1988; Matteson & Ivancevich, 1987; Quick & Quick, 1984). In summary, most models of organizational stress identify complex interactions between aspects of the individual and of the environment as causing work stress (e.g., Payne, 1988; Schaubroeck, Cotton, & Jennings, 1989). Caplan's (1971) and D. Katz and Kahn's (1979) seminal model on organizational stress differentiates components of occupational stress, including the objective and subjectively experienced environment. Stressors at work can be transient and acute or chronic (House, 1987). It is still not fully understood how individual characteristics interact with those of environments to determine the propensity with which stress and negative outcomes will be experienced (e.g., K. J. Smith, 1990). Of particular concern because of its potential for creating problems for individuals in the workplace is the combination of responsibility for outcomes without control over means to accomplish them (e.g., Landsbergis, 1988; see also Spector, 1987) and the general absence of social support as a means of ameliorating the effects of stress (see chapter 4).

Although there is far from universal agreement about how exactly to define sources of stress within the working environment (Newton, 1989) and the extent to which work and personal characteristics contribute differentially to undesirable outcomes (Harenstam, Palm, & Theorell, 1988), some reasonably clear patterns can be noted concerning the likelihood of enhancing a good person–environment fit. Perceived psychological stress appears to lower satisfaction with work (Hollingworth, Matthews, & Hartnett, 1988). Apparently, men and women do not differ per se in the experience of occupational stress (Himle, Jayaratne, & Chess, 1983; Martocchio & O'Leary, 1989), although the conditions that are more likely to cause stress may differ (diSalvo, Lubbers, Rossi, & Lewis, 1988; Greenglass, Pantony, & Burke, 1988; Zappert & Weinstein, 1985). Work stress itself can be caused by a variety of work conditions (see the next section) and by the interaction of particular predisposing individual characteristics and workplace demands.

Organizational Life Cycle and Periodicity Phenomena

Just as individuals have life cycles, so do organizations (Kimberly, Miles, & Associates, 1980). Although organizations share many commonalities, the types of issues likely to be salient to a young organization struggling to survive are often different in kind from those important to mature organizations struggling to retain market share. Organizations are similarly affected by business cycles in which there are periods of greater and lesser demand for their products or services.

Start-up periods for new organizations are notoriously stressful and, when the organization is quite small, more likely to require adjustment by employees to the idiosyncratic characteristics of owners and managers who for a while *are* the organization. Periods of economic downturn, coupled with threatened or actual layoffs, also elevate the stress levels. Therapists are wise to inquire whether there are any unusual stressors at work and whether changed or atypical working conditions may be contributing to the immediate personal distress.

Dysfunctional Working Conditions

Organizations also may vary in the extent to which they create or ameliorate stress (DeWolff & Winnubst, 1987; Murphy & Schoenborn, 1989; see also chapter 5). Jobs can be badly designed, supervisors can indeed be ogres or have excessively high power needs, and co-workers can be petty, vindictive, and antagonistic. Working conditions, particularly those characterized by high levels of responsibility with limited opportunities for control, can have demonstrable effects on individuals' health and psychological well-being (Krantz, Contrada, Hill, & Friedler, 1988).

On the other hand, dysfunctional employees themselves may not be aware of or accept responsibility for the extent to which their own shortcomings and personal characteristics may contribute to problems on the job. Part of the challenge of working with individuals experiencing job difficulties is assisting them in coping more effectively with challenging work circumstances.

Although this book was not written with the purpose of training clinicians in organizational diagnosis or redesign (see, e.g., Levinson, 1972), practitioners should keep in mind that the organization itself can to some degree be the source of (or at least a contributing factor to) individual psychological problems. Thus, defective job design (such as through role overload [Perrewe & Ganster, 1989] and underload [Cooper & Wills, 1989], role ambiguity or conflict [D. Katz & Kahn, 1979; Leigh, Lucas, & Woodman, 1988; Nicholson & Goh, 1983; Tracy & Johnson, 1981], poor supervision, and tolerated dysfunctional interpersonal relationships) may cause or contribute to problems experienced by individual workers. Mental health professionals specializing in this type of work may need to become accustomed to interacting with supervisors and other organizational representatives to gain a better understanding of the technical and interpersonal context in which the troubled employee's work takes place.

Are there systematic and presumably predisposing occupational and organizational characteristics that are likely to increase stress levels?[4] Although there is evidence that average stress levels differ among workers in different occupations (Fletcher, 1988; Payne, 1988; Pendleton, Stotland, Spiers, & Kirsch, 1989; Rimpela, 1989), this clearly does not imply that all workers in a particular occupation will experience higher stress levels than average. Furthermore, even within the same occupation, jobs may be designed in such a way as to exacerbate or ameliorate stressful conditions. In particular, work situations that impose conditions of ambiguity, conflict among alternative roles, and lack of social support are likely to heighten the stress levels contributed by the work itself.

Changing Working Conditions

Although the practicing mental health clinician to whom clients experiencing work difficulties are referred will generally not be

---

[4] This generalization appears to be true regardless of how organizational or occupational stress is defined. Currently, there is far from universal agreement on definitions.

in a position to change the client's working conditions (Donatelle & Hawkins, 1989), some sensitivity to the characteristics of work environments is nonetheless needed. If it is likely that characteristics of the job itself rather than of the client are accountable for the distress, then it may make little sense to undertake treatment independently of the work environment unless there are issues tangential to or concurrent with the work difficulties for which psychological intervention might be appropriate.

A number of so-called stress management programs that attempt to treat stressful working conditions have been put forth over the years (e.g., Bertoch, Nielson, Curley, & Borg, 1989; S. Jenkins & Calhoun, 1991; J. J. Smith, 1987; Steffy, Jones, Murphy, & Kunz, 1986). These programs purport to change either working conditions themselves or, perhaps more likely, the capacity of individuals to cope with stress inherent in the job. Reviews of the comparatively sparse outcome research on such programs have been mixed (Ivancevich, Matteson, Freedman, & Phillips, 1990; Pelletier & Lutz, 1989). Perhaps the most that can be concluded here is that if occupational stress is to be addressed on an organizational rather than individual level, care must be taken to assure that (a) stress is being experienced by employees in the work unit under review, (b) the organizational variables to be changed are ones that are problematic in the current situation, and (c) changing these variables is both possible and likely to have an impact on the perception of stress. Although there are many organizational changes that are unlikely to be harmful (such as decreasing role conflict or creating better communication avenues within the organization), there is no assurance that they will help alleviate organizational dysfunction, particularly if no systematic diagnosis has been made of the stressful conditions in the particular setting.

For the practicing clinician, then, assessment of individually experienced work difficulties should proceed with some understanding of and respect for the conditions in which the work takes place. Although it is unlikely that mental health professionals will be able to become intimately familiar with the working conditions with which their clients must interact on a day-to-day basis, clinicians with a referral base of clients from a small number of work organizations are advised to develop some first-

hand familiarity with the reality of these settings. Naive recommendations (e.g., "assign Mr. X to day shift" or "put Mrs. Y
in a job in which she will have no social contact") may thereby
be avoided.

Determining the Relevance
of the Work Context

In evaluating work problems, the therapist needs some expertise
in evaluating characteristics of the work context itself, if only as
reflected by the client's rendering of it. The client who claims
that the work situation is horrendous and who describes everyone in his or her life as also horrendous is presumably reflecting
more about the personal dynamics than about the work setting
itself. However, when a client presents with concerns about a
supervisor, the therapist must consider the following questions:
Is this plausible? How would I handle such a situation? Are the
client's own psychological dynamics likely exacerbating the situation? Is the solution to this problem more likely to rest with
a practical rather than psychotherapeutic intervention? The therapist, knowing that all work organizations harbor some degree
of power mongering (the differential influence principle) and
power controlling (the subrogation principle), may consider
whether the client is likely exaggerating the problems associated,
perhaps inevitably, with organizational life. Straightforward, in-
tuitive questions can help facilitate exploration through the
client's eyes of the nature of the problems. Relevant questions
might include the following: Has this problem arisen for others
at your work? [if so] How have others handled the problem?
Who has been most successful in your work setting in handling
the supervisor? How did they respond differently than you may
have?

Thus, in considering a client's complaint of a supervisor who
is described as tyrannical and offensive to everyone, the therapist, in effect, needs to determine whether this is primarily a
work context problem[5] or an individual problem (e.g., a chron-

---

[5] Of course, work context problems can themselves be heavily laden with

ically dependent personality type). As is the case in exploring a marital concern, review of the history of the situation may be valuable: How did you choose this line of work? How did you choose this particular setting? Do you feel like you are well-matched for this type of work?

Even if the therapist can establish that the individual's psychological dynamics are part or virtually all of the problem, inquiries about the perceived work situation can still provide useful information. Central issues can be explored using the client's version of events, regardless of its accuracy. Using his or her own understanding of the workplace context, the therapist can make apparently naive inquiries to both make a point and assist the client in considering an alternative view of the situation. For example, a therapist's dialogue with a client referred because of problems in the work setting might proceed as follows:

Therapist (T): Isn't everyone in the office expected to be at work on time? [The therapist tests reality here. Perhaps this is an office with lax or indifferent supervision.]

Client (C): Yes, but she [the supervisor] lets Maxine come late but not me.

T: She plays favorites? [The therapist assumes the client's side by attributing a possibly negative characteristic to the supervisor.]

C: Yeah.

T: How often do the two of you come in late? [The two "offending parties" are paired; can the client acknowledge that she does come in late and that part of the problem may reside with her rather than her supervisor?]

C: Not too much. I wasn't late at all for the last two weeks, but Maxine came in at 10:00. [The workday starts at 9:00.]

T: Did your supervisor—what's her name?

psychological significance. Even in a horrendous work situation, how, out of all possible working places and conditions, did the client end up in this particular context?

C: Susan.

T: Did Susan talk with Maxine about coming in at 10:00?

C: No, she didn't, and I don't think that's fair.

T: Is it possible that she spoke with her privately when you were not around? [The therapist engages in reality testing: Is the perception of unfairness rigidly held? Is it accurate?]

C: I doubt it. Her desk is right next to mine.

T: I wonder why Susan might single you out? [Although it is possible that the supervisor "plays favorites" and ignores one employee's work problems while chastising another, it generally would be unlikely, particularly in the large and sophisticated organization in which the client was employed. The therapist does not wish to antagonize the client by "taking sides" and so does not challenge her version of events, instead gently gathering additional information on this perception, hopefully without alienating the client.]

C: Beats me. I don't think she's fair.

T: Tell me, other than your supervisor, do you *like* your work? [A test of the "invisible hand" principle: Is the client otherwise well-suited to her work or, conversely, does she complain about everything?]

C: I used to. But I can't stand being treated unfairly.

T: Other than being late occasionally [ignoring, for the moment, the third mention of "unfairness," the therapist again gently tests whether the client can accept the idea that she may be at fault], do you *enjoy* your work? [Liking one's work can be an important source of personal power.] Are you pretty good at what you do? [Here, the therapist explores issues of perceived competence and self-esteem.]

C: I like it OK, I guess. The pay is good, I like getting away from the kids, and I've gotten awards in the past for being the best in my section. [Presumably the invisible hand has moved her to work with which she is reasonably well-matched.]

T: [smiles slightly, acknowledging and encouraging the client's positive, self-efficacious view] And how are things going in the rest of your life? [Is the work problem affected by nonwork issues?]

C: Not too bad. Jack [her husband] and I had some fights last year, but we're doing better now. The kids are all in school. Really, things are OK except for this problem at work.

T: So, it's mostly this issue of being late that's causing the problem? [Although it is possible that there is more to the home situation than what the client has indicated, the therapist for now brings the focus back to the referring problem.] Have you complained to Susan that you feel she treats you unfairly? [The therapist ostensibly takes the client's "side" while also exploring her practical problem-solving skills in the situation she has described.]

C: All the time. She doesn't listen.

T: What would it take to get her to understand things as you see them? [Again, how does the client think she best can cope?]

C: She would have to get off my case—she's always harping about something I did wrong. [Although this may well point to an individually oriented psychodynamic, such has yet to be established. Possibly the supervisor *is* being "unfair" to the client.]

T: And it seems to be just you that she singles out for this attention? [Is this plausible?]

C: [sheepishly, suggesting that she has "heard" the possibility that she may also play a role in this problem] I know I do some things to irritate her sometimes.

T: Like showing up late? [A bit intrusive, but here the therapist tests for psychological understanding.]

C: Not really. I'm only late when I have car problems or one of the kids is sick. [Because the client is somewhat defensive, the therapist backs off, having made the point.]

T: Sometimes it's tough to juggle all these responsibilities [taking the client's side]. Tell me, with all these problems you've had with Susan, what have you thought of doing? [Is the client planning to quit? Does she have any practical suggestions?]

C: I'd quit if I could, but we need the money. Jobs are tight these days. [The client's perception is accurate. She would have few employment opportunities in her immediate area and job classification if she quit before finding another job.]

T: So I guess you and Susan are stuck together—for awhile, anyway [client smiles]. [The therapist grants the possibility of her wish in fantasy but quietly reminds her that there's a need to solve the problem.] Suppose you had a co-worker with this problem. How would you tell her to handle Susan? [The therapist is testing for empathy and trying to help her consider options she may not spontaneously have generated.]

C: Quit! [laughs] No, I'm just kidding. I don't know. You tell me. [silence] I guess I'd tell her to go ask her why she's always picking on her and tell her to stop or she'll file a complaint.

T: Have you done that? [back to reality]

C: No.

T: I wonder why? [Is this an avoidant personality? Is the client reliving some family-of-origin dynamic?]

The therapist would then continue this seemingly practically oriented exploratory dialogue with the client to determine the extent to which it is personal problems or those presented by the workplace that require further work. The therapist is active but in an inquiring rather than intrusive way. Rather than give "advice," the therapist helps the client explore how she might proceed.

This chapter closes with a case illustrating the complexity of the interaction of individual and organizational dynamics. The case concerns not so much an individual with personality difficulties in the workplace as a subordinate struggling to cope with such an individual. The next chapter explores more systematically procedures for classifying problems that clients experience at work and for differentiating personal and organizational factors.

Case 2.1
The Problem Supervisor

Maggie was in her midthirties when she sought help for problems in her work. She had recently changed jobs after a short period of unemployment following dismissal from a job she had held for several years. According to the patient, she had quit her prior employment due to an overly personal relationship outside of work with a supervisor. When the client decided that the supervisor's authoritarian, critical style was not a healthy basis for sustaining a personal relationship and acted to cut back on her nonwork involvement with her, the supervisor suddenly became cold and distant at work and was increasingly critical of her work performance (which never before that had been criticized). In the new job, the client fretted that, although her work group was unusually supportive and ostensibly helpful to her, that her inadequacies would be "found out" and she would again be fired from her job. In fact, she was receiving great praise for her performance but was working overly hard to the extent of taking no breaks during the day and taking on others' work.

The client had had prior treatment and recognized that her abusive childhood dynamics were being replicated in the workplace complaints. Therapy revealed that her attraction to the overly enmeshed environment similar to that in which she had been raised reflected an attempt to work through her family-of-origin dynamics; her appropriate steps to curtail and contain the relationship, to bring it back to more of a business relationship, met, perhaps predictably, with narcissistic injury on the part of her supervisor.

Her decision to leave her job after repeated efforts on her part to reshape it was reframed by the therapist as a positive step in establishing her independence. Although working through the issues with her prior supervisor might have been preferable, in reality her ability to do so was highly limited because the supervisor held the power over her and showed no inclination to change, despite repeated efforts. In reality, the supervisor *was* the boss (differential influence principle), and although she could have gone to her supervisor's boss, the practical consequences might have considerable had she remained in that company.

Her fears on her current job were examined in light of the earlier experience. The good prior psychotherapeutic work provided the basis for rather quickly and successfully resolving the current work difficulties. She began to take breaks, to assert herself appropriately in her new workplace, and to set appropriate limits concerning her work duties. Vulnerability to abusive situations remained, but she became more adept at responding promptly and more appropriately when she recognized herself to be at risk.

Summary

Work dysfunctions result from a complex interaction of characteristics of the person and the work environment. Clinicians, particularly those with limited knowledge of work settings other than in the mental health field, should caution against automatically or simplistically applying psychodynamic explanations as the exclusive means for understanding work-related problems. What can be very exasperating to the industrial psychologist or the manager is the mental health professional's attempt to psychologize everything and to apply psychodynamic explanations even when the fit is procrustean.

Although the focus of this book is primarily on individual characteristics as they translate into work-related problems, it is important that the therapist keep the work context clearly in mind and note that even though the therapist will view the client's world largely through his or her own representation of it, at times it is the job itself or the work environment, not neurosis, that interferes with successful execution of the work role. In such cases, it is the work environment (or the client's engagement with this particular working role) that may need to be changed for progress to be made. Although therapists may not be in the position of directly changing the client's working environment, the more knowledge of real-life working conditions they have, the more likely they will be to avoid overly psychologizing conditions that are not solely the result of the client's own psychological dynamics.

3

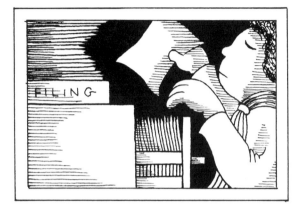

Diagnosis of Work-Related Dysfunctions

P sychological treatment presumes an understanding of what is being treated and the existence of some demonstrated relation between the intervention approach selected and the condition identified. The field of work dysfunctions counseling and psychotherapy is still in its infancy. At issue remains problem definition and taxonimization; the creation of a new diagnostic schema ultimately will allow categorization of presenting dysfunctions using generally accepted taxonomies of work-related psychological conditions. Intervention studies will be needed to allow selection of appropriate treatments from among well-validated, relevant therapeutic methodologies.

Although work-relevant psychological intervention techniques or approaches have been suggested and occasionally studied, there is much still to be done to create diagnosis-by-treatment methods that are adequately grounded in theory and

research. In this respect, the field of work dysfunctions counseling, much like that of career assessment (see Lowman, 1991b),
has been plagued by a premature focus on specific techniques,
interventions, or measuring devices, often without an underlying
understanding of the factors or conditions that contribute to work
dysfunction. The field currently needs (a) an adequate and reasonably comprehensive taxonomy of work dysfunctions, (b) epidemiological data on the prevalence of these dysfunctions
among various populations (see Fletcher, 1988; Mickleburgh,
1986), (c) clinical and research guidance to assist with differential
diagnosis, and (d) a matching of conditions and intervention
methodologies based on outcome research. Too often there is a
tendency for intervention approaches to be driven by particular
methodologies with which the clinician is familiar, with little or
no consideration of alternative explanations or intervention approaches. Differential diagnosis and outcome studies, then, are
among the first steps needed in the attempt to assure that the
client with work-related difficulties is properly counseled.

As with medical problems, the clinician treating work dysfunctions must start with an understanding of the types of problems with which clients present. Detailed description of the phenomenology of work problems is the most basic starting point
from which to develop taxonomies of work dysfunctions, from
which ultimately can be developed properly grounded theories
and relevant intervention methodologies. As with any branch of
clinical practice, the clinician must rule out alternative explanations of client dysfunction to be able to focus on and effectively
treat the presumed dynamic of the current presenting problem.

The systemic context in which work takes place must also be
considered to establish a proper understanding and diagnosis.
By all accounts, stress related to job conditions is on the increase
(e.g., Osipow & Spokane, 1984; Sauter, Murphy, & Hurrell,
1990), and job-stress issues are especially problematic for employers when they result in stress-related disability claims (Workers' Compensation, 1986). Such claims cost employers twice as
much ($15,000 per average claim, according to one report) as
nonpsychiatric claims (Farnhan, 1991). N. Cherry (1984b), for
example, found that in a sample of British women aged 26 at
the time of the original research and 32 at the time of follow-

up, about 40% of those working full-time reported significant nervous strain associated with their work, a figure similar to what she found for men.

It is well-established in the industrial/organizational and social psychological literature that job conditions can precipitate stressful conditions and negative psychological reactions at the individual level (see Beehr & Bhagat, 1985; Cottington & House, 1987; House, 1980; Ivancevich & Matteson, 1980; Millar, 1990; Osipow & Spokane, 1984). However, it is important to note that people who have experienced psychological dysfunction prior to their working may be the most vulnerable to job-related stress (N. Cherry, 1984a, 1984b). In an important early study of factory workers, House (1980) used a survey research methodology to demonstrate that subjective assessments of working conditions were associated with stress and the experience of negative psychological and physical conditions. House used subjective assessments of work conditions that are related, but not as directly as might be assumed, to more objective methodologies. In this and subsequent studies (e.g., Greenglass, 1988; Orth-Gomer & Unden, 1990), social support was shown to be a significant moderator of the effects of perceived stress, often ameliorating the negative consequences of bad working conditions. At the individual level, personality factors may also moderate the effects of stress (Keita & Jones, 1990; Levi, 1990), as may the stage in one's career (Hurrell, McLaney, & Murphy, 1990).

It is therefore important for the clinician to keep the client's work context firmly in mind in assessing work dysfunctions (see chapter 2). Characteristics of the job or working conditions can directly affect and ameliorate individual psychological consequences of stress at work. Work dysfunctions may therefore reflect characteristics of the person, the job, or (perhaps most typically) both.

An Explicit Assessment Strategy

Although an explicit strategy for assessing work-related psychological concerns is essential, current literature provides little systematic assistance for the formal psychological assessment of work-related disorders. The following clinical diagnostic principles are therefore suggested with an appropriate degree of tentativeness.

The client who consults a psychotherapist with a work-related problem may present with a variety of diverse initial complaints (e.g., E. Goldstein, 1984). Whereas one client may be quite direct in noting a problem with an irate supervisor, another may present with vague complaints of tiredness or general life dissatisfaction. Careful inquiry by the clinician will establish whether a work dysfunction underlies or is associated with the presenting complaints. However, because clinicians are often not well-trained in workplace issues and work dysfunctions, they may neglect to evaluate occupational issues as a standard part of a clinical intake interview.

Most counseling intakes, whether or not the presenting problems concern work, should include at least some assessment of the client's capacity to work.[1] The simple inquiry, "How are things going at work?" (for the employed client) or "How do you feel about not working?" (for those who are not currently employed), should be sufficient to open up the area for further inquiry and to encourage the client to discuss issues that may not seem obviously related to the experience of psychopathology, such as in a serious depression.

Having invited discussion of work issues, the clinician must, of course, know what questions to ask, which avenues to pursue, and what differential diagnostic issues are involved when occupational concerns are part of the presenting or underlying client difficulties. For this purpose, the clinician needs a taxonomy or systematic mapping of the domain of work-related dysfunctions. Unfortunately, no such consensually validated taxonomy currently exists.

---

[1] The failure of many epidemiological studies of mental health problems to include adequate measures of work functioning is a serious omission. For example, in their otherwise excellent study of depressive symptoms in a representative sample of community-residing adults, Blazer et al. (1988) included only one work-related symptom: "Had to stop work." This extreme symptom does not begin to account for the wide variety of work dysfunctions that could be indicative of depression, among other forms of psychological disturbance.

Traditional clinical diagnostic guidelines are of limited utility in assessing work and career dysfunctions. The *Diagnostic and Statistical Manual of Mental Disorders* (3rd ed., rev.; *DSM–III–R*; American Psychiatric Association, 1987) is not particularly helpful in assisting the clinician to diagnose work dysfunctions. The *DSM–III–R* formally incorporates only one diagnostic entity (Code V62.20, Occupational Problem) that is specifically relevant to work dysfunctions, although work problems figure indirectly in several other diagnoses such as adjustment disorder[2] and antisocial personality disorder. A single diagnostic category, particularly one assigned to the often third-party nonreimbursable Code V category, is not specific enough to be of much diagnostic assistance.[3] Yet, as of this writing, the epidemiological and research literature provide limited basis for expanding the category Occupational Problem in a scientifically acceptable manner (e.g., Blazer, 1989; Vaillant, 1984; Widiger & Trull, 1991).

Toward a Classification of Work Dysfunctions

Given the wide spectrum of work dysfunctions and the absence of generally accepted taxonomies of work dysfunction, the practicing clinician needs at the least some set of guidelines to assist in conducting the assessment process. Ideally, clinicians who aspire to treat work dysfunctions will have had as part of their professional training extensive experience in general clinical assessment issues and career and occupational assessment (see

---

[2] Category 309.23 of the *DSM–III–R* adjustment disorders is titled *adjustment disorder with work (or academic) inhibition*. However, adjustment disorder diagnoses apply only to psychological conditions that occur in response to identifiable psychosocial stressors that occur within three months of the stressor and that persist for no longer than six months, rather limiting requirements when applied to work dysfunctions. Moreover, there is no definition of *inhibition* as applied to work.

[3] This would be akin to lumping all affective dysfunctions into a single diagnostic category *depressive problems* and ignoring the substantial differences among various subtypes of affective dysfunction.

Lowman, 1991b, 1993a). This background and expertise will serve the clinician well in differentiating between the occupational misfit—whose case will often necessitate a formal assessment of abilities, interests, and personality characteristics—and the client for whom some other type of assessment, such as psychotherapy or career coaching, will be appropriate. At times, a formal or informal job analysis or at least information from the client's supervisors or co-workers may also be required to understand more explicitly and systematically the demands of the job or occupation compared with the client's strengths and limitations.[4] Is, for example, a client in trouble because the work is too difficult or demanding or because key aspects of his or her abilities are not being utilized?

The initial task of the clinician, then, is to (a) assess the type of work problems, if any, presented by the client and (b) determine the relation of such problems to other aspects of personality and psychopathology for purposes of (c) formulating a diagnosis and (d) developing an initial intervention strategy. D. Brown and Brooks (1985) appropriately noted that what is often called *career counseling* is not separable from, or somehow less important than, psychological concerns: Work issues *are* psychological issues and often are as, if not more, complex as other types of psychological difficulties (see also Blustein, 1987).

Although many career assessment issues (primarily those dealing with questions of occupational misfit) may call for detailed assessment of interests, abilities, and personality characteristics in contrast to job-related concerns, there is a whole range of work difficulties that do not assume occupational misfit. These relate to work issues that occur once the client is appropriately and reasonably happily established in an occupation or job in which there is no question of whether he or she is well-matched with this type of work or work setting. Such issues involve not so much a mismatch between person and occupation or between

---

[4] In some work dysfunction cases, sufficient relevant information about the current work situation can be obtained by interviewing the client, possibly supplemented (with the client's informed consent) by information provided by supervisors.

"We can't tell yet if it's a malfunction or a dysfunction."

Drawing by Koren; © 1991 The New Yorker Magazine, Inc.

person and organizational setting but problems in a particular phase of one's work that will probably not entail career change or major course correction. Procrastination, conflicts with co-workers, periods of limited productivity, and authority conflicts are all examples.

Of efforts thus far to taxonomize problems experienced by people in their work roles, one of the better descriptive efforts is that of Campbell and Cellini (1981), who relied on several sources of information for the development of a problem categorization of career and work problems. This effort is reproduced in Appendix A to this chapter.

This taxonomy provides a good start as a descriptive effort in summarizing a variety of types of problems that the practicing clinician may encounter. Its limitation, however, is the lack of a theoretical base and its grouping of work concerns on more of a chronological than a theoretical model (i.e., issues placed in the taxonomy on the basis of *when* various career issues are likely to arise in the life continuum rather than on any sense of *why* the difficulty is encountered). Moreover, those aspects of career difficulties with which the clinician is most likely to have relevant expertise (those relating to "characteristics of the individual"; II.A in this taxonomy), are not well elaborated. Thus, this taxonomy is extremely useful as a practical tool for thinking about career issues that may need evaluation or intervention. However, it is of less utility as a theoretical guide to the types of problems that a client may experience or how such problems group from a psychological perspective.

This chapter therefore provides and illustrates an alternative taxonomy of work dysfunctions that is intended to help the clinician differentiate issues for which career and work counseling are appropriate from those for which some other type of assessment and/or intervention will be appropriate. The term *work dysfunction* denotes any persistent difficulty or failure in the work role associated with psychological characteristics of the individual. Work dysfunctions can be independent of or interactive with the nature of the client's work or the organizational context in which the work takes place.

Distinctions in the Taxonomy

The taxonomy presented in Table 3.1 makes an initial distinction between psychopathology and work dysfunctions while recognizing that the two types of problems can coexist. The purpose of this distinction is to acknowledge (and to remind the practitioner and researcher alike) that psychopathology and work dysfunctions may or may not have orthogonal (uncorrelated) dimensions. The clinician's job is to assess the presence of psychopathology and its relation, if any, to work functioning. An equally important task of general practicing clinicians (including those who do not specialize in work issues) is to assess the presence of work dysfunctions and their impact on psychopathology.

Thus, for example, it is common for a depressed client to present with work concerns just as someone experiencing work issues may present with symptoms of depression. Indeed, work-

Table 3.1

*Toward a Clinically Useful Taxonomy
of Psychological Work-Related Dysfunctions*

I. Determining the relation between psychopathology and work dysfunctions
   A. Affecting work performance
   B. Not affecting work performance
   C. Affected by work performance
   D. Not affected by work performance
II. Disturbances in the capacity to work
   A. Patterns of undercommitment
      1. Underachievement
      2. Temporary production impediments
      3. Procrastination
      4. Occupational misfit
      5. Organizational misfit
      6. Fear of success
      7. Fear of failure
   B. Patterns of overcommitment
      1. Obsessive-compulsive addiction to the work role ("workaholism")
      2. Type A behavioral pattern
      3. Job and occupational burnout
   C. Work-related anxiety and depression
      1. Anxiety
         a. Performance anxiety
         b. Generalized anxiety
      2. Work-related depression
   D. Personality dysfunctions and work
      1. Problems with authority
      2. Personality disorders and work
   E. Life role conflicts
      1. Work–family conflicts
   F. Transient, situational stress
      1. Reactions to changes in the work role (e.g., new job) whose impact on the work role is time limited
   G. Other psychologically relevant work difficulties
      1. Perceptual inaccuracies

(continued)

Table 3.1 *(continued)*

III. Dysfunctional working conditions
    A. Defective job design (role overload, ambiguity, etc.)
    B. Defective supervision
    C. Dysfunctional interpersonal relationships

related problems appear to be one of the commonly encountered characteristics of the prodromal phases of at least some types of depression (Fava, Grandi, Canestrari, & Molnar, 1990; Lykouras, Iannidis, Voulgarie, Jemos, & Izonou, 1989) and can be a differentiating symptom indicating the severity of depression (D. C. Clark, Gibbons, Fawcett, Aagesen, & Sellers, 1985). From both theoretical and practical perspectives, it matters whether the psychopathology or the work dysfunction is judged to be primary because alternative intervention strategies may be required. Career assessment or work counseling with a severely depressed client, for example, may have to wait until the client is reasonably far along in the course of recovery from depression given that many ability and personality measurement results will otherwise be affected by the depression (see Lowman, 1991a). (The commonality of depression among people presenting with work dysfunctions also illustrates that work dysfunctions therapy requires professional training in mental health assessment and treatment. Without proper training, one risks misdiagnosing or inappropriately treating psychological impairment.[5])

Beyond this primary distinction, the taxonomy attempts to group presenting problems on the basis of an underlying dynamic or chief characteristic that contains implications for how

---

[5] Many who use the title *career counselor* may not have this training. Efforts at state-level regulation of the use of this title (e.g., Texas's Career Counseling Services Act, Article 5221-a8) have been largely unsuccessful. Professionals trained in counseling and psychotherapy are probably well-advised to use the title of the professional group of their primary training (e.g., psychologist or psychiatrist) rather than adopt the generic term *career counselor*.

the dysfunction may best be addressed. In the following section, I briefly discuss the major categories of the taxonomy. Later chapters discuss several of these specific classifications in more detail.

Determining the Relation Between Psychological Problems and Work Dysfunctions

This section of the taxonomy addresses the need in evaluating the work dysfunctions to differentiate the presence and relevance to work dysfunction of psychological disturbance. Although psychopathology may be present in clients presenting with work problems, it may or may not be relevant to problems experienced in the work role. Conversely, clients with work difficulties may or may not also experience psychopathology, at least as the term is traditionally defined and conceptualized. This section of the discussion of the taxonomy therefore addresses diagnostic issues important in assessing how psychopathology relates to work. The taxonomy notes that psychopathology may or may not affect work performance (I.A. and I.B.) and that conditions of the workplace may or may not affect or cause psychological distress (1C and 1D). This section discusses these issues in more detail.

It is well-established that serious emotional problems such as depression (Fava et al., 1990), schizophrenia (Meltzer, 1982), paranoia (Jorgensen, 1985), borderline personality disorders (at least for women; see Bardenstein, McGlashan, & McGlashan, 1988), and severe mental impairment in general are often accompanied by deficits, and in severe cases incapacity, in the ability to work (Massel et al., 1990). If psychotherapeutic or psychopharmaceutic treatment of the psychological problem is successful, work-related problems may improve spontaneously as conflicts are resolved or as psychotic conditions are controlled enough for reality functions to become increasingly available to the client. Rarely, however, is work performance or capacity the major concern of the treatment. At most in such cases, work is used as a metaphor for the client's disconnection with reality, and work counseling serves as a focus for stabilizing and increasing the client's reality orientation (e.g., R. R. Nelson & Condrin, 1987).

In contrast, when a client comes for assistance with psychologically relevant job or career concerns, work is likely to be the focal point that motivates the request for assistance, even if the clinician ultimately determines that the work concern is secondary (as, e.g., in the case of a client with borderline personality disorder or severe depression whose capacity to work has been negatively affected by psychopathology). In such cases, the clinician must determine which of the presenting or underlying concerns are primary and which are secondary in the problem presentation.

The research literature on how psychopathology affects work suggests the following with a reasonable degree of consensual validation:

1. A predictable percentage of the general population will experience diagnosable psychological dysfunction over the course of their lives (see T. A. Brown & Barlow, 1992; Dohrenwend et al., 1980; Gallant & Simpson, 1976; L. K. George, Hughes, & Blazer, 1986; Rush, 1982; Weissman et al., 1988). For example, in cross-sectional epidemiological studies, prevalence estimates suggested that at any time 3–8% of the populations studied will be experiencing depressive disorders compared with 13–20% who will be manifesting more circumscribed depressive symptoms (Blazer et al., 1988). Similarly, lifetime prevalence estimates for anxiety disorders are approximately 15% (Regier, Burke, & Burke, 1990).

2. Of those experiencing psychological dysfunction, the more disturbed individuals will not be in the workplace because their psychopathology is too severe and/or too disruptive of the work process (e.g., acutely disturbed hospitalized schizophrenics; see Massel et al., 1990).

3. The prevalence rates for work dysfunctions (with and without defined psychopathology) are currently unknown (Lowman, 1989; Mickleburgh, 1986), except as demonstrated in studies of employed people who have mental

health problems (which may or may not be related to their work; see Fletcher, 1988; Fraser, 1947; Kornhauser, 1965).

4. Psychopathology may or may not affect work performance. Some currently unknown subset of psychologically disturbed individuals are apparently able to function without impairment in the workplace (see Lowman, 1989).

5. Working conditions or the work itself may also affect the experience of psychopathology (e.g., job stress can generate stress and/or mental dysfunction, especially anxiety and depression; see, e.g., Quick, Bhagat, Dalton, & Quick, 1987; Quick & Quick, 1984).

6. Complex research designs (of the type not commonly found in the literature) are required to extract the relative contributions of psychopathology to work and of work to psychopathology. Such research requires large sample sizes drawn from what constitutes a low base-rate phenomenon.

7. Faced with work stress, those with a priori psychiatric symptoms (especially of anxiety and depression) may cope differently with the stressors than those without psychic distress (e.g., N. Cherry, 1984a, 1984b). Those with preexisting psychological difficulties apparently constitute a group that is at higher risk than those not so affected for work difficulties and symptoms of anxiety when under stress on the job.

Many individuals who seek professional assistance with career and work problems are experiencing varying degrees of depression or other clinical symptoms of psychological dysfunction. An initial diagnostic task of the clinician, therefore, is to determine whether the psychopathological symptoms preceded and are essentially independent of the work difficulties or whether they are a result of the career or work problems. In the former case, treatment of the psychiatric problems may be necessary either as part of the work issues counseling process or as separate from it. In the latter instance, addressing the work problems may prove effective in controlling the clinical symptoms.

The diagnosis and differentiation of career and work concerns assuredly can be a complex task. A decision tree outlining some of considerations and tentative suggestions for proceeding with differential diagnosis is provided in Figure 3.1.

More generally, the following steps should be followed in clinical assessment to differentiate clinical and work concerns.

1. The clinician should examine for psychopathology in the usual manner (clinical interview and formal psychological assessment [e.g., testing] when needed).
2. The therapist should inquire, as a routine intake practice, whether work performance is impaired, either through the impact of psychopathology on the job or the presence (related or not to psychopathology) of work dysfunctions.
3. When preliminary inquiries suggest that work is a problem, the clinician should conduct further evaluation to determine the course of action most clinically appropriate.
4. When both psychopathology and impairment of the ability to work are present, the clinician should determine which at that time is primary. That condition should be treated first, unless there is convincing reason to believe that the work issues and the nonwork issues can successfully be treated simultaneously (e.g., treating the work problems as a metaphor for larger life-pervasive issues).
5. If, over the course of treatment, the initial assumptions prove invalid (e.g., the clinician works with psychopathology first and the work problems do not self-correct), the clinician should consider reassessing the diagnosis and trying alternative approaches. If, for example, a depressive condition is successfully treated but the work problems remain, further assessment of the latter may be required. If, on the other hand, the clinician begins treating an apparently circumscribed work issue and the psychopathological condition does not improve, more direct intervention with the psychopathology may be required (e.g., "Yes, my job is better, but I'm *still* depressed").

From a clinical perspective, it should be clear that effectively differentiating psychological factors from other factors is conceptually and clinically complex. In practice, issues do not nec-

Figure 3.1

Clinical Decision-Making Aid

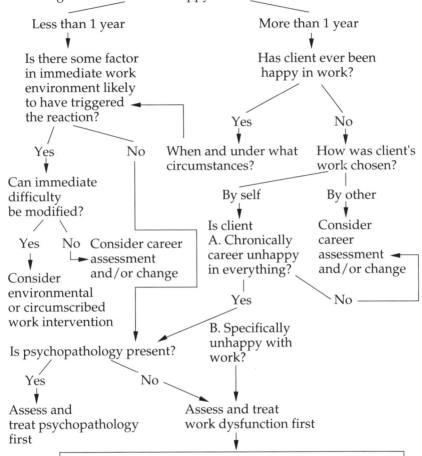

Evaluate possible changes in work functioning:
1. What are the perceived and actual costs?
2. How realistic is the anticipated change?
3. Can needs be achieved avocationally without major life disruption?
4. If not, are the needed precursors to change achievable?
5. How sincere, profound, and long-lasting is the commitment to change?
6. Is there a pattern of short-lived changes in the past?
7. If so, what dynamic is driving the pattern?

Note. This decision tree is intended to aid assessments of clients presenting with work dysfunctions.

essarily sort themselves out into conceptually distinct diagnostic entities. The following case is illustrative.

Case 3.1
The Unsociable Computer Technician

Trevor had earned engineering and computer technology degrees from some of the nation's most prestigious universities. However, his career progress had not matched his early academic accomplishments because, although technically proficient, he was never able to acclimate socially into his work group. Eventually, he sought outside assistance for his work problem.

Despite excellent and well-regarded research skills and an outstanding research record, he managed in most work settings rather quickly to assume a reputation for being unlikable and strange. Computer technologists as a group often manifest isolated, impersonal behavior, but this client's was unusual even for members of this occupational group. What led his colleagues to their conclusions regarding him was his persistent suspiciousness of others, inappropriate romantic overtures to female coworkers, imagining slights, grandiosity, and general social isolation.

Psychological evaluation revealed a very bright yet rigid nonpsychotic young man who, when under stress, regressed significantly. The client's family of origin had been very disturbed. Diagnostically, he probably fit best into a mixed personality-disorder classification with schizoid and paranoid features (see chapter 7). His psychopathology clearly predated his work problems, although the ineffective way in which the work problems were addressed when they arose in the workplace may have exacerbated his psychological difficulties.

Despite being terminated from two of his past employment positions, both at widely respected engineering research firms, he clung to the idea that he would be "rescued" by his present employer, despite the now-familiar work impairments. When this fantasy proved clearly untenable, he began to experience a serious depressive reaction and to consider making "wild" career shifts that, for him, were quite impractical choices.

Intervention in this case focused on raising the client's self-esteem so that he could better explore the inferiority underlying his social distance and expressed grandiosity. As in many such cases, treatment needed to be sensitive to reality issues of the workplace and the treatment of psychological dysfunctions. The work issues needed to be more than just "grist for the therapeutic mill" given that failure to attend to real-life work issues could have resulted in the client's termination or some other jeopardizing of the work role.

In Trevor's case, exploring family-of-origin dynamics revealed a perfectionistic, dominating mother and a distant, subservient father. Trevor's inappropriate advances toward women masked a deep-seated antipathy toward his mother for her dominance and control as well as anger at his father for not "rescuing" either Trevor or himself from the mother's control. Although this may suggest a psychodynamic rationale for the reported behavior, the workplace is generally not the preferred place to "act out" such conflicts. The potential workplace consequences are too severe and the results of possible job loss too disruptive of other aspects of life. The clinician in this case actively assisted the client in not further jeopardizing his position by inappropriate behavior that might have cost him his job. Although the client was still rather isolated from a "normal" social life after his intensive treatment, he had learned through therapeutic intervention more about his psychodynamics and ways to present himself more positively in his work setting. His became more directed toward goals in his work behavior and was able to sustain goal-directed performance and to minimize his self-destructive acts. Although he was still seen by many of his co-workers as aberrant, he provided his superiors no grounds for dismissal. After a time, the group's focus shifted to the quality of his work and away from the aberrations of his personality.

This case illustrates how the interaction of psychopathology in the workplace can be complex. In the next section, I introduce various components of my diagnostic taxonomy. In later chapters, each major type is elaborated in detail.

Patterns of Undercommitment

This grouping of work dysfunctions (2A in the taxonomy, discussed in detail in chapter 4) has in common the tendency to be underinvolved in work in a way that makes the individual less effective than his or her ability structure or career profile would otherwise suggest. Perhaps everyone underutilizes abilities to some extent, but inclusion in this classification implies that the pattern has become sufficiently dysfunctional to interfere with day-to-day work efforts. It is also important to differentiate transitory but perhaps predictable patterns of withdrawal (e.g., a writer finds herself unable to write for three months after concluding of a significant creative project) from those that are persistent or chronic (e.g., a "writer" who never gets around to writing anything because of constant procrastination).

The central issue in patterns of undercommitment is a failure to commit to requirements of the work role such that potential is not reached or there is a significant discrepancy between required job duties and prototypical job performance. Undercommitment patterns can be cyclical, occurring at sporadic intervals, or they can be persistent and typically characteristic of the individual's job performance. Both the individual and the employing organization suffer in not obtaining the best the individual is capable of on the job. Several common patterns of undercommitment are underachievement, temporary production impediments (blocks), procrastination, lack of occupational and organizational fit, and "fear of success" and "fear of failure" syndromes.

In *underachievement* patterns, there is a chronic discrepancy between the individual's ability to do the job and how he or she actually performs the job. Underachievement can be caused by a variety of issues, including passive–aggressive behavior. *Temporary production impediments* such as writer's or painter's blocks (or other general intrusions into the creative process) refer to a temporary or cyclically periodic inhibition in the work role in an individual who formerly performed at a higher level. *Procrastination* refers to a persistent and/or cyclical pattern in which an individual who is otherwise capable of doing the job repetitively avoids timely initiation and/or completion of work assignments or activities that must be initiated or completed by a particular deadline, real or perceived. Often, the individual waits until the last minute and then races to complete the various tasks quickly. By procrastinating, the individual may, for example, preserve the illusion of greater talent than has yet been manifested, may indulge in a thrill-seeking race to get assignments turned in just under the wire, or may passive–aggressively avoid timely or agreeable compliance with the requirements of those in authority.

Lack of occupational or organizational fit refers to individuals who are mismatched with their work or with the characteristic or predominant career profile of those in the group of organizational setting where the work is performed (see Lowman, 1991b, 1993a). Such patterns are often associated with underachievement on the job. Finally, various psychological conditions can also affect work performance, such as *fear of success* (Horner, 1968), in which the employee underachieves because of consciously or unconsciously perceived negative consequences associated with being "successful," including the perception that significant others may be dissatisfied or unhappy with the achievements. *Fear of failure*, or "hostile press" as it is sometimes termed, identifies energy withholding associated with concerns of not being successful in one's efforts; it may have diverse motivations.

Undercommitment syndromes share a failure to reach potential in one's work and a persistent, repetitive tendency to underrealize potential. For many affected, underachievement is accompanied by the sense of frustration that occupational rewards, which perhaps appropriately are seen as within the client's capability level, are not achieved. A discrepancy between potential and achievement, particularly when not due to issues of the client's apparent own choosing, can be the source of chronic frustration, disappointment, and anger.

In assessing undercommitment conditions, it is important to differentiate characteristics of individuals and individual reactions that reflect an appropriate coping mechanism for working within a dysfunctional organizational system. Ashforth and Lee (1990), for example, noted that withdrawal may be an effective coping strategy in certain bureaucratic organizations. In such situations, change of the work environment (e.g., through leaving it) may be a more expeditious change route than trying to change one's personal attitudes. The therapeutic goal in working with patterns of underachievement is to determine the motivating forces that account for the dysfunction and assist the individual in understanding and resolving the conflict so that it becomes less of an impediment to reaching desired work goals. Intervention characteristics will vary with the specific underachievement dynamics. Passive–aggressive behavior, for example, will best be handled in a different therapeutic way than one would treat a client who is mismatched with his or her current occupation, as in the following case illustration.

Case 3.2
A Misplaced Accountant

Sidney was 25 years old at the time he came for career assessment. He was extremely unhappy in his present work situation. As an accounting student in California, he had interned in a large accounting firm that subsequently offered him a job. Initially, he had been very challenged in his work at the company, but after a few months a need in another segment of the company forced him to be reassigned. In his new job, he was no longer conducting audits but was expected to design a new accounting system from scratch to meet the needs of the small business market. Whereas his previous work had been highly structured, there was very little explicit structure in this new position, and he was left alone most of the day to work on designing the new system. Working autonomously was typical of the accountants assigned to this section.

Sidney spent his days in increased frustration. He could not get accustomed to the absence of structure and the need to create something from nothing. Although his superiors had expressed no dissatisfaction with his work (in fact, they felt that he was a competent and reliable employee), Sidney felt he was about to be fired and began inquiries into alternative positions and companies. He became seriously depressed, showing vegetative signs (insomnia, weight loss, and decreased libido). His wife of six months became alarmed. Recognizing that he was in trouble and with the encouragement of his wife, Sidney sought out psychological assistance before making a radical job change.

Assessment showed Sidney to be a bright young man with vocational interests and abilities appropriate to his chosen profession of accounting. However, his personality data demonstrated that he was extremely constricted and lacking in imagination, being far better suited to working in a prescribed routine than to venturing off into something new and undefined. These were not neurotic conditions but ones of temperament (see, e.g., Gough, 1992).

With the help of his therapist, the client was better able to understand his career profile. He came to a prompt conclusion that he was misplaced in his present position but not in his occupation. As a result, he made a relatively minor "course correction" in his occupational choice, moving to a section of the organization involving auditing and the use of prescribed procedures rather than innovative ones. His depression quickly lifted.

Patterns of Overcommitment

Patterns of overcommitment refer to too intense identification with and involvement in the work role such that personal psychological (and sometimes physical) health is potentially impaired. Overcommitment does not become a work dysfunction, of course, until it is perceived by the employee as a problem or until the consequences of the overcommitment become problematic from a physical or mental health perspective. Because work patterns of overcommitment are often positively regarded and rewarded in the workplace, individuals manifesting difficulties in the overcommitment area often do not seek out help until physical or other psychological symptoms are manifest or until some key aspect of the work role changes (e.g., they are laid off in a corporate merger or economic downturn).

Three major syndromes are reviewed in chapter 5, which covers overcommitment patterns: (a) compulsive or obsessive–compulsive dynamics (sometimes called *workaholism*), generally combined with a narrow range of interests and associated with an addiction to the work role; (b) the Type A or coronary-prone personality pattern; and (c) job and/or occupational burnout. In obsessive–compulsive addictions to the work role, work may be one of many areas of compulsive behavior, or it may be the primary area to which the individual is rigidly attached. The wide study in the health psychology field of Type A behavior pattern, a syndrome examined in chapter 5, has identified it as a syndrome that may have important psychological consequences, independent of the now-controversial issue of whether it predicts to health difficulties, particularly in the coronary area. Finally, job or occupational burnout often reflects characteristics of the work itself as much as of people fulfilling the work role. People in social service "helping" roles appear especially prone to this condition.

Work-Related Anxiety and Depression

Although anxiety and depression can be associated with any work dysfunction and may be viewed more as being symptoms of other conditions than a separable category, the apparent pervasiveness of these conditions merit their inclusion as a separate category (Fletcher, 1988; Kornhauser, 1965). Chapter 6 reviews relevant literature on these topics.

Work-related anxiety can be specific to isolated aspects of the work role (such as with people experiencing trouble with the interpersonal aspects of a job to which they are otherwise well-suited) or can reflect a generalized condition. Work-related depression is a commonly encountered condition in assessing and treating work dysfunctions and needs careful evaluation to determine whether it should be treated before or after work problems.

Personality Dysfunctions and Work

Personality problems create some of the most emotionally volatile and difficult to manage workplace problems, affecting not just the individual but often others in the work section or organization. Often, these difficulties assume proportions greatly discrepant with the precipitating conflict as individuals get locked into dysfunctional interactions and as conflicts become publicly manifest in the organizational context. They may reflect longstanding characterological problems of the individual, dysfunctional authority patterns, or disordered peer relationships, among other psychological dynamics.

Because conflicts with authority are so frequently encountered in clients presenting with personality difficulties and work problems, they are given special attention in chapter 7. Characteristics of the individual and the supervision must be considered in evaluating such difficulties. In a case of conflict with authority in which the supervisee is the client, the problem may be as much an overcontrolling or otherwise incompetent manager as it may be a personality disorder of the client. All supervision involves the exertion of authority; some supervisors are simply better at exercising their control such that they do not create conflicts with their subordinates and leave the supervisory control more implicit than explicit. Similarly, except for those who work alone, most employees are subject to the exercise of authority. What the employee brings to the work situation in terms of prior authority problems, including unresolved conflicts with parental figures, will influence the likelihood of conflicts. However, in practice, it may more likely be the client who must accommodate to the working situation than the other way around. Authority problems are typically directed toward supervisors or managers, whereas other types of interpersonal conflict are typically directed toward peers or subordinates. Those who meet *DSM–III–R* diagnostic criteria of personality disorders are at risk for also experiencing problems in the work role. In chapter 7, each of the 11 current *DSM–III–R* personality disorders are reviewed in terms of their work role implications.

Subsequent chapters discuss in more detail several of these broad, cross-situational patterns of work dysfunctions; outline therapeutic principles; and use case examples to illustrate the complexities of diagnosis and clinical intervention techniques in actual practice. First, however, several additional work dysfunctions noted in the taxonomy are briefly noted.

Other Psychologically Relevant Work Difficulties

Life Role Conflicts

At times, stress on the job is due to stress off the job. Conversely, difficulties in the work role may cause the individual to experience stress in nonwork life. Although cited in the taxonomy and an important area of study (see, e.g., Zedeck, 1992), comprehensive treatment of this topic is not a focus of this book (see, however, Ulrich & Dunne, 1986, for a discussion of some of the therapeutic implications of conflicts between work and nonwork).

Transient, Situational Stress

Although situational work stress may be as troublesome to the individual as deep-seated behavioral difficulties at the time it is experienced, it is more amenable to crisis or short-term intervention and is generally short-lived. This type of stress includes reactions to changes in the work role (e.g., new job, new boss). Such short-term situationally delimited actions are not further discussed in this book.

Perceptual Inaccuracies

Perceptual inaccuracies occur in situations in which there is some significant difference between consensually validated views of the situation and the client's perceptions. This category does not refer primarily to severe perceptual distortion in which the individual psychotically distorts reality (which falls outside the scope of work dysfunctions). Perceptual inaccuracies instead refer to motivated, nonpsychotic discrepancies between perceptions of the client and those of the others in the work setting. An example would be a manager who always thinks that his supervisor is angrily opposed to his ideas when in fact it is the manager who is angry.

In clinically assessing clients with work dysfunctions, an accurate and unbiased perception of the dynamics of the work situation may be difficult to ascertain. Contrary to certain psychodynamic models, work treatment may often benefit from external views of the nature of the problematic behavior (assuming the client's written consent). A client's lament about grossly unfair treatment by a supervisor may need to be juxtaposed with the supervisor's own interpretation of the behavior. Although the clinician is generally in a poor position to assess the factual realities of different versions of the same events, some clinical judgment is required given that a client who perceptually distorts the truth or outright lies will require different therapeutic intervention than someone who is truly victimized by an exploitative work system.

In ruling out perceptual distortions, the clinician can ask straightforward, commonsense questions such as "How would you feel about my talking directly with your supervisor to get a better understanding of his side of things?", "Is it possible that your supervisor may be upset at your missing work so much while your husband was sick?", "Has this ever happened to you with other supervisors (or on other jobs)?" Experience with a multitude of work-related counseling situations in which cases have extended to known outcomes will also assist the clinician in improving clinical judgment in determining whether the client is accurately perceiving the dynamics of the work situation. The task of the clinician is to function as an ally to the client without taking sides.

Dysfunctional Working Conditions

Changing the nature of the job rather than of the person is advised when the nature of the work or working conditions are believed to be primary. As discussed in chapter 2, characteristics of the workplace or job itself may partly or wholly be responsible for conditions presented as work dysfunctions. Work dysfunctions caused by the context of the work or workplace include defective job design, defective supervision, and dysfunctional interpersonal employee relationships ("personality conflicts").

It is the initial responsibility of the clinician to make at least a preliminary assessment of the extent to which the client's psychological difficulties are caused by working conditions, by the individual's personal psychological dynamics, or by some complex interaction of the two. The clinician may well not be trained, interested, or available in making changes in the working conditions themselves. Nonetheless, the therapist of work dysfunctions needs to make a brief evaluation from the client's perspective of at least the nature of the working conditions.

When the working conditions are clearly dysfunctional (and perceptual distortions or motivational distortions associated with pending stress-related claims do not account for the client's views), the clinician should consider contacting the workplace or referring the client to a trained industrial specialist. Again, a wide breadth of clinical experience within a variety of work settings and with a variety of work-related presenting problems will assist the clinician in determining the most effective course of treatment. Commonsense questions that take a third-party perspective (e.g., "How is it that your supervisor only singles out you as a target for attack?" or "Have you made use of the grievance procedure in your workplace") may assist in determining whether it is the workplace itself or the client's departure from it that needs to be the focus of attention.

Summary

This chapter discusses issues important in clinically diagnosing work dysfunction conditions. Assessing the role and relevance of psychopathology to work dysfunctions can be a complex, although important, diagnostic consideration. To some degree, diagnosis of the nature of the work itself and its suitability to the client may also be required.

The two clinical taxonomies presented classify the types of work difficulties that clients may experience. Case examples illustrate applications of one of the diagnostic schemes to actual cases of work dysfunctions.

Appendix A
Campbell and Cellini's Taxonomy of Work Dysfunctions: Problem Categories and Subcategories

I. Problems in career decision making
   A. Getting started
      1. Lack of awareness of the need for a decision
      2. Lack of knowledge of the decision-making process
      3. Awareness of the need to make a decision but avoidance of assuming personal responsibility for decision making
   B. Information gathering
      1. Inadequate, contradictory, and/or insufficient information
      2. Information overload (i.e., excessive information that confuses the decisionmaker)
      3. Lack of knowledge as to how to gather information (i.e., where to obtain, organize, and evaluate information)
      4. Unwillingness to accept the validity of the information because it does not agree with the person's self-concept
   C. Generating, evaluating, and selecting alternatives
      1. Difficulty deciding owing to multiple career options (i.e., too many equally attractive career choices)
      2. Failure to generate sufficient career options because of personal limitations such as health, resources, ability, or education
      3. Inability to decide because of the thwarting effects of anxiety such as fear of failure in attempting to fulfill the choice, fear of social disapproval, and/or fear of commitment to a course of action

Note. From "A Diagonostic Taxonomy of Adult Career Problems" by R. E. Campbell and J. V. Cellini, 1981, *Journal of Vocational Behavior, 19,* pp. 178–180. Copyright © 1981 by Academic Press. Adapted by permission.

4. Unrealistic choice (i.e., aspiring to goals either too low or too high based on criteria such as aptitudes, interests, values, resources, and personal circumstances
5. Interfering personal constraints that impede a choice (e.g., interpersonal influences and conflicts, situation circumstances, resources, health)
6. Inability to evaluate alternatives because of lack of knowledge of the evaluation criteria (e.g., criteria could include values, interests, aptitudes, skills, resources, health, age, and personal circumstances)

D. Formulating plans to implement decision
1. Lack of knowledge of the necessary steps to formulate a plan
2. Inability to use a future time perspective in planning
3. Unwillingness and/or inability to acquire the necessary information to formulate a plan

II. Problems in implementing career plans
A. Characteristics of the individual
1. Failure of to undertake the steps necessary to implement plan
2. Failure or inability to successfully complete the steps necessary for goal attainment
3. Adverse conditions of or changes in family situation

III. Problems in organization/institutional performance
A. Deficiencies in skills, abilities, or knowledge
1. Insufficient skills, abilities, and/or knowledge on position entry (i.e., underqualified to perform satisfactorily)
2. Deterioration of skills, abilities, and/or knowledge over time in the position because of temporary assignment to another position, leave, and/or lack of continual practice of the skill
3. Failure to modify or update skills, abilities, and/or knowledge to stay abreast of job changes (i.e., job obsolescence following new technology, tools, and knowledge)

B. Personal factors
1. Personality characteristics discrepant with the job (e.g., values, interests, work habits)

2. Debilitating physical and/or emotional disorders
3. Adverse off-the-job personal circumstances and/or stressors (e.g., family pressures, financial problems, personal conflicts)
4. Occurrence of interpersonal conflicts on the job specific to performance requirements (e.g., getting along with supervisor, coworkers, customers, clients)

C. Conditions of the organization/institutional environment
   1. Ambiguous or inappropriate job requirements (e.g., lack of clarity of assignments, work overload, conflicting assignments)
   2. Deficiencies in the operational structure of the organization/institution
   3. Inadequate support facilities, supplies, or resources (e.g., insufficient lighting, ventilation, tools, support personnel, materials)
   4. Insufficient reward system (e.g., compensation, fringe benefits, status recognition, opportunities for advancement)

IV. Problems in organizational/institutional adaptation
   A. Initial entry
      1. Lack of knowledge of organizational rules and procedures
      2. Failure to accept or adhere to organizational rules and procedures
      3. Inability to assimilate large quantities of new information (i.e., information overload)
      4. Discomfort in a new geographic location
      5. Discrepancies between individual's expectations and the realities of the institutional/organizational environment
   B. Changes over time
      1. Changes over the life span in one's attitudes, values, life style, career plans, or commitment to the organization that lead to incongruence between the individual and the environment (e.g., physical and administrative structure, policies, procedures)

C. Interpersonal relationships
   1. Interpersonal conflicts arising from differences of opinion, style, values, mannerisms, etc.
   2. Occurrence of verbal or physical abuse or sexual harassment

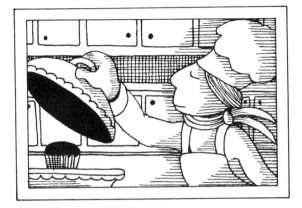

Patterns of Undercommitment

To achieve in any significant human endeavor is to assert one's independence, one's self (Krueger, 1984). For individuals having had benevolently perceived families of origin, achievement (although rarely effortless) is generally not the source of significant ambivalence or conflict. However, in patterns of adult undercommitment of psychogenic origin, asserting one's talent may invite conflict (see Weiss, 1990). To succeed by fulfilling one's own promise can come to be viewed as an issue of pleasing or frustrating the parent. Ambivalence toward a parent or mixed or disapproving messages (especially, for women, from the mother) can apparently cause conflict in the working role (e.g., H. G. Lerner, 1987; J. R. Miller, 1980; Moulton, 1985; Person, 1982; Teevan, 1983). Maternal depression has also been suggested as a source of work inhibition among women (see K. G. Cole, 1983). Success in such cases can become psychologically associated with giving in or relinquishing control by pleasing the parent and subconsciously letting the parent "win." The game can be tautly played, with a tension between showing just enough of one's talents to prove they are there yet not enough to succeed in the sense of lasting and prolonged occupational achievements. In a sense, it is a teasing game, often frustrating for those who must supervise or counsel the undercommitted worker.

The conditions of undercommitment may also be a source of great frustration to the client, who may feel that the job, work, supervisor, or career is holding him or her back from success perceived to be obtainable. Of course, rejections in school or the workplace may also influence the willingness to compete and risk one's self-esteem to an often-rejecting outside world over which one has little personal control. As Lyons (1992) put it in a memorable essay on rejections experienced by writers,

> There are ways of insulating yourself from rejection . . . risking little, wanting (and needing) nothing—but such protection reminds me of Swift's jibe at stoicism: that it supplies our wants by lopping off our desires, cuts off our feet when we need shoes. (p. 20)

Unfortunately for the undercommitted worker, the world of work does not wait for the resolution of psychic conflicts. Conflicts with authority, particularly in large organizational contexts, usually are resolved in favor of authority. The rallying catharsis that expression of antiauthority sentiments may generate among fellow employees is usually squelched with the sacrifice of the offending party. Changing this destructive pattern requires some understanding of the psychodynamics of undercommitment that are operative in particular cases. At least three subtypes, presumably reflecting different psychodynamic origins, can be identified: (a) anger that is misdirected at authority figures, (b) problems of self-esteem or self-doubt, and (c) fear or reluctance to compete. Other causes are also possible. From the extensive academic underachievement literature, for example, implicated factors include socioeconomic factors, sibling relationships, expectations of significant others such as teachers, inability to make a poor fit better over time, and characteristics of personality (see the excellent summary of research in this area by Mandel &

Marcus, 1988). In each case, the psychological issues involved may be complex and multiply determined. In addition to psychodynamic factors, undercommitment may be associated with the client's failure to find a career path that is personally motivating. Those who work in fields not compatible with their primary interests or abilities, or who simply have not yet found a work choice of interest, may be especially prone to experiencing undercommitment. Because the psychodynamics will vary from one case to another, the therapist needs to identify for each client the central themes associated with the particular pattern of undercommitment.

The following case illustrates many of the complexities of working with underachieving clients, particularly when there are long-standing entrenched personality issues.

Case 4.1
The Persistent Underachiever

Although Peter was 28 years old when referred, he looked closer to 18. He had bright blond hair that he wore in a frizzy hairstyle and through which he had dyed a jagged black streak. He wore earrings and dressed in a flamboyant, seemingly attention-seeking manner. He worked as a probation officer (nonsupervisory) in a large state bureaucracy. Peter came for his therapy appointments wearing his uniform, which was oddly irregular. He tested every limit and challenged the authority of his employer with dizzying regularity. At the time of his referral, he had had yet another altercation with his supervisor and had been put on medical leave until the event passed over. He was asked to remove weapons from his home and to sign an agreement stating that he would not harm his supervisor or himself, a request to which he readily consented.

The event precipitating the referral was the client's becoming irate with his Hispanic supervisor, whom he claimed was persistently rude to him. In particular, the client insisted that his supervisor call him by his surname and the title *Mister*. When the supervisor continued to call him by his first name, Peter filed grievances and became openly angry toward his supervisor, making veiled threats. At this point, Peter was referred to his employee assistance program and, ultimately, for counseling.

The client's mental health benefit plan authorized a fixed number of treatment sessions, which thereafter could be renewed. In this case, the client was initially given six sessions to address these complex issues. Anticipating a much larger and physically threatening man, the therapist was rather shocked when Peter arrived, rather sheepishly, to his appointment. Everything about his physical appearance said "rebel," yet there was something oddly likable about this curious young misfit.

A bright young man, Peter professed to take special pleasure in "breaking in" new supervisors in his work group. He had "initiated" several. Because he felt he knew the work rules and regulations much more thoroughly than they did, he felt that he could always trip them up on something, even if he did not have every detail exactly straight. Supervisors came to fear him (and therefore dislike him), a situation the client professed to love, enjoying his power and ability to intimidate. However, Peter was clearly ambivalent about being in this system and felt that it was beneath him intellectually, which in fact it was. Yet, he had enrolled in college only once, had sat through a few classes, and had concluded that he knew more than the instructor, that the students were intellectually inferior to him, and that he was making too much money to put up with this, as he indelicately put it, "bullshit."

As a client, Peter engaged with the therapist rapidly. He showed up promptly for every session dressed as colorfully as ever, paid his small copayment in cash, and shook hands at both the beginning and end of each session. What quickly emerged was a portrait of a chronic underachiever who was seemingly without effort or awareness following the occupational footsteps of his father, whom he professed not to respect. The depth of the character issues, combined with periodic substance abuse (acknowledged only later in the treatment), caused therapy to progress slowly.

The client had been raised in a family in which the father's work involved frequent moves. His parents had met abroad during wartime. The father was described as being a passive but somewhat angry and rebellious alcoholic who was chronically unhappy with his work situation yet unable to make any substantive changes in it. He was viewed as the mother's intellectual inferior, and the family myth was that the father was generally inadequate. Eventually, his parents divorced, and Peter began alternating between time with his penurious mother (whom he perceived as a talented underachiever) and her family of origin and time with a father whom he perceived to be inadequate and unsupportive. The client obtained a "good government job," choosing not to go to college despite having had good high school grades.

Major treatment goals in this case were to help the client keep his job, stop seeking so much inappropriate gratification of neurotic conflicts through his work, and, perhaps most important of all, begin taking steps to enable himself to prepare for a better fitting and more intellectually fulfilling career. Making sense of the wall of resistance that this client had created around any efforts to help him move beyond his present position benefited from a psychodynamic understanding of his family-of-origin issues.

In treatment, Peter proved to be an engaged client but one whose transference included the perception that the psychotherapist just "did not understand" how difficult change was for him. His narcissism made efforts to confront his patterns difficult. Finally, he dropped out of treatment, returning only when external circumstances (including the threatened loss of his job) forced him to acknowledge the seriousness of his estrangement and his substance abuse. Eventually, referral to an adult children of alcoholics group provided him with some perspective on the origins and commonality of his family stress, and he began to become slightly more sensitive to his behavior. Treatment, however, progressed on his own terms and schedule of readiness to change. After a period of six months of not attending therapy, the therapist wrote to indicate that the case would be closed after a certain date. The client subsequently developed a crisis at work and sought additional help. In fact, he had made substantial progress in his independent efforts at adjustment, slowly and with considerably more anxiety than he could acknowledge or share.

Until the latest cause for his referral, the client had not had any new problems at work, had stopped using most drugs, and was behaving much more compliantly at work, although he remained singularly misfit. At this point, treatment was rapid and improvement spontaneous. He began to accept responsibility for his own unhappiness at work and to make realistic plans to begin college. His few remaining sessions focused on termination, which this time proceeded appropriately. Today, the client is finishing a degree program and soon plans to assume a relevant position in which his skills and talents will be utilized more effectively.

Cultural, Familial, and Personality Factors in Undercommitment

Although psychodynamic explanations of patterns of undercommitment are valuable in particular cases for generating clinically relevant hypotheses, they also have limitations, particularly when they are applied mechanistically to a set of problems for which they were not originally developed (see Cavenar & Werman, 1981; Mallinger, 1978; Schecter, 1979; Wasylenki, 1984). A tendency to explain undercommitment exclusively in psychodynamic terms should be avoided. In all cases, the therapist should be familiar with the research literature on alternative, nonpsychogenic explanations of the phenomenon (see, e.g., Grieff & Munter, 1980).

Systemic and cultural factors must also be taken into account. Undercommitment is defined to some extent subjectively by an individual, with some standard of comparison, either explicit or implicit. The comparison standard may be the culture at large; one's peers, parents, or siblings; or some internalized, perhaps idealized, view of oneself. The family dynamics and context also need to be considered. Some studies have reported, for example, that undercommitment or relatively lower achievement by a husband compared with that of his spouse can be associated with a heightened increase in risk for spouse abuse (Hornung, McCullough, & Sugimoto, 1981).

Personality factors as much as ability differences may account for differential behavior among at least some types of underachievers and overachievers. Romine and Crowell (1981) found, in a study of academic overachievers and underachievers of equal ability, that the overachievers were nonprocrastinating, hard working, and serious—characteristics opposite to those of the underachieving group. Whether these differences extend to adult populations has not yet been empirically established. Other factors potentially associated with patterns of overachievement include birth order (Pfouts, 1980) and characteristics of the situation. For example, situations high in achievement expectations may be more likely to trigger achievement-related behavior among certain individuals. Bergman and Magnusson (1979) reported that among overachieving men, but not women, adrenaline levels were elevated in an achievement situation but not in a neutral situation.

Learned helplessness models (Dweck & Wortman, 1982; Seligman, 1975) and attribution models (Heider, 1958; Kelley, 1967; Weiner, 1982) also have relevance for understanding underachievement dynamics. Although people can and certainly do differ in what they bring to their work and career choices (e.g., their characteristic level of motivation and energy level), how they interpret what happens to them can also influence their expectation of achievement and the likelihood with which they initiate behavior likely to result in success. For some individuals, the opportunity to discover a relationship between personal effort and desired outcomes is absent or has become seriously impaired. This may occur, as in learned helplessness models, through a series of aversive experiences that occur in response to personally initiated effort.

In psychologically healthy patterns of achievement, individuals discover a contingency between their efforts and positive outcomes. They focus on aspects of the situation that they can control and adjust their expectations to be reasonably congruent with reality. When, over time, a person comes to believe that there is no association between effort and positive outcomes or that their efforts result in painful consequences, they may cease self-initiated effort. Covington and Omelich (1991) examined an important distinction made in the original models of need for achievement, namely the hypothesis that need for achievement results from a conflict between hoped-for success and the fear of failure. They identified four groups, empirically validated in a study of college students: success oriented (high in success seeking and low in failure avoidance), failure oriented (low in success seeking and high in failure avoidance), conflicted over-strivers (high in both success seeking and failure avoidance), and failure accepting (low in both success seeking and failure avoidance). In this model, it is the interaction of two conflicting individual dynamics that determines achievement-oriented behavior. Presumably, there can be change over time as either of the variables changes.

Attribution models also contribute to the understanding of underachievement patterns among adults. In attribution theory, what happens to a person may be less important than how the person interprets the event (or series of events over time). Underachievement patterns may result when positive outcomes are attributed to accidental features (e.g., luck) yet failure is attributed to the results of personal effort (Weiner, 1982). According to Weiner (1982), people seek explanations (i.e., attribute causality) for outcomes, especially under conditions of failure. They may attribute bad outcomes to chance factors such as mood, fatigue, or illness; to lack of effort; or to inability to perform the task. Problematic attributions that are likely to lead to patterns of underachievement include those in which individuals attribute blame to themselves for unfavorable consequences and belittle themselves for perceived shortcomings.

What also differentiates those who are likely to succeed is that they do not stop trying, even when they are initially unsuccessful and may experience as much failure as or more than those who abandon effort or settle for a lesser outcome. People more likely to fail seem to remember failures and forget successes (Dweck & Wortman, 1982) in addition to "giving away" the successes they earn while retaining their failures. Given that failure is an inevitable part of the achievement process, it is not so much the occurrence of failure that matters as how the individual chooses to interpret it. Attempts made despite failures enhance the likelihood of long-term successful outcomes.

General Diagnostic and Therapeutic Issues

Identification of a pattern of undercommitment obviously requires some indication that there is a discrepancy between ability and accomplishment.[1] The therapist should note that undercommitment patterns are not limited to those with few abilities. Gifted children and adults also experience the phenomenon (Gallagher, 1991).

In establishing a pattern of difference between ability and performance, objective assessment of the client's ability pattern has both its uses and limitations. Certainly, intelligence testing alone is not sufficient to establish undercommitment in all domains in which the phenomenon might occur. Undercommitment patterns may have little to do with the results of measures of general intelligence, contrary to the views of some (e.g., Spokane, 1993). Thus, writing, art, physical abilities, and the like are not predominantly predicted by intellectual factors, and classical ability testing of objective measures of cognitive abilities may have limited utility. Age at the time of assessment must also be considered. Certain patterns of achievement have characteristic levels of peak productivity and achievement (see Simonton, 1988, 1989). For example, a musician with demonstrated talent at age 16 who is failing to make progress and not practicing at age 19 may arouse in the psychologist greater cause for concern than may an aspiring writer or philosopher who at the same age appears to be floundering and not achieving. Some occupational pursuits simply take longer than others for the various components to gel or reach fruition. This particularly appears to be the case with occupations that require broad knowledge in diverse domains rather than focalized, somewhat unidimensional work.

The therapist's task in working with the undercommited is generally not to create change per se, particularly with a highly resistant client intent on making the therapist another super-

---

[1] Although some personality scales purport to measure underachievement (e.g., Felton, 1973), the clinician should not rely on such measures alone in establishing a pattern of underachievement.

egolike figure. Rather, the therapist's goal is first to contribute to the client's acceptance of self and factors influencing his or her behavior, particularly when the pattern has been ongoing. Even when long-standing undercommitment patterns can be changed rapidly, it is important for the therapist to be clear on what is being changed and why. The therapist should have a solid understanding of the psychodynamics driving the observed pattern of undercommitment and a plan for intervention. Alternative dynamics and various personality structures may call for different technical approaches.

The following sections identify and examine several specific patterns of undercommitment, review relevant literature, and provide illustrative case material.

Fear of Success and Fear of Failure

Fear of Success

Fear of success (FOS) and fear of failure (FOF) appear to be separable, if potentially interactive, constructs in understanding certain patterns of workplace undercommitment (Griffore, 1977a; Intons-Peterson & Johnson, 1980; Karabenick & Marshall, 1977; McElroy & Willis, 1979; Mulig, Haggerty, Carballosa, Cinnick, & Madden, 1985). Indeed, there is evidence that there may be overlap between these constructs (see Sadd, Lenauer, Shaver, & Dunivant, 1978). *FOS* refers to a persistent tendency to avoid behaviors that may be associated with achievement, particularly when success looms imminent, and to minimize accomplishments or attribute achievement to factors not controlled by the individual (see Horner, 1968, 1972; Kirkpatrick, 1982; Zuckerman & Allison, 1976). Low self-esteem, being preoccupied with external evaluation, and a competitive orientation have also been described as characteristic of those who experience FOS (Pappo, 1983).

Although still somewhat controversial, the FOS construct has generated a large body of literature, and there is evidence that it predicts at least to some degree real-life work and school undercommitment phenomena. Hoffman (1977), for example, reported in a follow-up study of women experiencing FOS that they reported 9 years after the initial measurement to be much more likely to have become pregnant when on the verge of success relative to a spouse or boyfriend. Goh and Mealiea (1984) reported that in a sample of female clerical workers, women with greater FOS were more likely to evaluate their job performance negatively, although it did not affect job tenure.

There is a diverse literature examining the differential impact of the FOS construct, beginning perhaps with Freud's early essay on "those wrecked by success" (Freud, 1915/1959). FOS may be more common among younger than older adult workers (Orpen, 1989; Popp & Muhs, 1982). Although the extent of a sex difference is not yet reliably established, it apparently interacts with the type of measurement technique used and the time of measurement. Hoffman's (1977) follow-up study of previously measured research subjects, for example, found that women generally experienced less FOS than at initial measurement, whereas men experienced more. Whereas many studies have reported a higher rate of FOS among women or girls than men or boys (Silva, 1982; Vanvaria, Agrawal, & Singh, 1981), others have not (Brenner & Tomkiewicz, 1982; Chabassol & Ishiyama, 1983; Curtis, Zanna, & Campbell, 1975; Kearney, 1984; O'Connell, & Perez, 1982; Wood & Greenfeld, 1979; Yamauchi, 1982), especially when the construct is operationalized in a complex manner (Intons-Peterson & Johnson, 1980). Evidence for racial differences is mixed and inconclusive (Esposito, 1977; Fleming, 1977, 1978, 1982; Gonsalves, 1983; S. R. Murray & Mednick, 1977; Popp & Muhs, 1982; Puryear & Mednick, 1974; Savage & Stearns, 1979).

Some of the contradictory findings in the literature may be due to age and population differences (workers vs. students), occupational or activity differences, cultural differences (e.g., Weinreich-Haste, 1978), and variations in method of measuring the construct (Gelbort & Winer, 1985; Hoffman, 1977, 1982; Juran, 1979; Moreland & Liss-Levinson, 1977; Paludi, 1984; Ward, 1978; Zuckerman & Wheeler, 1975). Projective stimuli have not consistently portrayed the degree of success depicted in the stimulus to which projections are made (Fogel & Paludi, 1984; Paludi, 1979) or the type of occupation in terms of whether it is male dominated or female dominated (e.g., nursing vs. engineering; Breedlove & Cicirelli, 1974; F. Cherry & Deaux, 1978; Janda, O'Grady, & Capps, 1978; Shapiro, 1979). In addition, a wide variety of measures of the construct have been reported in the literature, which encompasses both projective and objective methodologies (e.g., Griffore, 1977b; Ho & Zemaitis, 1981; Reviere & Posey, 1978; Zuckerman & Allison, 1976; Zuckerman & Wheeler, 1975). Projective measures of FOS may result in higher estimations of FOS than may objective measures (see Gelbort & Winer, 1985). In addition, cohort differences (Hoffman, 1974; Yogev, 1983) and variables possibly reflective of cohort differences (e.g., whether a woman had a working or nonworking mother) may also influence the experience of FOS (Gibbons & Kopelman, 1977; Gilroy, Talierco, & Steinbacher, 1981), as may unmeasured variables reflecting ability differences (Curtis et al., 1975; K. M. Taylor, 1982). Cultural differences are also relevant (Wang & Creedon, 1989).

Moreover, FOS may not be a unitary construct but may have embedded in it a number of dimensions such as certain types of anxiety and commitment (Daniels, Alcorn, & Kazelskis, 1981; Hyland & Dann, 1988; Illfelder, 1980; Sadd et al., 1978; A. H. Stein & Bailey, 1973) and masked subcomponents such as the fear of appearing incompetent (Brenner & Tomkiewicz, 1982). Sassen (1980) argued that it is not FOS per se that arouses conflict, especially for women, but the nature of the competitive environment in which "success" is pursued. Undercommitment is reported generally to be associated with elevated levels of anxiety, at least as related to the undercommitment stimulus (Sepie & Keeling, 1978). However, the cause of the anxiety may be important in determining the dynamics and intervention tactics clinically appropriate. Hoffman (1974) and others (e.g., Pfost & Fiore, 1990; Sancho & Hewitt, 1990) suggested that for women it is perceived affiliative loss that contributes to FOS and presumably to the experienced anxiety, whereas for men it is more likely to be a questioning of the value of success or achievement. In fact, anxiety concerning success may be triggered by a variety of feared stimuli. Balkin (1986) reported FOS concerning college achievement among males who were the first in their family to attend college. Indeed, Hyland (1989) attempted to abandon or at least reconceptualize FOS as a characteristic motive of individuals, substituting for the idea of FOS simply an attempt by individuals to compromise when confronted with competing goals.

FOS may also interact with other dimensions of personality, such as internal or external locus of control (LOC; R. Anderson, 1978; Feather & Simon, 1973; Goh & Mealiea, 1984; Ireland-Galman & Michael, 1983; Midgley & Abrams, 1974; K. M. Taylor, 1982), masculinity or femininity (Byrd & Touliatos, 1982; Cano, Solomon, & Holmes, 1984; Forbes & King, 1983; Kearney, 1982; Sadd, Miller, & Zeitz, 1979; Savage & Stearns, 1979), Type A or B personality (Loewenstine & Paludi, 1982), learned helplessness (Ris & Woods, 1983), need for power (E. Sutherland, 1978), and need for achievement (Piedmont, 1988). Subjects high in FOS and low in need for achievement may be especially prone to performance disruptions (Tresemer, 1976).[2] FOS may also be associated with lower internal motivation and intrinsic task motivation (Zuckerman, Larrance, Porac, & Blanck, 1980). In addition, and perhaps most important for practicing clinicians to keep in mind, FOS can also be influenced by environmental factors such as type of task (Marshall & Karabenick, 1977), role overload (Bremer & Wittig, 1980), family and community endorsement of high standards (Farmer, 1980), peers (Balkin, 1987; Balkin & Donaruma, 1978), and public- versus private-sector setting (Wood & Greenfeld, 1979).

Fear of Failure

Like its more extensively studied counterpart, FOF (often called *hostile press*) has been found to be a complex mixture of multiple components.[3] Atkinson and Feather (1966) identified a "failure

---

[2] Most studies of FOS, FOF, and the like concern, by implication, those who score at the extreme ends on relevant scales. Sorrentino and Short (1977) noted that the behavior of those who score in the midranges on such scales may be much more inconsistent and therefore difficult to predict.

[3] A large body of literature on test anxiety addresses constructs sometimes viewed as constituting FOF (see Hodapp, 1989; Sadd, Lenauer, Shaver, & Dunivant, 1978). Although test anxiety may embody FOF constructs, it is not the primary focus of this book. Moreover, the generalizability of test anxiety to adult FOF phenomena is unestablished.

threatened" personality, who may cope by taking on very low or very high levels of task difficulty (the former assuring "success," the latter, "excusable" failure). As conceptualized by Birney, Burdick, and Teevan (1969), FOF concerns a perception that one will not be able to reach a desired or previously set goal or desired success (see Latta, 1978) and that one will therefore be a failure, especially in the eyes of others (Becker, Cohen, & Teevan, 1975). Birney et al. (1969) noted that failure experiences can result in lowered self-esteem, a perception (or reality) of external punishment, and a sense of decreased social value. Anxiety and worry, resulting in day-to-day dysphoria and avoidance behavior (Stavosky & Borkovec, 1987), become associated with the experience of failure and the tendency to avoid situations in which one may not succeed; low self-esteem may result, and the self-concept may become less stable (see C. Goldberg, 1973; Hamm, 1977). FOF has been demonstrated to be associated with academic and (to a lesser extent) adult achievement problems (Skeen & Zacchera, 1974). Conceptually, the literature differentiates between FOF that is failure avoidant and FOF that is driven by the desire to succeed (Weeda, Winny, & Drop, 1985). When one expects failure, one may avoid it as being an aversive experience; when one wants very badly to succeed, the fear of failure may exceed the expected benefits associated with the desired success.

The person generally high on FOF measures may cease to try; may try to reach a goal using inappropriate strategies such as spending too long on a task (see Teevan, Zarrillo, & Greenfeld, 1983), particularly in situations in which achievement motivation is likely to be aroused (Teevan & Yalof, 1979); or may set goals within an overly restricted range (Teevan & Smith, 1975). Alternatively, the individual may withdraw prematurely from a goal (e.g., a career; see Vaitenas & Wiener, 1977) or may make riskier, "go-for-broke" decisions, raising the probability of failure (Hartnett & Barber, 1974).

From a psychodynamic viewpoint, although FOS and FOF may both result in task avoidance or undercommitment, the psychological dynamics of the two constructs appear to differ. People high in FOF may be more likely to be motivated by failure avoidance (Gastorf & Teevan, 1980) and may protect themselves

The "Bizarro cartoon" by Dan Piraro is reproduced by permission of Chronicle Features, San Francisco, CA.

by ascribing negative attributions to others (Saltoun, 1980). Individuals who are high in FOF may become more concerned with favorable impression management than with problem-solving efforts that might result in task accomplishment (see Cohen & Teevan, 1974). They may fail to initiate role-appropriate behavior or to take appropriate steps that would lead to fulfilling an achievement-oriented goal (Dapra, Zarrillo, Carlson, & Teevan, 1985).

There are a number of measures of FOF (e.g., Birney et al., 1969; Good & Good, 1975; Karabenick & Marshall, 1977; P. A. Richardson, Jackson, & Albury, 1984; Teevan & Fischer, 1974). There appears to be a sex difference, with women on average scoring higher on many measures of FOF (see V. E. O'Leary,

1974; Vollmer & Almas, 1974), although the issue has been less well-examined than it has for the FOS variable. Like FOS, FOF has been studied in reference to other personality constructs and correlates predictably with such variables as LOC (low FOF scoring in the more internal LOC direction; Brannigan, Hauk, & Guay, 1991) and Type A behavior (Burke & Deszca, 1982; Houston & Kelly, 1987). Moot, Teevan, and Greenfeld (1988) reported need for achievement to be independent of FOF. Environmental factors (e.g., absence of father in the home while growing up; voluntarily placing oneself in publicly competitive situations) may also be associated with higher levels of FOF (Greenfeld & Teevan, 1986; Teevan & Greenfeld, 1985). In one of the few studies in the literature dealing with FOF in an adult employed population, Gudjonsson (1984) found FOF scores to be highly correlated with scores on a neuroticism variable. The pattern of these findings, although limited, suggests that configuration analysis rather than single-variable study is probably the most productive route for future research.

Interventions With FOF and FOS

Clinically, the FOS and FOF constructs appear useful in certain situations for generating psychodynamic hypotheses when undercommitment or underachievement dynamics are present. However, the widespread presumption that women are overly prone to FOS or that this dynamic alone is sufficient to explain all undercommitment problems appears naive at best. Moreover, as L. M. Yuen and Depper (1987) appropriately noted, FOS can occur in the context of a variety of other types of pathology (e.g., narcissistic, borderline); each case must be considered in the clinical context in which it presents.

Sherman (1987; see also Hollinger & Fleming, 1984) noted that although FOS may be a useful psychological construct, it is not likely to be differentiated by the patient from other, related variables such as lack of confidence, low self-esteem, and low risk taking. A specific intervention for FOS may be less relevant than one for the perceived constellation of traits that might globally be termed *problems of self-confidence*. Reis (1987) identified the need to help young women identify factors that may cause them to behave in an underachieving manner, particularly in such areas as math and science. More generally, an activist role by the therapist in challenging incorrect assumptions about the likelihood of failure may be needed (e.g., Spillane, 1983).

Other approaches to intervention have been reported in the literature. Group treatment programs have reported positive results in lowering FOF (Rajendran & Kaliappan, 1990). The value of groups in countering the so-called impostor phenomenon, in which an individual feels that he or she has succeeded inappropriately and will soon be "found out" to be a fraud, has also been reported (Clance & O'Toole, 1987; J. A. Steinberg, 1986). Hypnotherapy has also been suggested (Gross & Gross, 1985), although Manganello, Carlson, Zarrillo, and Teevan (1985) found men high in FOF to be poor candidates for hypnotic induction.

One of the findings that emerges from the rather complex FOF and FOS literature is that subjective estimations of success and of the consequences of failure play an important role in both phenomena. Because the assumptions made about a feared or avoided situation by the client may not be articulated, even to oneself, it may therefore be important for the therapist to help the client make these assumptions explicit (e.g., "If I'm successful, no one will like me"; "If I fail, it will be a terrible, shameful tragedy"). Challenging false or unproved presumptions may assist the client in considering alternatives.

Performance, of course, is not always changeable, and the therapist needs to consider the role of ability in the FOS/FOF dynamic at hand. A person may desire to accomplish a particular occupational goal but may not have the capability to do so. Ability assessment in addition to clinical judgment may be needed to determine the realism of the espoused goal. Although the therapist needs always to be understanding of espoused goals, when the goals are demonstrably unobtainable because of ability deficits, the client may need assistance in creating more realistic goals (see Moses, 1989). Accomplishment of so-called lower level goals may be much more satisfying than the avoidance and fear associated with holding more ambitious, but clearly untenable and therefore frustrating, goals.

The therapist can help the client make choices about which situations require assertion and how much energy should be expended. People high in FOF or FOS may exert lower levels of effort to solve problems (e.g., Vollmer & Kaufmann, 1975). Thus, a strategic intervention may be assisting the client in exerting more effort and in setting appropriate targets. By increasing effort and receiving supportive assistance in attempting previously avoided but appropriate goals, the client's self-esteem may be raised, and he or she may expend greater effort in future such situations.

In other cases, self-esteem may be so low that it makes no sense to start with facilitating goal-directed behavior. Rather, intensive effort may need to be made toward enhancing self-acceptance before addressing any so-called external issues. For example, when family-of-origin issues are the central focus, the therapist may need to work with the client on these issues, postponing the FOF and FOS issues to a later date. Clinical judgment is required in each case to determine the appropriate intervention point and level.

Procrastination

Definition and General Characteristics

The various definitions of procrastination that have been offered in the clinical and research literature vary considerably, ranging from the merely self-descriptive to the criterion specific. Dell (1973), for example, studied 48 college males who "described themselves" as procrastinators. Milgram, Sroloff, and Rosenbaum (1988) offered the prosaic definition "putting off for tomorow [sic] what one should do today" (p. 197). These same authors differentiated between academic procrastination (by far the most systematically and empirically studied of procrastinating phenomena) and "neurotic indecision," the "repeated postponement of major life decisions" (p. 197). This distinction parallels that between procrastination as a state phenomenon (procrastinating about specific tasks and under specific circumstances) and procrastination as a trait phenomenon (a potentially crippling, broad-ranging, pervasive life characteristic).

Some empirical definitions have emerged that merely define procrastination as scoring at a certain level on an empirical measure of a construct (e.g., McCown, Petzel, & Rupert, 1987). Solomon and Rothblum (1984) defined procrastination as "the act of needlessly delaying tasks to the point of experiencing subjective discomfort" (p. 503), identifying one, but not the only, critical component of procrastination. Lay (1986) noted that a definition of procrastination needs to accommodate the tendency to postpone goal-relevant behavior, the extent to which the task is chosen or imposed and involves a pleasant or dysphoric task, the perceptions of what is needed to be done to complete the task, and other behaviors that occur between learning a task and completing it. Lay (1986) further noted that procrastination appears to involve deviations between what "ought" to be done to complete a task and what is actually undertaken. The procrastinator loses sight over time of priorities and the relevance of present actions to the accomplishment of high-priority, task-relevant behaviors.

This raises the important issue of differentiating between completion of isolated tasks and completion of an interrelated sequence of task-relevant behaviors necessary to accomplish some long-term project or goal. Thus, although some studies (e.g., Wesp, 1986) have found procrastination to be reduced by breaking up work into smaller bits (e.g., by having daily quizzes), more complex work may involve more intricately and interrelated behavioral patterns over time, and such subdividing may not so easily be applied.

For the purposes of this discussion, I define *work-related procrastination* as a persistent and/or cyclical pattern in which an individual who is otherwise capable of doing the work repetitively avoids timely initiation and completion of work assignments or activities that must be completed by a particular deadline, real or perceived, with dysfunctional consequences for failing to do so. Procrastination can vary in the extent of its dysfunctionality (which can be external or internal) and in the breadth of life areas affected. Complex patterns of procrastination suggest that there are sometimes utilitarian, if personally stressful, purposes associated with the behavior. For example, the actor Warren Beatty is described as following an interesting dynamic in his slowness to commit to certain movie productions: "Often . . . he won't commit himself to a particular project 'until the idea of not making it becomes so humiliating to me that I am filled with self-disgust at not doing it' " (Biskind, 1992, p. 60).

Most investigators (e.g., Rothblum, Solomon, & Murakami, 1986) agree that anxiety is aroused by procrastinating behavior. People who procrastinate on academic or work-related tasks do not necessarily do so on activities they find pleasurable. Either the task itself or the perceived or imagined consequences of completing the task are aversively charged. The therapist's first task, therefore, involves the attempt to understand what type of procrastinating behavior is being presented and the psychological components that may be causing its persistence.

The multidimensionality of procrastination has been reported in several studies. Lay (1987) differentiated among the following types of procrastinators: (a) a highly procrastinating, highly neurotic, and rebellious group who undertook projects they perceived to be very difficult and who experienced great stress and reported little progress in meeting their goals; (b) a low-energy "underachiever" group that perceived tasks to be of low difficulty and who reported apparently false progress toward goal achievement; and (c) an independent, intellectually curious group who may take on too many things and be overly self-focused. When men and women were analyzed separately, Lay (1987) found less differentiation among female than male procrastinators. The female procrastinators were more likely to experience poor organization, low energy level, low self-esteem, neuroticism, and low achievement needs.

McCown, Johnson, and Petzel (1989) administered measures of personality, depression, and Type A behavior pattern, along with time usage measures, to a group of persistent academic procrastinating undergraduates. They reported three "types" of procrastinators: a more seriously disturbed group (high psychoticism scores), an extraverted but neurotic group, and a depressed group.

McCown, Carise, and Johnson (1991) found a tendency for self-reported children of alcoholics to score higher on what they termed *trait procrastination*. They interpreted task avoidance in such populations to be rooted in the desire to avoid parental criticism. Other researchers have found procrastination to be associated with low self-esteem and anxiety (Beswick, Rothblum, & Mann, 1988; Effert & Ferrari, 1989), even among very young procrastinators (Morse, 1987). Solomon and Rothblum (1984), studying a college student population concerning procrastination on academic tasks, differentiated two major types of procrastinators: (a) a relatively homogeneous group that was generally anxious and depressed, had low self-esteem, feared failure, and therefore avoided task initiation and (b) a relatively diverse group of procrastinators who found the task being avoided to be aversive.

The role of the perceived unpleasantness of task in encouraging procrastination has been noted by other researchers (e.g., N. N. Harris & Sutton, 1983; Milgram et al., 1988). This implies at least two factors to be considered in assessing reported problems with procrastination: characteristics of the individual and characteristics of the task itself. Table 4.1 illustrates that tasks perceived to be imposed rather than voluntary (Milgram et al., 1988) and that tasks perceived to require more advance planning (Milgram, 1988) are more likely to generate procrastination.

Extent and Frequency of the Problem

The literature defining the extent to which procrastination is dysfunctional is rather limited. Hill, Hill, Chabot, and Barrall (1978) conducted a survey of procrastination among 500 university students and 150 faculty members. They found faculty members' reports of procrastination to be somewhat lower than students' (27% vs. 18% reported "frequent" or "usual" procrastination), but faculty's estimates of students' procrastination was higher than students' estimates of their own procrastination (and than faculty's estimates of their own procrastination; 42% of the students were estimated by faculty to frequently or usually procrastinate), with discipline somewhat moderating the estimates of procrastination by students. Students' reported pro

Table 4.1

Factors in Propensity to Procrastinate Associated With Three Groupings

Characteristics of the person	Characteristics of the task	Characteristics of the person–task match
Low self-esteem	Aversive	Fear of task failure
Conflicts with authority	Neutral	Fear of task success
Passive–aggressive	Positive	
Energy level		
Neuroticism		
Anxiety		
Type B personality		
Sex		

crastination increased with year in school. Few solutions were offered by the faculty concerning ways to decrease procrastination except for decreasing the breadth of the assignments and increasing the frequency of quizzes or assignments. Solomon and Rothblum (1984) found with introductory psychology course subjects that 46% reported that they procrastinated on term papers "nearly always" or "always," whereas 27.6% reported similar levels of procrastination on studying for exams and 30.1% on reading weekly assignments. The subjects varied in the type of assignment and procrastination, with longer term assignments (e.g., terms papers) generating more self-reported procrastination. In another study of academic procrastination, Rothblum et al. (1986) found that 40% of an introductory psychology course student sample reported high levels of procrastination.

Delay in completing isolated tasks is apparently a universal phenomenon (see Ellis & Knaus, 1977), but the number of individuals for whom the problem is sufficiently severe to interfere with workplace performance is unknown. Nonetheless, it appears that, at least for student populations, the more unstructured the task (e.g., term paper vs. weekly reading assignments), the greater the likelihood of procrastination.

Procrastination is apparently more common among the neurotically disturbed in general (Lay, 1986, 1987), although McCown et al. (1987) reported a nonlinear relation between scores on neuroticism (as measured by the Eysenck Personality Questionnaire; Eysenck, 1958; Eysenck & Eysenck, 1976) and procrastination (as measured by Aitken's, 1982, Procrastination Inventory). Higher neuroticism scores were associated with very high and very low levels of procrastination. McCown et al. also reported procrastination to be higher among extraverts than introverts. Procrastination may be higher for men, at least among those who are not of Type A personality (Milgram et al., 1988). Sex and age differences in procrastination behavior have not yet been reliably established, although one study (Lay, 1986) did report lower mean procrastination scores for an adult sample than for samples of university students. Also, Rothblum et al. (1986) found that female procrastinators were more likely than nonprocrastinators and male procrastinators to report test anxiety and physical symptoms of anxiety and that more women than men reported themselves to be high in procrastination (44.8% vs. 31.6%). According to Lay (1986), people who were high in procrastination did not differ in all areas in which avoidance is likely to be manifest but were more likely to be high in procrastinating on vocational and hobby-related activities, whereas those who were low in procrastination were likely to report the behavior in reference to home and family activities.

The following case illustrates some of the commonly encountered psychological factors in patterns of chronic procrastination.

Case 4.2
The Chronic Work Procrastinator

Marcella had a long history of procrastination when, at age 34, she elected to join a procrastination treatment group. She was regarded as an employee of high ability who was somewhat erratic in her work as a manager for a large corporation. Usually, she got her work done on time, but it was often at the expense of a tremendous surge of last-minute effort, the psychological effects of which were quite stressful for her.

In practice, Marcella wasted a great deal of time at the office. She tended to procrastinate especially on tasks that would be evaluated by others or that she considered boring, which, in fact, covered many of the tasks she was assigned. Although she found this style of working to be highly stressful, she felt powerless to change it. Often, she stayed up all night completing an assignment, thus producing a product of lower quality than she was capable of. Moreover, the anxiety and sometimes sheer terror associated with these last-minute races created havoc for her staff and her family. Reviewing with Marcella her pattern of procrastinating helped her identify some of the characteristic difficulties. Family-of-origin dynamics included a father whom she perceived to be aggressive and controlling and against whom she rebelled by slowing down whenever he demanded that Marcella produce on schedule. Identifying that this psychodynamic history was involved assisted her in recognizing that to some degree she was perpetuating a pattern of her youth. Further exploration indicated that Marcella was actually unhappy in her current line of work. She thus began to pursue another interest on a part-time basis, which enabled her to be more relaxed and less emotionally invested in her current career. Finally, therapy helped her identify a pattern of catastrophizing, in which she chronically expected the worst to happen. Waiting until the last minute on projects was to some degree a defense against recognizing that she anticipated doom (e.g., her perceived incompetency would be discovered or she would be fired).

Marcella procrastinated in therapy as well. She missed some appointments just as important insights were being gleaned and tended to act out conflicts by procrastinating on homework assignments. However, with the therapist's help she began to make improvement and eventually some significant life changes. At the end of treatment, she still procrastinated on occasion but could see the humor in her behavior at these times. Overall, her level of procrastination greatly decreased, and she described herself as considerably more relaxed in her work.

Effects of Procrastination

Solomon and Rothblum (1984) found no correlation in a university student sample between self-reported procrastination and course grades. Similarly, Lay (1986) found no association between scores on a measure of procrastination and grade point average, although procrastinators were more disorganized and more likely to return their survey late. This suggests that although procrastination may constitute personally dysfunctional behavior and may indeed be a source of considerable anxiety or depression, it may not necessarily result in poorer performance in a university student population. If confirmed in adult studies of work-related behavior, this may imply that enlisting the client's help in combatting procrastination may necessitate addressing the client's personal distress with and rejection of the personally aversive aspects of procrastination (termed *dysphoric affect* by Milgram et al., 1988). However, expecting negative outcomes to instigate a client's desire for change may be unrealistic. Moreover, given that quality of work may not be a motivator of change, psychological conflict concerning achievement and control may be more likely to motivate change than unhappiness with the final product. However, a feared decrease in quality may still be found. Thus, the therapist needs to determine whether the client's unconscious fantasy is that removal of procrastination would imply decreased work success. Ingrained ritualistic work habits, however dysfunctional, may be associated in the client's mind with dire and negative outcomes, the unreality or at least unproved nature of which may need to be aggressively challenged by the therapist. This may be the case particularly with clients for whom procrastination is part of a broader pattern of psychological disturbance.

The therapist should note that procrastination is not necessarily an inappropriate pattern of behavior. At times, postponement may be the best course of action. Waiting may allow time for fruition, resulting ultimately in a better final product. The "positive" aspects of procrastination are illustrated by the following writer's recounting:

The book took a year and a half to write. At least half of the chapters came out whole the first time. The biggest struggle was not with the actual writing, but working out the fear of success, the fear of failure, and finally burning through to just pure activity. The last month and a half I wrote seven days a week. I finished one chapter and began another. That simple. (N. Goldberg, 1988, p. 169)

Assessment and Psychodynamic Issues

Unfortunately, neither the clinical nor the research literature offers conclusive recommendations regarding assessment or treatment.

Psychodynamically, procrastination appears to embody a number of separable components including (a) failure to initiate task-relevant activity in a timely manner; (b) perseverance in inappropriate, and particularly perfectionistic, activities that prohibit tasks from getting completed; and (c) failure to complete tasks that have been initiated. Chronic procrastinators often have a work style of waiting until the last minute, at which point frenetic work activity may result in an inferior product (see Burka & Yuen, 1983) because they have invested less overall and less high-quality time (Lay, 1986, 1990). Boice (1989) noted that procrastinators tend to occupy themselves with irrelevant task activities and to use task performance "binging" as a way of compensating.

The therapist needs to understand the client's dominant and preferred features and to have some understanding of their motivational dynamics. In addition to clinical interviews, use of a procrastination log may prove helpful for this purpose (Lopez & Wambach, 1982; Strong, Wambach, Lopez, & Cooper, 1979). In addition, alternative diagnoses need to be ruled out, especially obsessive–compulsive personality dynamics, other forms of psychopathology (Dooley, 1987), or even neurological dysfunction (Strub, 1989).

Although formal, psychological assessment of the nature of the procrastination may not be necessary, a few instruments have been reported. These include the Tel-Aviv Procrastination Scale (Milgram et al., 1988), intended to be a measure of "everyday" procrastination; the Procrastination Inventory and Procrastination Log (Strong et al., 1979), a procrastination scale that includes a Rebelliousness scale to address the control factor reported among procrastinators (Lay, 1986); the Procrastination Assessment Scale–Students (Solomon & Rothblum, 1984); the Procrastination Inventory (Aitken, 1982); and other clinically useful forms (Burka & Yuen, 1983).

As part of the assessment process, the therapist should also determine the cause of the immediate referral (e.g., external or internal factors, a situation in which a job is on the line, or a self-referral prompted by personal unhappiness or distress). Assessment should also include determination of the extent to which the procrastination is common and repetitive or isolated and the extent to which it is part of a broader pattern of personality disorder or neuroses. In addition, the therapist needs to determine whether the client's seeking help for procrastination is a socially acceptable "cover" for seeking help for more deep-seated psychological dysfunction.

Because procrastination may result from either real or imagined inability to perform the task in question, the therapist should make some assessment of the client's capacity to perform the avoided behavior. Information may be elicited in the case of schoolwork by taking a brief history of current and past grades and standardized test scores, whereas for problems in work settings, the therapist may have to ask about recent and past performance evaluations. When there is doubt about the client's capacity to perform the work, additional information, including formal psychological or career assessment, may be required.

Psychological dynamics can be complex and overdetermined in individual cases of procrastination. Rorer (1983) identified fear or ambivalence regarding success as a factor in some types of procrastination. Mixed reinforcement patterns are present with many so-called positive outcomes, and anticipated or imagined consequences may be associated in the procrastinator's mind with task completion.

The issue of control is important in many formulations of procrastination and needs to be explored in the client's context. Not doing expected, required, or unpleasant work may be a way of expressing anger (e.g., Rorer, 1983). Thus, it may be important to understand who is likely (in the client's mind) to be "punished" or made angry by the procrastinating behavior or its consequences. Those with passive–aggressive personalities may fail to succeed, or do just enough to squeak by, despite having high ability levels, to unconsciously punish significant others who may have prematurely forced accomplishment or made love and positive reinforcement contingent on successful performance. In complicated cases of procrastination, the therapist should consider the psychological dynamics of the family of origin as a possible explanatory mechanism for withholding. However, from the perspective of therapy or intervention, the therapist should avoid an overly analytical or historically focused approach (see, e.g., Salzman, 1979). In particular, such approaches may merely protract if not exacerbate an already dysfunctional work style. Because a protracted assessment process may become just another instance of failure to break a persistently dysfunctional cycle, it is important that the therapist start treatment promptly, preferably on the client's first visit.

Finally, the nature of the procrastinated task itself must be considered. N. N. Harris and Sutton (1983) identified task discretion as a potential moderator of the relation between task and procrastinating behavior. They concluded that, for adults in real-life work settings, task assignments occur in the context of multiple tasks requiring simultaneous work or completion. Thus, the organizational context may affect the propensity if not the desirability of procrastination. Procrastinators also appear more likely to attempt to structure complex tasks by breaking them down into small and simpler pieces, perhaps never getting to the more difficult aspects (see McCown et al., 1987).

Treatment Issues

Although several studies have reported effective treatment of procrastination, no definitive conclusions can yet be drawn. The studies vary widely in the degree of rigor and extent to which procrastination is the primary emphasis. Several appear to address procrastination as a demonstration of the applicability or effectiveness of a particular treatment modality (e.g., rational–emotive, behavioral) or issue (Claiborn, Ward, & Strong, 1981;

Olson & Claiborn, 1990) rather than as a phenomenon in its own right (e.g., Silver & Sabini, 1981). Moreover, most studies have been conducted using college students not in the workplace rather than adult employed workers.

Several studies have addressed the efficacy of paradoxical approaches to the treatment of procrastination (see Strong, 1984). Lopez and Wambach (1982) compared two treatment approaches (paradoxical and self-control) with a control condition in studying 32 students who reported last-minute cramming some or all the time, who perceived their procrastinating problem to be a serious one, and who claimed to have been unsuccessful in changing it on their own. Both treatment methods were effective compared with the control condition, with the paradoxical group showing more improvement. Although many reasons may account for this finding, one is that the paradoxical approach cuts through the complex wall of resistance relatively quickly and permits the client to see that the often unconsciously anticipated consequences do not occur in the absence of procrastination. Shoham-Salomon, Avner, and Neeman (1989) found, in a study of the mechanism by which paradoxical approaches affect procrastinators, that those higher in reactance (the desire to restore a perceived threat to freedom; see Brehm & Brehm, 1981) were more likely to benefit from paradoxical treatment than were those low in reactance. Low-reactant subjects were also affected but apparently through an intervening cognitive mechanism of increasing a sense of control rather than through the paradoxical intervention itself. In another brief intervention study, Dowd et al. (1988) found high- and low-reactant college students to decrease procrastination as a result of both restraining and nonparadoxical interventions, although the latter produced more improvement. They found no significant differences between the effects of restraining and reframing interventions.

To the extent that procrastination results from a failure to prioritize tasks according to degree of relevance or importance, the skill of being able to identify and attend to high-priority over low-priority tasks appears to be trainable (see B. L. Hall & Hursch, 1981–1982). Bost (1984) found that a group of students on academic probation were helped by peer counseling on time management skills. McCown et al. (1987) argued for an educational approach in treating procrastinators, suggesting that those high in procrastination may need assistance in learning to tackle more challenging goals and budgeting a greater amount of time (see also Lay, 1990) than they think will be required to correct for an apparent tendency to underestimate the amount of time required to complete a task (Lay, 1988).

In clinical practice, it is recommended that the therapist carefully review with the client the reported patterns of procrastination, particularly stressing the need for specific examples of the currently problematic behavior. Vague and generally self-negating statements (e.g., "I always procrastinate"; "I don't know why I keep sabotaging myself") are less helpful for diagnosis than are specific, current examples (e.g., "I have a major work project due next week that I can't seem to get interested in"; "I haven't started a term paper that's got to be turned in Friday"). In the initial clinical assessment, the therapist needs to be sure that the procrastinating phenomenon is more or less isolated and not associated with conditions such as obsessional disorder (Salzman, 1979) in which the procrastinating behavior is merely symptomatic of a broader personality style or dysfunction.[4] An excellent as well as potentially therapeutic assessment device involves keeping a log of procrastinating events (e.g., Strong et al., 1979), which helps the client to become a better observer of the types of circumstances that trigger procrastination and the extent to which procrastination actually occurs.

In the absence of a definitive research base, the therapist might proceed generally in working with procrastinating clients as follows. A general understanding of the psychodynamics of the particular presenting pattern should rapidly be obtained. Focusing in excessive analytical detail on the problematic behavior may not be important and may indeed be counterproductive, except with very bright clients who may require some sort of rational understanding before they can participate in a therapeutic stratagem.

---

[4] Although a therapeutically similar treatment approach may be used with varying psychodynamics, the therapist may need to alter a particular approach or treat the so-called underlying condition before focusing on what in such cases may be merely symptomatic behavior.

Barring significant underlying psychopathology suggestive of psychosis or severe obsessional or other psychological disorders, the therapist should move rapidly to an activist stance in dealing with the procrastinating behavior. Therapy may otherwise become one more excuse by which the client avoids completing tasks. The therapist can pleasantly but actively challenge the client's false premises and develop a timetable for taking small steps toward the desired goal. Chronic procrastinators who are perfectionists and who set too high a standard for themselves and others may need encouragement to develop less grandiose, more realistic goals. When appropriate, settling for acceptable rather than idealized outcomes, at least in certain situations and contexts, can be a desirable goal. When there are more circumscribed dysfunctional work habits (e.g., underestimating the amount of time needed to complete tasks, tackling too simple tasks), an educative or educative–cognitive approach may be effective.

With some clients, it is especially important for the therapist to understand and bring to the client's attention the positive aspects of procrastination and defuse the concept that the client is a terrible failure or unworthy person because of the procrastinating behavior. A more effective interpretation is that the client avoids certain behaviors but not others for some good psychological reason, that the behavior is changeable at the client's discretion, and that the immediate treatment goal is to learn when procrastination is and is not appropriate. Because chronic procrastinators often are perfectionistic, self-blaming individuals with low self-esteem (Ellis & Knaus, 1977; Frost, Marten, Lahart, & Rosenblate, 1990; Ishiyama, 1990; Knaus, 1973; D. J. White, 1988), the therapist may help by reframing procrastination itself as a sometimes-desirable behavior that should not be summarily dismissed from the personality. Rather, it can be considered a style and approach to be selectively applied but in a manner under clear control of the individual. Thus, the therapist should not communicate to the client as a goal eliminating procrastinating behavior altogether; rather, a more productive goal may be modifying the behavior such that the decision to procrastinate is a reasoned choice associated with pleasure and productivity rather than pain. Aspects of procrastination the client may be helped to consider include not having to be rushed into a decision, the exercise of personal power and control, not having to risk external judgment, and simply being able to enjoy one's own schedule rather than having to adhere to one imposed by others. Procrastination can thus serve a useful purpose of withdrawal and, at certain phases of life, be productively regressive (see Giovacchini, 1975).

This formulation is particularly relevant in working with individuals who tend toward pleasure-negating behavior and do nothing in life but duty-inspired, work-related behavior and need permission to accept the more sensuous aspects of the self to enjoy work and life. Guided imagery may also be useful with such clients in avoiding resistance to behavioral approaches (D. J. White, 1988). The therapist's focusing with the client on what is found pleasurable and how often that behavior is undertaken may result in important discoveries about the psychodynamic motivations of the procrastinating behavior. While not requiring the client to abandon what the therapist may consider overly high standards, the therapist may encourage a simple reward schema in which the client does some self-enhancing, enjoyable activity in response to completing some small portion of an avoided task.

Because procrastinators may use therapy itself as a vehicle for further procrastination, keeping the focus on specific, real, and current examples of how procrastination is problematic is wise. Although it is important for the therapist to have some clear understanding of the psychodynamics motivating the procrastinating behavior, it is not necessarily important for the client to have that same understanding. Changing the problematic behavior, getting it under greater control, and accepting the inevitability and imperfections can become the client's goals. Setbacks or recurrences of the problematic behavior are viewed not as unexpected instances of personal failure but as part of the normal process of change. Reminding the client who has regressed of the positive aspects of procrastination can also be helpful, as can helping the client avoid negative self-labeling.

Given that procrastinators often have trouble with issues of control, the therapist should generally avoid battles for control. Some studies (e.g., Rothblum, Solomon, & Murakami, 1986) have found locus of control to be more externally than internally correlated with academic procrastination. Thus, the procrastinator may exert less effort because he or she feels less personal control over the outcome of a situation. Keeping the power issues between therapist and client implicit to the extent possible is generally recommended. The therapist's allying with the nonpunitive, pleasure-seeking side of the client's ego enhances the likelihood that power struggles will be avoided. Nonetheless, while keeping resistance in the background, the therapist still must be prepared to handle power struggles with underachievers whose dynamics center on displaced anger toward authority figures. Recognizing and validating the anger, particularly when displaced, may prove useful in helping the client move beyond it.

Because chronic procrastinators are often conflicted over pleasure seeking, the therapist may help by giving permission for nonwork and nonduty aspects of life. Particularly in cases wherein punitive, overly achievement-oriented dynamics have prevailed, the therapist should encourage the client to explore, understand, and accept the needs of the pleasure-seeking side. The reward strategy just mentioned (e.g., providing a reward to oneself for a small step toward accomplishing an avoided task; see Ziestat, Rosenthal, & White, 1978) can serve as an opportunity for exploring what the client finds rewarding, which those with restricted, conflicted personalities may need assistance in discovering.

Giving permission concerning the client's preferred work style is also something the therapist should consider when appropriate. Although steady, incremental progress toward a goal and rapid discharge of dysphorically charged activities may be the preferred working style of many, working in fits and starts is not always inappropriate, particularly in some of the creative occupations. Modulating rather than eliminating the periods of productivity and withdrawal may be a more appropriate goal.

Underachievement

In contrast to at least some patterns of procrastination, underachievement patterns are here conceptualized to refer to long-standing and persistent inability to achieve in the absence of inability to do so (the special case of writer's and other creative blocks is discussed in chapter 7). Two examples illustrate that underachievement can apply to those with high potential. In *Remembering Denny*, Calvin Trillin (1993) depicted the true-life case of Roger (Denny) Hansen, an athlete, an academic star at Yale, and subsequently a Rhodes scholar, who became only modestly successful in adulthood and, at age 55, committed suicide. In *Goat Brothers*, Colton (1993) depicted the case of a cohort of fraternity brothers, some of whom showed great promise in youth that was generally unfulfilled in adulthood. Complex interactions of abilities and personality characteristics are suggested to account for these adult outcomes.

In contrast to simple procrastination, underachievement is chronic rather than cyclical or deadline related. The phenomenon appears to have been better studied in school and academic settings (Mandel & Marcus, 1988) rather than in adult populations, the primary focus of this book.

Psychodynamic Factors

A number of psychodynamic factors have been conceptualized to explain underachievement. Family dynamics are identified by some clinicians and investigators as being primary. Neuroticism of families and key family members can certainly contribute to patterns of underachievement (Shepperson, 1982). Whether the underachievement pattern precedes and causes the neuroticism or the other way around has not been reliably established.

Psychodynamic factors will, of course, vary with each case. Psychoanalytically oriented writers have identified several themes in patterns of underachievement or "success inhibition," including fear of success, unresolved oedipal issues, projected parental anger, pathological narcissism (H. S. Baker, 1979; Krueger, 1984, 1990), and perceived fraudulence (Kolligan, 1990; Ulrich & Dunne, 1986).

A number of studies have examined various aspects of underachievement syndromes. Ilechukwu (1988) hypothesized sibling rivalry to be the cause of underachievement syndrome in some college students being treated for academic underachievement. H. S. Baker (1987), however, attributed underachievement in college students to internal structural deficits rather than to unresolved conflicts. Green, Fine, and Tollefson (1988) found no empirical differences in family functionality in families with gifted or underachieving boys aged 13–15 years. H. S. Baker (1979) identified the relevance of narcissistic personality factors in underachievement patterns, noting that, when confronted with setbacks in their studies or work, subjects with certain narcissistic personality patterns avoided the tasks rather than increased their efforts, thus failing to accomplish needed goals. Tesser and Blusiewicz (1987) hypothesized that underachievement in students may be conceptualized psychodynamically as a conflict between dependence and the desire to present oneself to the external world as being independent.

The following case illustrates issues involved when underachievement results from an apparent mismatch between the individual and a planned occupation.

Case 4.3
The Academic Underachiever

A student at a prestigious university, Carlton was currently on leave of absence due to academic problems. When he began therapy, he was decidedly unsure of himself but stubbornly persistent in his belief that he could not abandon his choice of majors (chemistry) or his plan to return to the university to obtain his bachelor's degree and pursue, initially, a career in high school teaching.

Compared with his peers in his chemistry program, Carlton was decidedly underachieving. However, he was competing at his university with some of the finest scientific minds in the country, few of whom had any aspirations for careers in high school teaching. He was branded by his faculty as not being a promising candidate for graduate school, and his grades in his chosen major were fair at best.

The career assessment for which he sought help revealed Carlton to be ill-suited to physical sciences but well-suited to social sciences. He was certainly bright enough to succeed at the university he was attending, but his current choice of majors had caused him to lose self-confidence and to wonder why he had done so well in high school science yet so poorly in college. Being asked to leave the university because of low grades was a serious blow to Carlton's self-esteem. Yet, at the time of the assessment, he remained committed to somehow getting back into the university and completing his major as planned.

Carlton's personal rigidity no doubt contributed to his persistence in a field that was, at the least, not his strong suit and that in college had brought him little happiness or success. His perception of himself as a persistent academic achiever caused him to cling to the "wrong" major rather than pursue new options.

Fortunately, Carlton responded with more flexibility after receiving the data from his career assessment, which among other things confirmed his earlier view of himself as being intellectually talented. Armed with this information, he was able to put his school "failure" in context and make plans to return to the university with a changed major. Although high school teaching might well be an interim goal for him on completion of his undergraduate degree, it was unlikely to hold sufficient motivational appeal for him over time.

Assessment Issues

Although psychodynamic explanations can be relevant in specific clinical casework, such models can be limiting if other factors are not taken into account in making an assessment. In conceptualizing patterns of underachievement, factors of ability, interests, and motivation (i.e., personality) must also be considered (see Cattell, 1987; Lowman, 1991b).

Underachieving gifted individuals may be underestimated by those around them, especially in school settings (see E. G. Hall, 1983). Formal assessment of interests, abilities, and personality characteristics may therefore be needed in many, if not most, cases to assess the client's potential and identify what is likely to be motivating to the client.

If it is established that abilities are present but are somehow not being well-utilized, the therapist will need to establish whether it is because there is not a good match with the individual's interests. If so, a job change may be a good idea. Alternatively, primary work activities can be conceptualized as the necessary means to fuel nonwork activities. The latter is particularly relevant to those with strong artistic interests and abilities (Holland, 1985) who are forced to take jobs they do not like given that there are very few jobs within their field of interest (see Lowman, 1991b).

There is no formulaic approach to determining areas of mismatch. Clinical and painstaking review of complex psychological assessment data is often necessary to establish such patterns. Involving the client in the process of data review can prove helpful.

The next two cases illustrate how complex and subtle certain patterns of underachievement can be. Sorting through the important and salient issues in treatment can require considerable effort.

Case 4.4
The Persistent Underachiever

Brian had recently been fired from his job in business administration when he came to the psychologist for help. A review of his work history showed that he had had some sort of problem with each of his jobs in the years since he graduated from college, all of which had been in the same general field. Although he was not totally mismatched with his field (he had a bachelor's degree in business and had done some work on an advanced degree), he seemed to have very little passion about it.

Exploration of his personal life revealed a similar pattern. He had had several relationships with women but only one that had been invested with much emotional commitment. This one ended with the woman leaving the relationship precipitously not long after they had moved in together. He suspected that she may have become involved with someone else just before leaving. Since the breakup, he had dated women who were "safe," who were more interested in him than he was in them. In each case, he broke off the relationship. Initial exploration of his childhood revealed no major traumas in upbringing. His father was a successful writer who also had some successful business activities on the side. His mother worked as a manager in a restaurant. The relationship between the parents was described as being generally absent of conflict. He described no serious sibling rivalry or anything that seemed to account for his current difficulties. Career mismatch of a subtle rather than radical nature was suspected as the source of his problems at this point.

Finally, however, he mentioned in passing that a friend had thought he had many of the characteristics popularly associated with the adult child of alcoholics phenomenon. He noted that, unknown to him at the time, his father had been an alcoholic and had received treatment in an inpatient facility. Further exploration revealed a subtle dynamic in which commitment both within and outside the family was unsafe and avoided. Positive self-presentation masked considerable hostility and resentment. Brian became better able to direct his efforts as the result of treatment and found himself becoming more passionately committed to things of his choosing in both his personal and his professional lives.

Case 4.5
The Chronic Underachiever

Mickey was 33 years old at the time of his referral. He had worked briefly in a series of jobs, none of which had lasted very long. He had been a carpenter, an assistant manager of a convenience store, and a licensed building contractor. He had briefly owned his own business, which did not succeed. Since then, except for occasional short-term employment on his father's properties, he lived frugally with friends who would allow him to stay with them for a period. Mickey stood to inherit a share of his father's estate, which consisted of a number of properties, currently managed by his sister (who had successfully kept her siblings from becoming involved with her management of the properties). His mother, who in the alcoholic literature might be called an *enabler*, reinforced the client's infantalized role by giving him just enough money to maintain dependency. The family perception persisted that this son was a "n'er-do-well" who seemed intent on besmirching the family's good name.

This attractive, well-dressed man was brought in for career assessment and counseling by his mother. He was superficially cooperative with the assessment process, attended all sessions in a timely manner (the assessment being paid for by his mother). However, he noted to his therapist at several points that he doubted that he would learn anything from this process. After all, he had been assessed before in his youth and had not found the process to be of much use.

Although he had little yet to show for it in life accomplishments, this was a very cognitively able man (Verbal IQ, 115; Performance IQ, 123; Full Scale IQ, 121) whose self-doubt and protective narcissism caused him not to test himself against appropriate career goals. The perception in his family of origin of being incompetent reinforced his self-doubt and reluctance to compete. Intervention in this case necessitated working with the family members as well as the individual. Seeing his potential revealed in a career assessment battery helped release him from a narrow and self-defeating view of himself and helped redefine him within his family-of-origin context.

In psychotherapy following his assessment, Mickey came to realize that the underachievement associated with the high promise he had manifested since his youth served as a protection. Through therapy, Mickey was helped to the realization that in his thirties, it was *he* who had not lived up to his potential. For years he had blamed others, particularly his father from whom he had been estranged, for his lack of success in his work. He thus sought psychotherapeutic assistance in working through this issue.

Why had he defended against the best that was within him and protected himself from a sense of competence, efficacy, well-being, and, ultimately, independence? For some, such behavior would serve as a self-punishing defense in a world given to rampant self-promotion. However, in Mickey's case, withholding achievement was both an angry and punishing defense. Regrettably, the defense was hurtful not just to others (e.g., his authoritarian father) but to himself as well.

Treatment Issues

Although underachievement may have many different psychological sources and may present with a variety of psychodynamic patterns, treatment goals are generally the same: to help the client initiate effort toward accomplishing personally meaningful goals. Because the ratio of attempts made to success appears to be relatively constant, those who risk fewer attempts are more likely to fail—attributions of an association between effort and results (Carr, Borkowski, & Maxwell, 1991; Nurmi, 1991; Singer, Grove, Cauraugh, & Rudisill, 1985; Warring, 1991). The therapist therefore aims to assist the client in increasing the attempts initiated, thereby increasing the likelihood of success. Unfortunately, conceptually identifying the therapeutic goal is far removed from achieving it in practice, particularly in the real world of accomplished resistances and multiple-motive situations.

In working with adult underachievement, the therapist is therefore well-advised first to obtain an understanding of the role that achievement and accomplishment play in the client's psychological makeup, including the various operative familial and personal factors. If the therapist can rule out inability (see Grayson, 1991) as the source of the underachievement, the therapeutic task is to assist the client in making sound judgments about career directions in his or her own life context. In this regard, a neutral stance toward achievement is perhaps the least likely to create conflict between therapist and client. The therapist in effect communicates that he or she wishes the best for the client but that what constitutes the "best" for one client will not be the best for another. The therapist is the "coach," not just another parentlike figure seen as applying pressure to achieve. Helping the client recognize the right to underachievement (the therapist's granting permission for the patient to underachieve) may, paradoxically, free the client to explore achievement on his or her own terms, not as something done to please the therapist.

Timing is also important in deciding how to intervene with such clients. The client may simply not be ready at the particular point in time to perform the avoided work or integrate the various aspects of self that may be required for productive accomplishment. The therapeutic alliance may at such points call for the therapist to avoid strong emphasis on the avoided goals or tasks and provide support for the client's own timetable for accomplishment ("When you're ready to, you will"). But regardless of the timing or whether the client is merely being resistant or avoidant, the therapist should avoid becoming another parental figure pushing for "success" that the client may feel unable to accomplish.

Exploring the client's fantasies associated with achievement can also be useful. Clients may fantasize that were effort systematically begun toward a long-desired goal, the result would be an unacceptably high commitment to work to the exclusion of other interests. Such patterns may be discerned from discussion of the client's leisure interests. The focus of the intervention may appropriately be on shorter term goals, with leisure-interest rewards provided when some small step has been made toward the goal. Because changing long-standing, resistant patterns of underachievement may challenge the client's psychological identity, the client may need assurances that change can occur on as rapid or as slow a timetable as feels comfortable and that fundamental changes in identity are unlikely.

Exploration of the client's current sources of pleasure and satisfaction may also identify clues as to what is likely to be motivating over time. Perhaps no energy has been directed toward certain goals because those goals have not been of interest. Caution against too-rapid change may help the client see the therapist as an ally.

Summary

Failure to achieve at the level of one's abilities can be caused by a number of factors, psychological (e.g., fear of success and fear of failure) and otherwise. Occasional procrastination becomes dysfunctional when it occurs characteristically or predominantly. Underachievement occurs in situations in which there is a persistent failure to achieve although the individual has the abilities to do so. Therapists can help their clients identify the phenomena of underachievement and ways in which it can be remediated. Creativity in working around entrenched sources of resistance may be needed. The therapeutic goal is to assist the client in increasing the number of achievement attempts so as to increase the likelihood of personal success or, at the least, to help the client make a conscious and deliberate, rather than neurotic, decision not to achieve.

5

Patterns of Overcommitment

P eople who are overcommitted to the work role would appear to endorse the old German proverb, *Rast ich, so rost ich* [When I rest, I rust]. As with patterns of undercommitment, overcommitment can be a matter of degree. There is a fine and sometimes imperceptible difference between work behavior that is appropriately achievement and success oriented and that which is overly compulsive, driven, and cheerless ("workaholism"; Naughton, 1987) and would be considered compulsive or obsessive–compulsive. Work overcommitment can be the price of success for an achievement-oriented, goal-directed careerist, or it can reflect a neurotically driven, joyless compulsivity.

Although overachievement has been called a curse by some (Molestrangler, 1975) and ways have been suggested for its reduction (Killinger, 1992), the societal rewards for compulsive and "successful" behavior should not be underestimated and must always be considered in determining how to intervene in a particular case (see Van Egeren, 1991). A practicing psychologist I met at an international conference fantasized about moving to the quiet, yet ambitious country in which the conference was being held. He boasted of earning more than $120,000 per year (still a respectable income at the time of this writing), yet in the next breath stated that he was abusing alcohol and drugs as a way of coping. "If the work is making you so unhappy, why don't you just cut back?" I naively wondered aloud. Alas, psychologists generally do not make the best patients (Freudenberger, 1983), even in casual curbside consultations; for some, overwork is about as positive an addiction as can be hoped for.

It is difficult to imagine very many occupational settings that would not value the typical features of work overcommitment, particularly in Holland's (1985) Enterprising occupations (see Lowman, 1991b). Yet, at the individual level, excessive involvement in one's work may come at the cost of considerable psychological (sometimes medical) distress and trauma. It follows that, of all the work dysfunctions considered, patterns of overcommitment may be the most difficult in which to make substantive change simply because there are so many positive outcomes associated with or perceived to be associated with this potentially dysfunctional behavior.

The overvaluation of work, often accompanied by compulsive qualities, is exemplified in fiction by the character of Bob Sterling in Thomas Wolfe's (1929) *Look Homeward, Angel*:

> Eugene began the year earnestly as room-mate of a young man who had been the best student in the Altamont High School. His name was Bob Sterling. Bob Sterling was nineteen years old, the son of a widow. He was of middling height, always very neatly and soberly dressed; there was nothing conspicuous about him. For this reason, he could laugh good-naturedly, a little smugly, at whatever was conspicuous. He had a good mind—bright, attentive, studious, unmarked by originality or inventiveness. He had a time for everything: he apportioned a certain time for the preparation of each lesson, and went over it three times, mumbling rapidly to himself. He sent his laundry out every Monday. When in merry company he laughed heartily and enjoyed himself but he always kept track of the time. Presently, he would

look at his watch, saying: "Well, this is all very nice, but it's getting no work done," and he would go.

Every one said he had a bright future. He remonstrated with Eugene, with good-natured seriousness, about his habits. He ought not to throw his clothes around. He ought not to let his shirts and drawers accumulate in a dirty pile. He ought to have a regular time for doing each lesson; he ought to live by regular hours. (pp. 480–481)

Life, in short, should be directed toward the accomplishment of well-defined goals and objectives, and pleasure is at best an adjunctive, clearly a circumscribed diversion.

Etiology of Work Overcommitment

Patterns of overcommitment to the work role can arise from a variety of sources (Rohrlich, 1981). The etiology of each case should be assessed by the clinician before deciding on an intervention approach. The clinician needs to assess whether the commitment to work is indeed excessive and therefore dysfunctional. Evidence suggests that people differ constitutionally in the amount of energy they typically have available, for both work and nonwork tasks (see Buss, 1988). Although a balanced life may be a noteworthy goal for psychologists, spouses, or moralists to espouse, the reality is that ambitious, responsible people do not typically get ahead by leading so-called balanced lives. However, only when the work role causes psychological or psychophysiological symptoms or serious disruptions in family or nonwork life are such individuals likely to seek psychological assistance.

In general, common psychological patterns associated with overcommitment to the work role include the following:

1. Neurotic compulsions to succeed based on an unhealthy sense of self-esteem or dysfunctional family-of-origin dynamics (Ottenberg, 1975);
2. Positive striving based on ambitious goals and/or high levels of energy;

The "Bizzaro cartoon" by Dan Piraro is reproduced by permission of Chronicle
Features, San Francisco, CA.

3. Obsessive–compulsive personality in which "doing" and
   activity serve neurotic ends (Naughton, 1987) and in which
   anxiety may be a key underlying dynamic (Andrews &
   Crino, 1991);
4. Failure to accomplish significant life goals on schedule, resulting in imbalance between occupational and nonprofes-
   sional goals;
5. High levels of ability that are purposely and productively
   directed toward productive or creative work;
6. Avoidance of what may be psychologically more stressful
   issues such as intimacy or closeness;
7. Shame associated with excessive blaming or other mistreat-
   ment as a child (Kaufman, 1985, 1989; Robinson, 1989);

8. Avoidance of anxiety-provoking nonwork or leisure roles and interests (Khanna, Rajendra, & Channabasavanna, 1988); and
9. A defense against discovery of a sense of pervasive psychological inadequacy for which excessive work may serve as a cover (Kolligan, 1990).

The origins of neurotic striving for success need to be at least briefly examined as part of the clinician's assessment process. Fenichel (1945) spoke of patients who

> pay the installments due their superego not by suffering but by achievements. Successes are thought of as undoing previous failures and guilt. Since no achievement succeeds in really undoing the unconscious guilt, these persons are compelled to run from one achievement to another, never being satisfied with themselves. They are the Don Juans of achievement. (p. 502)

Although such people will certainly be encountered in clinical practice, the therapist needs to ascertain whether a pattern of what appears to be overwork is neurotic or healthy. The a priori presumption that all apparently excessive commitment to the work role is necessarily neurotic (see, e.g., Aldrich, 1987) should be avoided. Moreover, much time can be saved by making an early determination of whether the client has any real interest in changing. If not, palliative interventions to assist the client through some externally precipitated anxiety may be most appropriate. Paradoxical stances may also be relevant for intevening with those overcommitted to the work role. These include the clinician's expressing skepticism about the depth or interest in changing what may be viewed as a successful way of life or requiring the client to identify compelling reasons for changing. Such tactics may assist the clinician in assessing strength of motivation and commitment to change before spending too much energy on change efforts that are unlikely to have any effect.

Differential Diagnosis

Differential diagnosis in patterns of overcommitment includes determining whether an obsessional, compulsive, or obsessive–

compulsive disorder or other form of psychopathology may be present and masked by the overcommitted behavior (see, e.g., Black & Noyes, 1990). Because sociopathic and obsessive–compulsive behaviors may also present as apparent overinvolvement with the work role, such personality dysfunctions should also be ruled out (see chapter 4). Overwork and leisure avoidance may also make patterns of depression.

Obsessive–Compulsive Patterns and Work

Although people with obsessive–compulsive diagnosis often suffer work dysfunctions (e.g., Steketee & Cleere, 1990; Steketee, Grayson, & Foa, 1987), not all those presenting with patterns of overcommitment meet DSM–III–R diagnostic criteria for obsessive–compulsive disorder (see W. N. Goldstein, 1985b). Furthermore, despite both obsessive and compulsive polarities being potentially problematic in relation to work issues (Solyom, Ledwidge, & Solyom, 1986), their psychological dynamics may differ from each other (Pitman & Jenike, 1989). Thus, the still-common practice of discussing "obsessive–compulsive" disorders as if they were one and the same may be problematic.

Although characteristics of parsimony, withholding, orderliness, and deficits in information-processing abilities (Frost, Lahart, Dugas, & Sher, 1988) may characterize compulsive individuals, obsessional traits may relate more to anxiety, indecisiveness, and uncertainty (see Garamoni & Schwartz, 1986; D. J. Stein, Hollander, DeCaria, & Trungold, 1991). Whereas obsessional disorders may well belong in the spectrum of anxiety disorders (see chapter 6), compulsive disorders may share more in common with personality disorders (see chapter 7). In a study of 26 patients with obsessive–compulsive disorder diagnosis, Steketee (1990) found that only one met the DSM–III–R criteria for compulsive personality disorder, whereas more than 25% met other personality disorder criteria. Solyom et al. (1986) studied 94 patients with obsessive–compulsive disorder diagnosis and found both obsessional and compulsive symptoms, but not obsessional or complusive traits, to affect occupational adjustment.

It must also be noted that surprisingly little research has been published about compulsive dynamics among nonclinical populations. Although some have argued against a continuum between so-called normal compulsivity and dysfunctional psychopathology (Pitman & Jenike, 1989), others (Victor, 1987) stress the normalcy and predictability of certain compulsive behaviors. Additionally, some studies have reported occupational differences in compulsivity, although more studies are needed before drawing substantive conclusions. Krakowski (1982), for example, reported high levels of compulsivity among physicians. In another study, Krakowski (1984) compared age-matched attorneys and physicians and found the latter group to be the more compulsive. Rhoads (1977) described those in "open-ended" occupations (including business executives, lawyers, physicians, accountants, clergy, and homemakers) as particularly prone to work compulsivity. Obviously, there are other occupational groups whose members would also be expected to have above-average work compulsivity. Other studies corroborate these findings for at least some of these occupational groups (e.g., H. E. Smith, 1982; K. J. Smith, 1990).

The following case illustrates how overcommitment to the work role (or, in this case, to *a* work role) can prove dysfunctional.

Case 5.1
The Overly Loyal Employee

Sarah was 38 years old and married at the time of the referral. She was referred by a friend because of stress and anxiety that was identified as relating to family problems. Although she did have some problems relating to her in-laws, it turned out that the primary difficulties were with her work.

Sarah was employed as an office manager for a busy radiologist who had opened a private practice after being employed as a professor at a prestigious university. She had worked with this physician for a number of years but had periodically quit after a flare-up occurred in which he seemed, almost intentionally, to provoke a protracted argument identifying some aspect of her work as being problematic. Her boss had experienced chronic difficulties in getting along with others, but Sarah had persisted in the relationship longer than was appropriate for either her career or her sense of self-esteem. However, each time she quit, she returned once again, sometimes after several months, during which she made little effort to find alternative employment.

The client found her boss's style often to be reprehensible and unprofessional. Although a well-trained physician, he tended to take on more duties than he could reasonably fulfill. Beyond this, however, he let radiology reports go undictated for weeks, leaving Sarah to fend the many resulting irate calls. This practice also wreaked havoc with the billing system in the office.

Entrenching herself further in a dysfunctional system, Sarah began to assume responsibility for overseeing her boss's personal finances, which were every bit as chaotic as those in his office. Despite making an excellent income and owning a very expensive house in a prestigious part of town, he continually failed to pay his bills; his utilities had been shut off and turned back on with some regularity. He paid his bills whenever he felt like it.

When Sarah complained to her boss about his behavior, as she occasionally did when she became disgusted with the work situation, she was made to feel "dumb." After a few years, she began to realize that her boss seemed to enjoy confrontation and conflict, too often provoking confrontative interactions. For her troubles, Sarah was paid a few dollars an hour over minimum wage and was never given a raise unless she demanded one, and then only after a protracted battle. She had no health benefits or retirement plan and over the past few years before seeking help had begun to feel used.

Each time Sarah quit her job, however, she became depressed and always ended up going back to her former employer, much like someone might who is neurotically addicted to a dysfunctional relationship. Prior to coming to work for her present employer, she had made up her mind to go to nursing school. Because she had been out of school for several years, she became frightened concerning her ability to compete but had nonetheless begun the training program and had done reasonably well in her studies. Not too far from the terminating point of her degree, however, she became ill and dropped out of school, never to return.

The client's family of origin had been chaotic. She was the oldest of four children in a family with an emotionally disturbed father. Although she had assumed a caretaker role, she moved out when she was 15 years old. Her adult relationship with her family had been rocky, with periodic confrontations followed by long periods of time in which she did not speak to them. This case illustrates the complexity of interaction between personal and workplace dynamics. The client had overly committed herself to an inappropriate work role, one replicating many of the dynamics of her family of origin, yet could not yet let go of her hopes of and compulsive commitment to this time making the situation right. The seemingly obvious repetition of her family dynamics in her relationship with her employer had gone unnoticed until brought to her attention by her therapist. A need to grieve the lost relationship with her father, and the loss of the similarly dysfunctional relationship with her boss, was of primary importance. Assisting her through the anxiety, depression, and resultant low self-esteem became a primary goal of the therapy. Over time, she did end her employment permanently, returned to school, and was able to follow a more appropriate course of action in her career.

Two Patterns of Overcommitment

In addition to obsessive–compulsive dynamics, this chapter discusses two particular overcommitment patterns or syndromes that go beyond traditional obsessive–compulsive disorders: Type A personality pattern and job burnout.

Type A Behavioral Pattern

Widely studied in the context of cardiovascular impairment, the so-called Type A behavioral pattern describes a syndrome highly relevant to work overcommitment (Friedman & Rosenman, 1974; Rosenman, Brand, Sholtz, & Friedman, 1976; Rosenman & Friedman, 1959; Rosenman et al., 1966; Strube, 1991). Garamoni and Schwartz (1986) identified many similarities between the Type A behavior pattern and the compulsive personality disorder, including features of excessive sense of time urgency (R. V. Levine, Lynch, Miyake, & Lucia, 1989; Strube, Deichmann, & Kickham, 1989; Winnubst, 1985), decreased coping skills for handling interrupted tasks (Kirmeyer, 1988), hostility (S. A. Yuen & Kuiper, 1991), rapid speech, low latency in responding verbally to others (Scherwitz, Graham, Grandits, & Billings, 1990), overcommitment to the work role (Chonko, 1983) apparently at the expense of nonwork activities (Burke & Greenglass, 1990; Tang, 1986), strong needs for control (Strube, Berry, & Moergen, 1985), perfectionism, and emotional constriction.

Type A behavior is apparently not a unidimensional trait (Begley & Boyd, 1985). Factors of Achievement Strivings (AS) and Impatience–Irritability (II) have been reported (Bluen, Barling, & Burns, 1990; Helmreich, Spence, & Pred, 1988). According to R. B. Williams and Anderson (1987), it is the latter component— especially uncontrolled, free-floating hostility (Dembroski, MacDougall, Costa, & Grandits, 1989; Saab, Dembroski, & Schneiderman, 1990) or so-called negative Type A pattern (R. B. Williams & Barefoot, 1988)—that appears to be the component of Type A behavior that has the most negative effects on physical health (Krantz, Contrada, Hill, & Friedler, 1988; R. B. Williams, 1989). Also, Type A behavior appears to interact with characteristics of the task or situation in determining whether there will be dysfunctional consequences. K. A. Lawler and Schmied (1987) found that the combination of Type A behavior and the perception of limited ability to control the situation was likely to have cardiovascular implications.

Fine-tuning the definition of Type A behavior is still needed to ferret out relations between particular aspects of the behavioral style and work outcomes (e.g., those who are high in anger and competitiveness vs. those high only in anger; see Gray, Jackson, & Howard, 1990). Recent research has suggested a genetic component to Type A behavior (e.g., K. A. Matthews, Rosenman, Dembroski, Harris, & MacDougall, 1984) that when first manifest in childhood may predict adult Type A behavior. In a longitudinal study in Sweden, MacEvoy et al. (1988) found characteristics in infants and youths of liveliness, sociability, and poor appetite to be associated with time urgency and irritability in adulthood. Furthermore, Type A children may describe their fathers as being more concerned with achievement and undervaluing their actual accomplishments, whereas Type B children may view their parents as themselves having more Type A behavioral characteristics (Blaney, Blaney, & Diamond, 1989). On the other hand, not all studies have found Type A behavior in youth to predict Type A behavior in adulthood (L. Steinberg, 1988).

A variety of instruments for assessing Type A and Type B behavior have been put forth. Although several measures of Type A behavior have been reported (see Blumenthal & Kamarck, 1987), including interviews (Scherwitz & Brand, 1990) as well as objective forms and scales for children and adolescents (see B. S. McCann & Matthews, 1988), the most widely used measures in the research literature to date are the Jenkins Activity Survey (C. D. Jenkins, Rosenman, & Friedman, 1966; C. D. Jenkins, Zyzanski, & Rosenman, 1971) and, to a somewhat lesser degree, standardized interviews. Alternative measures appear to assess similar phenomena, and the construct validity for such measures is generally good (Mayes, Sime, & Ganster, 1984; for exceptions, see H. Firth, McIntee, McKeown, & Britton, 1985). Recent developments in isolating the possible critical importance of hostility, particularly as measured by such scales as the Cook and Medley Hostility Scale (Ho; Swan, Carmelli, & Rosenman, 1991), point to important differences between generic Type A characteristics and the specific factors of Type A that may define the syndrome's most dysfunctional characteristics. Those who score high on the Ho scale appear to be more neurotic and may be at greater risk for cardiovascular difficulties (see Swan et al., 1991; R. B. Williams, 1989), although this contention is increasingly challenged.

Whether the specific occupation held moderates the relation between Type A behavior and role strain is unknown. However, Type A behavior is by no means limited to those in high-powered, executive-type positions. Evans, Palsane, and Carrere (1987) found work-relevant differences among bus drivers in both the United States and India on Type A and Type B behaviors. Although epidemiological data on Type A and Type B behavior in various occupations is currently limited, studies that have examined the proportion of people manifesting Type A behavior have typically reported that around 50% or more of occupational samples show Type A behavior (Fletcher, 1988; Nagy & Davis, 1985). Helmert, Herman, Joeckel, Greiser, and Madans (1989), using Bortner Scale scores of greater than or equal to 57 as a criterion of Type A personality, found that 15.9% of the males and 12.8% of the females were of Type A in a German general population sample. Of course, the nature of the sample would be expected to influence the proportions of Type A and Type B behavior. Boyd (1984) sampled chief executive officers and found that 82% of the respondents completed the Jenkins Activity Survey in the Type A direction, and Greenglass (1991) found a sample of professional women to be predominantly Type A. A self-selection phenomenon is presumably at work through which people with prior predispositions to Type A characteristics seek out work roles that call for active, if not overcommitted, work behavior.

In addition, gender or masculine/feminine sex roles may moderate certain relations between Type A behavior and role strain (Auten, Hull, & Hull, 1985; L. J. Baker, Dearborn, Hastings, & Hamberger, 1988; Bedeian, Mossholder, & Touliatos, 1990). Although some researchers (e.g., Thompson, Grisanti, & Pleck, 1987) have suggested a general elevation of Type A behavior in males compared with females, this hypothesis appears to be neither universal nor reliably established. Type A behavior appears to interact in a complex manner with other factors, such as the type of activity toward which Type A behaviors may be directed (Burke, 1985), the number of hours worked (Sorensen et al., 1987), relationships with locus of control, and, for women, masculine sex role orientation (L. J. Baker et al., 1988).

Although there is some controversy about associations between physical consequences and Type A behavior, this section is concerned not so much with the cardiovascular implications of the construct as with the implications of Type A behavior for work-related behavior and performance. In the workplace, Type A workers are apparently more likely to experience stress (at least subjectively, if not objectively; see Ganster, 1986; Rahe,

1975) than non-Type A workers (L. J. Baker, Dearborn, Hastings, & Hamberger, 1988; Cooper & Roden, 1985; Houston & Kelly, 1987). Questions remain as to the mechanism that connects Type A behavior and stress and concerning the situations among adult workers that are likely to engender stress in those scoring high on Type A behavioral scales. For example, are Type A workers more likely to experience stress in a slow-moving job in which the characteristics do not match their hard-driving personality style?

Other studies also support the finding that Type A workers are more likely to experience stress on the job with consequences of work dysfunction (Evans et al., 1987; Greenglass, 1990; Kushnir & Melamed, 1991; V. J. Sutherland & Cooper, 1991). In a study of nurses, Jamal (1990) found that those higher in Type A behavior pattern reported the most job stress and identified the job characteristics most commonly associated with stress (role ambiguity, role conflict, etc.). Type A behavior pattern also moderated the relation between job stressors and negative outcomes, with Type A workers being more likely to be negatively affected by work stressors.

Some contradictory results have also been reported. Froggatt and Cotton (1987) concluded that any enhanced job stressors that Type A workers reported were because they were more likely to seek out highly demanding work situations. On the other hand, Kushnir and Melamed (1991) found Type A workers and Type B workers not to differ in their stress reactions to low role-overload conditions (except when they experienced low levels of control, in which case more psychic stress could be expected). Newton and Keenan (1990) reported that Type A workers experienced *less* strain when job demands increased than did Type B workers in a sample of engineers in Great Britain.

Type A and B workers appear also to differ in their interpersonal relationships at work (Sorensen et al., 1987) and outside work (Blaney, Brown, & Blaney, 1986) and in their use of social support to moderate the effects of stress. Greenglass (1988) reported that Type B workers were more likely to use social support as a means of coping with stress, whereas Type A workers were more likely to use instrumental (goal-directed) approaches. These studies may imply that Type A workers to some extent create their own stress on the job and are less likely to know how to ameliorate its effects, at least through the use of social support (see Orth-Gomer & Unden, 1990). A related finding by L. K. Clark and Miller (1990) showed that Type A workers were more likely than Type B workers to want to work alone on a task when offered the opportunity to work with someone else and were more likely to see little value to be added by a partner. Modification of such personal behaviors may therefore be an important part of changing Type A behavior, assuming that change is desired or needed.

The extent to which Type A behavior is associated with other characteristics of personality, demographic variables (including sex, race, age, and marital status), occupational membership, and various characteristics and levels of ability is not yet established. Evidence suggests that Type A behavior varies by social class, being higher in groups of higher socioeconomic standing (Helmert et al., 1989). Type A behavior is apparently also more likely to be associated with compulsive personality dynamics (Garamoni & Schwartz, 1986), impulsivity, and extraversion (Buss, 1988).

The role of family dynamics has been noted by some investigators (e.g., P. A. Martin, 1981). Excessive striving in the work role by one spouse (historically, the male) may result in overcommitment to the work role at the expense of the family and general undercommitment to family and other nonwork roles. Blaney et al. (1986) found that the combination of Type A husbands married to Type B wives was particularly likely to be stressful.

The relation between Type A behavior and work or school performance also has yet to be conclusively established. Studies reporting positive associations between Type A and performance (Boyd, 1984; Fekken & Jakubowski, 1990; M. S. Taylor, Locke, Lee, & Gist, 1984) contrast with those showing negative associations (Diekhoff, 1984; Evans et al., 1987; Jamal, 1990; Matteson, Ivancevich, & Smith, 1984). This may partly reflect occupation–individual interactions; Type A behavior may be more adaptive in certain occupations (e.g., white-collar managerial jobs with opportunities for advancement) than in others (e.g., blue-collar occupations with no or little opportunity for advancement where goal-directed behavior may be the source of peer rejection or ridicule).

The exact relations among these variables appear to be complex and somewhat confounded. Confounding factors include (a) the many aspects of behavior that are included in the Type A behavioral pattern as typically defined (Bluen et al., 1990; Helmreich et al., 1988; Spence, Helmreich, & Pred, 1987), (b) the fact that Type A workers may behave differently than Type B workers in being more goal directed (L. J. Baker et al., 1988; Greenglass, 1988; K. V. Jones, 1985), and (c) the apparently higher incidence among Type A workers of psychological difficulties that could affect work outcomes (e.g., depression and anxiety; see Bluen et al., 1990; Dearborn & Hastings, 1987; R. A. Martin, Kuiper, & Westra, 1989). Moreover, if Type A workers are more productive in their work than Type B workers, the mechanism of such an association needs to be examined. Type A workers appear to spend greater time on their work (Byrne & Reinhart, 1990; J. H. Howard, Cunningham, & Rechnitzer, 1977), although they may not necessarily perform their work better (see Burke & Weir, 1980). In addition, they appear to respond faster (Damos, 1985; Damos & Bloem, 1985), have a preference for greater task variety, and set higher goals for themselves (Kirmeyer & Biggers, 1988; C. Lee, Earley, Christopher, & Hansen, 1988; Tang & Liu, 1989).

Such behaviors, of course, would likely enhance the probability of occupational success, although Yarnold, Mueser, and Lyons (1988) found that higher level work outcomes for Type A workers compared with those of Type B workers took place only in conditions in which Type A workers thought they would be held personally accountable for the results. Furthermore, only certain aspects of Type A behavior may account for differential achievement outcomes. Helmreich et al. (1988) reported that, of the Type A dimensions, only AS and not II was associated with positive outcomes in a sample of male academic psychologists.

The relation of Type A behavior and job satisfaction has not been reliably established; findings of positive and negative correlations between job satisfaction and Type A behavior have been reported (e.g., Dearborn & Hastings, 1987; Kushnir & Melamed, 1991; V. J. Sutherland & Cooper, 1991). In a more specific study of job satisfaction and Type A behavior, Day and Bedeian (1991) found Type A behavior to be associated with higher intrinsic, but not extrinsic, job satisfaction, whereas Bluen et al. (1990) found only the AS dimension, not the II dimension, to predict job satisfaction. Moreover, Type A and Type B are not binary, discrete constructs. More may be known about individuals at the extremes of the Type A–B distribution than about those who score in the midrange (see Lundberg, Hedman, & Melin, 1989).

Issues involved in intervention with Type A personality are discussed later in this chapter. The following case illustrates what sometimes happens when there is interruption in the work role of someone whose primary commitment is to that aspect of life.

Case 5.2
The Unemployed Compulsive Worker

An attractive, never-married, middle-aged woman, Beth consulted a psychologist when she was dismissed from her executive assistant job after her firm merged with another. Bright, articulate, and hard-driven, Beth became depressed over the job loss and focused her attention on trying to find another job—a frustrating effort that had not been going well owing to the poor state of the economy. Although initial interviews with a number of companies had been promising, she had not had any definite offers and was panicked that she would remain unemployed. She was irate that her company had "mistreated" her after her years of faithful and productive service.

Initial exploration indicated that her striving masked a rather deep-seated, shame-driven anxiety and that her work activities had been effective in protecting her from deeper experiences of humiliation, estrangement, loneliness, and anger. Exploratory inquiries suggested that this client had no interest in probing these "deeper" issues, that at the time of referral reemployment would most expeditiously reconstitute her defenses, and that intrusive unconscious probing would only intensify further her defenses and accelerate her departure from treatment. A brief course of supportive treatment was therefore undertaken and a few suggestive seeds planted in her conscious mind about some psychological issues that she might address at a later date.

Not unexpectedly, given her overcommitment to the work role, the client promptly found new employment. After the few sessions of counseling she had attended while in crisis, her successful search for another job enabled her to escape the experience of anxiety by recommiting herself to the work role. She discontinued treatment.

Job and Occupational Burnout

Rarely in social science literature does a construct such as *burnout* have as much popular as well as research appeal. In the few years since the term was originally introduced in the psychological literature (see Freudenberger & Richelson, 1980; Maslach, 1982; Pines, Aronson, & Kafry, 1981; Pines & Maslach, 1978), hundreds of research articles have been published, and probably thousands more have appeared in the popular press. Jobs and activities as diverse as teaching (Lowenstein, 1991), nursing (McGrath, Reid, & Boore, 1989), dentistry (Burns, 1986), academic administration (Sommer, 1973), psychotherapy (Farber & Heifetz, 1982), and working with the mentally challenged (P. Edwards & Miltenberger, 1991) and with youth sports programs (Cohn, 1990; Rotella, Hanson, & Coop, 1991) have been considered to be at risk for burnout. Burnout has been suggested to cause outcomes from employee turnover, to patient abuse (Pillemer & Bachman-Prehn, 1991), to coronary heart disease (Appels & Schouten, 1991), to general health problems (Golembiewski & Munzenrider, 1991; Kahill, 1988), to family problems (Bacharach, Bamberger, & Conley, 1991). In short, the term has entered the national vocabulary, indicating both the presence of something to which the general public can obviously relate and a construct with the danger of being overly diffuse or confounded.

However, the concept of burnout was identified long before its "discovery" by psychologists. Graham Greene's (1960) book *A Burnt-Out Case* presented the case of a renowned architect, Querry, who randomly traveled to an African leper colony in a blind attempt to cope with symptoms that closely matched to-day's psychological construct of burnout. As Querry put it,

> chiefly I wanted to be in an empty place, where no new building or woman would remind me that there was a time when I was alive, with a vocation and a capacity to love. . . . A vocation is an act of love. . . . I've come to the end of desire and to the end of a vocation. Don't try to . . . make me imitate what I used to perform with passion. And don't talk to me like a priest about my duty. A talent . . . should not be buried when it still has purchasing power, but when the currency has changed and the image has been superseded and no value is left in the coin but the weight of a wafer of silver, a man has every right to hide it. (pp. 46, 50)

Is the construct of burnout psychologically viable? In the minds of the public, the answer is apparently a decided yes. For psychological researchers, there is more uncertainty (Gold, 1984a). Meier (1984) found evidence of relatively good construct validity for the notion of burnout but noted considerable overlap among burnout, depression, and various elements of job satisfaction. Similarly, Handy (1988) identified considerable overlap between burnout and occupational stress constructs. Brill (1984) proposed an operational definition of burnout that excludes psychological difficulties, including depression and marital problems, which is somewhat at odds with empirical findings in the literature.

Most researchers report that burnout is a multidimensional construct (Blostein, Eldridge, Kilty, & Richardson, 1985–1986; Perlman & Harman, 1982). Some researchers have found support for a three-component model that divides burnout into its presumed psychological dimensions: *emotional exhaustion, depersonalization,* and *personal accomplishment* (Belcastro, Gold, & Hays, 1983; Gold, 1984b; R. T. Lee & Ashforth, 1990; Malanowski & Wood, 1984; Maslach & Jackson, 1984). Although researchers have found promise for the three-factor model (e.g., Meir, Melamed, & Abu-Freha, 1990; Pierce & Molloy, 1990a), some studies have noted that there are complex interactions between components of the model and their impact on individuals' lives. Leiter (1990) found emotional exhaustion to be related more to family issues than to work issues, depersonalization to both family and work, and personal accomplishment to work. On the other hand, McGrath, Houghton, and Reid (1989) found burnout to be related more to job stress than to sources of personal stress. At least some studies have demonstrated that burnout is more likely to be associated with high (if not excessively high) standards, including the desire to have an impact on important social problems (Burke & Kirchmeyer, 1990).

On the other hand, several studies have suggested the primacy of emotional exhaustion in the burnout construct. J. E. Wallace and Brinkeroff (1991), however, found only emotional exhaustion to serve as a valid and reliable component of burnout, whereas Brookings, Bolton, Brown, and McEvoy (1985) found emotional exhaustion and depersonalization scales not to be empirically distinct. Although Koeske and Koeske (1989) agreed that exhaustion was the primary aspect of burnout, they also found personal accomplishment and depersonalization to be separable scales on the Maslach Burnout Inventory (Maslach & Jackson, 1981), although they did not concur that they should be regarded as elements of burnout. Other researcher have found work stress to be related only to emotional exhaustion in a sample of teachers (Friesen, Prokop, & Sarros, 1988; Maslach & Florian, 1988); the other two components of burnout were related to recognition and status factors.

Concerning individual differences, burnout is reportedly higher among younger, more junior individuals (Ackerley, Burnell, Holder, & Kurdek, 1988; Burke & Greenglass, 1989a; Gillespie & Numerof, 1991; Kottkamp & Mansfield, 1985; Masterson-Allen, Mor, Laliberte, & Monteiro, 1985; J. W. White, Lawrence, Biggerstaff, & Grubb, 1985) and among Whites compared with Blacks (Matteson & Ivancevich, 1987). At least some studies have shown a sex difference, with men scoring higher than women on burnout (Maslach & Jackson, 1985), at least on the depersonalization scale (Burke & Greenglass, 1989b; Greenglass & Burke, 1988; Greenglass, Burke, & Ondrack, 1990; Ogus, Greenglass, & Burke, 1990). However, in other samples, the sex difference has been in the opposite direction (e.g., Caccese & Mayerberg, 1984; Etzion, 1984, 1987; Etzion & Pines, 1986;

Fuehrer & McGonagle, 1988; Hendrix, Cantrell, & Steel, 1988; Hetherington, Oliver, & Phelps, 1989), with women scoring higher than men on burnout, at least on the emotional exhaustion scale (Gaines & Jermier, 1983). Several studies reported no sex difference (Etzion, 1984; Kirkcaldy, Thome, & Thomas, 1989; McDermott, 1984; Shinn, Rosario, Morch, & Chestnut, 1984).

The complexity of the relation between gender and burnout is illustrated by a study by Etzion (1984), which reported men to be more vulnerable to job-related burnout and women to overall life-factors burnout. Men and women may also differ in what generates burnout and in how they handle burnout components when they encounter them. Izraeli (1988) found that burnout in male workers was more strongly related to doubts about their work performance than was the case for female workers. Women may be more likely than men to experience conflict between family and work as a cause of burnout and to have social support moderate the experience of burnout; for men, work stress alone may be more determinative of burnout (Etzion, 1984; Greenglass & Burke, 1988). However, having children may also moderate the experience of burnout. Maslach and Jackson (1985) found employees with children to be at lower risk for job burnout than those without. In contrast, Greenglass et al. (1990) found that, for men, the addition of children to work stress significantly increased the likelihood of burnout.

In addition to the differences in causes of burnout for men and women, occupational differences presumably interact with gender to moderate the propensity for burnout and the ability to cope with factors predisposing to burnout. Lemkau, Rafferty, Purdy, and Rudisill (1987), for example, found that in a sample of male and female physicians, women reported themselves to be more sensitive to hurt feelings than did men, but the men were more likely to experience a discrepancy between their actual and their ideal accomplishments at work.

Finally, men and women may differ in their coping strategies for handling burnout symptoms, with men apparently choosing a more active, direct (and possibly more effective) strategy (Etzion & Pines, 1986). On the other hand, Greenglass et al. (1990) reported better skills for coping with potential burnout among women than men.

In summary, no inherent sex differences in job-related burnout have been reliably established (Gold, 1985; Himle et al., 1983; Maslach & Jackson, 1985), and it is likely that other factors may more likely account for any observed sex differences (e.g., whether the sex experiencing the higher burnout is in the majority or minority in a particular occupation; characteristics or perceived characteristics of the job as rated by the respective sexes).

Interactions of burnout and such psychological variables as internal or external locus of control (with externals more likely to experience emotional exhaustion and lower senses of personal accomplishment) (Ganster & Fusilier, 1989; Glogow, 1986; McIntyre, 1984; St. Yves et al., 1989), compulsive personality (Lemkau, Purdy, Rafferty, & Rudisill, 1988), Type A or Type B personality (Mazur & Lynch, 1989; Nagy & Davis, 1985; Nowack, 1986, 1987), hardiness (Nowack, 1986; Topf, 1989), anxiety and depression (Jayaratne, Chess, & Kunkel, 1986), feeling types (who are more affected by low social support) and thinking types on the Myers-Briggs Type Indicator (Myers & McCaulley, 1985), perceived self-competence (Jayaratne & Chess, 1986), self-esteem, social introversion, and obsessional characteristics (McCranie & Brandsma, 1988) are unclear. Career orientation may also influence burnout propensity (Burke & Greenglass, 1988; Cherniss, 1985).

Several measures of burnout are available (e.g., Arthur, 1990; Emener, Luck, & Gohs, 1982; D. L. Ford, Murphy, & Edwards, 1983; Gold, Bachelor, & Michael, 1989; Gold, Roth, Wright, & Michael, 1991; Maslach & Jackson, 1984; Pines et al., 1981; Seidman & Zager, 1986–1987), although there is reported discrepancy between some of the symptomatology of burnout and what is measured in some of these instruments (see Paine, 1984). By far the most widely used measure of burnout is the Maslach Burnout Inventory (Maslach & Jackson, 1981, 1984). Other scales include the Staff Burnout Scales (J. Jones, 1980a, 1980b, 1981; see also Arthur, 1990), the Staff Burnout Scale for Health Professionals (Brookings et al., 1985; J. Jones, 1980a), the Staff Burnout Scale for Police and Security Personnel (J. Jones, 1980b), and the Tedium Scale (Pines et al., 1981; Stout & Williams, 1983). Corcoran (1986) found the Maslach and Pines measures to be highly correlated, although the construct validity of the subscales was more problematic. Some scales have purported to measure burnout in specific settings such as hospices (Masterson-Allen et al., 1985; Tout & Shama, 1990) or with specific occupational groups such as speech language pathologists (Fimian, Lieberman, & Fastenau, 1991). Whether this multiplicity of instrumentation is really needed or is measuring anything conceptually distinct is not reliably established (Golembiewski & Munzenrider, 1988). Kahill (1988) appropriately noted methodological problems associated with some of the burnout measures.

Occupations appear to differ in their propensity to engender burnout in their members (Burke, Shearer, & Deszca, 1984). However, some occupations that might be considered a priori high in burnout may on examination be no higher than others, and it may not be the occupation itself so much as certain characteristics commonly associated with the profession that yield higher rates of burnout. Anson and Bloom (1988) found no significant differences in burnout levels among samples of prison guards, probation officers, firefighters, and emergency medical technicians, although a study by P. A. Wallace, Roberg, and Allen (1985) found intraoccupational differences among police, with narcotics officers at highest risk for burnout.

The actual incidence of burnout, however defined, among various occupations is not reliably established. Mohler's (1983) sample of air traffic controllers reported that about 9% of the sample (in a group characterized by high levels of hypertension and substance abuse) experienced psychological burnout from their jobs. Ackerley et al. (1988) reported that a third of their sample of licensed psychologists reported high levels of emotional exhaustion and depersonalization on the Maslach Burnout Inventory, whereas Kahill (1986) found that in a sample of 255 psychologists, 6.3% of the subjects were considered to be burned out, a finding generally consistent with figures reported by Farber (1985, 1990), who estimated a 2–6% incidence rate of burnout among psychotherapists. Penn, Romano, and Foat (1988) found "low to moderate" levels of burnout among those in human service professions. In a study of more than 900 public school teachers, Hock (1988) reported that 40.8% of the sample had moderate or high levels of burnout, whereas Nagy and Davis

(1985) found that 33% of junior high school teachers and 10% of elementary school teachers met criteria of burnout and Farber (1984) reported that 10–15% of a sample of suburban teachers were "already burned out," with another 20–25% reported as being vulnerable to burnout. In still another study of teachers, Belcastro and Hays (1984) reported that about 20% of their sample was classified as burned out. Whitehead (1986) reported that in a sample of probation workers, virtually all employees reported experiencing emotional exhaustion, typically about once a month. This may imply that problematic burnout is a matter of degree, not a dichotomous differentiation, and that identifying those who experience burnout in a way that jeopardizes their job performance is a high priority. Clearly, however, the wide variability of reported burnout across samples points to sample-specific, if not occupation-specific, differences.

The helping and public service professions are seemingly at greatest risk for burnout (e.g., Borg, 1990; Farber & Heifetz, 1982; Kilburg, Kaslow, & VandenBos, 1988; D. B. Matthews, 1990; Rafferty, Lemkau, Purdy, & Rudisill, 1986), although other occupational groups that generally experience high stress (e.g., air traffic controllers; see Mohler, 1983) also are reported to experience high rates of burnout. The reported high incidence of burnout among social service workers may merely reflect the fact that such groups have been intensively studied or, perhaps more likely, the impossibility of the tasks that these workers take on, combined with the low salary levels for some of these occupations. Certainly other high-demand, high-stress occupations besides those named are also prone to burnout. The social service occupations may be at special risk, however, because it appears that these workers are exposed to stress without influence, a factor that is especially implicated in the burnout process. Not surprisingly, in this model, some studies (see Burke & Greenglass, 1989a) have demonstrated that it is the lower, not the higher, organizational levels that are more prone to burnout.

The effects of burnout on work performance are predominantly negative. Burned-out workers may cope by withdrawal and rigidity in decision making (McGee ,1989); however, they may not self-rate their job performance as being affected because denial may be part of the pattern (Zedeck, Maslach, Mosier, &

Skitka, 1988). Although burnout may also result in greater absenteeism and turnover (Harris, 1988; Jackson, Schwab, & Schuler, 1986; Kahill, 1988; Masterson-Allen, Mor, & Laliberte, 1987)
and in increased risk of physical impairment (Belcastro, 1982;
Belcastro & Hays, 1984), the relations to specific aspects of burnout appear to be complex. H. Firth and Britton (1989) reported
in a longitudinal study different predictors of burnout at its different stages. Short-term absences were predicted by burnout
scores early on, emotional exhaustion and perceived lack of support predicted absenteeism in the next year of employment, and
leaving the job was predicted by depersonalization in the next
two years. This would imply that differential aspects of burnout
would predict consequences of work dysfunction at different
phases of employment.

Characteristics of the work and of the work organization may
also influence the propensity for burnout (Golembiewski & Munzenrider, 1988; Matteson & Ivancevich, 1987). A major job and
organizational factor implicated in burnout and stress more generally is work stress that is perceived as resulting from such job
features as role ambiguity, conflict, and overload (Cooper &
Payne, 1988; Dignam, Barrera, & West, 1986; Eisenstat & Felner,
1984; Friesen & Sarros, 1989; Hills & Norvell, 1991; Jackson,
Turner, & Brief, 1987; Kottkamp & Mansfield, 1985; Pierson &
Archambault, 1987; Schwab, Jackson, & Schuler, 1986), particularly when coupled with real or perceived lack of control (Kirkcaldy et al., 1989; Leiter, 1991; Mazur & Lynch, 1989; Pierce &
Molloy, 1990b; Syme, 1990) and lack of social support (Melamed, Kushnir, & Meir, 1991; R. R. Ross, Altmaier, & Russell,
1989; Russell, Altmaier, & Van-Velzen, 1987) especially from
one's supervisors (Constable & Russell, 1986; Savicki & Cooley,
1987). However, the type of social support available may determine whether it has an impact on decreasing burnout. Himle,
Jayaratne, and Thyness (1991) found only instrumental and informational support, not support of an emotional or approval-
giving variety, to be effective in ameliorating burnout. This finding needs replication and has been criticized on methodological
grounds (L. S. Miller, 1991). Organizational climate (James &
Jones, 1974; O'Driscoll & Schubert, 1988) and type of work setting may influence the extent of burnout. In the social services,

working in an agency setting (versus private practice) is apparently much more likely to be associated with burnout (Raquepaw & Miller, 1989).

The causal relations between specific job variables and burnout has not always been well-established. Although many studies have suggested a correlation between burnout and job commitment (Jackson et al., 1987; Leiter & Maslach, 1988) and between burnout and job dissatisfaction (Grigsby & McKnew, 1988; Jayaratne & Chess, 1986; McDermott, 1984; Penn et al., 1988), Wolpin, Burke, and Greenglass (1991) presented evidence suggesting that burnout causes job dissatisfaction, not the other way around. According to this model, the work characteristics (role conflict, overload, etc.) cause burnout, which in turn causes job dissatisfaction. Other studies have reported a longitudinal change process, with burnout being associated with a lowering of self-esteem over time (Golembiewski & Kim, 1989; Golembiewski, Munzenrider, & Carter, 1983; see also Burke & Deszca, 1986). Golembiewski's phase model of burnout specifically proposes a three-step sequential model of burnout: Work conditions result in depersonalization, which results in a lower sense of accomplishment, which in turn causes emotional exhaustion and burnout (Golembiewski & Munzenrider, 1988; Golembiewski, Munzenrider, & Stevenson, 1986).

The mechanisms by which job conditions interact with personality variables to cause burnout and its presumed psychological consequences also remain to be established (see Burke, 1987; Dignam & West, 1988). Leiter and Maslach (1988) suggested that emotional exhaustion precedes depersonalization, which in turn leads to burnout. Other models are also possible.

Intervention Approaches

Because of the positive and societally sanctioned rewards associated with compulsive behavior and overachievement syndromes, change is not easy. People seeking mental health assistance are likely to be individuals who (a) have lost their employment and thus their major, if not only, source of self-esteem; (b) have lost (or are threatened with losing) their spouses or significant others because of their unavailability in the relationship; (c) are experiencing drug or alcohol abuse adopted as a means of coping with excessive stress associated with the overcommitment pattern; (d) have had a health crisis (e.g., myocardial infarction) possibly at least partly attributable to compulsivity; or (e) are typically of middle age or beyond who have reached a point at which they are unhappy with their life-style and seek change as part of a midlife transition or crisis.

Although there is considerable literature on the treatment of obsessive–compulsive disorder (e.g., Andrews & Crino, 1991), little of it specifically addresses the work role. Various interventions have been proposed for dealing with overcommitment patterns (generally with very little data on their efficacy), including enforced rest, psychotherapy focused on reeducating the client to the relative importance of work and nonwork and attending to physical and emotional needs (Rhoads, 1977), and very specific dietary interventions. If anxiety is a critical component of obsessive–compulsive dynamics (e.g., Mavissakalian & Michelson, 1983; Salzman, 1979), therapeutic methods directed at its reduction would appear to be more likely to have positive effects than those that do not take account of this factor.

Type A behavior and burnout, two variations of overcommitment, differ in their dynamics and therefore in appropriate intervention. Whereas Type A behavior appears primarily to embody characteristics of individuals, burnout is more likely initially to involve characteristics of the job. Of course, in both cases personal and situational attributes can interact. Particular jobs and job settings can be more or less demanding of Type A behaviors, and those psychologically at risk may have more trouble with working conditions that imply higher levels of burnout. How to proceed in each particular case must rest on the clinician's careful assessment of the factors at play in the immediate situation (Jayaratne & Chess, 1984).

Modifying negative Type A behavior appears to be difficult unless some external threat (e.g., myocardial infarction) has forced the individual to consider life changes; even then, such clients are often known to be resistant to and noncompliant with treatment recommendations (Rhodewalt & Fairfield, 1991). Although some studies have reported a decrease in Type A behavior with specific therapies (e.g., Burrel, Sundin, Strom, & Ohman, 1986; Woods, 1987), too many (e.g., Yoder, 1987) have merely been suggestive of a particular treatment method or approach with little if any evaluation of outcome data. In spite of thorough literature reviews on Type A intervention outcomes (Price, 1982; Suinn, 1982), there is no convincingly identified standard treatment protocol that can be recommended (see also Levenkron & Moore, 1988; Roskies, 1987). However, promising components include relaxation methods (Suinn, 1982), stress management methods (Roskies, 1987), straightforward educative techniques (for a good summary, see Matteson & Ivancevich, 1987), and behavioral and group approaches (Powell & Thoresen, 1987). One difficulty in existing studies is that the interventions are often not for a sufficient duration to be likely to have impact on the behavior (Price, 1982).

Most techniques put forth thus far in the literature are multimodal (see Price, 1988), including both cognitive and relaxation components. However, modification of the hostility components of the syndrome appears to be particularly important (Dembroski et al., 1989; Saab et al., 1990; Rosenman, 1990; R. B. Williams, 1989; R. B. Williams & Anderson, 1987; R. B. Williams & Barefoot, 1988). Allowing the client to have control, or at least perceived control, in the treatment may also enhance the likelihood of its being effective (see Rhodewalt & Fairfield, 1991).

Other factors should also be considered in modifying Type A behavior. Price (1982) discussed three clinical states in which Type A workers often find themselves: playing "superman" (taking on unrealistic goals and assignments), anger, and depression (when, predictably, personal efforts are ineffective in reaching overly idealized goals). Because of the role that family dynamics may contribute to Type A behavior patterns, efforts to change the overly work-involved individual may need to be made in the context of the family situation. Groups seem particularly well-suited to Type A intervention (Roskies, 1987). Values counseling—namely, helping the client put the work role in context and move away from overly ambitious striving (particularly when associated with little sense of personal satisfaction)—is a therapeutic strategy that is effective with many such clients.

It is difficult on the basis of current literature to isolate the effective components of treatment when behavioral change is observed (see Roskies, 1990). A small number of controlled studies have been conducted. Bennett, Wallace, Carroll, and Smith (1991) reported that, compared with a control group and a stress management program, a program specifically directed toward Type A characteristics was more effective in reducing Type A behaviors and in reducing blood pressure. Seraganian, Roskies, Hanley, Oseasohn, and Collu (1987) found that behavioral reactivity was lowered by a stress management program but not by exercise alone, although neither intervention affected physiological reactivity (see also Roskies et al., 1986), with the latter having no effect on excessive psychophysiological reactions to mental stress. Razin, Swencionis, and Zohman (1986–1987) found modest improvement in Type A behaviors as the result of a group cognitive–behavioral intervention program, with most improvement noted for those highest on Type A behavior prior to intervention and for men.

Workplace factors appear to be at least as important as individual differences in understanding the construct of burnout. To the extent that emotional exhaustion is a major if not primary factor in burnout, addressing the job components associated with it may be significant (Riggar, Garner, & Hafer, 1984). For some seriously afflicted employees, temporary withdrawal from the job (or certain phases of it) may be necessary (Ursprung, 1986). For others, less drastic approaches may be taken, including physical exercise, relaxation techniques (Watkins, 1983), and other exhaustion-combatting activities; viewing the job and what one can realistically accomplish in it more objectively; and reducing role overload, ambiguity, and conflict. Zastrow (1984) noted that individuals in high-stress situations can also be assisted in changing their perceptions about distressing events that occur at work and that might otherwise contribute to burnout. At this time, there is no validated targeted approach through which specific symptoms or conditions can be paired with specific interventions.

Few controlled studies have evaluated the effectiveness of various burnout-reduction programs. Higgins (1986), who used the Maslach Burnout Inventory as a criterion, reported that scores on emotional exhaustion scales decreased as the result of participation in either of two stress reduction programs, one focusing on physical relaxation techniques and the other an amalgam of rational–emotive counseling and assertiveness training (even though there is some evidence that assertiveness is unrelated to burnout; see Nagy, 1985). There was no difference in the relative effectiveness of the two programs. Pines and Aronson (1983) found a small effect six months later for a one-day group intervention on burnout.

Although a number of methods have been suggested, primarily group intervention programs in the workplace (Bair & Greenspan, 1986; M. Richardson & West, 1982; Spicuzza & deVoe, 1982), most are broad-spectrum programs that encompass multiple components and have yet to receive adequate research evaluation to establish their effectiveness and generalizability.

Some clinicians have identified the role of humor and helping the client learn to be less controlling and more accepting of lack of control (e.g., Gibson, 1983). Because overcommitted individuals are often bright and may therefore be able to appreciate some of the absurdity of the situations into which they repetitively place or find themselves, humor directed to their areas of vulnerability may be effective. In response to a compulsive client's statement of needing to spend more time at the office to finish a project, the therapist might respond, "I'll bet your family will enjoy that" or "I suppose you're the only one in your office who can do that job." Mild sarcasm by the therapist in working with a client in a well-established therapeutic relationship does have its use, particularly when other approaches are ineffective or when the client is not likely to perceive the behavior as rejecting. Paradoxical interventions (e.g., a "duty" to play) may serve a similar purpose.

Giving the client permission to enjoy himself or herself may also be a valuable contribution. Exploration of the family-of-origin dynamics often reveals a contingent environment in which the client had to "perform" either to get praise and acceptance or in which overwork was the principal means of escaping from traumatic situations at home. The therapist's introduction of choice in helping the client focus on what he or she wants and what kind of life he or she wants to live can be very productive.

Clinically, certain conflicts can predictably be expected to be manifest in the transference. Most likely, if the client engages in treatment, it will become another type of "work." To the extent that the therapist attempts to create a nonthreatening, all-accepting environment for the client, the client will inevitably test the authenticity of that plan. Most likely the tests will be over anger-arousing events, given that anger is often a prominent defense among the overcommitted. For example, the client may become upset at the lack of progress, often when the defenses are threatened, and may attack the therapy process (seldom the therapist directly), wondering, "I understand this, but what am I going to *do* to change it?"

Acceptance of the client means acceptance of the dysfunctional aspects as well. A therapist who is put off by overcommitment to the work role or by compulsive behavior and who attempts, even in a subtle manner, to communicate frustration or exasperation with the client will likely alienate the client. Indeed, part of what the overcommitted person often is skilled at doing (without so realizing) is alienating others. Because the defensive pattern is deeply ingrained and has societal value, even subtle derision may communicate rejection to a client with whom a relationship has not been clearly established. Rejection is generally well-known to these individuals, especially in interpersonal situations.

A more workable stance is for the therapist to assist the client in understanding the positive aspects of the defensive behavior and in coming to understand that there is at least some choice in adulthood about how to live one's life. The idea of choice may not be something that naturally occurs to the client. Simple educative functions may therefore be worthwhile in assisting the client in understanding that recreation is a natural and necessary part of living. Simply because recreational activities may not have been sanctioned in childhood does not mean that the individual is stuck forever being a drudge. Because such clients are often "duty bound," the use of homework assignments directed at the problematic behavior (e.g., "When my anger is uncontrollably expressed, I must take my wife out to dinner";

"For every five hours of work, I must spend at least 30 minutes waking time in recreational activities") may be clinically effective.

Because overwork often presents in counterdependent personality types, the therapist needs to respect the likely depth of the underlying dependency needs. The client's unconscious fear of identity loss in the event of loosening up some control is not a trivial or insignificant matter. The therapist who pushes too aggressively for "change" rather than moving quietly and in an accepting manner may find the therapy abruptly ended as the client's vulnerability becomes exposed. The following case is illustrative.

Case 5.3
The Overcommitment and Depressed Worker

The reader will recall the case in chapter 1 of Paul, a dysfunctional, if reluctant, government bureaucrat. At the time of his referral, Paul had been placed on disability leave because of psychological stress and was convinced that he might have to take early retirement. Having become a government employee rather late in his career, he could not easily cope with not being able to control all the impinging external circumstances. He had become seriously depressed. Treatment with this highly traditional, conservative, and work-oriented man proceeded surprisingly smoothly. The depression that was so severe that it caused him to be removed from work by the referring source proved very amenable to brief, problem-focused treatment.

Despite the initial recommendations of the referring source that the client be seen twice weekly, intervention turned out to be quite brief and surprisingly uncomplicated. In treating this case, the therapist listened very closely to the litany of woes about the client's job and carefully reviewed and sympathetically attended to each physical complaint, which, at the time of the initial referral, were numerous. In fact, the somatic complaints were not trivial: The client had been hospitalized at least four times for medical problems at least partly suggestive of a psychogenic etiology.

In treatment, whenever mention was made of a somatic complaint, the therapist had the client describe the symptoms in great detail and expressed sympathy and concern about these unfortunate occurrences. Soon, however, the discussion always returned to the work conditions, about which the client was justifiably outraged even though his calm, gentlemanly manner masked his rage, to both himself and others. In the past, Paul had attempted to deal with his chronic job frustration by working ever harder, oblivious to the fact that he truly controlled very little of the situation he was in.

Paul had no natural interest in introspection and would probably never have come to see a psychotherapist if his deteriorating condition had not resulted in his referral. The therapeutic goal, of course, was not for him to develop significant insight about his situation but for him to get over his psychological symptoms and get on with his life. The therapist therefore applauded the client's great persistence and tenacity and strong desire to forge ahead and to be successful, as he had tried to do all his life. However, the therapist gently but persistently wondered aloud whether the client might be going about the task in the wrong way.

The therapist assumed a cognitive stance and made a detailed, lengthy explanation differentiating the things that Paul could and could not control in his situation. The list of factors in the work situation that were under his direct control turned out to be rather short. Yet, with help in reframing his situation, Paul began to see new options. For example, it was clear that laying off workers was something he dreaded doing and felt very badly about. (The client was not a natural supervisor and came to this role as the only way to rise within the system.)

The therapist made the case that the client's current situation of waiting for headquarters' ax to fall left little for him to control. An alternative was that he consider taking proactive responsibility for getting costs in line with revenues by proposing earlier layoffs. Although, for a variety of reasons, he chose not to do this, the mere intellectual contemplation of alternatives broadened his perspectives and livened his outlook. The therapist also attempted to validate the client's anger, agreeing with him that his work situation was poorly conceived.

However, although he sided with the client's justifiable view of himself as a victim, the therapist noted that there were aspects of the situation that were directly in the client's control and that in these areas he was behaving inappropriately. Thus, although the client could not control the circumstances of his work, he certainly could control whether he played golf or went dancing with his wife. In these areas, he was less a victim because he held personal responsibility. (This approach would likely work, of course, only with someone for whom responsibility was an important value.) The therapist helped the client to realize that many aspects of his work situation were totally outside of his control, just as those in his personal life were much more within his control. In addition, work and play metaphors were intertwined, with the paradoxical effect that play became something he could control and to which he had not been dutifully enough committed.

Within a few weeks of his initial therapy session, the client resumed golf (a formerly favorite activity that he had avoided for months), went out to dinner with his wife, discontinued his "as needed" antidepressant medication, and successfully survived two "setbacks" at his office during which he reexperienced anxiety. There was danger, of course, that the changes were being made too rapidly and would as quickly vanish, leaving the client where he had started or worse. The therapist therefore tentatively suggested that the client consider returning in two weeks rather than one (with the proviso that he call at once if anything came up that he could not handle) and indicated that setbacks were a normal part of the change process and indeed were indications of improvement. Thus, the client was in a sense placed in a "therapeutic bind" in which failure to improve was tied to his not trying hard enough to control the things that were within his realm of responsibility, whereas the predictable setbacks were signs of improvement.

Within two sessions of his initial visit, the client was back at work (after a hiatus of several weeks). Once he survived the first week, he adjusted quickly and rapidly to a newly perceived situation. His previously restless sleep improved, as did his appetite, and he experienced at follow-up no recurrence of the work problems. The client was seen for a total of five sessions.

In an effort to alleviate the client's anxieties about subsequent failure, the therapist offered him one optional additional session up to a certain point several months later and additional treatment should there be a need. The client did not request further treatment, and follow-up showed him to be functioning well at work.

Although it would be nice to believe that patterns of overcommitment can be generally resolved this quickly, in reality, many are stubbornly resistant to change because the characteristics embodied by the type are so adaptive in our culture. Thus, it is unlikely that the typical overachiever or person who works too hard is likely to come in for treatment, barring a significant health or personal crisis.

One final case illustrates problems encountered in clinical practice and interventions with people who are overcommitted to the work role.

Case 5.4
Fear and Loathing at Work

At age 40, Mark came to treatment complaining of severe overwork, unhappiness with his family life, and fear that he might be laid off from his job. A professional manager, Mark worked in a company that was going through serious retrenchment typical of the times. Although the specialty of his own job ensured reasonable security, his section's workload had increased significantly as a result of cutbacks in other areas. Unwilling to complain to upper management for fear of jeopardizing his position, he suffered in silence while finding himself growing increasingly angry at his subordinates and his family.

The client had been raised as the only child of wealthy but austere and, in his recollection, rejecting parents. He had been sent off to boarding schools at a young age and while home had been raised mostly by servants. After graduating from college, he took a position in another city and soon after met his wife, a warm and spirited woman. After a few years of marriage, they had a child, which the client found to be much more disruptive of his peace and tranquillity than he had imagined. Although he loved his child, he unrealistically insisted on things being peaceful and quiet whenever he was working at home, which was frequently. When, contrary to his wishes, his wife became pregnant again, he became chronically angry at her. With the birth of the second child and the ensuing chaos, his desire for order and quiet became totally unrealistic.

Over time, his work situation deteriorated as he tried increasingly to manage an ever-escalating degree of work while facing at the end of each day even greater chaos. Although the client had some very legitimate concerns about his work situation, his avoidant manner left his co-workers upset, puzzled, and wondering what they were doing wrong. He was generally quiet and agreeable when dealing with his superiors.

This complicated case necessitated short-term, nonintrusive intervention on a variety of levels. The initial focus of the treatment was on the difficulties at work. The client was helped to see that his anger had been misdirected and that if he wanted to change the situation, he would need to do so much more directly. By examining the realities of his work situation, including the fact that he had other employment options in spite of the recessionary economy, the client was freed to express some of his concerns directly to upper management. He asked for, and to his surprise received, assistance in managing the workload in his section. Although technically competent, some of his employees were not putting in the overtime he felt necessary, whereas he was putting in excessive amounts of overtime, much to the consternation of his wife. Giving him permission to be more direct with his subordinates about what he expected and needed served two purposes: It lessened his workload while assisting his employees in feeling more a part of the team.

Mark's home situation was much more difficult. Although a central theme involved unexpressed anger and developmental failures in not having had the opportunity to have been childlike at the appropriate time, direct confrontation of these dynamics may have been premature. Instead, using the same ostensibly matter-of-fact, problem-solving approach, the client was helped to put his home situation in context. When he was able to understand that there were choices, that his needs for peace and quiet were not unreasonable (although could not continuously be met when there were young children in the house), the client's self-confidence increased, his self-blaming (projected onto his wife) decreased, and it became possible to introduce the idea that his unmet dependency needs in his family of origin were being partly triggered by the presence of his two young children. All his years of unmet needs came into sharper focus, and he became able to realize that, although those needs would never be met through his parents, there were other outlets for them in adulthood, including through nurturance of and play with his own children. By focusing on this dynamic, the client realized that there was choice involved in his adult life, namely, concerning the kind of family he wished to have.

Although these issues were obviously complex, it is worth noting that this therapy took only six sessions. In spite of the fact that each of these issues could have been explored at much greater length, at the end of the employee assistance allotment of sessions, the client declined referral. On follow-up, he reported himself to be doing well, and although the work organization was still in turmoil, the presenting problems had resolved themselves and he was more happily relating to his wife and children.

Summary

Although those overly committed to work can be frustrating to work with in psychotherapy, they can also be rewarding. Because they are often bright, successful, and highly motivated individuals, they are generally able to learn quickly and readily understand the therapeutic issues at least conceptually. The therapist may have the opportunity to address non-work-related issues as well as work-related ones, serving as a guide, not a director, who can give the client permission for enjoyment. Because many therapists are themselves overworked, perfectionistic, and overcommitted individuals who get too little pleasure out of life, work with clients who have similar problems may arouse some of the therapist's own anxieties about the work role. Providing a model of the unpressured but productive worker whose work exhibits a positive drive rather than expression of displaced hostility may be the first challenge for the therapist.

6

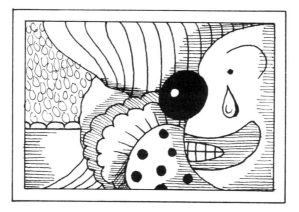

Work-Related Anxiety
and Depression

T his chapter addresses work issues associated with two commonly encountered clinical manifestations of work dysfunction: anxiety and depression. Although both are apparently quite common, they are not always considered to be separable constructs and have been shown in some studies to exhibit moderate to high correlations (e.g., Meier, 1991; Warr, 1992). Many of the studies on the psychological effects of work on individual mental health pair anxiety and depression together, assuming them to be more or less interchangeable (e.g., Donat, Neal, & Addleton, 1991; Shankar & Famuyiwa, 1991) or simply lump them together into a "mental strain" factor (e.g., Arsenault, Dolan, & Van Ameringen, 1991). Although the two constructs are indeed related both conceptually and empirically, it still makes sense to consider each separately.

Anxiety and Work

Anxiety, according to McReynolds (1973), has been experienced persistently throughout history, reflecting "an inevitable part of the human condition" (p. 131). As with its occurrence in other contexts, anxiety concerning one's work can be transient and situational (e.g., the type encountered in a job interview), or it can be almost incapacitating, preventing one from getting to the workplace or completing a workday without major disruptions. The dread may be so great that the client avoids work altogether. In between are multiple variations. A commonly shared theme, however, is the experience of dysphoric affect and the general tendency to avoid situations engendering the anxious feelings (e.g., Sharma & Acharya, 1990).

Types of Anxiety

Although the *Diagnostic and Statistical Manual of Mental Disorders* (3rd ed. rev.; American Psychiatric Association, 1987; *DSM–R–III*) diagnostic system includes a variety of specific anxiety disorders (e.g., phobias, panic disorders, and generalized anxiety disorders) that potentially relate to work issues, anxiety has been studied primarily in reference to relatively circumscribed performances (such as music performance), with specific types of anxiety-creating factors (e.g., technology, see H. Kahn & Cooper, 1991; or periodic role overload, see Berkhoff & Rusin, 1991) or to analogous, presumably work-related conditions (such as test anxiety among students). In clinical applications of anxiety to workplace issues, the task is to identify anxiety both as it relates to characteristic behavior over time and as it relates to behavior during more delimited performances. Because a substantial literature of work and career anxiety does not yet exist, studies of other settings or concerning other types of problems must often be extrapolated to the workplace. A work-specific anxiety research literature remains to be created.

Still, there is much that is potentially relevant in studies of generic anxiety and of the specific effects of anxiety on analogous achievement situations. Early models (Spielberger, 1975) differentiated anxiety as a trait (which apparently decreases with age;

see Costa & McRae, 1988) from anxiety that is situation specific—the enduring "trait–state" distinction. Other widely studied models of anxiety identified characteristics of situations (e.g., the loss or start of a job) as being inherently stress engendering (Holmes & Rahe, 1967). The "stressful events" approach to anxiety, although productive, has increasingly been questioned for its failure to identify differential responses to the same stressor (Laux & Vossel, 1982; Schonfeld & Ruan, 1991). Moreover, it is the capacity to cope with anxiety-arousing situations that may differentiate those who are successful in handling difficult external circumstances from those who are not (Lazarus, 1966, 1973; Lazarus & Folkman, 1991).

Anxiety does not appear to be a unidimensional phenomenon that can be described accurately and universally by one model, nor is the relation between anxiety and performance clearcut or unambiguously established. The conceptualization of anxiety itself has moved from the widely accepted notion of an inverted U-shaped curve (high and low states of anxiety associated with poorer performance) to models based on complex interactions of cognitive (Darke, 1988), affective (Neiss, 1988b), and somatic (Burton, 1988) or psychobiological (Neiss, 1988a) states. People may cognitively perceive themselves to be anxious, experience physiological reactions to anxiety, or both (Fremouw, Gross, Monroe, & Rapp, 1982).

Several researchers (e.g., Weinberg, 1990) agree that anxiety is multidimensional, with cognitive, affective, and (at least in the case of physically oriented performances such as sports or acting) psychophysiological elements. Steptoe (1989) also demonstrated that performance anxiety can be part of a more generalized concern with career stress, including the tendency to exaggerate the importance to one's career of any single performance.

Concerning its effect on performance situations, however, anxiety, whether of a state or trait nature, generally serves to lessen the quality of the performance (W. E. Collins, Schroeder, & Nye, 1991; S. Hamilton, Rothbart, & Dawes, 1986) and to be associated with increased levels of job stress (e.g., Augestad & Levander, 1992). Two components of anxiety relevant to achievement situations have persistently been identified, particularly in the test anxiety literature: a cognitive component ("worry") and a physiological component ("emotionality") (Liebert & Morris, 1967; Wine, 1982). The cognitive factor refers to the cognitive perceptions and attributions a person makes to himself or herself about a performance (e.g., "I don't know why I can't do this any better"; "I'm an inadequate person for not being able to perform this task"; "I'm no good at it, no matter how hard I try"). Physiological components refer to the bodily reactions associated with anxiety states; they are relatively transient and generally unstable, decreasing as the anxiety precipitant is removed. Moreover, although anxiety reduction efforts affecting this component may reduce the subjective sense of anxiety, such amelioration is reported to have little impact on performance (Wine, 1982). The cognitive aspects of anxiety, in contrast, tend to be stable over time (Wine, 1982) and to be the major source of decreased performance. The cognitive components are also amenable to change efforts (Beck & Rush, 1973).

On the other hand, it cannot be assumed that performances across all types of tasks are equally compromised by cognitive attributions. For example, in artistic and creative occupations, interpretation of external reality through one's own self and experiences may constitute an important part of the creative process. This process may indeed tap into self-doubts and questioning, both of which may be put to productive use.

In clinical practice, the therapist must identify the particular pattern of presenting anxiety and determine whether it is clearly limited to one or a small number of situations at work or whether it is suggestive of wide-ranging anxiety of which work is only one affected area. Assessment must also include the history of the condition. Anxiety of relatively recent onset, even if chronic, may in adult populations be more likely to be situation specific and may be more easily treatable than longstanding anxiety present before the client entered the workforce (N. Cherry, 1978, 1984a).

Performance Anxiety

Performance anxiety is typically situation specific and can be directly relevant to work. It can affect a variety of performance areas or be limited to certain aspects of work. For example, a business executive may be well-suited to the role of management and generally well-adjusted in interacting with peers but may experience "stage fright" when making an important presentation to superiors.

Performance anxiety has been well studied only in a few professions and occupationally relevant activities. Most studies have addressed anxiety as a factor in such performance areas as sports (Cooley, 1987; Maynard & Howe, 1987; Vealey, 1990); mathematics (Adams & Holcomb, 1986; Siegel, Galassi, & Ware, 1985); music (Steptoe & Fidler, 1987; Sweeney & Horan, 1982; Tobacyk & Downs, 1986); and, among students, testing ("test anxiety"). Anxiety has also been examined for its impact on specific aspects of work such as perceptual detection ability (Singh, 1989). Various types of working conditions, especially role ambiguity and role overload, have also been demonstrated to increase the likelihood of work-related anxiety (Srivastava, 1989).

Although performance anxiety may be localized, it may also reflect life-long patterns associated with work difficulties, as the following case illustrates.

Case 6.1
The Unintentional Trailblazer

Madeline was about 50 years old at the time of referral and worked for a manufacturing organization where she was one of a few female employees and the only female supervisor. Far from being an intentional trailblazer, Madeline had reluctantly assumed her position after working in low-level clerical positions because it paid well and because she was determined to prove that she could support her four children on her own after divorcing her first husband, an unreliable alcoholic. Her children were all grown at the time of her referral for work-related problems, and she was more or less happily remarried. Although there were some minor problems in her relationships with her extended family and she had been overly involved in the lives of her grown children, her problems were clearly centered in the workplace when she came for treatment.

The client had been working in a physically dangerous part of the organization for a number of years. She was conscientious and had been regarded by management and her co-workers as an excellent employee. The client felt that her co-workers were often lackadaisical in their execution of their duties (e.g., not making outside checks when they said they had) and generally lacking the vigilance and care with which she approached her job. Because the work involved running processes that had potential to be highly destructive, there was some reality base to her fears, although her fears did seem mildly exaggerated.

She and a fellow employee, whom she had befriended, were among the only women in the organization. However, when she rather than this co-worker was promoted to acting supervisor, problems began to develop. The co-worker was experiencing marital and family problems and had begun actively resisting Madeline's authority. She violated work rules almost in defiance of Madeline's authority, made faces at her behind her back, and had become so difficult for Madeline to handle that Madeline had become fearful of going to work.

Analysis of the situation demonstrated that the co-worker resented Madeline's promotion and had never accepted that the client and not she had been promoted. Although she challenged Madeline's authority, it was never quite to the point calling for disciplinary action. As the difficulties persisted, the client became anxious about even being in the presence of her co-worker and felt that, because she was in contention for a permanent promotion to the position she now held in an acting capacity, she could not complain or even obtain a reality check with her supervisors, lest she be considered ineffectual.

In treatment, it became clear that this overly anxious woman had inappropriately personalized the situation. She viewed her co-worker's behavior as a betrayal and could not respond to the situation objectively. With her therapist's help, she was able to examine the situation from the perspective of the co-worker and to grieve the loss of the relationship she once had with a person whom she considered to be her friend. This enabled her to abandon the unconscious hope of returning to things as they were. Because the client was probably generally success phobic, she was not ready at that time to work with the broader issues, and as she gained control of the immediate precipitating situation, she discontinued therapy.

The experience and treatment of anxiety among those in selected artistic occupations has been fairly widely studied, perhaps most widely in adult occupational performance. Wesner, Noyes, and Davis (1990) surveyed 294 musicians (157 women, 137 men) and found the experience of performance anxiety to be common, especially among women, although it was indicated to be a serious detriment to performance in only a small percentage of subjects. Commonly reported symptoms of performance anxiety among the musicians in this study included poor concentration, rapid heart beat, tremors, sweating, and dry mouth. Also relying on a survey methodology, Dews and Williams (1989) found musicians to report commonly experiencing performance anxiety; most of these musicians frequently sought help from friends or instructors rather than professional counselors.

It must be noted that anxiety among performing artists presumably does not occur independently of a predisposition to psychological disturbance, especially affective disorders (see Andreason & Canter, 1974; Andreason & Powers, 1975; Cooper & Wills, 1989; D. W. Goodwin, 1988; Jamison, 1992; Lockwood, 1989; Lowman, 1991b; see also chapter 8). Cooper and Wills (1989) examined the effects of stress on performance anxiety among popular male musicians ($n = 70$). Common sources of stress included having both too much and too little to do and problems with work and nonwork relationships. However, the musicians as a group were also elevated on measures of psychological dysfunction on the Eysenck Personality Questionnaire.

That performance anxiety can lead to undesirable effects when untreated was suggested by D. B. Clark (1989), who noted that musicians' anxiety about their performance can lead to the overuse phenomenon, often associated with a radical or precipitous change in playing habits presumably intended to cope with the anxiety. In working with musicians (and possibly with other performing artists who make use of their hands), physical assessment may need to co-occur with psychological assessment (see Manchester, 1988).

Other Factors in Performance Anxiety

Anxiety, performance or otherwise, does not appear to be a uni-dimensional phenomenon that can be described accurately and universally by one model, nor is the relation between anxiety and performance clearcut or unambiguously established. A number of situational factors are involved in the experience of anxiety. Barrell, Medeiros, Barrell, and Price (1985) identified five elements present in the experience of performance anxiety: (a) the perceived presence of significant others, (b) the possibility of visible (public) failure, (c) a need to avoid failure, (d) the uncertainty of the outcome, and (e) the extent to which the task calls for focus on self. Each of these factors would be expected to contribute to the experience of anxiety in work contexts; by implication, each may provide a potential avenue for intervention in alleviating such anxiety.

Performance anxiety can also be part of a more generalized concern with career stress, including the tendency to exaggerate the importance to one's career of any single performance (Steptoe, 1989). Moreover, anxiety related to one's work may differ depending on the nature of the task (see P. J. Lang, Levin, Miller, & Kozak, 1983; Weerts & Lang, 1978) and those in whose presence (real or imagined) the performance is to be made (e.g., those perceived to be in authority or peer conditions; see Barrell et al., 1985; Darke, 1988; Leon & Revelle, 1985).

The role of an audience, in particular the fear of negative evaluation by others (see Hartman, 1984), may be especially important in certain types of performance anxiety. Craske and Craig (1984) found that for pianists anxiety played an influential role primarily in conditions in which the audience was perceived to be evaluative. Although performance anxiety may be experienced at various stages of one's career, it may decline with added experience (Kranz & Houser, 1988; Steptoe & Fidler, 1987) as self-confidence in the anxiety-arousing task increases.

The relation of ability level to performance anxiety has also been noted by researchers. Dew, Galassi, and Galassi (1984) found, in a study of math anxiety, that more anxiety variance was accounted for by ability factors than by math anxiety or more generalized anxiety per se. Most studies of performance anxiety fail to control for or even measure ability level as a possible determinant or covariate of anxiety. Equally important to consider is the client's *perceived* ability to perform, which may differ significantly from, yet be as important as, actual ability in producing anxiety and determining the perceived difficulty of the task (Adam & Van Wieringen, 1988). In a study examining extreme levels of ability, H. G. Levine and Langness (1983) reported that the mentally challenged populations compared with nonmentally challenged populations exhibited considerably more anxiety in playing a competitive sport (basketball).

The tenacity of negative misperceptions bears significantly on actual ability level (see Lowman, 1991b). In clinical populations, the tendency to underestimate actual ability level and maintain a self-view of inadequacy can be doggedly persistent. In one such case, a bright, able graduate student maintained a patently false view that he was only of average intelligence. He experienced anxiety in contemplating continuing his graduate studies, fearing that his inability would be discovered or that he would fail in his academic work. Such cases may require exploration of the accuracy and adequacy of the self-concept and the psychodynamic origins of the misperception. In this case, for example, the client was the youngest in a large family of highly accomplished and highly achieving parents and siblings, whom he used as his perhaps overly high standard of comparison.

The role of cognitive belief factors has been identified in several studies. Anticipated dread can have as much or more effect than the actual feared stimulus. Tobacyk and Downs (1986) found that among student musicians with elevated scores on a measure of irrational beliefs, higher levels of anxiety were experienced a few days before a juried performance. Assisting a client who is concerned about dreaded situations at work may necessitate carefully identifying the most dreaded stimuli and designing an intervention program related to these concerns. Aggressive cognitive or behavioral treatment involving massed, imploded exposure to the feared stimuli may be helpful when obsessive–compulsive disorder is the cause of the avoidance (Egli, 1992).

Trait Anxiety and Work Performance

Generalized (rather than narrowly specific) anxiety is a more serious condition than occasional performance anxiety and presumably predisposes the client to the experience of anxiety in a variety of work settings. Moreover, work disinterest or impairment may be a prodromal sign of a major affective or anxious disorder (Fava, Grandi, Canestrari, & Molnar, 1990); this implies the need to clinically differentiate between generalized anxiety that is part of a more pervasive psychopathological syndrome and anxiety that is secondary to work dysfunctions.

A common distinction in the clinical and research literature differentiates between state and trait anxiety (Spielberger, 1975), the latter being associated with cross-situational dysfunction. Several studies have, in essence, extended this differentiation to the world of work and performance. Bond and Omar (1990) demonstrated that undergraduates scoring high in social anxiety performed more poorly on an experimental task. Hatcher and Underwood (1990) reported that in a sample of Baptist ministers, those highest in state anxiety were more likely to experience higher levels of self-criticism and lower self-concepts than those not high in trait anxiety. That the relation between state anxiety and performance may be more complex than a simple correlation was suggested by Froehle (1989), who demonstrated that, in a group of graduate counseling students, those scoring high in state anxiety exhibited poorer performance only under conditions perceived to be threatening. When threat was absent, the performance did not vary according to state anxiety.

Although other studies (e.g., S. E. Kahn & Long, 1988) also point to connections among self-concept, trait anxiety, and work stress, few have explored the issue of causality. Does trait anxiety exist before employees come to the workforce and conditions there exacerbate a priori psychic states, or is there something about stressful work that causes employees to become anxious (see D. Wilson & Mutero, 1989)? N. Cherry's (1978, 1984a) longitudinal research in England suggests that the former explanation is more likely.

Newer models of anxiety have yet to be systematically examined for their career and workplace implications, but a few findings are suggestive. Some studies have found that somatic anxiety may be less important in understanding the impact of anxiety on performance than may cognitive anxiety and that the complexity and duration of the task may also be influential (e.g., Burton, 1988). Task complexity may also influence the extent to which anxiety interferes with performance. More anxious subjects appear to do worse on simple tasks but to be faster (although less accurate) on complex tasks (Leon & Revelle, 1985).

Thus, a variety of factors can potentially affect an individual's experience of anxiety. The therapist should consider at the least the elements listed in Table 6.1 in attempting to understand the particular dynamics at hand and before determining a course of treatment.

Intervention Issues

Interventions with clients suffering performance anxiety have been extensively examined in the behavioral literature; this topic

---

Table 6.1

Summary of Diagnostic Dimensions Important in Assessing Work-Related Anxiety

Characteristics of the task
   High or low stress
   External people present or absent
   High or low status relevant to task
   Certainty/uncertainty of the outcome

Characteristics of the person
   Level of trait anxiety
   Level of state anxiety relevant to the anxiety-arousing task
   Actual and perceived ability level relevant to the task to be
      performed
   Experience level relevant to the anxiety-arousing task
   Need to avoid failure
   Cognitive attributions
   Helplessness

---

appears to lend itself to behavioral and cognitive approaches in which the symptom is viewed as an isolated phenomenon rather than as symptomatic of a broader pattern of psychosocial dysfunction (see, e.g., Kendall, 1984).

Behavioral paradigms such as stimulus exposure and guided mastery have been applied to an assortment of symptomatic conditions, often with positive results. S. L. Williams and Zane (1989) found, in treating clients of a specific phobic group (agoraphobics) who exhibited performance anxiety, that assisting them in working with the feared stimulus (guided mastery) proved superior to merely exposing them to it (stimulus exposure). Kendrick, Craig, Lawson, and Davidson (1982) compared behavioral rehearsal with cognitive approaches (self-instruction and attention focusing) in a performance-anxious group of pianists. At follow-up, both treatment methods were more effective than a waiting-list comparison condition, but the cognitive intervention was more effective than the behavioral rehearsal method. Kirsch, Wolpin, and Knutson (1975) found that in vivo flooding (repeated practice of a feared speaking assignment at a higher level of difficulty than the actual feared speaking task) was more effective than implosion (sudden, intensive exposure to the feared stimulus) or successive approximation (gradually increased difficulty levels). However, all three methods were more effective than a control group condition.

Positive results have also been reported for stress inoculation training in moderating self-reported stress levels (Cecil & Forman, 1990; Hytten, Jensen, & Skauli, 1990). Effectiveness may be improved when such intervention is combined with an exercise component (Long, 1988). In using modeling tapes to treat phobias, some researchers (e.g., Lineham, Rosenthal, Kelley, & Theobald, 1977) have found that exposure to more diverse stimuli beyond the immediately feared one is more effective than exposure to models showing only the feared stimuli.

In assessing clients suffering performance anxiety, the therapist should undertake as an important first diagnostic step an analysis of the type of anxiety present. Generalized anxiety conditions are unlikely to be responsive to the same type of intervention as more localized anxiety conditions (e.g., speaking anxiety). The goal is to (a) determine the likely causes of the presenting problem or productive impediment and (b) design an intervention that is likely to be responsive to that type of problem. Determining whether anxiety is commonly experienced as part of a broader career concern can have important therapeutic implications. It is also important to keep in mind the type of career pattern in which the performance anxiety is manifest. Intervention with a client with high control needs in an enterprising occupation (Holland, 1985) who is frightened by having to give a talk to key executives may call for a different strategy than that with a client in the arts who has difficulty performing before live audiences. Fogle (1982) cautioned against the use of physical relaxation procedures with musicians and argued instead for the use of such procedures as cognitive desensitization (i.e., shifting the focus of attention from inappropriate, destructive worrying about "bad" outcomes or the experience of anxiety itself to content and task-relevant or performance-relevant cues). Cognitive therapies in general have been reported to be effective in treating anxiety disorders (Chambless & Gillis, 1993).

For localized anxieties, behavioral or problem-focused approaches (including paradoxical and symptom prescriptive approaches) may be good places at which to begin. The direct, symptom-focused approach can be particularly helpful. Rather than colluding with the client's commonly experienced self-perception that the performance condition points to a generalized difficulty or flaw in character, personality, or ability, the therapist presents precisely the opposite construct: Because anxiety is a natural response to stressful conditions and the expectation of stress-free situations in work contexts is unrealistic and irrational, the goal is not to make a basic change in personality or character but to more productively handle a natural event inherent in the work setting. Steptoe (1989) noted that in working with musicians, helping the client see the limited importance of any one performance can potentially serve to decrease performance anxiety associated with stage fright.

Studies by Bond and Omar (1990) and Motley (1990) illustrate this approach. In considering public speaking anxiety, Bond and Omar differentiated between those who conceptualize public speaking as a performance and those who view it as a means of communication. The latter group was much less subject to speaking anxiety. Similarly, the therapist may assist clients in reframing their purpose in activities that they associate with anxiety. For example, to view one's role as a speaker not as "giving a speech" but as attempting to communicate with and motivate others may help the client move the focus from self to task and, in the process, become less anxious. At the same time, helping the client set realistic expectations (e.g., "I should never experience speaking anxiety" vs. "Anxiety is something everyone experiences, even the most talented; I am no different") may defuse some of the anticipatory anxiety associated with such undertakings. Nagel, Himle, and Papsdorf (1989) found that a six-week intervention program combining progressive muscle relaxation, cognitive therapy, and temperature biofeedback training was more effective than was a waiting-list condition with a small sample ($n = 12$) of male music students who suffered performance anxiety. Interestingly, their anxiety reportedly decreased as the result of treatment not only in their musical performances but also in taking tests and other domains in which anxiety might intervene.

Psychopharmaceutical approaches have also been shown to be effective in blocking the experience of certain types of performance anxiety (Lader, 1988). Lockwood (1989) noted that β-adrenergic blocking agents may be used without medical supervision. However, careful coordination of the physical and psychological interventions is suggested.

Other therapeutic approaches have been shown to be effective with defined, delimited anxiety-arousing situations. Some evidence has been published on the use of hypnosis (A. Miller, 1986) and symptom prescription (J. Katz, 1984) in treating performance anxiety. D. Y. Lee, Rossiter, Martin, and Uhlemann (1990) reported treatment of performance anxiety using paradoxical and nonparadoxical approaches, with no significant differences between the two when using a 45-minute "counseling" intervention. Others have advocated a multimodal approach (e.g., Rider, 1987). Group "stress reduction" approaches involving relaxation training have also shown promise in treating employees in certain types of stressful work situations (Schloss, Sedlak, Wiggins, & Ramsey, 1983).

Finally, perhaps the least examined avenue for treatment may be the improvement of skill level. Practice and overpreparation may be the most effective remedies for performance anxiety. These methods are especially likely to be helpful when there are defined or perceived deficits in ability. This issue has received some attention in the behavioral literature, especially in the treatment of phobias. Thus, when real or perceived ability deficits underlie and are thought to account for performance anxiety, improvement of the skill may prove more effective than focus on the experienced symptoms alone.

Intervention to change conditions of the job itself that may be causing or exacerbating job-related anxiety should also be considered in selected cases. Promising candidates for systematic variation include increasing behavioral control over a task[1] (Perrewe & Ganster, 1989; Statham & Bravo, 1990), social support (S. Davis, Jayaratne, & Chess, 1985; House, 1980), job redesign, and preventive selection of more stress-resistant individuals.

In summary, differential diagnosis of the type of work-related anxiety presented must precede selection of a treatment approach. Generalized anxiety that also manifests in work problems appears to be a different phenomenon than anxiety localized to one aspect of work or life.

Although the therapist needs to have a good understanding of the type of performance anxiety experienced by the client, this understanding does not necessarily need to be communicated to the client. The therapist may wish to raise questions that test the client's conceptualization of the problem to the extent that they further the therapist's diagnosis (e.g., "It seems like just before a big performance, your body reacts with fear. Do you suppose more experienced violinists have a similar reaction?"). The purpose of such an inquiry is to test the therapist's understanding of whether the anxiety is felt only in actual performances or is a characteristic that pervades even practice. The inquiry implicitly offers the client a face-saving way out of the anxiety—almost a therapeutic double bind. For example, if more

---

[1] However, this factor may be moderated by age, at least with some work groups (see Perrewe & Anthony, 1990).

experienced violinists also experience the same thing, then who is the client to complain about it as a relative novice? On the other hand, it may be viewed as just part of the costs of working as a professional musician. The therapist needs then to observe the client's reactions to such an interpretation to determine the next steps that might be appropriate. If the response is essentially hostile, the therapist can graciously acknowledge the inappropriateness of the question and move on to other avenues for exploration.

The next case illustrates how obsessive–compulsive dynamics can interact with anxiety in creating work-related problems. It also illustrates the frequently complex interaction of psychological dynamics, which may not fit neatly into a single diagnostic entity.

Case 6.2
The Anxious and Obsessive Worker

Bob was approaching 40 at the time of his referral for evaluation because of problems in his work as a driver and messenger for a large corporation. Although Bob was described by all as being extremely conscientious, he had had a number of recent accidents on the job while driving company vehicles. Increasingly, the client was ruminative about what tasks needed to be done on the job. He had begun to ask supervisors over and over about previously made assignments, continually calling in to verify delivery addresses. According to his supervisors, he had attempted to cover up the several minor accidents in which he had been involved. His supervisors, genuinely concerned about his well-being, worried that he might be experiencing some serious health or mental difficulty and referred him for medical evaluation. These evaluations, including visual acuity tests, were essentially within normal limits, and the physician therefore referred the case for psychological evaluation.

Bob's work history indicated that he had been employed in a manufacturing position for about 20 years and was then suddenly laid off without notice when his previous employer went through a period of serious economic decline. At the time of the psychological assessment, Bob was preoccupied with financial difficulties and worried about another possible layoff, a prospect he had become convinced was imminent.

The client cooperated well with the mental health evaluation. However, his response rate was extremely slow on most of the measures: For example, he took several hours to complete the Minnesota Multiphasic Personality Inventory (MMPI; Dahlstrom, Welsh, & Dahlstrom, 1972). He was ruminative and repeatedly asked if the evaluation procedure was being done to get him fired. Despite multiple assurances that this was not the purpose of the assessment, he continued to obsess about this possibility.

Mental status evaluation was essentially within normal limits; intellectual limitations were suggested. The client indicated that he had done "fairly well" in school (he held a high school diploma) but was very vague concerning the particulars of his education. Although obsessive worry was manifest about his current finances, a review of his actual income compared with his expenses showed little objective cause for alarm. His spouse worked, his three children were grown and out of the house, and the mortgage on his home was almost paid off. However, he was earning considerably less than he had in his prior manufacturing position.

The client was not on medication at the time of the assessment, although he stated that he had problems with his nerves ("I've been right hyper lately"), which he believed had deteriorated in the past six months. Bob denied prior psychological history or treatment. When asked about his automobile accidents, he attributed them to problems with his nerves and trouble concentrating. He acknowledged memory problems, occasional sleep disturbance, and an occasional excess of energy. There was no history of mania or serious depression.

Psychological testing revealed no evidence of organicity on a brief screening measure. However, on the intelligence measure (Wechsler Adult Intelligence Scale–Revised; Wechsler, 1981), Bob scored 82 ($\pm$ 5.2), 86 ($\pm$ 7.4), and 84 ($\pm$ 4.4), with little variability on the subtest scores. He scored in the 27th, 21st, and 5th percentiles on the reading, spelling, and arithmetic subtests, respectively, on an achievement test (Wide Range Achievement Test–Revised; Jastak & Wilkinson, 1984). In completing the

MMPI, he was slightly guarded, perhaps appropriate to the evaluation context. His MMPI elevations on scales 7, 2, 1, 8, and 0 suggested obsessive worry and clinical depression. Projective testing revealed constriction and persistent rumination. The following Thematic Apperception Test (Murray, 1943, 1965) response to Card 1 is illustrative of his obsessional defenses:

> It's a young boy who's wanting to take violin lessons but he don't know how well he can do. He's thinking about attempting to try the violin but he's having second thoughts. [What is the outcome?] The outcome is he's thinking if he gets real good he could be successful. [What happens?] To me, I think he finally makes up his mind to play and believes in his mind he can learn and be successful at it.

On the projective psychological tests, the client manifested considerable ambition and striving for success, which contrasted with his more modest level of abilities. He stated on an incomplete sentence measure that his greatest fear was "how successful will I become," noting that he secretly "had desire of become a famous individual of success." In contrast, he viewed himself as a failure in his current working situation. Although no psychotic features were noted on any of the projective or other tests, his obsessional and ruminative characteristics were clearly dysfunctional. He tended to view even trivial issues as being of "great" and exaggerated importance.

The client's accidents appeared to be due to his obsessional worrying, which appeared to be tied to fears of losing his job. As a result of this dysfunctional obsession, he required constant reassurances that he was doing the right thing. His work problems were not caused by excessive commitment to the work role but by anxiety. Ironically, this anxiety contributed to the creation of the very phenomenon he most feared.

The goal for treatment was to decrease the client's anxiety and obsessional rumination and assist him in retaining his job. The client's obsessional and anxious behavior appeared to be amenable to medication management. He was referred to both a psychiatrist and a counselor for short-term, pragmatically oriented work- and fear-control strategies. The primary intervention concerning his work was made with his supervisors, who were given suggestions on how to manage his obsessional behavior in the workplace. On follow-up, the client had successfully returned to his job and had decreased his obsessive ruminations.

This case illustrates the importance of differentiating obsessive from compulsive psychological dynamics and other relevant patterns. Although some features of excessive commitment to an exaggerated self-view were present in this case, the client's problems were more appropriately viewed as reflecting anxiety and obsession rather than overcommitment or a compulsion.

Depression and Work Performance

Given that depression is considered by many to be the "common cold" of psychological problems (Charney & Weissman, 1988), it is not surprising that depressive features are frequently found as part of the presenting symptoms of work-related difficulties. Estimated from epidemiological data to affect 8–12% of men and 20–25% of women, the life expectancy experience of serious depressive reactions (Charney & Weissman, 1988) virtually assures that workplace issues of many people will be affected at some time by depression. High-level workers are not immune, and indeed may be especially vulnerable, to the experience of work-related depression. Phelan et al.'s (1991) study of professional and managerial employees found, in a sample of 1,523 married employees, 124 cases of symptoms that could be characterized as major depression (48 of which were first-time episodes) (see also Warr, 1990). However, despite the apparent frequency of the phenomena and the plethora of writings on the subject of depression and affective disorders, it is still possible to examine dozens of textbooks on the subject and find no mention whatsoever of the work role.

Several aspects of depression have already been discussed in chapter 3, which this section supplements. It should first be noted, however, that people who are unemployed but wanting to work are at higher risk for depression than are those who are employed (Brief & Nord, 1990a; Fryer & Payne, 1986; Warr,

1987).[2] Moreover, for certain populations, work can itself be a means for managing depression and preventing more severe depression from occurring, for example, in response to negative life events (see, e.g., Edbril & Rieker, 1989).

On the other hand, depression can also cause problems in the work role. Studies have increasingly found the subjective experience of depression to be associated with problems in the work role (e.g., C. J. Firth & Hardy, 1992; Snapp, 1992). Work disinterest may itself be an early sign of depression, whether caused by work or not. Depression in general, and presumably also in the workplace, is experienced more commonly by women than by men (Charney & Weissman, 1988) and among workers who are younger or older workers than those who are middle-aged (Warr, 1992). Women in professional roles (e.g., physicians, ministers) may be especially susceptible to work-related depression (e.g., Heim, 1991; Rayburn, 1991).

At least three primary types of depression are identified by *DSM–III–R*: major depression (296.2), dysthymia (or depressive neurosis, 300.4), and, although not an affective disorder per se, adjustment reaction with depressed mood (309.00). In addition, bipolar disorders, which combine manic and depressive features, have been studied in reference to work with respect to creative and leadership occupational roles. In such groups, bipolar disorders are apparently common, especially among the highly successful and well-known (F. K. Goodwin & Jamison, 1990; Hershman, 1988; Jamison, 1989).

The following case illustrates the psychological consequences associated with work loss and subsequent work in an area in which one is not trained or lacks special interest.

Case 6.3
The Depressed and Passive Employee

John was in his late thirties when he sought help for difficulties in his work role. Trained as a graphic artist, he had been laid

---

[2] Although the effect of unemployment on mental health is an important topic in its own right, it is not a primary focus of this book.

"Come in, come in, Cartwright. I'm entering my exuberant phase and I need your dour skepticism."

Drawing by Stan Hunt; © 1986 The New Yorker Magazine, Inc.

off from a job in this area that he had held for a number of years and had been working in retail sales for a number of months and finding it exceedingly unpleasant. However, he had little idea of how to find a better fitting job or how to adapt his current job to make it more to his liking.

The only one in his family to move away from the small northern town where he was raised, John had left for the broader horizons of a larger city. He obtained a job doing ad layout for a large grocery store chain and then assumed the role of art director for a small magazine where he became involved in many different aspects of the job. Although he worked for the magazine for a number of years, it fell on hard times in a recessionary period and ultimately he was dismissed.

The client tried to survive financially by doing freelance work, but he had very little business sense and was not very successful in getting work. Both because of his period of unemployment and because a significant number of friends had died from AIDS, he became seriously depressed. Finally, after several years of unemployment he declared bankruptcy, accepted financial support from his family, and took a very low-level position that gave him a small paycheck and some structure for his time. Then having health care benefits, he sought counseling assistance, but began therapy only after obsessively phoning the future therapist with questions about various aspects of the treatment.

Assessment revealed a significantly depressed man whose work was at the center of his immediate problems. Yet, the client was very reluctant to consider new employment alternatives. Because of either his depression or his characterological style, he had become a chronic naysayer, seeing only why career change possibilities would not work rather than how they might work. Although his attitude was not hostile, it did reflect a defensive stance toward change.

John had few friends (except through his past employment), had no stable relationships outside work, and met many of the diagnostic criteria of schizotypal personality (see chapter 7). His immediate reaction to any suggestion was that he simply "couldn't do it." When vigorously challenged on these assumptions, he maintained a passive stance.

At his work, he had progressed from his initial job to one in which he was in charge of the scheduling department. Although he rather enjoyed the obsessional detail of the job and had made a few changes to improve the operations, he had found no outlet either at work or in his nonwork life for his creative talents. He had not thought to tell the management of this company (which had a graphics art department) that he would like to be considered for employment in that section of the organization. Few in the company knew of his past experience as an art director.

With his therapist's prodding, John began to consider some changes that he might make in his employment to improve his situation. Each suggestion was met with considerable resistance. Although antidepressant medication was recommended as an interim way to manage his immediate depression, John resisted this suggestion as well. Finally, owing to his therapist's persistence, John made some small steps toward improving his work situation. Eventually, he let management know of his talent in art. He was allowed to fill in on occasion in the firm's graphic arts department, although no vacancies were available for a full-time position. Eventually, he began to do some freelance work on his own. His depression became more manageable as he started conceptualizing alternatives. At the end of treatment, he remained reserved, distant, and somewhat obsessional and op-positional but was not depressed and had begun seeking realistic employment alternatives.

Although clients obviously can be depressed in their work because of a variety of reasons having nothing to do with work, there are many aspects of work that can influence depression, even when nonwork life is going well. These include problems with supervision (Golding, 1989); demanding work (Holt, 1982), particularly when coupled with limited ability to make relevant decisions (Braun & Hollander, 1988); ambiguity of authority; perceived or real lack of social support (H. Firth & Britton, 1989); corporate instability (Little, Gaffney, Rosen, & Bender, 1990); and even such physical conditions as exposure to toxic solvents (Bendiksen & Bendiksen, 1992; Brozgold, Franzblau, & Borod, 1992; McCrank & Rabheru, 1989; Ng, Ong, Lam, & Jones, 1990; Singer & Scott, 1987). Indeed, many of the working conditions that place the employee at risk for depression appear to be variants of learned helplessness models of depression in which individuals have perceived responsibility but not control over their work environment (e.g., Seligman, 1975; see also Dweck & Wortman, 1982).

Depression, of course, can be affected by both work and nonwork factors. Depression can lower work performance, although its manner of operation may be more complex than imagined. S. Fischer (1991), for example, found that although depressed subjects were more likely to have an overall negative impression of their performance, they did not evaluate their individual performances any more negatively than did nondepressed subjects. Ulrich and Dunne (1986) identified a discrepancy between what is sought after occupationally and the estimation of what has actually been achieved as often being a crucial therapeutic issue in work-related problems. In other words, it is the subjective impression that matters most, and people who are high achievers may still experience depression from the discrepancy between what they have accomplished and what they have sought to accomplish.

Research suggests that work-related depression can be independently influenced by both work and nonwork factors. Frone, Russell, and Cooper (1991) investigated the relation between stress-related depression and both work and nonwork stressors in a sample of well-educated, employed managers. Contrary to popular belief, they found work and family stress to have very little synergistic effect on depression. Both factors made separate, but not interactive, contributions. Similar findings were also reported by Phelan et al. (1991).

Work-related depression, sometimes termed *acedia*, has been considered by some to be endemic to a postindustrial society that places primary emphasis on work and money and is limited to a narrow definition of sources of self-esteem (Bartlett, 1990). Certain occupations and positions appear more prone to job-related depression than others. High levels of psychological "burnout," possibly a form of work-related depression (see chapter 5), have been reported among workers in the helping professions (Holland, 1985). Studies show that physicians (Kalra, Rosner, & Shapiro, 1987; Krakowski, 1985), psychiatric nurses (deLeo, Magni, & Vallerini, 1982), home care providers (Stoneman & Crapps, 1988), health and mental health care workers (Belfer, 1989; H. Firth, McKeown, McIntee, & Britton, 1987; Hilliard & Riemer, 1988; Kahill, 1988; R. J. Lang, Gilpin, & Gilpin, 1990), teachers (Bloom, 1983; Kyriacou & Pratt, 1985; Schonfeld, 1990), and police officers (Girodo, 1985; Reiser & Geiger, 1984) are at high risk for work-related depression.[3] Other researchers have reported differential incidence of work-related (or at least occupation-specific) depression. Krakowski (1984) compared samples of physicians and attorneys and found the former group to be much more compulsive and prone to depression than the latter. Alfredsson, Akerstedt, Mattsson, and Wilborg (1991)

---

[3] This is not, of course, to imply that other professions or occupations are immune from the effects of stress (e.g., K. J. Smith, 1990) but merely that occupations in social service areas appear to be at higher risk than some other occupational groups.

found night security guards also to be higher than expected risk for depression and other nervous disorders.

Although studies rarely control for direction of causality, certain features of the job or work environment appear to be more highly associated with work-related depression. These include the frequently encountered job stressors of role strain, role overload, and role ambiguity (D. Katz & Kahn, 1979; V. Sutherland & Davidson, 1989). Although there are limited data concerning these factors specific to the workplace, women appear to be at higher risk for depression than do men (Braun & Hollander, 1988; Greenglass & Burke, 1988; Lowe & Northcott, 1988; Zappert & Weinstein, 1985; regarding "burnout," see Etzion, 1987; see also chapter 5), a finding similar to that for the general population (Lowman & Parker, 1988).[4]

Although jobs and occupations appear to differ systematically in the propensity of their members to report work-related depression, it is important to note that individual workers also differ in their capacities to tolerate dysfunctional working conditions (Strelau, 1989), some being more "hardy" than others. Given that subjective evaluation of what constitutes stress varies, employees in similar working conditions may differentially experience (or at least report) stress, anxiety, or depression (see Mo-

---

[4] Whether this finding, at least in work-related depression, is due to a real sex difference or to secondary factors (e.g., lower pay, discrimination, role conflict between work and family) that in turn result in negative affect has not been established (see Greenglass, 1985). Particular personality characteristics (e.g., Type A personality, external locus of control, use of avoidance as a means of coping with role overload or stress) may also predispose the individual to work-related stress (Bluen, Barling, & Burns, 1990; Fusilier, Ganster, & Mayes, 1987; R. A. Martin, Kuiper, & Westra, 1989; May & Revicki, 1985; D. L. Nelson & Kletke, 1990; O'Neill & Zeichner, 1985; Revicki & May, 1985). However, the specific nature of the relation may be complex, and support for the relation is not always found (e.g., Bruch, Pearl & Giordano, 1986). Bluen et al. (1990) found only the impatience–irritability dimension but not the achievement striving dimension on Helmreich, Spence, and Pred's (1988) adaptation of the Jenkins's Activity Survey (Jenkins, Zyzanski, & Rosenman, 1971) to predict depression. Age, or at least amount of experience in a job, may also affect depression given that personal control may increase with age and experience in the occupation (e.g., May & Revicki, 1985).

towidlo, Packard, & Manning, 1986). Moreover, positive as well as so-called negative events may precipitate work-related depression (e.g., Giannandrea, 1985). At best, knowledge of the occupation, work characteristics, and sex of the individual only indicate demographic risk factors and perhaps propensity for work dysfunction, including depression. Similarly, knowing that certain aspects of jobs (e.g., role ambiguity or low social support) are associated with higher levels of stress or anxiety says nothing about whether that factor is operative in the immediate case or situation. Individual clinical assessment, both of the person and, to the extent possible, the work itself, is essential in each case to understand the dynamics of the immediate situation. Table 6.2 identifies several variables important in assessing work-related depression.

The differential impact of stressors in one's work and nonwork life on the experience of depression has received relatively little

---

Table 6.2.

Summary of Assessment Dimensions Important in Evaluating Work-Related Depression

Characteristics of the task
  Perceived control
  Perceived social support
  Role ambiguity
  Role conflict
  Perceived alternatives to present work situation
  Exposure to toxic solvents
  Role overload

Characteristics of the person
  Internal versus external locus of control
  History of depression
  Nonwork depression
  Use of avoidance as a defense
  Perception of options
  Perception of effort–outcome contingencies
  Helplessness

systematic research attention. Kandel, Davies, and Raveis (1985) studied the relation of work and nonwork stressors in a sample of women. Although they found more stress overall in work roles (including housework) than in family roles, when stress in the family role was experienced, it was more likely to result in depression. Relations among various sources of strain appeared complicated, with work stress decreasing the impact of marital stress but stress in the parental role increasing the impact of occupational stress.

Intervention Issues

In treating the depressed client, the therapist should routinely assess concerns that the client may have with the work role (as outlined in chapter 3). Having detected problems in the work role related to depression, the therapist must determine the source of the stress and whether the cause of the depression is work alone or work acting in combination with another factor. Pertinent diagnostic questions to this end include the following: Is the client in the wrong occupation or in a wrong position in the particular organization? Is there a problem with a particular supervisor? Are co-workers or supervisors seen as nonsupportive? What objective and subjective aspects of the position may be amenable to change?

Often, as a result of the depressed client's perceived inability to cope with the work situation, he or she will have generated few options concerning alternative ways to handle the presenting difficulties. Using sound judgment and a presumably clearer head than the client's, the therapist can suggest in a tentative, questioning manner a variety of alternatives that may not have occurred to the client. Examples include the following: Have you thought about trying to switch to a department that has another supervisor? How about going back to school on a part-time basis so you can get out of this mess? I wonder why it is that you stay in such an unpleasant job? The therapist need not be an expert in the client's particular line of work to address process issues and to assist in generating alternatives. However, the therapist must be knowledgeable about the psychological dynamics of jobs and the ways in which work influences individual behavior.

Although a wide variety of approaches might be attempted in counseling clients suffering from work-related depression or anxiety, they generally reduce to changing the person, changing the job, or some combination of the two. As with stress reduction programs, therapy of work-related depression that aims to change the person while ignoring characteristics of the work that may be causing the psychological dysfunction is problematic. Although such therapy may reduce individual strain and at least temporarily decrease depression or anxiety, also changing the work itself (i.e., modulating work aspects of depression) may have a greater, longer lasting impact. Moreover, people already experiencing job difficulties may be in greater need and may experience more positive results from intervention efforts (see J. Firth & Shapiro, 1986).

Although it is obviously not always possible to remove stressors from a job or occupation, a persistent finding in the literature suggests the positive role of social support in coping with and moderating the effects of depression (see, e.g., Caplan, 1971; Fusilier, Ganster, & Mayes, 1987). Low levels of perceived social support, particularly for those in occupations perceived to be stressful, are associated with higher levels of psychological problems, including depression (Mohler, 1983).[5] In addition to social support, life-style and positive health habits, including physical fitness (Sothmann, Ismail, & Chodepko-Zapjiko, 1984), can apparently moderate the effects of occupational stressors such as role ambiguity and overload and stressful life events (Steffy, Jones, & Noe, 1990) assuming they are duplicated in work-related depression. Revicki and May (1985) found, in a sample of middle-aged physicians, that family social support, but not co-worker social support, moderated the relation between work stress and depression. Thus, the therapist treating cases of work-related depression in which the stressors are not changeable may need to assist the client in creating such sources of support and/

---

[5] Although most studies have reported social support to moderate the relation between work strain and negative personal and work consequences, there are exceptions. Kaufmann and Beehr (1986) found results that are contrary to this model.

or positive health behaviors, either through the workplace or outside of it.

Important as social support may be in modifying effects of work-related stress such as depression, it may not be sufficient or applicable in all cases. This is demonstrated by studies that refute the effectiveness of simplistic approaches to management of work-related depression that proffer a single intervention as universally applicable. For example, in a study concerning the negative mental health consequences (including depression) among male bus drivers in Britain following that industry's deregulation, Duffy and McGoldrick (1990) found that although support and a sense of involvement moderated the negative impact of the organizationally mandated changes (including depression), so too did the type of bus driven (moving from double-decker to smaller buses). Other studies have demonstrated negative outcomes concerning stress at work (e.g., Ganster, Mayes, Sime, & Tharp, 1982) but have not necessarily shown specific effects on depression or anxiety (see also Pelletier & Lutz, 1991).

Once the therapist has established (if only as a working hypothesis) that work issues are primary in a client's depression, that aspect of life generally becomes the primary focus of the therapy for at least a period of time. The therapist actively intervenes to help the client discover new ways of handling the perceived work difficulties, if necessary (and always with the client's consent) contacting workplace officials to gather more data or to suggest ways of improving the work situation. Although there are exceptions, it is generally best for the depressed employee to maintain work involvement because in most cases it improves the long-term prognosis (see Devereaux & Carlson, 1992).

The next case illustrates how both work and nonwork factors can influence work-related depression.

Case 6.4
The Overworked Attorney and Underinvolved Husband

Stanton was 29 years old when he came for assistance because of marital difficulties. Constant stress, combined with his wife's depression, had put sufficient strain on the marriage that outside help was considered the only possible antidote to divorce.

In the course of the evaluation, Stanton was discovered to be an overachiever at work. He felt that there was no substitute for anything but superior performance at work. In fact, Stanton was spending about 80 hours or more a week at the office, and although he was very highly regarded by his superiors and on a fast track for earning a partnership in the prestigious law firm where he worked, he centered his entire life on the work world, arriving home thoroughly exhausted and agitated at his wife. He had increasingly withdrawn into himself, experiencing anger and frustration in his home life, which led him to bury himself even deeper in his work. The strain on himself and on his marriage was considerable.

Exploration of the marital dynamics revealed relevant family-of-origin dynamics. Stanton was the middle child of a highly conflicted family in which the parents had fought voraciously for years before obtaining a very messy divorce during the client's teen years. His wife had come from a family with a very aggressive mother and a rather passive father. Although she identified with her husband's ambition, she felt that it went too far. When she considered herself neglected, she complained and became irritated with her husband.

In the initial assessment, the couple was interviewed separately. Because his wife had a recurrent history of major depression, Stanton feared that his behavior might trigger another episode. Yet, he found what he experienced as her constant need for attention as being meddlesome and intrusive into his career goals. Further exploration of his career situation, however, demonstrated that he was compulsively going through the expected rituals of overcommitment at the office but was experiencing little joy or pleasure in his work. His withdrawal at home had been a depressive reaction to the demands and pressure he felt at work. When asked to grade his performance, he gave himself a "C" as a husband and an "F" for taking care of his own needs.

Further exploration of his family-of-origin dynamics showed that he was carrying the dynamic of shame in the family. Whereas his two siblings had acclimated themselves to rather unprestigious jobs and careers, he followed the admonitions of his father, with whom he strongly identified, to be successful and achieve, no matter what. In college, although shorter than many players, he had tried out for the basketball team and, almost totally on the sheer force of his determination and persistence, managed to make the team and occasionally to play in competitive games.

As an attorney, he competed just as he had in college, fiercely determined to be successful, no matter what. He could not then see that his own self-esteem was the victim of this race and that his father's unfulfilled ambitions drove his desperate chase for success, which left him feeling depressed rather than effective, despite his achievements. With his therapist's prompting, he was able to identify his lack of fulfillment at work. In slow, barely perceptible steps, he cut back on some of the ferocity of his work commitment. The unidimensional boss for whom he worked reacted warily at first but gradually accepted that Stanton could be a valued employee but lead a somewhat more balanced life. Eventually, however, Stanton sought employment elsewhere and began to enjoy much more the time he spent with his wife.

As this case demonstrates, when work is not judged to be the primary cause of depression, effective treatment may still have a positive impact on work. C. J. Firth and Hardy (1992) studied 90 depressed adults who were experiencing work stress and found that psychotherapy improved their perception of their work. Moreover, because nonwork and work factors apparently contribute separately to depression at work, separate assessments and possibly interventions to address these issues may be necessary. In part, the therapist may need to help the client juggle competing priorities and make conscious decisions about how to live. The therapeutic process may therefore involve helping the client identify and make decisions about implicit premises about work (e.g., "Work [or money] is everything"; "My family takes secondary priority to my work"; "It is not possible to do my work and to be a good parent"). Helping the client adjust occupational goals in the interests of a balanced life may be part of the therapeutic agenda. When factors outside the client's control have caused depression, reframing the situation to help the client learn what is and is not within his or her control in the situation may be desirable.

Depression as a reaction to or cause of work dysfunctions is so common in clinical referrals that the therapist of work dysfunctions should have specialized expertise in its treatment. This chapter concludes with a final case illustrating the types of depression related to work that the therapist may encounter.

Case 6.5
An Impaired and Depressed Artist

An artist in his thirties at the time of referral, Tom had the look of a broken and defeated man, with little sense of mission or purpose. He had been injured in an automobile accident and had spent the better part of a year under his physician's orders not to paint because of the physical sequelae of the accident. Although he presented as clinically depressed at the time of the assessment, he also displayed a well-entrenched perception of himself as an unjustly treated victim against whom some aspect of the world was always attempting, almost plotting, to perpetuate unhappiness. A curious string of calamities had preceded his injury, and it seemed that bad things continually happened to this talented man and, strangely, always appeared to deteriorate into catastrophes.

Clinical investigation revealed a talented artist whose forte was the integration of realism with modern art. His highly stylized paintings manifested a strikingly creative talent, yet history suggested that Tom had never been very commercially successful in part because he had gotten involved with agents whom he felt had taken advantage of him and in part because of his perfectionism. In addition to his doctor's advice, Tom was reluctant to use his talents because of a hand tremor that occurred after he worked with a brush for a relatively short period of time. He requested assessment to determine if there was some other career for which he might be suited.

Psychological testing showed Tom to be depressed at the time of assessment. However, his abilities were relatively unaffected by the depression or by the physical sequelae of his accident. He was cognitively able and had special talents in art. Rather than suggesting a new field of endeavor, the therapist suggested that Tom continue with his chosen profession but consider returning to school to get advanced training that might enable him to teach in this area—an alternative that would make fewer demands on his physical condition.

With curious obstinancy, Tom spent much time obsessing about what he should do next in his work. Eventually, with the help of his therapist, he took what appeared to him to be a risky course of action and returned to school. He did very well in spite of his continued hand tremor (untreatable with medication or other medical interventions), which made completing the studio courses difficult. He eventually obtained an advanced degree and secured a teaching position. Tom's depression improved slowly but steadily, and over time he was able in therapy to work on family-of-origin issues that affected his somewhat chronic sense of failure and underachievement.

Summary

Work-related anxiety and depression are complex and multidetermined phenomena. Performance anxiety and generalized anxiety can both be related to work concerns. The former has been more thoroughly examined in the literature and may lend itself more readily to treatment. The frequency with which depression occurs in connection with work-related issues suggests that psychotherapists need to become familiar with differentiating depression that is caused by work problems from work problems that are caused by depression. When work is the source of depression, correcting the difficulties in the work situation may cause the depression to spontaneously lift. In cases in which work problems are caused by the depression, successful treatment of depression may ameliorate the work concerns, or the work concerns may effectively be dealt with as a circumscribed problem after the depression has been successfully treated.

Personality Disorders and Work

I n this chapter, *personality disorders* includes not only character or personality disorders in the formal diagnostic sense of that term (e.g., *Diagnostic and Statistical Manual of Mental Disorders*, 3rd ed., rev. [*DSM–III–R*], American Psychiatric Association, 1987; Millon, 1990) but also persistent difficulties in successfully negotiating the work role because of character problems. The client experiencing difficulties of this type usually exhibits long-lasting and generally cross-situational[1] behaviors and attitudes that conflict with the roles and values of the workplace. Although people who do not meet formal diagnostic criteria for personality disorders may exemplify the types of problems discussed in this chapter, there is also evidence that people with formally diag-

---

[1] However, see Amodei and Nelson-Gray (1991) for another view on the presumption that people with personality disorders behave consistently across situations.

177

nosed personality disorders are particularly likely to experience work-related problems (e.g., Dowdall & Goldstein, 1984–1985; Palinkas & Coben, 1988). Unfortunately, however, the workplace implications of personality disorders have been largely unspecified, and much of the literature on personality disorders (e.g., Kernberg, 1984; Lion, 1981; Millon, 1981; Millon & Klerman, 1986) contains scant, if any, mention of the work role,[2] implying either that work does not matter to the pathology or that there is no reason to regard the personality aberration as existing differently in the workplace than outside of it.

Millon (1990), one of the major contemporary theorists of personality disorders, identified four areas of clinical functioning in which problems that are prototypical of personality dysfunction occur: (a) expressive acts, (b) interpersonal conduct, (c) cognitive style, and (d) regulatory mechanisms. Generally, personality disorders are believed to include a persistent, transituational style of ineffective interactions with others that is often rather impervious to substantive change. Personality-disordered individuals typically have little understanding of or sensitivity to their impact on others and behave characteristically in a way that others may find interpersonally offensive or otherwise objectionable. Although the behavior of people with personality dysfunctions is often self-defeating, it tends to be symbolic of characteristic conflicts or concerns. The ability of people with personality disorders to regulate their own behavior is limited given that they typically act in a way directed at getting their own perceived needs met, often at the expense or oblivious to the needs of others. Although somewhat dependent on the specific disorder, the deficiencies often have a structural component in which there may be weaknesses in the ego's ability to interact

---

[2] A few conditions such as antisocial and passive–aggressive personality disorders specifically mention work role difficulties as part of the diagnostic criteria used to establish the condition (e.g., inability to sustain the work role), but even with these diagnoses there has been very little attention to this aspect of the disorders in the literature. An exception to this generalization is the work of Masterson (1988), who at least acknowledged the role of work in the healthy personality and considered how personality dysfunctions may interfere with normal, healthy development of the ability to work.

effectively with the outside world (Giovacchini, 1976). In the workplace, people with personality problems can cause considerable difficulty for both the organization and ultimately themselves. The following case illustrates this point.

Case 7.1
A Bright and Shining Flop

Ralph, a key manager in a large manufacturing organization, was generally viewed by his peers and subordinates as being technically brilliant but temperamentally difficult. He had graduated with a technical degree from a prestigious university and had held several jobs, generally for a few years each, before assuming the position from which he was ultimately to be fired.

Hired to help with the start-up of a new manufacturing facility, he chronically angered subordinates and superiors with his brusque and abrasive style. Although much of what he stated was technically accurate, some was not. The force with which he espoused his views and the aggressiveness with which he responded to questions and challenges suggested that his views were strongly held and presumably correct. Few dared to challenge him and risk his inevitable and condescending wrath.

Although advised on several occasions by his peers and subordinates to pay more heed to the impact that his style had on others, his arrogance and sense of superiority prohibited him from taking these admonitions very seriously, assuming he ever really heard them. In his own mind, Ralph was the rational and "correct" person in any altercation, and those who dared to challenge him were simply wrong because, had he stopped to think about it (which, characteristically, he did not), they were less intelligent than he. Yet, as a result of technical problems, Ralph's department experienced serious production problems, making it the focus of intense and unrelenting scrutiny by higher levels of management within the corporation.

Ultimately, Ralph became his own worst enemy. After a disagreement with a senior manager, which included a shouting match, the manager moved to fire Ralph. Only through the intervention of his one remaining highly placed ally in the company was he kept on at all and then only in a makeshift position.

After a few months in this role, even his sponsor could not protect him and, after renewed conflict with the senior manager, this bright and shining star was predictably fired.

What led to Ralph's demise? Obviously, job performance factors contributed to his dysfunctional behavior, perhaps exacerbating his basic defensive orientation. But even more important, Ralph's personality style contributed to his downfall. Indeed, he had faced similar difficulties in other organizations before. As one who was reputed to have considerable ability in solving technical problems, Ralph did not know how to motivate people and managed always to say just the wrong thing so that blame and self-protectiveness were aroused rather than support or a sense of commonality. It was his difficulty in learning from experience and his almost literal inability to comprehend the message that his approach to others was a problem that ultimately caused his downfall.

The presence of personality disorders, with or without other psychopathology, generally worsens the prognosis for treatment or change (Shea, Widiger, & Klein, 1992). Reich and Green's (1991) review of 21 studies of the influence of personality disorders on treatment outcome found the overall effect to be predictably negative, a finding partially supported by Shea et al.'s (1990) research with depressed populations. Although patients with major depression who also had personality disorders showed poorer social adjustment and more residual depressive symptoms than did depressed patients without personality disorders, there was no difference between the two groups on follow-up in their work functioning (Shea et al., 1990).

Personality patterns relevant to work dysfunction can include all of the standard *DSM–III–R* formal diagnostic groups, reflecting such dimensions as impulsiveness (Buss, 1988), narcissism (Masterson, 1988), paranoia, avoidance (Reich, Noyes, & Yates, 1989), and interpersonal isolation (Mollinger, 1980). *DSM–III–R* formally identifies 11 major categories of personality disorder: avoidant, dependent, obsessive–compulsive, passive–aggressive, antisocial, borderline, histrionic, narcissistic, and (of a somewhat more severe nature) paranoid, schizoid, and schizotypal disorders.

Several significant issues remain to be settled in establishing the independence of these entities from one another and from Axis I conditions and the empirical validity of the symptom lists said to characterize each of the conditions (see Benjamin, 1987; Frances & Widiger, 1986; Gorenstein & Newman, 1980; Hirschfeld, Shea, & Weise, 1991; Jenike, Baer, & Carey, 1986; Lilienfeld, VanValkenburg, Larntz, & Akiskal, 1986; Livesley & Schroeder, 1991; Perry, O'Connell, & Drake, 1984; Plakun, 1987; Reich, 1990b; Shea et al., 1992; Widiger, Freiman, & Bailey, 1990; Widiger & Shea, 1991; Wulach, 1983). Moreover, personality disorders can coexist with Axis I conditions (e.g., J. Morrison, 1989; Peters, 1990; Stanley, Turner, & Borden, 1990), although the presence of personality disorders appears to indicate a worse prognosis, poorer social adjustment, and more negative reactions from others (Reich & Green, 1991; Shea et al., 1990; Steketee, 1990).

The seasoned clinician involved with workplace issues will recognize immediately the domain of which I write, whether personality problems are formally diagnosed or represent a sub-diagnostic trend. Examples include the employee who loses job after job because of conflicts with authority, the worker who cannot conform to work expectations of arriving to work on time and complying with behavioral rules, the malevolent supervisor who misdirects large amounts of subordinates' energies into managing their rage and opposition (see Levinson, 1992), the co-worker who is chronically difficult to get along with, the "impaired" professional (Guy, 1987; Kilburg, Kaslow, & VandenBos, 1988; Kilburg, Nathan, & Thoreson, 1986; Swearingen, 1990) who engages in sexual and other exploitation of clients (experiencing little remorse until being caught, then suddenly developing awareness of "impairment" and the need for outside help), and the supervisor or co-worker who chronically blames others and who is able to see only the negative in everyone but himself or herself. Personality disorders apparently account for a sizable proportion of psychiatric casualties at work (e.g., Dowdall & Goldstein, 1984–1985; Lowman, 1989; Palinkas & Coben, 1988) and may be overrepresented in those seeking workmen's compensation (Gordon, Eisler, Gutman, & Gordon, 1991). Personality disorders and unresolved early interpersonal relationship difficulties can combine to make work one more arena in which the difficulties are potentially "acted out."

However, because personality-disordered individuals may also be talented and productive in other aspects of their work, their behavior may be tolerated in the workplace beyond what would otherwise be expected. In this context, it is useful to recall that in the current psychiatric nosology, character or personality disorders can coexist with other forms of psychopathology (Frances & Widiger, 1986; Kendall & Clarkin, 1992). Analogously, personality problems in the workplace can also coexist with other personal characteristics; there may also be relatively unaffected areas of work life. It is when the work itself calls for interpersonal behavior as part of the job duties (e.g., support of or cooperation with subordinates or co-workers is important) that such behavioral patterns may become especially problematic. In other words, the combination and interaction of personality disorders and other relevant characteristics (e.g., intelligence and interest patterns) may determine whether problems are encountered in the workplace (Lowman, 1989, 1991b; Mandes & Gessner, 1986).

The possibility that the workplace itself may create or exacerbate such psychological difficulties needs to be considered. Kets de Vries and Miller (1991) identified leadership styles that may reflect "neurotic" organizations.[3] Bowler, Mergler, Rauch, Harrison, and Cone (1991) reported that personality and other disturbances were found among female microelectronics assemblers who had been exposed on the job to certain organic solvents. Although this study did not control for psychopathology, it at least introduces the idea that aspects of the workplace may cause or contribute to mental health difficulties, including personality disorders.[4]

---

[3] There is, of course, a danger of reductionism in asserting that organizations "behave" like individuals. This model may be more useful as a metaphor than as an exact descriptor of the behavior of organizational entities.

[4] Although this area is ripe for additional research, care must be taken not to overgeneralize from the limited data now available. Furthermore, there is at least limited evidence that prior disposition may play at least as large (if

Differential Diagnosis

Although psychopathology nosological schemes, particularly the *DSM–III–R*, may be conceptually useful, they are somewhat limited for addressing personality disorders in the work context. First, the *DSM–III–R* personality disorder nosological system was not established with workplace difficulties in mind. Second, the system imposes a somewhat arcane if not archaic model of personality dysfunction on a new territory that is has not been well-researched, particularly with reference to workplace applications. Finally, the *DSM–III–R* requirement that personality disorders meet a certain number of conditions could inappropriately eliminate from further consideration many types of work difficulties.

Although clients may present with personality disorders *and* work dysfunctions, the link between the two should be specifically established as part of the diagnostic process and not be merely the object of casual speculation. The presumption cannot be made that because diagnostic criteria for a personality disorder are met the client will necessarily experience difficulty in the work role or, conversely, that the client with character difficulties that do not meet *DSM–III–R* criteria for personality disorder will not experience work difficulties. The former situation is particularly true for sociopathic-like dysfunctions that, at least at mild levels, may be functional and adaptive in certain work settings where such behavior may facilitate advancement and goal accomplishment (Lowman, 1987). There are also individuals who, although meeting *DSM–III–R* criteria for personality disorders, may treat work as an island of relative quiescence, perhaps the one area of life in which things are orderly and predictable or in which the external behavioral checks and balances force a facade of positive adjustment.

---

not larger) a role in psychological dysfunction than the workplace itself (see, e.g., Bouchard, Lykken, McGue, Segal, & Tellegen, 1990; N. Cherry, 1978, 1984a; Keller, Bouchard, Arvey, Segal, & Dawis, 1992; Moloney, Bouchard, & Segal, 1991). Thus, simplistic presumptions that attribute individual personality dysfunction primarily or exclusively to working conditions should be regarded with some skepticism.

Of course, within the work setting there are reasons why conforming, nonpathological behavior may more likely be displayed and maladaptive behavior suppressed. Internalized behavioral controls, often lacking in at least certain forms of personality disorder (Millon, 1990), are generally well-articulated by the nature of the work setting itself, and the consequences of noncompliance can be immediate, obvious, and severe. For some, it may take several jobs (and other punitive life experiences in response to the problematic behavior) before the reality of behavioral rules is grasped. Then, adaptive learning may finally occur despite there being no clear change in the underlying character pathology or predispositional tendencies.

A few suggestions may aid the clinician in diagnosing character pathology with workplace implications. To be considered a personality disorder with workplace relevance, the problematic condition or set of characteristics should be persistent across a variety of situations including the workplace, should demonstrably interfere with the implementation of the work role, and should be relatively unresponsive to efforts at change and control through informal or advisory methods used in routine supervision (i.e., the condition does not "self-correct"). The inability to learn from experience, to adapt appropriately to new situations or conditions, and to consider the reactions of others are all characteristics that are likely to characterize personality disorders with workplace relevance.

General Issues

Problems With Authority

One area that presents particular opportunity for conflict for the personality-disordered individual concerns the hierarchical nature of work organizations and the fact that some individuals in the workplace will characteristically exert power and control over others. Indeed, some of the most crippling and common barriers to productive accomplishment occur in the context of the relationship of employees to people in authority. The sources of such difficulties can rest with the individual (e.g., Wilke, 1977), the organization, or some interactive combination. This section considers the psychological dynamics associated with interventions suggested for individual-centered authority conflicts.

Most work settings inevitably involve hierarchical layers in which people have authority over others. Within these layers, individuals vary in their preference for types of relationships with authority. Dependent personalities, for example, may prefer others to be in a superior position to them both in their work and personal lives. At work, they may look to their supervisors or co-workers to provide direction and close oversight. Such individuals may essentially seek a "good parent" who will provide them with nurturance, care, and direction. When the passive–dependent employee is assigned to a job or organization in which the work situation matches these expectations (i.e., need to take orders, do one's job, accept direction), things may go well. However, when the job situation becomes less paternalistic or a new supervisor arrives who is less directive, the employee may respond by attempting to reinstate the structure.

For others, unresolved family-of-origin conflicts or personality styles create animosity toward those in authority. The supervisor–supervisee relationship may become a battleground for proving the ineptitude of the supervisor or for asserting the subordinate's apparent independence of those in authority. Because supervisors may or may not govern competently, characteristics of the supervisor must also be considered in assessing individual cases. For the bright subordinate paired with a less competent or overly controlling superior, many opportunities exist for conflict. Passive–aggressive behavior, in which work is sabotaged without direct confrontation and in such a manner that responsibility can never quite be established, is one way in which the authority may be opposed.

Authority problems at work presumably stem from the same intrapsychic sources as do authority problems in other aspects of life such as marriage or parental relations. As in assessment with all work dysfunctions, two contributing factors must be evaluated: the role of predispositional factors and the role of the work situation itself. Jobs vary in the degree of supervision they inherently require and in the manner in which the supervision is implemented. Individuals whose family-of-origin conflicts are severe and unresolved will likely have problems with authority and will typically create a problem if one does not already exist.

Most obvious and most frequent are authority issues associated with perceptions of overly controlling supervision. The supervisor–supervisee relationship, perhaps inevitably, has the potential for reenacting family-of-origin dynamics, complete with siblings (co-workers), parents (supervisors), and even grandparents (senior administrators). Just as the parental role can be developed in a variety of styles, so too can the supervisory role. The myth of a single superior style of supervision is as false as the idea that there is only one appropriate or "right" parenting style. Individual personality and ability characteristics will interact to determine how the supervisory role is implemented.

Although it may be true that the enlightened supervisor bends his or her style to reflect characteristics of the person being supervised (the so-called contingency theory of leadership), in fact, people gravitate to supervisory and subordinate roles not randomly but based on certain characteristics of personality and ability. This implies that the role repertoire for manifest supervisory behavior will be limited both by the personality and ability restrictions of the person and by the formal and informal rules governing such role prescriptions in the particular setting. In any individual, the range of behaviors is not likely to be great.

The supervisee, particularly one without aspirations of great upward mobility goals, does not always bring a realistic sense of what is and is not possible and may project wishes, wants, fears, and other needs onto both the supervisor and the work setting more generally. Just as the very young child projects fantasized wishes onto parents and authority figures, the subordinate employee may respond to the work situation with all the diversity of feelings associated with the child's role.

The diagnosis of authority conflicts in a given work situation should generally begin with an assessment of the realities of the complaints. If multiple complaints of abuse of authority repeatedly come from the same segment of a work organization or from a particular supervisor's workers, the issue is likely less of the client's personality and more of the supervisor's characteristics. In such cases, the therapeutic intervention might best be systemic if the context allows the therapist access to the problematic supervisor. Alternatively, it may be directed at helping the troubled employee learn how to adjust and work with (or around) such a supervisor. Pragmatic issues may also assume high priority (e.g., helping the supervisee consider realistic available options such as switching to another section of the firm, becoming more assertive). In some cases, the only resolution may be for the employee to seek other employment.

In the case of problems with authority related to personality problems, differential diagnosis is especially important. Seemingly intractable personality disorders can be difficult to change. Therefore, short of personality restructuring, can an individual prone to authority conflict improve? The quality of the transference and the rapidity with which it is manifest provide important clues about the effectiveness of various therapeutic interventions.

Intervention Issues

Although the overall prognosis for clients with personality disorders and work dysfunctions is not highly optimistic (Dowdall & Goldstein, 1984–1985; Drake & Vaillant, 1985; D. Edwards & Berry, 1973), a variety of treatment interventions have been suggested, including psychodynamic therapy (Stricker & Gold, 1988), cognitive–behavioral therapy (Beck & Freeman, 1990), and inpatient multimodal treatment (Gralnick, 1979; Greben, 1983). Before developing an intervention plan with a personality-disordered client in the work context, the therapist must first assess the immediate situation, the extent of the reality base, and the amenability of both the individual and the situation to change. By and large, personality disorders are believed to be relatively impervious to therapeutic efforts, although more research is needed to determine whether certain therapies work best with particular types of personality difficulties. For example, in working with people experiencing major depression, Shea et al. (1990) reported that cognitive–behavioral approaches were most effective with a subset of patients who also had personality disorders. Others have suggested that psychotropic medications may be helpful for those needing mood control (Van der Kolk, 1986).

Whether of organic or functional origin, personality disorders at work call for identification and modification of the problematic behavior. Because people with problematic personality patterns often make a positive contribution to the workplace and indeed may generate quite a following with considerable (if divisive) loyalty, care must be taken in approaching the problematic behavior. If the goal is to preserve the individual in the work or organizational context, persistent care must be taken to assure that the intervention is of sufficient strength to address the problem but is not so blunt as to trigger even greater destructive or sabotaging behavior on the part of the client.

Specific Personality Disorders

A review of some of the work implications of current *DSM–III–R* personality disorders follows. Despite the aforementioned problems with the *DSM–III–R* classification and categorization system of personality disorders, the *DSM–III–R* structure is still useful because it provides a terminology with which clinicians are likely to be familiar and because there are work behavior implications for many of these diagnostic categories.

Avoidant Personality Disorder

Avoidant personality disorder is a relatively new diagnostic entity that may not be conceptually distinct from other disorders such as dependent disorder (Reich, 1990b) and schizoid disorder (Livesley & West, 1986; Livesley, West, & Tanney, 1986; Overholser, 1989; see also Akhtar, 1986; Millon, 1986). Individuals with avoidant personality disorders have as a primary difficulty failure to engage with others when relationships with others are both desired and feared (Reich et al., 1989). Because they usually have difficulty in initiating routine social intercourse with others (Stravynski & Greenberg, 1985a, 1985b), they are often impaired in jobs requiring such behavior. Accompanying somaticization, anxiety, and social phobia symptoms may also be experienced (Flynn & McMahon, 1984; Merskey & Trimble, 1979; Turner, Beidel, Dancu, & Keys, 1986). At the extreme, these individuals may avoid work altogether, particularly if it imposes a requirement of frequent contact with others.

Individuals with avoidant personalities may also perceive everyday situations to be more fear-laden than they actually are and may be particularly sensitive to perceived rejection by others (Renneberg, Goldstein, Phillips, & Chambless, 1990). Such people may also gravitate to relatively obscure, low-level occupational roles in which there is little need to interact with others. When this pattern exists in a person who is also ambitious in an organizationally based career, intrapsychic conflict often results. On the other hand, a well-defined work situation with minimal interpersonal contact can be compatible with this personality style (except when simply being in the work situation itself necessitates extensive day-to-day contact with others).

Job analysis of the client's work role may therefore be an appropriate initial step, especially in situations in which the prognosis for changing the job or the individual is not encouraging. Appropriate understanding of the work role may allow the therapist to help the client negotiate a low-threat job that requires minimal social interaction. A nonthreatening, supportive coaching role by a sensitive therapist is important (see, e.g., F. D. Lewis, Roessler, Greenwood, & Evans, 1985).

No method of intervention has been demonstrated to permanently remove the symptomatology of avoidant personality disorder as defined by *DSM-III-R* criteria so that improvement is maintained and generalized over time. The intervention that incorporates cognitive and behavioral therapy (Heimberg & Barlow, 1991) may have effects of longer duration than psychopharmaceutical intervention (Mattick & Newman, 1991), although positive results have been reported for the latter type of treatment (e.g., with alprazolam) (Deltito & Stam, 1989; Reich et al., 1989; Reich & Yates, 1988). Group approaches have also shown promise (Alden, 1989; Renneberg et al., 1990). Interestingly, social skills training (Stravynski, Grey, & Elie, 1987), intended to address the central behavioral concern of avoidant personalities, has not been shown to have a consistent advantage over alternative treatment modalities (see Alden, 1989; Stravynski, Lesage, Marcouiller, & Elie, 1989).

Dependent Personality Disorder

The dependent personality disorder encompasses an apparently common diagnostic entity (Alnaes & Torgersen, 1988) that may overlap considerably with avoidant personality disorder (Reich, 1990b; Trull, Widiger, & Frances, 1987). Individuals with dependent personality disorder are thought to look to others to provide structure and direction and readily assume guidance proffered by others. They seek through affiliative ties the approval of others, even in everyday decisions, and fail to initiate appropriate behavior in situations in which assertiveness is required (R. P. Greenberg & Bornstein, 1988b; Millon, 1981). Because their self-esteem is closely tied to the approval of others, they are easily hurt by others and by the threat of (or actual) abandonment by others.

Although both sexes may be affected by dependent personality disorders, women apparently experience the pattern more frequently than do men (Symonds, 1976), although this finding has not been confirmed in all studies of psychiatric patient groups (Reich, 1987). Families of origin of these people may be characterized by high levels of control combined with limited expression of emotions (Head, Baker, & Williamson, 1991), although men and women with dependent personality disorders may differ in their early family environments (Reich, 1990a). Individuals with dependent personality disorders have been reported to be especially prone to depression (Chodoff, 1973; Mezzich, Fabrega, & Coffman, 1987; Overholser, 1992), somatic disorders (Greenberg & Bornstein, 1988a), and panic disorders (Reich, Noyes, & Troughton, 1987).

No studies were found addressing the behavior of dependent personalities in the workplace. However, it can be hypothesized that dependent personalities, like avoidant ones, gravitate to lower level jobs within organizations or to dependent positions under someone more powerful and that they seek support and assistance from others in a manner that might be perceived as excessive. Sensitivity to slights and rejections and oversensitivity to criticism, real or perceived, may combine to make the employee with a dependent personality experience strain in the workplace. On the other hand, corrective emotional experiences and a sensitive supervisor willing to work with the dependent person may enhance the chronically strained sense of self-esteem and provide a constructive identity that supersedes relationships with others.

Passive–dependent personality types who experience acute symptoms may respond well to antidepressant medications (Deltito & Perugi, 1986; Lauer, 1976) and to supportive psychotherapy. More intrusive psychotherapy can be directed at increasing the independence of the dependent personality, thus lessening the need to look to others to provide direction. Millon (1981) offered a good prognosis for dependent personality types in that these individuals are likely to have had supportive relationships and to seek help through others to meet their dependency needs.

Work difficulties generally center on resentment of co-workers and supervisors who may feel exploited by the strong dependency needs and the possible failure to initiate goal-directed actions when they are necessary. By being tolerant and providing a good role model, the therapist can encourage the client to assume and experiment with more active and goal-directed behavior.

Obsessive–Compulsive Personality Disorder

Critical dimensions of the obsessive–compulsive personality that are potentially relevant to work include perfectionism (D. A. Clark & Bolton, 1985; Sorotzkin, 1985; see also Pirot, 1986) and high needs for control (Mallinger, 1984; Salzman, 1979; Starcevic, 1990), coupled with resistance to demands made on the individual by others (Mallinger, 1982). These people tend to neglect family members, often viewing them as extensions of themselves (Pietropinto, 1986). They are typically excessively devoted to their work activities (Chonko, 1983; Pietropinto, 1986). Other characteristics attributed to the obsessive–compulsive personality include indecisiveness, restriction in the range of emotional expressiveness, experience of dysphoric moods (Davies & DeMonchaux, 1973), and reliance on such *DSM–III–R* defense mechanisms as isolation (W. N. Goldstein, 1985b; Pollak, 1979, 1987; von der Lippe & Torgersen, 1984) and social avoidance

(Turner, Beidel, Borden, Stanley, & Jacob, 1991). Subtypes of obsessive–compulsive personality disorder may also exist, with varying degrees of adjustment, vocational and otherwise (Cornfield & Malen, 1978), such as seen in those individuals manifesting impulsive behavior (Hoehn-Saric & Barksdale, 1983) or a failure of self-control (Reed, 1977). The prevalence of this disorder was reported by Nestadt et al. (1991) to be about 1.9% of the general population, being more common among men than women (Nestadt et al., 1991; Reich, 1987).

General aspects of diagnosis and treatment of this type of disorder in relation to work disfunction were discussed in chapter 5, noting the conceptual and diagnostic differences between the obsessive–compulsive personality disorder and the obsessive–compulsive neurotic disorder (see, e.g., Crino, 1991; Mavissakalian, Hamann, & Jones, 1990; Steketee, 1990). As discussed, there is considerable positive reinforcement in the culture, particularly of compulsive characteristics, as related to work, and the therapist must be sure that the behavior is indeed problematic from the perspective of the client and the client's work environment. It is the rigid adherence to such behavioral patterns, even in the face of repeated evidence that they have become dysfunctional, that presumably transposes potentially positive or at least culturally valued characteristics into ones that are problematic in the workplace (Ingram, 1982).

Treatment in the work context must be approached with particular care given that there is generally little inherent incentive for changing personality characteristics that may be perceived to be closely tied to workplace success. However, if the personality style and defenses fail (e.g., the client experiences depression [Vaughan, 1976] or physical symptoms), the client may have more motivation to seek changes through treatment.

Supportive treatment may be effective in dealing with immediate crises; more substantive focus on the entrenched personality features may require longer term or at least more indepth psychotherapy. Some cases may respond well to behavioral or group psychotherapy or psychotropic medication (Crino, 1991; Mavissakalian & Michelson, 1983; Thoren, Asberg, Cronholm, Lennart, & Traskman, 1980; Wells, Glickauf, & Buzzell, 1990), particularly when depression or severe anxiety is experienced. However, Jenike (1990) argued that drugs and behavioral treatment are more effective with obsessive–compulsive neurotic disorder than with obsessive–compulsive personality disorders. Differential effectiveness of alternative treatment methodologies with the latter has not been established (Salzman & Thaler, 1981).

Passive–Aggressive Personality Disorder

The essential component of passive–aggressive personality disorders is superficial compliance masking opposition and noncompliance. In the work context, those with passive–aggressive personalities may avoid work, complain about the unfairness of their workload, and challenge (often indirectly) those in authority (American Psychiatric Association, 1987; J. T. McCann, 1988). Such behavior in the workplace can be very destructive and can generate animosity among co-workers and supervisors alike.

People with passive–aggressive personality disorders presumably have learned that it is less safe to confront disagreement head-on than it is to assert themselves in a more indirect way (M. Cole, 1984). Although clients with many types of psychological conflict may manifest passive–aggressive behavior, those with passive–aggressive personality disorders are distinguished by their persistent overreliance on these types of defenses. Subtypes may exist, including those motivated primarily by anxiety reduction and those including more resentful and vindictive behavior (Perry & Flannery, 1982). Some researchers have contended that passive–aggressive personality disorder is itself a subtype of narcissistic personality disorder (Rosenberg, 1987). In any event, a variety of other conditions can coexist with passive–aggressive disorders, including bulimia (Yates, Sieleni, Reich, & Brass, 1989) and conversion disorders (Fishbain, Goldberg, Labbe, Steele, & Rosomoff, 1988).

Treatment with such clients can be frustrating because there may be strong resistances to change coupled with superficial compliance. However, some positive results have been reported, even with relatively brief treatment modalities (Oldham, 1988). Helping the client to identify and giving the client permission to have directly aggressive responses may be particularly important aspects of intervention (Bonds-White, 1984).

In the workplace, there is generally little tolerance for passive–aggressive behavior. Yet, because the worker with a passive–aggressive personality is often expert at deflecting blame, he or she may succeed in this defensive style for some time, particularly if employed by a large, bureaucratic organization that tolerates blame attribution and low levels of performance. Those dealing with such employees may need to use direct confrontation, written instructions, and strict accountability if informal counseling methods prove ineffective.

Antisocial Personality Disorder

The antisocial personality disorder, apparently more the province of men than women (Bland, Orn, & Newman, 1988; C. K. Lee et al., 1990; H. E. Ross, Glaser, & Stiasny, 1988), is characterized by a flagrant disregard for the rights and feelings of others. With a restricted range of cognitive ability or curiosity, someone with an antisocial personality may have limited capacity for understanding the feelings and reactions of others (Virkkunen & Luukkonen, 1977). Substance abuse is a frequent accompaniment of antisocial personality or antisocial behavior (Alterman & Cacciola, 1991; Helzer & Pryzbeck, 1988; Koenigsberg, Kaplan, Gilmore, & Cooper, 1985; Kofoed & MacMillan, 1986; C. E. Lewis & Bucholz, 1991; Schubert, Wolf, Patterson, Grande, & Pendleton, 1988; S. S. Smith & Newman, 1990; Stabenau, 1990) and may worsen the prognosis[5] (J. J. Collins, Schlenger, & Jordan, 1988; Hasin, Grant, & Endicott, 1988; Mather, 1987), especially when drugs are abused (Liskow, Powell, Nickel, & Penick, 1990). Such people may also be at risk for lowered longevity (R. L. Martin, Cloninger, Guze, & Clayton, 1985) and suicide (Dyck, Bland, Newman, & Orn, 1988; Garvey & Spodey, 1980).

---

[5] Conversely, individuals with antisocial personality disorder who are also substance abusers may experience more trouble in the control of their drinking (see Yates, Petty, & Brown, 1988).

The individual with antisocial personality disorder as defined by *DSM–III–R* must have manifested cruel and/or irresponsible behavior prior to age 15 that has remained a problem into adulthood (Bailey, 1985). The employment arena may therefore be just one more aspect of life in which this dysfunctional behavior is manifest. People with this disorder often quit jobs precipitously, fail to conform to work rules (such as attendance), and become unemployed (American Psychiatric Association, 1987; Bland, Stebelsky, Orn, & Newman, 1988). Yet, the worker with an antisocial personality, particularly the male, may be well-protected by a positive self-regard that transcends considerable evidence that it is unearned (Sutker, DeSanto, & Allain, 1985). Wright (1987) postulated an underlying shame basis for antisocial personality disorder, suggesting that underneath the external positive self-regard lies considerable self-degradation.

DSM–III–R criteria for diagnosis of antisocial disorders have been criticized for their length and the number of conditions necessary to establish the diagnosis (Hare, Hart, & Harpur, 1991). Some researchers (e.g., Jordan, Swartz, George, Woodbury, & Blazer, 1989) have identified subtypes of antisocial personality patterns, including those related to substance abuse (Gerstley, Alterman, McLellan, & Woody, 1990) and those most

"Tell me, do you respond to treatment?"

Drawing by Rini; © 1992 The New Yorker Magazine, Inc.

typical among women. Other researchers have identified multiple factors involved in the antisocial personality domain (Harpur, Hare, & Hakstian, 1989).

Differential (and concurrent) diagnosis must consider many types of conditions, including narcissistic personality disorder (Plakun, 1987; Wright, 1987), somaticization disorders (Lilienfeld et al., 1986), affective disorders (Reich, 1985; Thorneloe & Crews, 1981), and borderline personality disorder (Perry, 1986). Care must also be taken concerning establishing the diagnosis given that self-report measures of antisocial personality may not concur with behavioral or observational measures (see, among others, Hare, 1985; Hasin & Grant, 1987; Perry, Lavori, Cooper, Hoke, & O'Connell, 1987; Schroeder, Schroeder, & Hare, 1983; however, see also Cooney, Kadden, & Litt, 1990).

There is a fine and not always perceptible line dividing antisocial behavior, antisocial personality, and trends in that direction in the workplace. Low levels of regard for the rights of others when combined with focused, goal-directed efforts may seemingly lead to advancement and positive rather than negative work outcomes (e.g., Lowman, 1989; Harrell & Harrell, 1972). The therapist therefore may be unlikely to receive a referral for someone with antisocial personality traits and work dysfunctions unless that individual has run into trouble with the law or authority structures or is suffering situational depression in response to some perceived external constraint. At least among managerial populations, such employees are likely to be adept at verbally defending themselves and not readily amenable to change.

For some antisocial personality disorders, the apparently natural diminution of symptoms with time and age may be as effective as any therapy in decreasing the virulently negative aspects of the disorder (Arboleda & Holley, 1991), particularly given that responsiveness to traditional forms of psychotherapy, including inpatient treatment, is generally poor (Gabbard & Coyne, 1987). Some researchers (e.g., Kellner, 1986) are more optimistic about the possibility of successful intervention with antisocial personality disorders. It is possible that the ability to form a relationship is a critical variable in predicting whether such interventions will prove efficacious (Gerstley et al., 1989).

Case 7.2
A Fired Family Member

Sam was in his early thirties when he was referred by his family's business, which was about to fire him. He was a son of the owner, who was letting him go after policy disputes between the son and other key managerial staff who were not family members.

Verbally facile, Sam was somewhat muted in the expression of his anger at the time of his referral. There was no love lost between he and his father, although he blamed the executives around him (whom he perceived as not wanting to change to meet new market demands), rather than his father, for his demise. The referral source in the workplace reported that Sam had tried to move too quickly to instigate change and had alienated most of his superiors.

The client's history revealed considerable delinquent behavior as a youth, which had forced his transfer from a fashionable private school to a military one. He had manifest unruly, sometimes cruel, behavior in high school. He then pursued a bachelor's degree and graduated with a passing but undistinguished record in an area for which he had little passion. He worked as a securities broker and then formed his own company, which survived for a time. Finally, he joined the family business.

Psychological testing showed occupational interests in the Enterprising–Conventional–Investigative area. He was very bright, with a high IQ and excellent scores on several other cognitive ability tests (including the Watson-Glaser Critical Thinking Appraisal [G. Watson & Glaser, 1980] and the Raven's Standard Progressive Matrices [Raven, Court, & Raven, 1977]). Ability tests also showed excellent strengths in other areas, including aesthetic judgment, music, and perceptual speed and accuracy.

On several personality measures, he scored in the dominant direction. However, his low scores on the Socialization scale of the California Psychological Inventory (Gough, 1987) and on the Q3 and Superego Strength scales of the Clinical Analysis Questionnaire (Krug, 1980) suggested unresolved conflicts, probably with authority. Some of his personality tests suggested a more creative than conforming personality. Although his external behavior was verbally sophisticated, his strong tendency toward rebelliousness made it difficult for him to work effectively within a conforming framework. His response to Card 1 of the Thematic Apperception Test (H. Murray, 1943, 1965) illustrated his conflicts concerning achievement:

> This kid is sitting looking at the violin, trying to learn. He is frustrated. The kid to me is going to break the violin and throw it out. If not, maybe he'll learn. [He had to be asked about the outcome of the story.] The kid will pick up and learn how to play. I do not detect a long-term love of the instrument. He wonders, Can I play this? Is it possible? Can it be done?

Some elements of this story stand out. The boy is trying to learn while passively observing the instrument and experiencing frustration, to which his first response is reactionary and impulsive. The original ending to the story is indeterminate, with no real commitment to either violent or more goal-directed behavior. When, at the examiner's request, he was prompted for an outcome, a bit more optimism and complexity ensued, with even self-doubting, possibly masked reactions.

One interpretation of this story is that the client's almost violent response to frustration masks both a desire for mastery and considerable self-doubt. When his drives are stymied, his immediate response is to react spontaneously, emotionally, and with rage. He views an end result he wants but when success is not immediately forthcoming, reacts with impulsive anger. However, when pressed by the enforced structure of the assignment, he becomes more self-revealing.

Another story expands these themes and helps identify possible underlying psychological dynamics. To Card 8BM of the Thematic Apperception Test, he created this story:

> This looks like a dream. It looks like the boy in the foreground is dreaming. This appears to be his older brother or a young father. The surgeon is performing surgery. This is very early medicine. The son is very controlled, unemotional, almost cold in thinking what the future will be like. [Again, the client had to be asked to generate an outcome.] He is not going to

make it. The son is on his own at an early age. It looks like he will inherit a substantial position or business. Looks like a royalty situation, more English than American, the early— late—19th or early 20th century. It reminds me of Tom Watson [a key founder of IBM] for some reason.

Although on one level this story reflects potentially healthy sublimation as a defense for handling overt aggression, perhaps the most noteworthy and personally revealing feature is the placement of the son on his own "at an early age." Although creature comforts are abundantly provided by his father's demise (in reality, the client was from a wealthy family), there is no warmth, only control and isolation. Again, Sam had to be prompted for an outcome, suggesting that he may experience trouble with planful actions and may therefore need assistance in creating relevant actions to generate and accomplish long-term goals.

Intervention in this case was oriented to databased feedback on the results of career assessment (the purpose of his contact with the psychologist) to help him better understand what had caused difficulties for him in his general orientation. Although Sam could not directly acknowledge it, he was very hurt by the prospect of being fired from his father's company, seemingly another in a series of rejections by his father. Current career options were reviewed, and the client declined any suggestion of need for ongoing assistance. By focusing exclusively on the career issues, however, it was possible for the therapist to assist him in obtaining a more sober and realistic view of what had happened to him thus far in his career and to direct his considerable energies and abilities toward more appropriate goals. Although this client did not continue psychotherapy, he did call the assessing psychologist from time to time and through this contact appeared to obtain nurturance and guidance directly relevant to his work and indirectly relevant to his personal life.

Borderline Personality Disorder

The borderline personality diagnosis includes a constellation of attributes, including impulsiveness and intense, but highly ephemeral, relationships with others. Those with borderline personality disorder experience a high rate of suicide attempts, pathological anger, and other intense emotions and often report identity problems (personal identity often being diffuse) (W. N. Goldstein, 1985a; Kernberg, 1984; Masterson, 1988; Millon, 1981, 1990; Snyder, Pitts, & Pokorny, 1986). One result may be chronic underlying loneliness and effective isolation from others. Preferred borderline defenses include splitting (Berg, 1990), in which attributes are divided and projected onto alternative objects, each of which may be perceived in an "all-or-none" manner. The borderline personality, while including highly unstable characteristics, is thought itself to be rather stable over time, not necessarily degenerating into psychotic or other severe forms of psychopathology (Gunderson & Zanarini, 1987). Although some believe this disorder to be more frequent in women than men, others have found it to be no more common among women (Reich, 1987). When combined with dysthymia, the borderline personality may imply greater impairment in the work role (Rippetoe, Alarcon, & Walter-Ryan, 1986).

Few studies were found specific to the borderline client's work role. A gradual pattern of decline in the work role has been identified by some researchers (Snyder, Pitts, & Pokorny, 1986). Salz (1983) presented a model of work dysfunctions of the borderline client that is tied to inhibition in exploratory behavior and in the ability to perform autonomous adult roles. Domash and Shapiro (1979) hypothesized that dysfunctional thinking patterns, including dogmatism and grandiosity, lead to work and achievement difficulties.

Therapy with borderline clients is notoriously difficult, complicated by persistent tendencies toward splitting and "acting out" conflicts of behavior outside the therapy relationship, which may include personally dangerous behavior (D. B. Clark, 1989; Kernberg, 1984; Masterson, 1990; Millon, 1981, 1990). Masterson (1990) argued that in such cases the therapist must actively intervene to confront the out-of-therapy behavior as an essential vehicle for addressing the personality difficulties. Countertransference in the therapist must carefully be managed (Meissner, 1982–1983). Others have advocated cognitive and behavioral approaches to the treatment of borderline clients (Freeman & Leaf, 1989; Linehan, Hubert, Suarez, Douglas, & Heard, 1991).

Workplace behavior of employees with borderline personality disorder requires careful (and sometimes frequent) management. Although the employee with a borderline disorder may be prone to divisive interpersonal work relations (e.g., splitting the "good" and the "bad" onto different people), supervisors and others in the workplace may need to compare notes and develop a united policy in handling such employees. Although the knowledge of such a condition may facilitate tolerance of periodic emotionality, particularly if regressions are occasional and stress related, the borderline employee needs gently but directly to be confronted with what is unacceptable about the problematic work behavior. For some, an ongoing relationship with a therapist who is expert in working with such conditions may need to be strongly encouraged.

Histrionic Personality Disorder

Histrionic personality disorder is thought to be characterized by an other-directed character style in which flamboyance, excitement-seeking and attention-seeking behavior, and exaggeration are used in an attempt to maintain rather superficial relationships for purposes of getting needs met by being cared for by others (American Psychiatric Association, 1987; Millon, 1981; Pfohl, 1991). When such needs are not met, the histrionic personality may become petulant or develop conversion symptoms (deLeon, Saiz-Ruiz, Chinchilla, & Morales, 1987; Drossman, 1982; Slavney, Teitelbaum, & Chase, 1985). Some researchers (e.g., Standage, Bilsbury, Jain, & Smith, 1984) have attributed the histrionic disorder to difficulties in social role taking such that these people may be poor at understanding how their behavior is viewed by others in the environment.

Although many studies (e.g., Reich, 1987; Stangler & Printz, 1980) have reported this disorder to be more prevalent among women than men and although there is general consensus that hysterical characteristics are more commonly ascribed to women than men even by mental health professionals (Slavney, 1984), the data are not universally consistent (see, e.g., Nestadt et al.,

1990). Furthermore, Chodoff (1982) aptly noted that hysterical personality characteristics may be seen as a caricature of femininity that develops under conditions of male domination. Others have identified an apparent sex bias in the diagnosis of women with this disorder (M. R. Ford & Widiger, 1989; S. Hamilton, Rothbart, & Dawes, 1986). Moreover, cultural differences may influence the form that hysterical symptoms take (e.g., Makaremi, 1990; Pierloot & Ngoma, 1988).

Nestadt et al. (1990) reported a prevalence rate of 2.1% in the general population, although more people may manifest hysterical symptoms without the personality disorder (Marsden, 1986). Although those with a histrionic personality disorder may be at increased risk for depression, they experience less severe depression, manifest less anxiety, and have less severe illness than nonhysterical patients (Paykel, Klerman, & Prusoff, 1976).

In the workplace, hysterical personality traits are likely to prevent an individual from moving upward within the organization. Attention-seeking behavior and superficial charm in the absence of substantive accomplishment may make for mutual frustration, and the employee may react with impotent anger if he or she perceives that her or his accomplishments have been undervalued.

Interventions should be reality focused to help the individual identify the reality of the work situation as perceived by others, particularly those in authority, and to help the individual develop better skills in the workplace so that there is less need to look to omnipotently perceived others to get needs met.

Supervisors working with such employees may need to be highly supportive of work-relevant, positive behavior but somewhat neutral when excessive praise and attention are sought apparently for their own sake. Gentle, reality-based guidance (as, stylistically, might be given a child; e.g., "I really appreciate your effort, but you need to work a little harder on this project on your own to make sure it's completed by the deadline") may protect the employee's self-esteem while refocusing the histrionic characteristics to work-related causes. Histrionic employees' characteristics may prove adaptive when directed at work requiring positive enthusiasm unfettered by complexity (e.g., some types of sales and marketing).

Narcissistic Personality Disorder

People with narcissistic personality disorders or traits often experience problems with intimacy (Kirman, 1983) and are frequently described by others as being grandiose (Berg, 1990; Gunderson, Ronningstam, & Bodkin, 1990; Ronningstam & Gunderson, 1988, 1989, 1990, 1991), self-focused (Raskin & Shaw, 1988), self-important, indifferent to the feelings and reactions of others, and expecting unearned high praise no matter what the actual effort or result (American Psychiatric Association, 1987; Blechner, 1986; Grey, 1987; Gunderson, Ronningstam, & Smith, 1991; Kohut & Wolf, 1978; Messer, 1976; Mitchell, 1991; Ronningstam & Gunderson, 1988). With their sense of entitlement and grandiosity, they do not understand or perceive that others do not share their inflated view of their competencies and worth.[6] Dysfunctional behavior associated with such personalities may include substance abuse (Woodham, 1987) and pathological gambling (Rosenthal, 1986).

Retrospective diagnoses of actual and fictional characters in terms of narcissistic personality abound (e.g., Lake, 1988; Marohn, 1987; Mitchell, 1990, 1991; D. F. Nelson, 1988; Orland, Orland, & Orland, 1990; Wolf & Wolf, 1979); often, such real and imagined characters suffer an unfortunate or dramatic demise. Because such characters (imagined or real) *believe* that they are highly accomplished, they may direct little effort toward self-improvement (Millon, 1981); the capacity for self-deception may be high. They often have difficulty differentiating self from others and wish from reality, such that events are constructed and interpreted on the basis of wishes and desired outcomes rather than actual reality or sensitivity to the feelings and reactions of others (Lawner, 1985). Paranoid features may also be part of the disorder (A. Wilson, 1989).

Underlying the inflated self-view, of course, is likely to be a very fragile sense of self-esteem, masking intense feelings of

---

[6] This statement is true for at least one major type of narcissistic personality disorder. Gabbard (1989) reported a second type of narcissist who *is* aware of the impact that his or her behavior has on others.

shame and inadequacy (A. P. Morrison, 1983; J. O'Leary & Wright, 1986). Moreover, some researchers have suggested that grandiosity, narcissism, dominance, and hostility form a cluster of traits, with grandiosity serving as a means of containing hostility (Raskin, Novacek, & Hogan, 1991).

Although the evidence is limited, there is some indication of a sex difference in favor of men (Carroll, 1989; Philipson, 1985; Wright, O'Leary, & Balkin, 1989), although men and women may differ on average in the specific aspects of narcissism that are manifest and that cause distress (J. O'Leary & Wright, 1986; Richman & Flaherty, 1988; P. J. Watson, Taylor, & Morris, 1987).

The diagnosis of narcissistic personality may be established through clinical interview or psychological testing. Raskin and Terry (1988) developed a Narcissistic Personality Inventory (see also Emmons, 1987; Mullins & Kopelman, 1988), and various profiles measuring this construct have been developed, including the Minnesota Multiphasic Personality Inventory (Raskin & Novacek, 1989), the California Psychological Inventory (Wink & Gough, 1990), and the Thematic Apperception Test (Shulman & Ferguson, 1988; Shulman, McCarthy, & Ferguson, 1988).

In some occupations, narcissism is apparently common and may even be the norm (e.g., Meloy, 1986), although empirical research has not always supported popular notions of which occupational groups (e.g., psychotherapists) are excessively populated with narcissists (J. Z. Clark, 1991; M. J. Miller, Smith, Wilkinson, & Tobacyk, 1987). Moreover, complex patterns may belie apparent occupational group characteristics. For example, Carroll (1987) found business students who were male and high in power needs also to be high on a measure of narcissistic personality. Although Fast (1975) correctly noted that the narcissist may gravitate to creative work and away from goal-directed action, such attraction may be at least as much related to the perceived prestige value of creative work as to psychodynamic explanations of such appeal. To the extent that work or studies call for attention to detail and actual as opposed to perceived accomplishment, the narcissist may be at a disadvantage (H. S. Baker, 1979).

In the workplace, the grandiose style may be inappropriate and even result in termination (causing serious narcissistic injury to personal pride) or a rocky road of continual confrontations concerning the discrepancy between real and perceived accomplishment. On the other hand, those with narcissistic personalities may also be found among charismatic leaders (Post, 1986), with a continual search by the narcissist for adulating followers who will confirm their sense of omnipotence. Biscardi and Schill (1985) found a relation between narcissism and Machiavellianism (Biscardi & Schill, 1985).

Effective treatment with such cases requires the creation of a therapeutic relationship, which is difficult because it is commonly impeded by the personality characteristics of the narcissist (Adler, 1979, 1980; Spitzer, 1990). From this relationship, the client may over time be helped to construct a more reality-based (if less grandiose) sense of self and personal accomplishments. Masterson (1990) argued that therapy with such clients should be directed toward the interactions between the therapist and the client, emphasizing the feelings of vulnerability in the therapeutic relationship. Kernberg (1989) suggested that the pathological grandiose self first (if gradually) be dissolved, helping the client subsequently to develop a true sense of self. The fragility of the underlying personality structure must be taken into account; confrontation, even of a gentle nature, may cause premature injury to the client's self-esteem (R. Fischer, 1989).

In the presence of work dysfunctions, the therapist may need to strike a fine balance between more accurate environmental perception (with the risk of being perceived by the client as taking the "side" of supervisors or co-workers) and ego support. Recognizing the limited self-esteem underlying individuals with narcissistic personality may protect the therapist from excessively strong countertransference reactions (Kirman, 1983; Kohut, 1971; Madonna, 1991) and from prematurely aggressive intervention. Overall, the difficulties of working with and obtaining lasting change with such individuals should not be underestimated.

The next case illustrates some of the frustrations of working with narcissistic individuals who experience work dysfunctions. Engaging them in treatment can be difficult, particularly if they have been referred because of difficulties in the work role.

Case 7.3
A Legend in Her Own Mind

A self-important, well-coiffed woman in her fifties who worked in computer sales, Louise was mandatorily referred under her company's employee assistance program (EAP) by her supervisor. She appeared with great reluctance at the psychologist's office, impeccably dressed and coiffed, wearing expensive, dangling gold jewelry. She was extremely upset with her supervisor for requiring her to participate in the EAP.

To hear her tell it, Louise's role in forming the branch of her employing organization was critical. Although she was indeed one of the employees at this company location with the longest tenure, her role had essentially been that of a salesperson, not a manager. She had been moderately effective in that role but had had minimal organizational impact. Now, her productivity was down, and her regal style was creating problems for her supervisor, her co-workers, and a few of the company's clients.

Her supervisor perhaps erred in mandating EAP referral for so resistant a potential client. However, he did not want to fire her but increasingly found her self-serving, defensive views divisive. Although angry at having been required to participate in the EAP, the client talked excessively in the assessment session, and it was with great difficulty that the evaluating therapist managed to get her to leave the session at the end of her appointed time. Her dominance of the session expressed her need to control and protect herself from her rage and narcissistic injury at having been sent for counseling.

Although the client could not be enticed to undergo therapy (which would have required acknowledging a personal flaw, something she could not have tolerated), she instead reported back a few weeks after her initial visit that she and her supervisor had met, worked through their differences, and developed a more effective working relationship.

Paranoid Personality

The primary characteristics of the paranoid personality include a tendency toward suspiciousness, heightened sensitivity to nonverbal (LaRusso, 1978) and negative (Heilbrun, 1973) cues, chronic and excessive jealously, external attribution of blame, belief in hidden (and generally malevolently perceived) motives in others (Thompson-Pope & Turkat, 1988; Turkat, Keane, & Thompson-Pope, 1990), lack of cooperation with others (Turkat & Banks, 1987), and secretiveness (Akhtar, 1990; American Psychiatric Association, 1987). An underlying dynamic of shame, fear of passivity, and perceived inadequacy may constitute a core psychodynamic component (Colby, Faught, & Parkison, 1979; Meissner, 1979; Sparr, Boehnlein, & Cooney, 1986), which may be masked by overtly presented misperceptions of grandiosity and excessive influence (Romney, 1987). Paranoid features may overlap with narcissistic ones (Jette & Winnett, 1987; A. Wilson, 1989).

At their best, paranoid personalities may be seen as manifesting appropriate vigilance in pursuit of worthwhile objectives; at their worst, they are viewed as hostile, defensive, and stubborn. Positions of perceived powerlessness may contribute to the belief of externalized control and foment the development of paranoid dynamics (Mirowsky & Ross, 1983). When the paranoid personality is frustrated (e.g., when their rather grandiose expectations are not met), intense anger or depression may be unleashed (Bonime, 1982; Lasaga, 1980). Projection is a favored defense, namely, attributing one's own motives and behavior to someone else (although not all studies have supported this formulation; see Chalus, 1976). Paranoid personalities are apparently more common among men than women (Reich, 1987).

People with paranoid personalities may be quite successful in their work, and, depending on the specific circumstances, may actually be seen by others as leaders (deVries, 1977). Because people with paranoid personalities may be able to channel considerable energies in the direction of goal accomplishment or counter perceived enemies' threats, they may achieve considerable success at work, particularly if the work itself is basically compatible with their personality style. Thus, in highly competitive industries and jobs that call for combativeness against well-defined "enemies," paranoid personality styles may be functional. However, behavior that is not kept in check or suspicion that is directed toward co-workers and subordinates can result in considerable negative fallout.

Paranoid personalities are viewed as generally difficult to change through intervention (Conte, Plutchik, Picard, Karasu, & Vaccaro, 1988; Sparr, Boehnlein, & Cooney, 1986). Acute paranoid episodes may require management with medication. Long-term therapy based on a slowly developing, trustful relationship may prove most effective in moderating this style. Accepting the client despite cold, questioning, sometimes vengeful, jealous, and suspicious behavior may arouse difficult countertransference issues.

A few practical suggestions can be made for managing those with paranoid personality disorders in the workplace. Care should be taken to keep workplace assignments rational and straightforward. Suspicious questioning of others' motives and of reasons for assignments should be expected and may be countered with quiet, calm explanations of the real-life rationales for particular assignments. Because people with paranoid personalities are generally intelligent, they may respond well to tight logic and an apparently stubborn refusal to back down or avoid the paranoid personality. Keeping the likely underlying shame dynamic in mind may assist those interacting with paranoid personalities to be more accepting of them and to attempt to engage them on neutral rather than overly charged territory.

When stress exacerbates the paranoid condition, supervisors and co-workers may wish to differentiate for the employee the real and imagined nature of the perceptions. False perceptions should be calmly labeled as such and the employee encouraged in a calm but firm manner to comply with relevant organizational regulations and policies. If acutely problematic behavior persists, mandatory referral to a mental health professional should be considered. Although a supervisor may tolerate a certain amount of mildly abusive comments, he or she should take care not to be unduly tolerant given that this may discourage respect. Knowing the limits and boundaries of tolerated behavior may assist the paranoid employee in maintaining work behavior within acceptable boundaries.

Treating people with paranoid personalities may prove frustrating. Too ingratiating a role can send the client fleeing from the threat of intimacy, whereas one perceived to be overly negative can cause the client to aggressively attack. The following case illustrates the issues.

Case 7.4
A Paranoid Personality At Work

A 27-year-old man, Thomas was referred for counseling after a volatile conflict with his supervisor. Although a supervisor himself, Thomas viewed his role as having been exploited by his own manager. He had applied ten times to be transferred out of the section but had been inevitably turned down each time. Interviews with the supervisor who had referred him indicated that his concerns were not well-founded.

In light of Thomas's paranoid tendencies and perceptions of victimization and exploitation, the therapist proceeded cautiously to avoid unduly arousing the client's suspicion. While attempting to form a relationship with the client, the therapist gently noted that the client's manner of approaching his supervisor might partially account for the negative reaction he had experienced. Active denial and a sense of rejection ensued. The therapist patiently examined the client's hurt feelings resulting from his perception of having been criticized and then withdrew to more neutral territory to await the next opportunity to capture the client's attention and interest.

Over the course of his brief therapy, Thomas was engaged into at least a working relationship if not a fully therapeutic one. When, in the course of the treatment, it became apparent that cocaine abuse was responsible for an exacerbation of his symptoms, his therapist was able to assist in getting him into a drug detoxification program. After completion of the program, the client continued for a period in therapy. The paranoid dynamics remained at the end of this work-related intervention, but the client was better able to manage his behavior in the workplace and to accept, if grudgingly, the authority of his supervisor. His supervisor was pleased that Thomas was able to be kept on in the job and with the fact that his problematic behavior was more under control.

Schizoid and Schizotypal Personality Disorders

Schizoid and schizoptypal disorders are more severe than many of the other personality disorders. They have as central characteristics avoidance of others, severe deficits in relating to others, generalized withdrawal from life, and cognitive skills deficits (Walsh, 1990), although none of these are generally as severe or psychotic as in the Axis I condition of schizophrenia (Kendler, 1985). Among the personality disorders, schizotypal conditions may overlap with borderline conditions (George & Soloff, 1986; Stone, 1983; Widiger, Frances, Warner, & Bluhm, 1986) and obsessive–compulsive conditions (Jenike, Baer, & Carey, 1986; Stanley, Turner, & Borden, 1990). Schizoid and schizotypal personality disorders may also deteriorate into psychotic conditions, and there is limited evidence that poor work adjustment may be associated with greater likelihood of later schizophrenic decompensation (Fenton & McGlashan, 1989). Those with schizoid personalities would be expected to have limited desire for and interest in close relationships with others, to be somewhat insensitive to the reactions of others, and generally to be seen as cold and aloof. Schizotypal personality disorder adds to this cognitive distortions and more bizarre behavior (American Psychiatric Association, 1987; M. Stone, 1985).

Neither of these two types of personality disorder is likely to be found with any frequency in the work setting unless a job is quite autonomous or is a low-level position in which aberrations of behavior do not create serious problems. Therapeutic approaches may need to emphasize supportive, reality-based interventions rather than methods appropriate for more neurotic conditions (Robbins, 1988), and considerable care must be taken in not moving too aggressively before there is some relationship on which to build. The fragility of the defenses needs to be respected. Psychotropic medications may prove beneficial in at least certain phases of treatment (e.g., Serban & Siegel, 1984).

At work, such employees require both interpersonal distance and quiet, nonthreatening support. Such personalities may be well-suited to isolated, presumably low-level jobs with limited complexity. Positions in which monitoring can be impersonal (e.g., by computer) and in which there is some structure and pacing inherent in the work itself may be especially suitable. During acute episodes of schizoid disturbance, prompt referral for supportive counseling and/or psychopharmaceutical management may be needed.

Summary

Personality disorders will likely account for a large portion of work dysfunctions resulting from mental health problems. Although the prognosis for interventions with clients suffering personality disorders is generally poor, the workplace may potentially provide an oasis for relatively normalized behavior in an otherwise problematic life. Nonetheless, accommodations will still need to be made, and maintenance more than recovery may be the most probable end result. Close coordination between the therapist and the workplace may increase the likelihood of therapeutic effectiveness and workplace adjustment. With proper management, the workplace itself may ultimately prove more effective than therapy in "treating" many of the personality disorders.

8

Work Counseling With the Creative

The Creative Context

E ven if it were true that everybody has some creativity, that originality is a continuous rather than dichotomous variable, and that under the right circumstances or environmental influences we could all be more innovative (e.g., Amabile, 1990), some people have demonstrably more "creativity" than others. Some have more than others of whatever it is that makes people able to generate the new and different—to give readers, viewers, consumers, and participants new perspectives and allow them to experience emotions more deeply or perhaps for the first time.

What is creativity? As Spearman (1930) wrote, "The term 'creating' means the bringing into existence of that which did not ever exist previously; it signifies much the same as originating, generating, producing, making, and the like" (p. 1). More recently, Mumford and Gustafson's (1988) construct of a "creativity syndrome" astutely identified several important components of creativity that cut across diverse areas of generative production. Note, though, that creativity can span a wide range of domains and talent. Whereas there are very few people in any era or any field who merit the designation "genius," there are many who could be considered "creative." The latter exist in large enough numbers that practicing psychotherapists will encounter them routinely among their clients. Perhaps too much of the literature has focused on highly noted cases such as Emily Dickinson (Hirschorn, 1991), William James (Anderson, 1987), and Walt Whitman (Gutman, 1987) and not enough on people who make so-called lesser contributions of a creative nature but who still face psychological problems in their creative expression.

Why single out creative people as a specific population whose work difficulties merit special focus? Although the work of creative people may be no more or less important than that of other occupational groups, there appears to be some predictability to work issues that arise for those whose business it is to generate the new and different and to shape the society of the future. If civilization is deeply indebted for its progress to such individuals, whose struggles and contributions may forever be inadequately recognized, then psychotherapists who desire to counsel those with work dysfunctions should be prepared to help such clients cope with their probably inevitable periods of frustration and difficulty. Such efforts serve not only the creative themselves but societal functioning and long-term productivity as well.

If the great creators are ultimately held in exalted esteem by society (as Rothenberg, 1990a, contended), they are not necessarily honored at the outset of or often during their careers. As Sandblom (1989) noted,

> A true artist must be a pioneer and runs the risk of becoming a pathfinder without fans or followers. Some artists can be totally crushed by lack of appreciation and give up creative work; others, mentally stronger, like Cezanne, will stubbornly continue their lonely road, far from the madding crowd. (p. 36)

Creativity is publicly regarded with considerable ambivalence. Typically, society most reveres those whose creativity has already made them part of the establishment—whose works, often radical and rejected at the time of their initial conception, have passed the test of time. This usually means that the creative work has been validated by others with supposedly relevant expertise and then consensually accepted by the wider society as being "important." The viewer, reader, or consumer can then participate in the product of creativity from a comfortably safe distance. Such an appreciation can itself be an act of social compliance in that the audience may value only that which is ultimately judged important or sensible by others (see N. Branden, 1962). And although the recognized creator may be well-regarded, those who are in the process of establishing themselves as creative talents are frequently treated with skepticism and derision by a public that considers itself superior. Yet, society depends for its survival on new directions and new solutions to the complex problems presented by each age and time.

If the creative individual is often rejected by society, the process of generating the truly creative idea or product itself places the creator by definition at or beyond the edge of the border of accepted thought, practice, or understanding. As Michener (1991) put it in his novel *The Novel*,

> The artist must always be somewhat opposed to society— against received knowledge. He must be prepared to explore strange alleyways, to rebuke accepted wisdom, to confuse and challenge and reconstruct new patterns. The artist is by nature a semi-outlaw. Van Gogh assaults our sense of color, Wagner our inherited ideas about what acceptable sound is. . . . People at large don't want artists, don't understand them, never find them totally acceptable till they're dead. . . . [They are] athwart the grain, and the moment they [try] to conform to the grain, they [lose] their forward thrust—they [are] doomed to mediocrity. (pp. 213–214)
>
> An artist is a creative man who cannot and indeed should not lead a normal life. He should find sustenance from trusted friends like himself. His task is to provide society with a fresh and sometimes necessarily acid portrait of itself. (p. 215)

Truly creative work can be psychologically threatening and anxiety creating to both society more generally and the creator (see Rothenberg, 1990a, 1990b). It forces a reconceptualization of thoughts or feelings. Almost by definition, the creator challenges and refuses to accept current views of what constitutes reality, appropriate behavior, or established solutions to persistent problems. The creator generally works with greater effort, with smaller immediate reward, and with less social acceptance than do those in most other occupations. The creative efforts of a few in any generation result in spectacular fortunes (although rarely at the outset of the career) and phenomenal public or professional recognition; most, however, do not.

The truly creative person lives and works at the edge of the old and the new; loneliness and psychological distress are frequent companions (Tick, 1987). Other aspects of the creative personality that may differentiate the individual from the larger society and contribute to a sense of differentness include homosexuality, which is apparently more common among creative individuals than among the general population (see Rothenberg, 1990b). Although homosexuality is by no means a necessary condition for creativity, neither is it unexpected. Its apparently higher incidence among creative individuals may add to the basic tendency to see oneself as different from the mainstream and contribute to the artist's sense of separateness, sometimes making intervention more complex.

The creative person may work for low to nonexistent wages (or work in a personally undesired occupation or job to support the artistic "habit") and may lack assurance of stability or positive outcome. Even well-established creative people, such as in the performing arts, speak of the feeling with each project that it may well be their last. And because creative people generate more unusual ideas and juxtapositions, failure is likely to be encountered with some predictability (Albert & Runco, 1990).

Artists are commonly neglected during their careers, only to be held in high esteem by the public after their death. However, it is the esteem of other artists that may be of greater importance and sustaining power. The case of Joseph Conrad is illustrative:

> Born in 1857 in the Polish Ukraine, to impoverished landed gentry with a family history of courageous, if reckless, pa-

triotism, Joseph Conrad (ne Jozef Teodor Konrad Nalecz Kor-
zeniowski) became in the course of his difficult lifetime a
paragon of the post-Flaubertian literary artist: the writer of
idiosyncratic and obsessive genius who is neglected for most
of his career by the general reading public, but celebrated by
his fellow writers; the virtual martyr to this art who exhaust
himself in its service, as in the worship of an inscrutable
god.[1]

Often working in isolation (Kavaler-Adler, 1991) and relative
poverty,[2] creative individuals may be rejected for what to them
is the most important aspect of their lives. Vacillating between
productive peaks and infertile valleys, artists would seem naturally in need of what psychotherapy has most to offer: understanding, acceptance, and assistance in productively living what
is often a difficult life. Yet, artists are also typically individualists,
often having little interest in interpersonal relationships and being
willing to function quite independently from others (Lawrence,
1962).

Engaging in psychotherapy and thus relying on an outsider
for aid may not therefore happen readily or without a struggle.
Although the narcissistic features of creativity may be compatible
with the introspection required by many forms of psychotherapy,
the artist may lack the willingness to engage with another and
share issues of the creative product (which may at times be like
a surrogate child; see Corney, 1988). In effect, psychotherapy
may violate the life and work conditions that the artist has come
to expect if not require. Penetrating this wall of professional
isolation should therefore be approached with care.

---

[1] From "The Man Who Detested the Sea" [review of *Joseph Conrad, A Biob-
liography*], by J. C. Oates, *The New York Times Book Review*, 1991, April 14, p.
15. Copyright © 1991 by The New York Times Company. Reprinted by permission.

[2] Actors Equity, for example, recently reported that only 41.4% of its 35,252
paid members nationally worked at least one week in the previous year (Weber,
1993).

The Emotional Needs
of the Artist

Freedom and autonomy to create, coupled with the discipline of directed effort and the expectation of predictable failure in the pursuit of perhaps ultimate "success" are important aspects of many types of creative effort. The sensitive artist will likely suffer many crises and much alienation over the career course and is almost always highly and intrinsically invested in the work (Amabile, 1990). Indeed, it is the work, not the rewards of the work, that the artist values (Csikszentmihalyi, 1990). In fallow periods, when creative productivity is absent or lagging or, ultimately, when a talent enters its inevitable denouement or diminution, the artist may be especially vulnerable and most in need of outside assistance, including the type that a psychotherapist can provide. Rachel Hecker, a Houston artist, described such a period as follows:

> I was taking a break from painting; my work had started to feel repetitive and that's horrible—like living death. During that time off, I tried to think about what was important for me about painting, what was missing and what was making it a kind of joyless experience. I realized that I hadn't included the possibility of discovery in my work; I was making paintings that were either so theoretical or so meticulous in their design and craft, that I knew exactly what the image should be like before I made it; making the image felt almost machine-like. . . . I want to invest my work with a sense of possibilities and new discoveries in that way.[3]

The problems that creative people experience in their work do not necessarily differ in kind from the problems of those less creative. Boredom, alienation, and the experience of work that is joyless are concerns hardly unique to artists. What is different is that for the artist there is often little separation between person

---

[3] From "Rachel Hecker, Artist," *Houston Press*, 1991, July 18, p. 6. Copyright © 1991 by the Houston Press. Reprinted by permission.

and work: "My art, *c'est moi.*" Because the artist's product is closely tied to individual identity, periods of work dysfunction may weigh more heavily on the psyche and may more directly call for outside intervention. The experience of personal rejection associated with rejection of one's work can be associated with self-consciousness and vulnerability, both aspects of shame (C. Goldberg, 1988).

Moreover, the creative individual works within a social context, imposing his or her own talent against the known constraints in which a talent must operate. As Gleick described,

> Creative artists in modern times have labored under the terrible weight of the demand for novelty. Mozart's contemporaries expected him to work within a fixed, shared framework, not to break the bonds of convention. The standard forms of the sonata, symphony and opera were established before his birth and hardly changed in his lifetime; the rules of harmonic progression made a cage as unyielding as the sonnet did for Shakespeare. As unyielding and as liberating— for later critics have found the creators' genius in the counterpoint of structure and freedom, rigor and inventiveness.[4]

Perhaps because there are so often few extrinsic rewards to go around, creative individuals are often described as experiencing professional jealousy and resentment of one another. As John Cheever (1991) put it, "The rivalry among novelists is quite as intense as that among sopranos" (p. 330). Professional jealousy occurs, of course, in many occupational contexts. Among artists, many factors may account for heightened jealousy, including differential rewards that may seem to occur independent of talent (with people of popular appeal but perceived lower talent sometimes earning much larger rewards than those whose work is more esoteric). In addition, the strong views that artists hold concerning what constitutes good and bad art may make them sensitive to feeling that others' work is less worthy than

---

[4] From "Part Showman, All Genius," by J. Gleick, *The New York Times Magazine*, 1992, September 20, p. 44. Copyright © by The New York Times Company. Reprinted by permission.

their own. Finally, artists may simply experience normal feelings more intensely.

Much understanding of artists' work dysfunctions can be gained by exploring their interpersonal relationships with other artists and with important individuals in their lives who may not themselves be creative. When there is persistent rivalry, jealousy, and excessive competitiveness, these issues may need to become a part of the therapeutic exploration. Professional jealousies do not necessarily have their origins in sibling rivalries in the family of origin.

Finally, artists can be markedly impractical when it comes to day-to-day affairs of living. Idealism in values and work (to which there is often an intense, if not excessive, commitment) may make for good art but strained interpersonal relationships, particularly when one's life partner or associates are forced to contend with the more mundane aspects of living. Furthermore, self-absorption and personal narcissism may combine to create intense involvements and unique perspectives that may be alienating in an interpersonal sense, thus increasing the artist's estrangement from others.

Diagnostic Issues

Within such a context, creative occupational pursuits call for certain characteristics of interest, ability, and personality (see Lowman, 1991b) that almost by definition alienate the artist from the status quo and from mainstream thinking (see also Gough, 1992). Artists, whatever their specific art form, are apparently far more likely than people in general to suffer psychological disturbance, especially affective disorders (see Andreason & Canter, 1974; Andreason & Powers, 1975; Jamison, 1989, 1992; Martindale, 1989; Prentky, 1989; for another view, see Rothenberg, 1990a). This is illustrated by the case of the late novelist Graham Greene, about whom his fellow writer Paul Theroux wrote in an obituary,

> He had a comic side that was so profound it verged on sadness (comedy is very near to tragedy, he often said) and

touched mania. In his autobiography, he was frank about the mania; he went further and described how he was a manic–depressive, his bipolar nature having been responsible for novels as diverse as "Travels with My Aunt" and "The Heart of the Matter," giddiness on the one hand, gloom on the other. . . . I think he liked putting on his mask and being a fictional character. . . . Temperamentally, he was much like the central character, Bendrix in "The End of the Affair"—a lonely man, capable of great sympathy but with a sliver of ice in his heart. I feel lucky to have been his friend, but I doubt that I knew him—I don't think anyone really did.[5]

The artist may be estranged from others in part because of rejection by them, but the benefits to the artist of isolation and distance should not be underestimated. A preference for being *un*known by others may keep alive the idea that the artist is somehow special and different, that creativity somehow occurs within a different species or universe than that unfortunately inhabited by the less creatively endowed.

The heightened emotionality and sensitivity of those with creative talents is well-noted (see Martindale, 1989, who postulated a general theory of oversensitivity and disinhibition among the creatively talented). Lester (1990) studied the cases of 13 well-known novelists and poets who committed suicide and in another study (Lester, 1991) 70 American writers who either committed suicide or experienced chronic alcohol abuse. Chronic depression and substance abuse, along with doubts about one's ability, were prominent in the histories, a finding similar to ones noted by other researchers (e.g., Dardis, 1989; D. W. Goodwin, 1988; Ludwig, 1990; Rothenberg, 1990b). In an analysis of longevity rates among the creative, Kaun (1991) found that writers tended to live shorter lives than people in other occupations.

Talent often comes at the price of emotional disquietude. Creative people in general appear to be at risk for emotional dis-

---

[5] From "Theroux: An Edwardian on the Concorde: Graham Greene as I Knew Him" by P. Theroux, *The New York Times Book Review*, 1991, April 21, p. 15. Copyright © 1991 by The New York Times Company. Reprinted by permission.

turbance and for leading lives characterized, at least partly, by emotional turmoil. Whether this is because creative individuals experience more emotionally trying experiences or because they simply respond more intensely to regular experiences is unclear. Moreover, whatever the increased risk for suicide, most writers and artists do not commit or attempt suicide. Although suicide is always a risk to be considered with any psychotherapy client (particularly in cases of affective disorder), it certainly is not inevitable with all creative clients.

Is it possible to be creative but not neurotic or substance abusing? Presumably so, with examples such as writer–attorney–insurance executive Wallace Stevens coming to mind (Martindale, 1989; see also Kerr, Shaffer, Chambers, & Hallowell, 1991). As Schiff (1992/1993) put it,

> Crazy artists, or flamboyant ones, can be strangely comforting. We feel we understand where their visions come from, we're lulled by the symmetry of turbulent art and turbulent lives. But what about those other, more enigmatic figures, the placid and the sane, the middle-class, burgher-like souls who betray no evidence of the visionary within until they apply paint to canvas—or pen to paper . . . ? (p. 158)

Nonetheless, the emotional conflict and intense reactions that make for excellence in creative pursuits so often cause problems for the creative individual that the therapist should query carefully in instances of their reported absence. The therapist in such cases should determine whether the client's behavior is masking neurosis or other emotional disturbance, putting forth a facade to the therapist or in the work, or experiencing a conflict reported to affect the personal life and be unrelated to work life when it is actually a displacement of a creative, work-related conflict.

Careful assessment and evaluation of the sources of the immediate conflict are suggested, as is obtaining a detailed psychological history charting prior episodes of mental dysfunction. The history should include assessment of current and past substance abuse given that such difficulties are often part of the lifestyle of many in the creative professions. Intensive treatment of substance abuse may be needed before more intensive individual work on areas of conflict is possible.

Treatment Approaches

General Issues

Although the work and life situation of the artist can cause serious personal pain and estrangement, the therapist must be clear that the goal of treatment is not necessarily the removal of neurotic conflict or the creation of a life devoid of psychological pain or distress. Psychotherapy directed toward the goal of creating a "well-balanced," quiescent life devoid of inner conflict would appear to be missing the point. Neurosis and affective disorder are the frequent (for some, continual) companions of the creative (Prentky, 1989). And although I concur with Rothenberg's (1990a) formulation that the creative process usually occurs independently of mental illness and is not necessarily helped by it, the removal of conflict, neurotic or otherwise, is not necessarily the goal of psychological treatment.

Rather, the psychotherapist's goal in working with creative individuals may best be conceptualized as including (a) acceptance and validation of the creative aspects of the person (which may not have occurred in the client's formative years and indeed which may not be occurring in the client's adult life), (b) channeling of neurotic conflicts into productively creative work, (c) emotional support during creatively infertile periods, (d) greater awareness and understanding (but not necessarily change) of psychological conflict, and (e) assistance in interacting more effectively with the "real world" with which the creative individual is often ill-prepared to deal.

Thus, the therapist aims at the least to dampen the dysfunctional aspects of conflict or neurosis, not necessarily to remove conflict altogether. Other relevant therapeutic goals include helping such clients successfully weather periods of emotional upheaval and characteristic lulls in the creative process. This may call for supportive and/or interpretative psychological counseling but not necessarily life-style change or personality reorganization.

It should also be noted that if the client is acutely psychotic or is experiencing a life-threatening emergency, more radical intervention may be needed before the individual is able to work on in-depth understanding. In such cases, the creative aspects of the individual are relevant but tangential. The focus must first be on containing the immediate crisis (i.e., addressing suicidality, substance abuse, or psychosis as a primary treatment goal). Focus can then shift to work-related issues if they are relevant. However, even in treating a severely impaired creative client, the therapist must be sensitive to the nuances of the creative work process.

Presumptions concerning the work of other occupational groups should not automatically be assumed to apply to the work of creative individuals. Although depression or substance abuse may cause the creative client to present as if the work were not a central life interest, quite the contrary is usually the case. Often, it is the artist's perceived inability to be creatively productive that precipitates a depressive episode or encourages substance abuse as a way of coping. The therapist needs to respect and understand the creative process and be able to communicate sensitivity to, and preferably appreciation for, the vicissitudes of creativity. This may be easier for the therapists who are themselves artistic and who struggle with the ups and downs of writing or performing.[6]

The goals in treating work dysfunctions of creative clients should be continuously defined as the therapy proceeds. Given that creative individuals typically respond poorly to direct efforts at control, they may resist therapy that they perceive to imply a long-term relationship with no end in sight. It therefore may be more advantageous to present treatment as focusing on the presenting difficulties and symptomatic relief. More in-depth in-

---

[6] Interestingly, the occupational interest code ascribed to clinical and counseling psychologists by Holland's (1985) interest schema is Social–Investigative–Artistic (Holland, 1990). In the artistic interest area are found most of the so-called creative occupations.

tervention may then follow. Open-ended, overly analytical approaches may play into the resistance, allowing the client to avoid coming to terms with what is creating the immediate difficulty.

Therapeutic techniques such as reframing or reconceptualizing may be particularly appropriate for creative clients, who are often intense, acutely perceptive, and sensitive. Building on the fundamental narcissism that often accompanies creativity (e.g., Fine, 1980, 1984), the therapist might present anxiety as a badge of honor of creativity while helping the client understand that the conflicts are currently working against rather than for the client's creative efforts. Assisting the client in channeling what might in some contexts be viewed as neurotic characteristics (e.g., self-absorption, intensely focused concentration, isolation, depression) into productive creative outlets may serve therapeutic goals. The therapist may help the client become less perfectionistic and more accepting of his or her own flaws as well as those in the world more generally (Rothenberg, 1987).

Creative individuals can be quite persuasive and dramatic with their presenting complaints. It is important for the therapist not to overreact or inappropriately become part of the drama. Although the intensity of the client's pain can be quite real, the therapist must not become too enmeshed in the client's alarmed view of the world. In the artist's exquisite sensitivity may be intense focus on the belief that he or she has no productive creativity left and that because the state of the world in which the artist must create is so dismal and appreciation so limited, there is no hope. It is the therapist's task to keep focus on productive accomplishment, past and future. Empathizing with the depth of the client's current feelings does not mean accepting despair as the inevitable condition of the artist.

The therapist should seek an expertly struck balance between pushing the client toward a goal just beyond his or her current state and empathically communicating an in-depth understanding of the client's current withdrawal and despair. It is on the therapist's more optimistic and accurate perceptions of reality that a depressed or otherwise withdrawn creative client may need to rely to experience initial therapeutic progress.

The creative process itself may provide a useful focus for therapy with the creative client. With writers, for example, work specimens might be examined in the therapy session and the client given specific homework writing assignments. These might begin with simple tasks such as (for an avoidant writer) sitting at the writing desk for 15 minutes a day and writing at least a sentence or paragraph to bring to the next session. The goal of the therapist is often to serve as the ego force for the client to get the creative process back on track.

For other creative clients, the task may simply be to ride out a depressive interlude after completion of a major work. Sanctioning the idea of a vacation from creative productivity and a specific decision *not* to work for the present may be helpful during certain phases of the creative process. In such instances, the therapist should seek to normalize the ups and downs of creativity and help the individual accept that new experiences, information, and explorations of relationships are all relevant to the creative process.

Case 8.1
The Conflicted Sculptor

Brenda was an aspiring sculptor who came for counseling because she was unhappy with the small income she was making in her work. Her husband was generally supportive of her efforts but following a downturn in his business was feeling some financial pressure despite their being quite comfortable. The therapist asked Brenda to bring in samples of her work.

She brought to the next session an assortment of photographs of her work. Although each revealed obvious talent, the pieces differed significantly in their interest level. Ones that dealt with subjects with which she was familiar and psychologically invested were compelling and interesting in a way that the others were not. The therapist pointed out this discrepancy, with which Brenda fully concurred, noting that it was psychologically stressful to her to be what she thought was so self-revealing.

This led to exploration of her fears, which appeared exaggerated, as might be expected given that much of the association between an artist's work and his or her personal dynamics is visible only to those few who know the intimate details of the artist's life. In fact, this was the central creative issue for this talented artist. She was conflicted between revealing and withholding her innermost secrets (presumably, a shame dynamic; see Kaufman, 1985, 1989), the latter at the expense of her work.

There was no artful solution in this case. The therapist worked with the client on the underlying issues that disturbed her. However, she resented the intrusion into areas that she had become accustomed to concealing. Because she was not ready to change, the issue was not forced. (With creative individuals, perceived control must be very carefully managed.) She continued to sculpt, more aware of the conflict; later, when she was prepared to address the conflict, she returned to the therapist and rather quickly worked through the issue. Her creative work subsequently improved.

In general, the therapist must respect the delicacy of the creative process without becoming intimidated by it. Although artists can be fragile, they are rarely brittle and do not break as easily as the therapist might imagine. In addition to basic talent and temperament for creative work and inspiration, there is much that is mundane about the day-to-day creative process. As Rachel Hecker, a Houston artist, put it,

> There's a myth that artists go into their studio and that some kind of magic happens. My experience is that art is incredibly blue-collar. You have to work your ass off and think real tough and it doesn't end; you sweat. There's nothing glamorous about it. I've heard so many artists—mostly middle-aged men—talk about the magic, and people seem to want to buy into that kind of myth . . . An awful lot of the work is training and just practicing your craft. If there's any magic, it has to do with making something that hasn't been in the world before; for me, that's a very private moment. If there's magic, it only lasts for about one second. If I really started believing in the magic, then I wouldn't have to do all this work.[7]

---

[7] From "Rachel Hecker, Artist," *Houston Press*, 1991, July 18, p. 6. Copyright © 1991 by the Houston Press. Reprinted by permission.

Good timing, important in any psychotherapy, is especially relevant in working with the creative client. Too much pressure can result in stubborn resistance, whereas too little can fail to facilitate the therapeutic process. The creative client may need to be encouraged to continue the creative effort rather than wait until further along in the treatment process. There is a time to push and a time merely to be supportive; the therapist needs to know which is which.

Following the death of novelist–philosopher Ayn Rand, for example, a number of biographies appeared describing an apparently neurotic emotionality inconsistent with the image of the implacable moral heroine that Rand so consistently portrayed (see, e.g., B. Branden, 1986; N. Branden, 1989). After the completion of each of her significant novels, for example, she apparently spent much time in angry withdrawal, crying and nonproductive. After the publication of *Atlas Shrugged*, which she regarded as her premiere work, Rand never wrote another novel. Her personal life, always complex, seemingly deteriorated as she increasingly surrounded herself with fawning supporters and unchallenging admirers. Although she attributed "rescuing" her life to Nathaniel Branden, from whom she later dramatically broke off, it is unclear whether the aid Nathaniel Branden described in his memoir of their relationship (N. Branden, 1989) was in fact helpful or harmful to her creative pursuits. Indulgence in negative emotions can be dysfunctional, even for as apparently tyrannical an individual (and formidable a creative talent) as Ayn Rand.

A creative client is first a psychotherapy client, who like any other must be treated with the same compassion and firm assertion of therapeutic method. Countertransference feelings of being reluctant to "push" such clients, being intimidated by their fame or notoriety, or allowing for too long their feelings of despair or serious depression to go unchallenged do the client, creative or not, no favor and may unproductively prolong the therapy or result in its premature termination. Therapists who have some creative abilities themselves will have an easier time seeing the client as a hurting, distressed individual. Above all, the therapist must not fall in love with the client's work; in the context of psychotherapy, the focus is on the client, not his or her work.

To be effective in working with the creative client, the therapist should establish credibility with the client by communicating at some real emotional level an affinity, appreciation, and understanding of the creative process, with all its vicissitudes and personal anguish. Part of the therapeutic process includes cutting through the special defense of "differentness" that the client may feel while accepting the client on his or her own terms. At times, the creative client may need to be pushed, cajoled, or almost dragged across creative resistances and prevented from dwelling on negative perceptions. As Ayn Rand's first biographer, Barbara Branden (1986), noted, at the very end of her life, Rand started writing a screenplay of her novel *Atlas Shrugged*. Branden wrote,

> as she sat at her desk and the weeks passed and the stack of pages grew, she knew that she was alive again. She was writing fiction, and she wondered why she had ever stopped. She was living in *her* world again, and she wondered why she had ever left it. (p. 396)

It is impossible, of course, to know whether Rand would have produced more fiction had those in her immediate environment been less indulgent of her emotional reactions. It is conceivable that she had simply exhausted her creative ideas and that the manifest negativism and depression were some sort of grief reaction to diminished creative powers or energy. Still, therapeutic passivity in the face of long-standing emotional turmoil is rarely a preferred course of action. Rather, it may be effective for the therapist to side with the nonresistant aspects of the personality and challenge the resistant ones. At times, blunt and direct comments on the avoidant behavior may be needed. Such an approach can work, however, only if the therapist has first clearly demonstrated a fundamental sympathy with the creative process and somehow validated for the client acceptance of the complicated sense of self that is the usual lot of the creative person. To the extent that only one artist can criticize another, the therapist may need to strike a balance between support and encouragement, on the one hand, and active efforts to push through resistance to continued work, on the other, regardless of whether the therapist is an expert in the client's specific area of work.

Neither the depths of depression nor the heights of mania experienced by creative people should be underestimated. Evidence lies in the biographies of many movie stars and artists (see, e.g., Cheever, 1991). However, neither should the transitory nature of any negative reaction be forgotten (although the client may be unable to recall the nondistressed condition). When in the midst of a serious depression, the creative client may temporarily lose what he or she most values, the capacity to generate that which is new and unique. The therapist represents the latent optimism that at the end of this despair, the client will once more be productive, if not at the height of creative powers, or at least able to grieve the loss of an important, life-defining identity.[8]

Although there are those creative clients who delight in the introspection of long-term analytic methods, chronic introspection can itself serve as a defense. The fear of loss of creativity or (a variation on this theme) the fear that the therapist may somehow belittle or otherwise undermine the client's creative gifts (see Gedo, 1990) may frequently serve as resistance to treatment. Most knowledgeable observers have noted these fears to be unfounded (e.g., Rothenberg, 1990a). As Fenichel (1945) noted,

> Often artists are afraid of losing their creative abilities if their unconscious conflicts, the source of their creativeness, were analyzed. No absolute assurance can be given that an impairment of creative abilities through analysis is impossible. However, experience shows that neurotic inhibitions of creation are removed by analysis much more frequently than creativeness. Still, one must admit that in a certain minority of artists, neurosis and work seem to be so closely interwoven that it seems impossible to remove the one without impairing the other. (pp. 578–579)

---

[8] There are apparently predictable courses of creative talent, and the demise of talent is not necessarily unexpected. In a study of dancers, Kogan (1990) found that although the predictable course was for the dancer's career to be done by his or her late twenties, those giving up their career looked back on it favorably, not as something once had and lost but as an opportunity to have been part of an important and worthwhile enterprise.

In my experience, when the fear of loss or diminution of creativity is a factor in working with a creative client, it needs to be identified explicitly and as soon as it becomes manifest as a potential source of resistance. Generally, a simple acknowledgment of the client's fear is sufficient to keep the therapy on track. For others, however, a firm and embedded source of resistance requires careful exploration and may constitute a prolonged focus of a particular phase of the therapy. Assessment should establish whether such clients are resistant because of serious underlying ego weakness, major depression, or other major psychopathology. In such instances, the therapist may need to work creatively around the resistance or confront the underlying issue squarely (e.g., through psychopharmaceutical treatment of a depressive or psychotic condition). When the fear appears neurotically motivated, the therapist may wish to explore with the client fantasies of what life would be like without the cherished creative gift. However, as a practical matter, the client will generally know whether the therapist is supportive of creative people and creative work and will respond accordingly. Those who do not find the messy complexities of creativity and creative people appealing might do best to consider referring such clients elsewhere.

The role of humor in therapy with creative clients should also be considered. Being able to lightly tease a "stuck" artist and to commiserate on the vagaries of the creative process may encourage the playful elements so often found in the work of creative people. But although creativity may call for humor and playfulness in considering apparently fixed or at least intractable problems, artists themselves may not be particularly playful, particularly when they are troubled. The therapist's being playful and engaging when appropriate in humorous exchanges may help the client become "unstuck" and break through some of the resistance.

It is also important for the therapist not to treat the artist as "special" in a way that detracts from the therapy. Creative clients may be well-known, at least in a local area. Their very celebrity may be part of a complex relationship that makes it difficult for them to know where they stand with others. The therapist's sharing that glamour is generally unhelpful. To some extent, these clients must be viewed as "just another client," who happens to be creative and experiencing psychological or work dysfunction. To become too enamored with the mystery or the so-called glamour of the creative process may make it difficult for the therapist to push when pushing is called for and to resist accepting the perhaps brilliantly expressed but necessarily wrong pessimistic view of all effort as futile.

Treating Creative Blocks

Periods of creative block, in which the individual feels unable to be productive, either fully or partly, apparently occur with some predictability among creative individuals. Differential diagnosis should clarify whether the client is experiencing a serious pattern of depression in which the work inhibition is the secondary result or the predictable downward part of a creative cycle or a period of more substantive decline in creative powers (Simonton, 1988, 1989, 1990).

Although Fine (1984) opined that "if the normal individual does not want to work or cannot work, we say he needs a vacation; if the artist does not want to work, we say that he is blocked" (p. 27); in fact, blocks in creative work occur with apparent regularity and are not necessarily tied to volitional choice or avoidance. How long the creative block lasts, whether it is associated with underlying depression or other psychopathology, and what affective and cognitive attributions are associated with it will help determine the severity of the problem and the need for professional intervention.

Because creative highs and lows are so frequently described in the arts, especially among writers, the therapist working with the creative client should routinely inquire about the historic pattern that has been experienced by each client. Recurring patterns to the blocks may provide the therapist with some gauge as to the likely length of time that the block might be expected to continue. Identifying what has been effective in handling such situations in the past may also provide useful therapeutic clues.

In addressing creative blocks among writers, several recent publications may be of use to the therapist. Rose (1984) defined writer's block as "an inability to begin or continue writing for reasons other than a lack of basic skill or commitment" (p. 3). Clinical assessment needs to establish that there really is such a thing as "block," as opposed to a quiescent period in which germination is taking place.

As discussed in chapter 4, creative blocks are really a special instance of undercommitment more generally. Assessment of the block should establish the severity and chronicity of the perceived inability to work, the circumstances that seem to trigger it, and the depression (if any) associated with it. A creative block presumably exists only if the client has something of a track record of artistic productivity preceding the block; otherwise, what is presented as a creative block may simply be the posturing of someone aspiring to a supposedly prestigious creative role for which talent may be lacking.

The paradox in working therapeutically with the artistic individual is that the work itself is largely autonomous and individualized as opposed to the therapeutic process, which necessarily involves interaction with another person. To benefit from

Drawing by Mort Gerberg; © 1991 The New Yorker Magazine, Inc.

psychotherapy, the client must, in essence, give up some of his or her immediate control in the interests of an assumed long-term increase in personal control.

When experiencing a creative block, the individual has shut down the artistic productive process, often for reasons that appear to be outside of personal control. Because the individual may perceive locus of control at such times to be external (see Foon, 1987), the therapist may need to work with the client to identify those aspects of behavior, however few, that are still in volitional control. While sanctioning and identifying with the "artistic predicament," the therapist's aggressive challenging of the client's erroneous presumptions about what aspects of the problem are within personal control may have the effect of increasing hope and eventually assisting the client in taking small steps that ultimately become cumulative and help the client move beyond the block. If highly entrenched blocks do not respond to such approaches or to paradoxical attempts to work around them, other, less direct treatment interventions may be necessary.

Case 8.2
The Blocked Writer

Christopher, a freelance writer, complained of a circumscribed block that was preventing him from completing his assignments on time. His clinical history showed this to be part of a pattern of perfectionism and self-doubt that typically occurred in the middle phases of writing assignments.

The therapist first engaged Christopher's intellect and curiosity by expressing wonder at the predictability of the block occurring only in the middle stages of writing assignments. He offered the interpretation that Christopher's writing pattern mirrored the problems he had in relationships, in which he would quickly become infatuated but then precipitously leave after a few months. In both cases, he seemed to have trouble completing the middle phase. Early in treatment, the therapist asked Christopher to spend five minutes a day at his writing desk and record his observations of his responses. He was instructed that under no circumstances was he to begin an avoided task.

The client initially complied with this request. He brought to the weekly sessions acutely self-observant, well-written notes on his personal reactions to the experience, imagining himself as an outsider watching a great painter struggle with what to put on the canvas. The therapist complimented Christopher on his observations and style and reiterated his instruction not to take pencil to paper on any avoided assignments. For three sessions, Christopher dutifully and rather cheerfully brought in his notes. On the fourth session, however, after rescheduling the appointment twice, he came in sheepishly, saying that he had no notes for the session. In fact, he had sat down to do the assignment but found himself instead working on an avoided task. The therapist feigned upset. Did the client not want to get better? Did he not want to be rid of his procrastination problem? How can he presume he wants to get better when he has refused to do the assignment?

At this point, the therapist instructed him to try harder next time and then doubled the assignment: Christopher was to spend 10 minutes a day on his observations but again not to work on his assignments. If Christopher would have complied, the therapist would have effusively complimented him on what an excellent and compliant patient he has been while richly praising the writing style. By the fifth session, however, Christopher delightedly admitted, "I know what you're doing and it's no longer necessary. I'm writing as before." He had become unstuck.

In effect, with this client, as with many procrastinators in general, the state of being "stuck" was due to dread of some horrible consequence or was a means of expressing or resisting control (by others or by circumstances). The therapist, in this case, aligned with the negative side of the ambivalence and, in essence, set up a paradoxical condition in which writing became the noncompliant behavior. Because writers are generally quite autonomous and suffer structure or authority cheerlessly, aligning a mandate with the avoidant behavior leaves the client no choice but to "rebel" by performing the avoided behavior. In effect, the client became "re-primed" and could continue working in his usual, if somewhat neurotic, style.

A final case reminds us that the perceived *lack* of creativity, particularly when it is expected, can be a source of consternation.

Clients may exaggerate the perceived need for creativity and may underestimate their own talents, as the case of Zarit illustrates.

Case 8.3
The Critical Writer

Zarit, a young man in his early thirties at the time of referral, consulted a psychologist with concerns of what career path to take at the conclusion of his doctoral studies in English literature. Ability testing showed marked talent in areas relevant to literary criticism (in which a standard is applied to the works of others) but not in areas of verbal and ideational fluency and other aptitudes often found in creative profiles.

Because Zarit had experience in literary criticism, he wondered whether he should pursue job opportunities in this area or consider a career in original writing. He viewed himself as having good style and technique (particularly when writing about others' work) but felt that he was unlikely to make much of an original contribution to his field. He felt that if he pursued a creative writing career, he would always be found lacking (particularly when compared with the many talented writers in this field). He viewed his alternative as pursuing a postgraduate career involving more teaching and scholarly work.

Explorations of the client's fantasies suggested that his perceived dichotomization of original writing and creativity was unrealistic and that an initial position requiring literary criticism could always be supplemented by also writing original work as an avocation; pursuing creative writing alone would be very risky. Moreover, his idea of creativity was overly demanding. He compared himself primarily with world-renowned writers rather than with the many authors who also served by raising the standard of writing through their expert criticism. In addition, he did have a special talent, namely, preparing highly complex reviews with historical reference. This skill was in short supply.

Although the client came to realize that he might never become a premiere writer in his field, he came to appreciate the talent he did have. He also came to realize that he had more career choices available to him than he at first suspected.

Concluding Comments

In one sense, the creative client in psychotherapy is just another client. While respecting the powerful defense of "differentness," of seeing oneself as isolated and alienated from the rest of the world, the therapist must also address the psychological problems directly and substantively. Failure to intervene aggressively, for example, in cases of obvious manic depression or other serious psychopathology simply because the client is well-known or works in a so-called glamorous occupation is to abandon the psychotherapeutic responsibility. Certain psychological problems arise with characteristic predictability in the course of psychotherapy. The fear of loss of creativity (and thus control), the likelihood of affective disorders, estrangement from modal values, a self-view as a martyr of sorts in maintaining artistically high standards, and an expectation (and reality) of chronic rejection are all aspects of the psychotherapeutic relationship that can be expected to occur with greater than chance probability.

Although not the easiest population with whom to work, creative individuals can be among the most rewarding because their potential contribution is so great and they tend to approach the therapeutic process with unusual perspectives, as they do other aspects of their lives. The task of the psychotherapist working with creative clients, as with clients more generally, is to assist the individual in becoming more able to fulfill personal potential and more able to make volitional choices rather than respond neurotically to externally imposed conditions. Creative clients, however, differ from other clients in often being more dramatic and having greater potential if successfully assisted.

Summary

There are many issues to be considered in treating work dysfunctions of creative individuals, and certain psychodynamics (e.g., perfectionism, isolation, fear of loss of creativity and control) occur with some regularity. Therapists treating work dysfunctions of creative individuals can expect certain types of psychological disorders (e.g., affective disorders, work blocks of psychogenic origin) to occur with regularity. Intervention approaches need to be sensitive to the creative temperament of the artist but simultaneously direct and nonintimidated by the client's creative talent. Therapists who are themselves creative may work best with this population.

Toward a Psychotherapy
of Work Dysfunctions

R egarding the future course of research and practice in the psychology of the work dysfunctions, I envision a future in which

- every mental health professional has at least minimal competency in conducting a diagnostic evaluation that includes assessment of the psychological state of the client's work role, and psychotherapists untrained in work issues are considered to be as ill-prepared as those now who are not qualified to address marital or sexual concerns;
- mental health professionals' involvement in career and work issues is motivated less by anticipated profits than by professional necessity and personal interest;
- clients' work is viewed by mental health professionals of all varieties as more than a subtext for paying the psychotherapy bills;

- specialty clinics are widely available to assist in work issues diagnosis and intervention;
- workplaces throughout the nation and ultimately the world have teams of competent professionals that can be assembled as needed to create programs in the workplace for treating and preventing work-related problems;
- every man, woman, and adolescent has affordable access to competent assessment and counseling about work-related concerns.

Although this is a vision of the future, it is not radically removed from what is possible over the next decade or so. Promising starts have already been made in the creation of a research base in a surprising number of areas relevant to assessment and psychotherapy of work dysfunctions. Integration and diffusion, at least as much as new discoveries, are the agenda of the present.

Current State of Research and Practice

If the review in this book of work dysfunctions counseling and psychotherapy seems exhaustive (if not exhausting), in fact the field of work-issues counseling and psychotherapy is considerably larger than one might suspect. Much of the literature has been overly oriented to research rather than practice concerns, diffusely located, and insufficiently concerned with intervention issues. Nonetheless, much work has been done. Although this book has focused on integrating that literature and providing a research-based guide for practitioners, there remains more to be done in specific areas and in the process of integration.

A central theme of this book is that characteristics of individuals that combine to create work dysfunctions do not exist separate from those of organizations and occupations. In counseling clients who present with work-related concerns, the therapist must to some extent evaluate the client's workplace, even if evaluation must occur outside the actual work context. In treating work dysfunctions, the therapist must caution against allowing a psychological view to mask from consideration other factors that may be germane. Ignoring features of the work itself or the work context that may be the primary source of the client's difficulties is a common error of psychotherapists beginning to treat work dysfunctions.

Although analogies of the work setting that use the family as a metaphor have some relevance, they have limitations as well. On the one hand, both work and the family are powerful sets of relationships that are life defining. On the other hand, an unhappy and dissatisfying work relationship can be abandoned with somewhat greater ease than can one's family. Furthermore, the purpose of work is the accomplishment of some external productive task, not procreation or emotional satisfaction. Family connotes unchosen binding, an entity that is more tolerant of a range of emotional reactions and that contains elements running deeper than those of work relationships; removal from the unit occurs only with great emotional cost. Whereas family connotes tolerance of irrationality and, with children, expectation of irresponsibility (as well as responsibility), work (at least in theory) emphasizes rationality and, in most organizational contexts, conformity with well-defined behavioral expectations.

Recurring Assessment Issues

Determining whether work dysfunctions exist independently of, in combination with, or secondarily to psychopathology is an important concern in routine differential diagnosis. The therapist, if not the client, needs to be clear on the plan for addressing work-related difficulties and, when appropriate, psychological difficulties unrelated to work. In cases in which both psychopathology and work dysfunctions are present, it is useful to have some sense of which is primary and how the one relates to the other. For example, a client who is clinically depressed, unemployed, and about to experience a divorce may need help in determining which is the most pressing issue and which will be the initial focus of the therapy. On the other hand, clients whose work difficulties are not circumscribed to narrowly focused, delineated areas but are part of a broader, overarching conflictual life theme (e.g., reluctance to commit oneself) may benefit from working on the central theme or conflict, addressing both work and nonwork issues.

It is always the therapist's task to keep the general dynamic firmly in mind and to interpret behavior (work related or not) in light of the central theme. However, in manifesting resistance or transference issues, the client may attempt to alternate the focus between significant life concerns or may undermine genuine progress made in one domain by lamenting lack of progress in another. In one case, a client came to me for treatment shortly after being terminated from his job. Ostensibly, he sought help in formulating new career directions. Preliminary assessment showed that the client's family-of-origin dynamics were important factors in his failure to commit to a career in which he could excel. However, he resisted attempts to explore these dynamics as being relevant to his immediate need to get his career back on track. Yet, when the focus was put on the work issues, he eluded therapeutic scrutiny, seeking "practical" advice for questions to which he already had answers.

A second major diagnostic issue concerns the reality or factual basis of work-centered complaints about perceived inadequacies in the job or work context. Additional, reality-based data (which may or may not be appropriate to obtain) can aid the therapist in determining the validity of the client's complaints about the workplace, just as information from another family member can aid the therapist in understanding family-of-origin dynamics of an individual client. Many workplaces are notoriously mismanaged, and supervisors may be plainly incompetent, just as some parents are better or worse than others. The difference between work dysfunctions and family-of-origin conflicts is that the former generally occur in the present and therefore have more immediacy. In the context of counseling that is short term or involves immediately pressing situations (e.g., a threatened termination), the accuracy of the perceived reality of the work complaints may indeed matter and may, with the client's consent, be the subject of direct inquiry.

Recurring Intervention Issues

In the psychotherapy of work dysfunctions, however, conservatism is recommended in considering bringing such outside contacts into the therapeutic relationship. The quality of the therapeutic relationship depends to some extent on the client perceiving the therapist as being on his or her side, and in many models of therapy, self-discovery is the goal. Thus, assuming the validity or at least perceived validity of the client's understanding of the work situation may be a better stance than unnecessarily or prematurely bringing in outside parties. Of course the therapist can still raise questions or interpretations, particularly when there is reason to doubt the reality of the client's presentation of a work concern, but can do so in the context of a private relationship between two parties attempting to understand and work through issues at hand. Besides, if the client's psychological dynamics are the source of the work-related problems, chances are good that they will present themselves in the therapeutic transference or in a pattern of reactions that will become apparent with time.

This points to another central issue mentioned earlier: The therapist must guard against overly psychological or psychodynamic interpretations of work dysfunctions except when there is clear and compelling evidence that such factors are the driving force behind the problems at work. Although this may sound contradictory to the advice just given, the following example illustrates that it is not. A client presenting with depression and complaints of being "burned out" at work may be manifesting secondary work-related depression or may simply be exhibiting common symptoms of burnout. The therapist confronting such a case might intervene on several levels. Suggesting a job or career change, at least on a temporary basis, is one practical, perhaps well-founded way to proceed. Recommendations of other practical ways to handle the problem (e.g., physical exercise and vigorous nonwork activities as antidotes to the emotional exhaustion associated with the job) may also be appropriate. In still other cases, assisting the client in exploring reasons for the career choice or the tendency to become overly involved with impossible goals (e.g., "curing" poverty) followed by depression when personal efforts are ineffective may also be appropriate. These courses might be pursued over the course of therapy, particularly when there are a number of associated issues stemming from the client's family-of-origin dynamics (e.g., an older child always stuck in a caregiving role).

Short-term, behaviorally focused interventions have particular utility for treating many work dysfunctions provided that more complicated psychopathology or character disorders are not present or, at the least, that the broader, contextual issues are kept in mind. Metaphorical approaches that encapsulate a central dynamic of the person through the presenting work concerns may also prove effective. The therapist may need to work around lifelong characterological issues when working with clients experiencing both personality disorders and work dysfunctions.

Prevention

What can be done to prevent or at least minimize work dysfunctions? This book has suggested a number of approaches. The quality of fit between the individual and the career, a source of stress when absent or minimal, is to some extent determined on its own timetable; with some careers, quality of fit takes longer to emerge than with others. Nonetheless, parents can encourage children to follow their interests and experiment with alternative roles by providing a supportive home environment. Home environments that assist individuals in developing high levels of self-esteem by providing a diversity of sources of respect assist young adults in nonambivalently pursuing career goals.

Within the context of the work environment, organizations can assist employees by using hiring practices that attempt to select employees who are well-suited to their job duties and career path (although this must occur within legislative constraints), by providing career counseling and alternative career paths when difficulties are encountered, and by providing mental health counseling programs for employees who are under stress to encourage early psychological intervention when needed.

Practical career counseling and career management can also be helpful for some individuals, including those with relatively pervasive personality disorders. For example, stern warnings about the real-life work consequences of continued aberrant work behavior may be as instructive and influential in working

with certain personality disorders as may long-term psychotherapy. Such employees may be more highly motivated to be
compliant when facing job loss or restriction.

Of course, it is not only characteristics of individuals that contribute to work dysfunctions. Jobs can be poorly designed, supervisors nonsupportive or incompetent, and demands unreasonable. Occupational mental health professionals who are
knowledgeable about characteristics of the workplace will be
called on increasingly to intervene to make the workplace more
conducive to positive mental health, effective interpersonal work
relationships, and less stressful working conditions.

Training Needs

In whose professional turf does the treatment of work dysfunctions fall? Because work is so integrally a part of the life of today's
clientele, no discipline can rightfully claim work issues as its
exclusive province. For some time, the field of counseling psychology has considered the general area within its domain. Such
exclusivity, however, is unwarranted. Psychotherapists from a
variety of backgrounds can effectively counsel individual clients
about work dysfunctions provided that they have relevant
knowledge, some experience in the area, and reasonable affinity
with the types of issues characteristically raised. Psychologists
of several types (clinical, counseling, industrial/organizational,
and school), psychiatrists, and social workers all have important
contributions to make to this field and should be encouraged to
obtain the training necessary to make solid clinical and research
contributions.

Of what would that training consist? Ideally, practice in clinics
specializing in work and career issues would be part of the training experience of all psychotherapists. That is unlikely to happen
at present, however, simply because there are far too few such
clinics in which the training could take place and too few competent instructors to oversee the training. Over time, relevant
coursework and "work dysfunctions clinics" or specialty areas
in every psychology clinic, medical school training program, and
social work program would ideally be developed. Integrated pro-

grams, for example, in industrial psychology (current models of which too often have no adequate individual focus) and clinical or counseling psychology may also prove useful. Specializations in occupational psychiatry and occupational social work hopefully will become more common. In the interim, and especially for those already practicing their profession, seminars, comprehensive study programs, and supervised practica will be of assistance.

Next Steps

A perhaps surprising conclusion one may draw from this review is that there is already a fair amount of material with which to work. What is noteworthy is that there are actually rather large bodies of literature on the work dysfunctions in isolated areas. Thus, for example, Type A behavior, performance anxiety, and burnout all have quite extensive literature on which to draw. However, far more of the research in these and other areas of work dysfunctions concern one or another technical issue in defining, describing, and measuring the relevant constructs. Comparatively, there is scant research on how therapeutically to address such concerns and, except rarely, little literature on the differential effectiveness of alternative treatment approaches.

This finding may simply reflect the natural state of development of a field that is moving, if slowly, from description to construct definition to intervention methodologies. However, there is also some indication in this area that researchers and practitioners have once again gone their separate ways, the former group knitting elegant, tapestrylike sweaters for use by natives in the tropics, the latter fighting off dungeons and dragons with whatever weapons, however antiquated and ill-suited to the battle, that happen to be at hand.

Not surprisingly, much work remains. Still needed is more extensive research concerning the efficacy of various methods of treating work dysfunctions. Moreover, many variables relevant to work problems have been studied in isolation from one another, as if Type A behavior, for example, occurred in a different universe than burnout. Cleaner, neater, and no doubt faster studies are generated with such an approach, but their clinical utility in working with complex, real-life behavior of people who may be (for example) depressed, underachieving Type As with marital difficulties is limited.

The taxonomy presented in this book provides one way of attempting to group psychologically relevant work dysfunctions according to the commonalities of the presenting difficulties. Refinement of this taxonomy can occur as new findings emerge and additive or alternative groupings become clearer. It is hoped that future iterations of psychiatric diagnostic systems such as the *Diagnostic and Statistical Manual of Mental Disorders* (3rd. ed., rev.; American Psychiatric Association, 1987) will take into account more of the work role in all its complexity.

Finally, the accumulation of case knowledge to assist in the generation of a clinical literature will be greatly assisted by practitioners who make the effort to summarize their findings in conducting psychotherapy and counseling with clients experiencing work dysfunctions. The field of counseling and psychotherapy has clinically summarized cases of every imaginable (and some salaciously unimaginable) versions of love and hate relationships. However, no comparable clinical literature of work dysfunctions yet exists. I hope that this book will make a start in that direction, an avenue needing more traffic by individuals like the readers of this book. Such potential contributors should be warned, however, that the "reward" for such efforts may well be the wrath of those who claim to have gotten there first.

On the contrary, charting the phenomenology of work dysfunctions of our own clients is a noble and valued contribution. However modest the personal contribution, this enterprise helps create a signature quilt of knowledge from which ultimately sound tenets of practice can emerge. From such patches of learning and scraps of experience, whether published in journals and books of prestigious or more humble origin, there can emerge over time an artful psychotherapy of work dysfunctions. At stake is nothing less or more than the health and well-being of our clients' work and, therefore, their lives.

References

Ackerley, G. D., Burnell, J., Holder, D. C., & Kurdek, L. A. (1988). Burnout among licensed psychologists. *Professional Psychology: Research and Practice, 19,* 624–631.

Adam, J. J., & Van Wieringen, P. C. (1988). Worry and emotionality: Its influence on the performance of a throwing task. *International Journal of Sport Psychology, 19,* 211–225.

Adams, N. A., & Holcomb, W. R. (1986). Analysis of the relationship between anxiety about mathematics and performance *Psychological Reports, 59,* 943–948.

Adler, G. (1979). The myth of the alliance with borderline patients. *American Journal of Psychiatry, 136,* 642–645.

Adler, G. (1980). Transference, real relationship and alliance. *International Journal of Psycho-Analysis, 61,* 547–558.

Aitken, M. (1982). A personality profile of the college student procrastinator (Doctoral dissertation, University of Pittsburgh, 1982). *Dissertations Abstracts International, 43,* 3A.

Akhtar, S. (1986). Differentiating schizoid and avoidant personality disorders. *American Journal of Psychiatry, 143,* 1061–1062.

Akhtar, S. (1990). Paranoid personality disorder: A synthesis of developmental, dynamic and descriptive features. *American Journal of Psychotherapy, 44,* 5–25.

Albert, R. S., & Runco, M. A. (1990). Observations, conclusions, and gaps. In M. A. Runco & R. S. Albert (Eds.), *Theories of creativity* (pp. 255–269). Newbury Park, CA: Sage.

Alden, L. (1989). Short-term structured treatment for avoidant personality disorder. *Journal of Consulting and Clinical Psychology, 57,* 756–764.

Aldrich, C. K. (1987). Psychiatric interviews and psychological tests as predictors of medical students' success. *Journal of Medical Education, 62,* 658–664.

Alfredsson, L., Akerstedt, T., Mattsson, M., & Wilborg, B. (1991). Self-reported health and well-being amongst night security guards: A comparison with the working population. *Ergonomics, 34,* 525–530.

Alnaes, R., & Torgersen, S. (1988). DSM–III symptom disorders (Axis I) and personality disorders (Axis II) in an outpatient population. *Acta Psychiatrica Scandinavica, 78,* 348–355.

Alterman, A. I., & Cacciola, J. S. (1991). The antisocial personality disorder diagnosis in substance abusers: Problems and issues. *Journal of Nervous and Mental Disease, 179,* 401–409.

Amabile, T. (1990). Within you, without you: The social psychology of creativity, and beyond. In M. A. Runco & R. S. Albert (Eds.), *Theories of creativity* (pp. 61–91). Newbury Park, CA: Sage.

American Psychiatric Association. (1987). *Diagnostic and statistical manual of mental disorders* (3rd ed., rev.). Washington, DC: Author.

American Psychological Association. (1992). Ethical principles of psychologists and code of conduct. *American Psychologist, 47,* 1597–1611.

Amodei, N., & Nelson-Gray, R. O. (1991). Cross-situational inconsistency in the behavior of compulsive and histrionic personality disorders: An analogue study. *Journal of Psychopathology and Behavioral Assessment, 13,* 127–145.

Anderson, J. W. (1987). Why did William James abandon art? *Emotions and Behavior Monographs, 4,* 279–303.

Anderson, R. (1978). Motive to avoid success: A profile. *Sex Roles, 4,* 239–248.

Andreason, N., & Canter, A. (1974). The creative writer: Psychiatric symptoms and family history. *Comprehensive Psychiatry, 15,* 123–131.

Andreason, N., & Powers, P. S. (1975). Creativity and psychosis: An examination of conceptual style. *Archives of General Psychiatry, 32,* 70–73.

Andrews, G., & Crino, R. (1991). Behavioral psychotherapy of anxiety disorders. *Psychiatric Annals, 21,* 358–360.

Anson, R. H., & Bloom, M. E. (1988). Police stress in an occupational context. *Journal of Police Science and Administration, 16,* 229–235.

Appels, A., & Schouten, E. (1991). Burnout as a risk factor for coronary heart disease. *Behavioral Medicine, 17,* 53–59.

Arboleda, F. J., & Holley, H. L. (1991). Antisocial burnout: An exploratory study. *Bulletin of the American Academy of Psychiatry and the Law, 19,* 173–183.

Arthur, N. M. (1990). The assessment of burnout: A review of three inventories useful for research and counseling. *Journal of Counseling and Development, 69,* 186–189.

Arsenault, A., Dolan, S. L., & Van Ameringen, M. R. (1991). Stress and mental strain in hospital work: Exploring the relationship beyong personality. *Journal of Organizational Behavior, 12*, 483–493.

Ashforth, B. E., & Lee, R. T. (1990). Defensive behavior in organizations: A preliminary model. *Human Relations, 43*, 621–648.

Atkinson, J. W., & Feather, N. T. (1966). *A theory of achievement motivation.* New York: Wiley.

Augestad, L. B., & Levander, S. (1992). Personality, health, and job stress among employees in a Norwegian penitentiary and in a maximum security hospital. *Work and Stress, 6*, 65–79.

Auten, P. D., Hull, D. B., & Hull, J. H. (1985). Sex role orientation and Type A behavior pattern. *Psychology of Women Quarterly, 9*, 288–290.

Bacharach, S. B., Bamberger, P., & Conley, S. (1991). Work–home conflict among nurses and engineers: Mediating the impact of role stress on burnout and satisfaction at work. *Journal of Organizational Behavior, 12*, 39–53.

Bailey, J. E. (1985). Differential diagnosis of posttraumatic stress and antisocial personality disorders. *Hospital and Community Psychiatry, 36*, 881–883.

Bair, J. P., & Greenspan, B. K. (1986). TEAMS: Teamwork training for interns, residents, and nurses. *Hospital and Community Psychiatry, 37*, 633–635.

Baker, H. S. (1979). The conquering hero quits: Narcissistic factors in underachievement and failure. *American Journal of Psychotherapy, 33*, 418–427.

Baker, H. S. (1987). Underachievement and failure in college: The interaction between intrapsychic and interpersonal factors and the perspective of self psychology. *Adolescent Psychiatry, 44*, 441–460.

Baker, L. J., Dearborn, M., Hastings, J. E., & Hamberger, K. (1988). Type A behavior in women: A review. *Health Psychology 3*, 477–497.

Balkin, J. (1986). Contributions of family to men's fear of success in college. *Psychological Reports, 59*, 1071–1074.

Balkin, J. (1987). Contributions of friends to women's fear of success in college. *Psychological Reports, 61*, 39–42.

Balkin, J., & Donaruma, J. A. (1978). Contributions of family and friends to fear of success in men. *Journal of Psychology, 100*, 279–283.

Bardenstein, K. K., McGlashan, T. H., & McGlashan, T. H. (1988). The natural history of a residentially treated borderline sample: Gender differences. *Journal of Personality Disorders, 2*, 69-83.

Barling, J. (1990). *Employment, stress and family functioning.* New York: Wiley.

Barrell, J. J., Medeiros, D., Barrell, J. E., & Price, D. T. I. (1985). The causes and treatment of performance anxiety: An experiential approach. *Journal of Humanistic Psychology, 25*, 106–122.

Bartlett, S. J. (1990). Acedia: The etiology of work-engendered depression. *New Ideas in Psychology, 8*, 389–396.

Beck, A. T., & Freeman, A. M. (1990). *Cognitive therapy of personality disorders.* New York: Guilford Press.

Beck, A. T., & Rush, A. J. (1973). A cognitive model of anxiety formation and anxiety resolution. In C. D. Spielberger & I. G. Sarason (Eds.), *Stress and anxiety: Vol. 10. A sourcebook of theory and research* (pp. 349–365). New York: Hemisphere.

Becker, R. E., Cohen, R. J., & Teevan, R. C. (1975). Hostile press and a survey of fears. *Psychological Reports, 37,* 463–466.

Bedeian, A. G., Mossholder, K. W., & Touliatos, J. (1990). Type A status and selected work experiences among male and female accountants. *Journal of Social Behavior and Personality, 5,* 291–305.

Beehr, T. A., & Bhagat, R. S. (1985). *Human stress and cognition in organizations.* New York: Wiley.

Begley, T. M., & Boyd, D. P. (1985). The relationship of the Jenkins Activity Survey to Type A behavior among business executives. *Journal of Vocational Behavior, 27,* 316–328.

Belcastro, P. A. (1982). Burnout and its relationship to teachers' somatic complaints and illnesses. *Psychological Reports, 50,* 1045–1046.

Belcastro, P. A., Gold, R. S., & Hays, L. C. (1983). Maslach Burnout Inventory: Factor structures for samples of teachers. *Psychological Reports, 53,* 364–366.

Belcastro, P. A., & Hays, L. C. (1984). Ergophilia . . . ergophobia . . . ergo . . . burnout? *Professional Psychology: Research and Practice, 15,* 260–270.

Belfer, B. (1989). Stress and the medical practitioner. *Stress Medicine, 5,* 109–113.

Bendiksen, M. S., & Bendiksen, I. (1992). A multi-dimensional intervention for a toxic solvent injured population. *Journal of Cognitive Rehabilitation, 10,* 20–27.

Benjamin, L. S. (1987). Use of the SASB dimensional model to develop treatment plans for personality disorders: I. Narcissism. *Journal of Personality Disorders, 1,* 43–70.

Bennett, P., Wallace, L., Carroll, D., & Smith, N. (1991). Treating Type A behaviours and mild hypertension in middle-aged men. *Journal of Psychosomatic Research, 35,* 209–223.

Berg, J. L. (1990). Differentiating ego functions of borderline and narcissistic personalities. *Journal of Personality Assessment, 55,* 537–548.

Bergman, L. R., & Magnusson, D. (1979). Overachievement and catecholamine excretion in an achievement-demanding situation. *Psychosomatic Medicine, 51,* 181–188.

Berkhoff, K., & Rusin, W. (1991). Pediatric house staff's psychological response to call duty. *Journal of Developmental and Behavioral Pediatrics, 12,* 6–10.

Bertoch, M. R., Nielson, E. C., Curley, J. R., & Borg, W. R. (1989). Reducing teacher stress. *Journal of Experimental Education, 57,* 117–128.

Beswick, G., Rothblum, E. D., & Mann, L. (1988). Psychological antecedents of student procrastination. *Australian Psychologist, 23,* 207–217.

Beutler, L. E., Nussbaum, P. D., & Meredith, K. E. (1988). Changing personality patterns of police officers. *Professional Psychology: Research and Practice, 19,* 503–507.

Birney, R. C., Burdick, H., & Teevan, R. C. (1969). *Fear of failure.* New York: Van Nostrand Reinhold.

Biscardi, D., & Schill, T. (1985). Correlations of narcissistic traits with defensive style, Machiavellianism, and empathy. *Psychological Reports, 57,* 354.

Biskind, P. (1992). Chronicle of a life untold. *Premiere, 5,* 54–62.

Black, D. W., & Noyes, R., Jr. (1990). Comorbidity and obsessive–compulsive disorder. In J. D. Maser & C. R. Cloninger (Eds.), *Comorbidity of mood and anxiety disorders* (pp. 305–216). Washington, DC: American Psychiatric Press.

Bland, R. C., Orn, H., & Newman, S. C. (1988). Lifetime prevalence of psychiatric disorders in Edmonton. *Acta Psychiatrica Scandinavica, 77*(Suppl. 338), 24–32.

Bland, R. C., Stebelsky, G., Orn, H., & Newman, S. C. (1988). Psychiatric disorders and unemployment in Edmonton. *Acta Psychiatrica Scandinavica, 77*(Suppl. 338), 72–80.

Blaney, N. T., Blaney, P. H., & Diamond, E. (1989). Intrafamilial patterns reported by young Type A versus Type B males and their parents. *Behavioral Medicine, 15,* 161–166.

Blaney, N. T., Brown, P., & Blaney, P. H. (1986). Type A, marital adjustment, and life stress. *Journal of Behavioral Medicine, 9,* 491–502.

Blazer, D. (1989). Current concepts: Depression in the elderly. *New England Journal of Medicine, 320,* 164–166.

Blazer, D., Swartz, M., Woodbury, M., Manton, K. G., Hughes, D., & George, L. K. (1988). Depressive symptoms and depressive diagnoses in a community population. *Archives of General Psychiatry, 45,* 1078–1084.

Blechner, M. J. (1986). Entitlement and narcissism: Paradise sought. *Contemporary Psychoanalysis, 23,* 244–255.

Bloom, R. B. (1983). The effects of disturbed adolescents on their teachers. *Behavioral Disorders, 8,* 209–216.

Blostein, S., Eldridge, W., Kilty, K., & Richardson, V. (1985–1986). A multidimensional analysis of the concept of burnout. *Employee Assistance Quarterly, 1,* 55–66.

Bluen, S. D., Barling, J., & Burns, W. (1990). Predicting sales performance, job satisfaction, and depression by using the Achievement Strivings and Impatience–Irritability dimensions of Type A behavior. *Journal of Applied Psychology, 75,* 212–216.

Blumenthal, J. A., & Kamarck, T. (1987). Assessment of Type A behavior pattern. In J. A. Blumenthal & D. C. McKee (Eds.), *Applications in behavioral medicine and health psychology: A clinician's source book* (pp. 3–37). Sarasota, FL: Professional Resource Exchange.

Blustein, D. L. (1987). Integrating career counseling and psychotherapy: A comprehensive treatment strategy. *Psychotherapy, 24,* 794–799.

Bohle, B. (1967). *The home book of quotations.* New York: Dodd Meade.

Boice, R. (1989). Procrastination, busyness and bingeing. *Behaviour Research and Therapy, 27,* 605–611.

Bond, C. F., & Omar, A. S. (1990). Social anxiety, state dependence, and the next-in-line effect. *Journal of Experimental Social Psychology, 26,* 185–198.

Bonds-White, F. (1984). The special it: II. Treatment of the passive–aggressive personality. *Transactional Analysis Journal, 14*, 180–190.

Bonime, W. (1982). The paranoid and the depressive: Dynamic correlations. *Contemporary Psychoanalysis, 18*, 556–574.

Borg, M. G. (1990). Occupational stress in British educational settings: A review. *Educational Psychology, 10*, 103–126.

Bost, J. M. (1984). Retaining students on academic probation: Effects of time management peer counseling on students' grades. *Journal of Learning Skills, 3*, 38–43.

Bouchard, T. J., Lykken, D. T., McGue, M., Segal, N. L., & Tellegen, A. (1990). Sources of human psychological differences: The Minnesota Study of Twins Reared Apart. *Science, 250*, 223–228.

Bowler, R. M., Mergler, D., Rauch, S. S., Harrison, R., & Cone, J. (1991). Affective and personality disturbances among female former microelectronics workers. *Journal of Clinical Psychology, 47*, 41–52.

Boyd, D. P. (1984). Type A behaviour, financial performance and organizational growth in small business firms. *Journal of Occupational Psychology, 57*, 137–140.

Branden, B. (1986). *The passion of Ayn Rand*. Garden City, NY: Doubleday.

Branden, N. (1962). Social metaphysics. *The Objectivist Newsletter, 1*, 47, 50.

Branden, N. (1989). *Judgment day: My years with Ayn Rand*. New York: Avon Books.

Brannigan, G. G., Hauk, P. A., & Guay, J. A. (1991). Locus of control and day-dreaming. *Journal of Genetic Psychology, 152*, 29–33.

Braun, S., & Hollander, R. B. (1988). Work and depression among women in the Federal Republic of Germany. *Women and Health, 14*, 3–26.

Breedlove, C. J., & Cicirelli, V. G. (1974). Women's fear of success in relation to personal characteristics and type of occupation. *Journal of Psychology, 86*, 181–190.

Brehm, S. S., & Brehm, J. W. (1981). *Psychological reactance: A theory of freedom and control*. San Diego, CA: Academic Press.

Bremer, T. H., & Wittig, M. A. (1980). Fear of success: A personality trait or a response to occupational deviance and role overload? *Sex Roles, 6*, 27–46.

Brenner, O. C., & Tomkiewicz, J. (1982). Sex differences among business graduates in fear of success and fear of appearing incompetent as measured by objective instruments. *Psychological Reports, 51*, 179–182.

Brief, A. P., & Nord, W. R. (1990a). The absence of work. In A. P. Brief & W. R. Nord (Eds.), *Meanings of occupational work* (pp. 233–251). Lexington, MA: Lexington Books.

Brief, A. P., & Nord, W. R. (1990b). Work and the family. In A. P. Brief & W. R. Nord (Eds.), *Meanings of occupational work* (pp. 203–232). Lexington, MA: Lexington Books.

Brill, P. L. (1984). The need for an operational definition of burnout. *Family and Community Health, 6*, 12–24.

Brookings, J. B., Bolton, B., Brown, C. E., & McEvoy, A. (1985). Self-reported job burnout among female human service professionals. *Journal of Occupational Behaviour, 6*, 143–150.

Brown, D., & Brooks, L. (1985). Career counseling as a mental health intervention. *Professional Psychology: Research and Practice, 16*, 860–867.

Brown, D., & Brooks, L. (1990). *Career choice and development: Applying contemporary theories to practice* (2nd ed.). San Francisco: Jossey-Bass.

Brown, T. A., & Barlow, D. H. (1992). Comorbidity among anxiety disorders: Implications for treatment and *DSM–IV*. *Journal of Consulting and Clinical Psychology, 60*, 835–844.

Brozgold, A. Z., Franzblau, A., & Borod, J. C. (1992). Cognitive and affective aspects of multiple chemical sensitivities: A case study. *Neuropsychology, 6*, 59–70.

Bruch, M. A., Pearl, L., & Giordano, S. (1986). Differences in the cognitive processes of academically successful and unsuccessful test-anxious students. *Journal of Counseling Psychology, 33*, 217–219.

Budman, S. H. (Ed.). (1981). *Forms of brief therapy*. New York: Guilford Press.

Burka, J. B., & Yuen, L. M. (1983). *Procrastination: Why you do it, what to do about it*. Reading, MA: Addison-Wesley.

Burke, R. J. (1985). Career orientations and Type A behavior in police officers. *Psychological Reports, 57*, 1239–1246.

Burke, R. J. (1987). Burnout in police work: An examination of the Cherniss model. *Group and Organization Studies, 12*, 174–188.

Burke, R. J., & Deszca, E. (1982). Career success and personal failure experiences and Type A behaviour. *Journal of Occupational Behaviour, 3*, 161–170.

Burke, R. J., & Deszca, E. (1986). Correlates of psychological burnout phases among police officers. *Human Relations, 39*, 487–501.

Burke, R. J., & Greenglass, E. R. (1988). Career orientations and psychological burnout in teachers. *Psychological Reports, 63*, 107–116.

Burke, R. J., & Greenglass, E. R. (1989a). It may be lonely at the top but it's less stressful: Psychological burnout in public schools. *Psychological Reports, 64*, 615–623.

Burke, R. J., & Greenglass, E. R. (1989b). Sex differences in psychological burnout in teachers. *Psychological Reports, 65*, 55–63.

Burke, R. J., & Greenglass, E. R. (1990). Type A behavior and non-work activities. *Personality and Individual Differences, 11*, 945–952.

Burke, R. J., & Kirchmeyer, C. (1990). Initial career orientations, stress and burnout in policeworkers. *Canadian Police College Journal, 14*, 28–36.

Burke, R. J., Shearer, J., & Deszca, E. (1984). Correlates of burnout phases among police officers. *Group and Organization Studies, 9*, 451–466.

Burke, R. J., & Weir, T. (1980). The Type A experience: Occupational and life demands, satisfaction, and well-being. *Journal of Human Stress, 6*, 28–38.

Burns, R. C. (1986). Endodontic burnout. *International Journal of Psychosomatics, 33*, 17–23.

Burrel, G., Sundin, O., Strom, G., & Ohman, A. (1986). Heart and lifestyle: A Type A treatment program for myocardial infarction patients. *Scandinavian Journal of Behaviour Therapy, 15*, 87–93.

Burton, D. (1988). Do anxious swimmers swim slower? Reexamining the elusive anxiety–performance relationship. *Journal of Sport and Exercise Psychology, 10,* 45–61.

Buss, A. H. (1988). *Personality: Evolutionary heritage and human distinctiveness.* Hillsdale, NJ: Erlbaum.

Byrd, L. M., & Touliatos, J. (1982). Experimental manipulation of the "motive to avoid success." *Perceptual and Motor Skills, 55,* 1327–1331.

Byrne, D. G., & Reinhart, M. I. (1990). Work characteristics, occupational achievement and the Type A behaviour pattern. *Journal of Occupational Psychology, 62,* 123–134.

Caccese, T. M., & Mayerberg, C. K. (1984). Gender differences in perceived burnout of college coaches. *Journal of Sport Psychology, 6,* 279–288.

Campbell, R. E., & Cellini, J. V. (1981). A diagnostic taxonomy of adult career problems. *Journal of Vocational Behavior, 19,* 175–190.

Cano, L., Solomon, S., & Holmes, D. S. (1984). Fear of success: The influence of sex, sex-role identity, and components of masculinity. *Sex Roles, 10,* 341–346.

Caplan, R. D. (1971). Organizational stress and individual strain: A sociopsychological study of risk factors in coronary heart disease among administrators, engineers, and scientists. (Doctoral dissertation, University of Michigan, 1971). *Dissertation Abstracts International, 32,* 6706b–6707b.

Carr, M., Borkowski, J. G., & Maxwell, S. E. (1991). Motivational components of underachievement. *Developmental Psychology, 27,* 108–118.

Carroll, L. (1987). A study of narcissism, affiliation, intimacy, and power motives among students in business administration. *Psychological Reports, 61,* 355–358.

Carroll, L. (1989). A comparative study of narcissism, gender, and sex-role orientation among bodybuilders, athletes, and psychology students. *Psychological Reports, 64,* 999–1006.

Cattell, R. B. (Ed.). (1987). *Intelligence: Its structure, growth and action* (rev. ed.). Amsterdam: North-Holland.

Cavenar, J. O., & Werman, D. S. (1981). Origins of the fear of success. *American Journal of Psychiatry, 138,* 95–98.

Cecil, M. A., & Forman, S. G. (1990). Effects of stress inoculation training and coworker support groups on teachers' stress. *Journal of School Psychology, 28,* 105–118.

Chabassol, D. J., & Ishiyama, F. I. (1983). Correlations among three measures of fear of success. *Psychological Reports, 52,* 55–58.

Chalus, G. A. (1976). Relationship between paranoid tendencies and projective behavior. *Psychological Reports, 39,* 1175–1181.

Chambless, D. L., & Gillis, M. M. (1993). Cognitive therapy of anxiety disorders. *Journal of Consulting and Clinical Psychology, 61,* 248–260.

Charney, E. A., & Weissman, M. W. (1988). Epidemiology of depressive and manic syndromes. In A. Georgotas & R. Cancro (Eds.), *Depression and mania* (pp. 26–52). New York: Elsevier.

Cheever, J. (1991). *The journals of John Cheever.* New York: Knopf.

Cherniss, C. (1985). Stress, burnout, and the special services provider. *Special Services in the Schools, 2,* 45–61.

Cherry, F., & Deaux, K. (1978). Fear of success versus fear of gender-inappropriate behavior. *Sex Roles, 4,* 97–101.

Cherry, N. (1978). Stress, anxiety and work: A longitudinal study. *Journal of Occupational Psychology, 51,* 259–270.

Cherry, N. (1984a). Nervous strain, anxiety and symptoms amongst 32-year-old men at work in Britain. *Journal of Occupational Psychology, 57,* 95–105.

Cherry, N. (1984b). Women and work stress: Evidence from the 1946 birth cohort. *Ergonomics, 27,* 519–526.

Chodoff, P. (1973). The depressive personality: A critical review. *International Journal of Psychiatry, 11,* 196–217.

Chodoff, P. (1982). Hysteria and women. *American Journal of Psychiatry, 139,* 545–551.

Chonko, L. B. (1983). Job involvement as obsession-compulsion: Some preliminary empirical findings. *Psychological Reports, 53,* 1191–1197.

Claiborn, C. D., Ward, S. R., & Strong, S. R. (1981). Effects of congruence between counselor interpretations and client beliefs. *Journal of Counseling Psychology, 28,* 101–109.

Clance, P. R., & O'Toole, M. A. (1987). The imposter phenomenon: An internal barrier to empowerment and achievement. *Women and Therapy, 6,* 51–64.

Clark, D. A., & Bolton, D. (1985). Obsessive–compulsive adolescents and their parents: A psychometric study. *Journal of Child Psychology and Psychiatry and Allied Disciplines, 26,* 267–276.

Clark, D. B. (1989). Performance-related medical and psychological disorders in instrumental musicians. *Annals of Behavioral Medicine, 11,* 28–34.

Clark, D. C., Gibbons, R. D., Fawcett, J., Aagesen, C., & Sellers, D. (1985). Unbiased criteria for severity of depression in alcoholic inpatients. *Journal of Nervous and Mental Disease, 173,* 482–487.

Clark, J. Z. (1991). Therapist narcissism. *Professional Psychology: Research and Practice, 22,* 141–143.

Clark, L. K., & Miller, S. M. (1990). Self-reliance and desire for control in the Type A behavior pattern. *Journal of Social Behavior and Personality, 5,* 405–418.

Cohen, R. J., & Teevan, R. C. (1974). Fear of failure and impression management: An exploratory study. *Psychological Reports, 35,* 1332.

Cohn, P. J. (1990). An exploratory study on sources of stress and athlete burnout in youth golf. *Sport Psychologist, 4,* 95–106.

Colby, K. M., Faught, W. S., & Parkison, R. C. (1979). Cognitive therapy of paranoid conditions: Heuristic suggestions based on a computer simulation model. *Cognitive Therapy and Research, 3,* 55–60.

Cole, K. G. (1983). Daughters' reactions to maternal depression. *American Journal of Psychoanalysis, 43,* 291–300.

Cole, M. (1984). How to make a person passive–aggressive or The Power Struggle Game. *Transactional Analysis Journal, 14,* 191–194.

Coles, R. (1977). *Privileged ones: The well-off and the rich in America*. Boston: Little, Brown.

Collins, J. J., Schlenger, W. E., & Jordan, B. K. (1988). Antisocial personality and substance abuse disorders. *Bulletin of the American Academy of Psychiatry and the Law, 16*, 187–198.

Collins, W. E., Schroeder, D. J., & Nye, L. G. (1991). Relationships of anxiety scores to screening and training status of air traffic controllers. *Aviation, Space, and Environmental Medicine, 62*, 236–240.

Colton, L. (1993). *Goat brothers*. New York: Doubleday.

Constable, J. F., & Russell, D. W. (1986). The effect of social support and the work environment upon burnout among nurses. *Journal of Human Stress, 12*, 20–26.

Conte, H. R., Plutchik, R., Picard, S., Karasu, T. B., & Vaccaro, D. (1988). Self-report measures as predictors of psychotherapy outcome. *Comprehensive Psychiatry, 29*, 355–360.

Cooley, E. J. (1987). Situational and trait determinants of competitive state anxiety. *Perceptual and Motor Skills, 64*, 767–773.

Cooney, N. L., Kadden, R. M., & Litt, M. D. (1990). A comparison of methods for assessing sociopathy in male and female alcoholics. *Journal of Studies on Alcohol, 51*, 42–48.

Cooper, C. L., & Payne, R. (1988). *Causes, coping and consequences of stress at work*. New York: Wiley.

Cooper, C. L., & Roden, J. (1985). Mental health and satisfaction among tax officers. *Social Science and Medicine, 21*, 747–751.

Cooper, C. L., & Wills, G. I. (1989). Popular musicians under pressure. *Psychology of Music, 17*, 22–36.

Corcoran, K. J. (1986). Measuring burnout: A reliability and convergent validity study. *Journal of Social Behavior and Personality, 1*, 107–112.

Corney, M. R. (1988). Treatment of early narcissistic disturbance. *British Journal of Psychotherapy, 5*, 159–171.

Cornfield, R. B., & Malen, R. L. (1978). A multidimensional view of the obsessive character. *Comprehensive Psychiatry, 19*, 73–78.

Costa, P., & McRae, R. R. (1988). Personality in adulthood: A six-year study of self-reports and spouse ratings on the NEO Personality Inventory. *Journal of Personality and Social Psychology, 54*, 853–863.

Cottington, E. M., & House, J. S. (1987). Occupational stress and health: A multivariate relationship. In A. Baum & J. E. Singer (Eds.), *Handbook of psychology and health: Vol. 5. Stress* (pp. 41–62). Hillsdale, NJ: Erlbaum.

Covington, M. V., & Omelich, C. L. (1991). Need achievement revisited: Verification of Atkinson's original 2 × 2 model. In C. D. Spielberger, I. G. Sarason, Z. C. Kulcsar, & G. L. Van Heck (Eds.), *Stress and emotion: Vol. 14. Anxiety, anger, and curiosity* (pp. 85–105). New York: Hemisphere.

Craske, M. G., & Craig, K. D. (1984). Musical performance anxiety: The three-systems model and self-efficacy theory. *Behaviour Research and Therapy, 22*, 267–280.

Crino, R. D. (1991). Obsessive compulsive disorder. *International Review of Psychiatry, 3*, 189–201.

Csikszentmihalyi, M. (1990). The domain of creativity. In M. A. Runco & R. S. Albert (Eds.), *Theories of creativity* (pp. 190– 212). Newbury Park, CA: Sage.

Curtis, R. C., Zanna, M. P., & Campbell, W. W. (1975). Sex, fear of success, and the perceptions and performance of law school students. *American Educational Research Journal, 12*, 287–297.

Dahlstrom, W. G., Welsh, G. S., & Dahlstrom, L. E. (1972). *An MMPI handbook: Vol. 1. Clinical interpretation* (rev. ed.). Minneapolis: University of Minnesota Press.

Damos, D. L. (1985). The relation between the Type A behavior pattern, pacing, and subjective workload under single- and dual-task conditions. *Human Factors, 27*, 675–680.

Damos, D. L., & Bloem, K. A. (1985). Type A behavior pattern, multiple-task performance, and subjective estimation of mental workload. *Bulletin of the Psychonomic Society, 23*, 53–56.

Daniels, J. L., Alcorn, J. D., & Kazelskis, R. (1981). Factor analysis of the Cohen Fear of Success Scale. *Psychological Reports, 49*, 839–842.

Dapra, R. A., Zarrillo, D. L., Carlson, T. K., & Teevan, R. C. (1985). Fear of failure and indices of leadership utilized in the training of ROTC cadets. *Psychological Reports, 56*, 27–30.

Dardis, T. (1989). *Thirsty muse: Alcohol and the American writer.* New York: Ticknov & Fields.

Darke, S. (1988). Effects of anxiety on inferential reasoning task performance. *Journal of Personality and Social Psychology, 55*, 499–505.

Davies, T. W., & DeMonchaux, C. (1973). Mood changes in relation to personality and the excretion of 3-methoxy-4-hydroxy-mandelic acid. *Psychosomatic Medicine, 35*, 205–214.

Davis, R. V., & Lofquist, L. H. (1984). *A psychological theory of work adjustment: An individual differences model and its application.* Minneapolis: University of Minnesota Press.

Davis, S., Jayaratne, S., & Chess, W. A. (1985). A comparison of the effects of social support on the incidence of burnout. *Social Work, 30*, 240–244.

Day, D. V., & Bedeian, A. G. (1991). Work climate and Type A status as predictors of job satisfaction: A test of the interactional perspective. *Journal of Vocational Behavior, 38*, 39–52.

Dearborn, M. J., & Hastings, J. E. (1987). Type A personality as a mediator of stress and strain in employed women. *Journal of Human Stress, 13*(2), 53–60.

DeCarlo, D. T. (1987). New legal rights related to emotional stress in the workplace. *Journal of Business and Psychology*, 313–325.

deLeo, D., Magni, G., & Vallerini, A. (1982). Anxiety and depression in general and psychiatric nurses: A comparison. *International Journal of Nursing Studies, 19*, 173–175.

deLeon, J., Saiz-Ruiz, J., Chinchilla, A., & Morales, P. (1987). Why do some psychiatric patients somatize? *Acta Psychiatrica Scandinavica, 76,* 203–220.

Dell, D. M. (1973). Counselor power base, influence attempt, and behavior change in counseling. *Journal of Counseling Psychology, 20,* 399–405.

Deltito, J. A., & Perugi, G. (1986). A case of social phobia with avoidant personality disorder treated with MAOI. *Comprehensive Psychiatry, 27,* 255–258.

Deltito, J. A., & Stam, M. (1989). Psychopharmacological treatment of avoidant personality disorder. *Comprehensive Psychiatry, 30,* 498–504.

Dembroski, T. M., MacDougall, J. M., Costa, P. T., & Grandits, G. A. (1989). Components of hostility as predictors of sudden death and myocardial infarction in the Multiple Risk Factor Intervention Trial. *Psychosomatic Medicine, 51,* 514–522.

Denison, D. R. (1990). *Corporate culture and organizational effectiveness.* New York: Wiley.

Devereaux, E., & Carlson, M. (1992). The role of occupational therapy in the management of depression. *American Journal of Occupational Therapy, 46,* 175–180.

deVries, M. F. (1977). Crisis leadership and the paranoid potential: An organizational perspective. *Bulletin of the Menninger Clinic, 41,* 349–365.

Dew, K. H., Galassi, J. P., & Galassi, M. D. (1984). Math anxiety: Relation with situational test anxiety, performance, physiological arousal, and math avoidance behavior. *Journal of Counseling Psychology, 31,* 581–584.

DeWolff, C. J., & Winnubst, J. A. M. (1987). Stress in the working situation. In B. M. Bass, P. J. D. Drenth, & P. Weissenberg (Eds.), *Advances in organizational psychology: An international review* (pp. 43–57). Newbury Park, CA: Sage.

Dews, C. B., & Williams, M. S. (1989). Student musicians' personality styles, stresses, and coping patterns. Performance and stress. *Psychology of Music, 17,* 37–47.

Diekhoff, G. M. (1984). Running amok: Injuries in compulsive runners. *Journal of Sport Behavior, 7,* 120–129.

Dignam, J. T., Barrera, M., & West, S. G. (1986). Occupational stress, social support, and burnout among correctional officers. *American Journal of Community Psychology, 14,* 177–193.

Dignam, J. T., & West, S. G. (1988). Social support in the workplace: Tests of six theoretical models. *American Journal of Community Psychology, 16,* 701–724.

diSalvo, V., Lubbers, C., Rossi, A. M., & Lewis, J. (1988). The impact of gender on work-related stress. *Journal of Social Behavior and Personality, 3,* 161–176.

Dohrenwend, B. P., Dohrenwend, B. S., Gould, M. S., Link, B., Neugebauer, R., & Wunsch-Hitzig, R. (1980). *Mental illness in the United States: Epidemiological estimates.* New York: Praeger.

Domash, L., & Shapiro, R. (1979). Dysfunctional patterns of thinking in the borderline personality. *Journal of the American Academy of Psychoanalysis, 7,* 543–552.

Donat, D. C., Neal, B., & Addleton, R. (1991). Situational sources of stress for direct care staff in a public psychiatric hospital. *Psychosocial Rehabilitation Journal, 14,* 76–81.

Donatelle, R. J., & Hawkins, M. J. (1989). Employee stress claims: Increasing implications for health promotion programming. *American Journal of Health Promotion, 3,* 19–25.

Dooley, A. M. (1987). A developmental approach to diagnosis. *Clinical Social Work Journal, 15,* 328–333.

Dowd, E. T., Hughes, S. L., Brockbank, L., Halpain, D., Seibel, C., & Seibel, P. (1988). Compliance-based and defiance-based intervention strategies and psychological reactance in the treatment of free and unfree behavior. *Journal of Counseling Psychology, 35,* 370–376.

Dowdall, G. W., & Goldstein, M. S. (1984–1985). Occupational problems, unemployment and mental illness: How a community mental health center deals with job troubles. *Journal of Applied Social Sciences, 9,* 37–57.

Drake, R. E., & Vaillant, G. E. (1985). A validity study of axis II of *DSM-III. American Journal of Psychiatry, 142,* 553–558.

Drossman, D. A. (1982). Patients with psychogenic abdominal pain: Six years' observation in the medical setting. *American Journal of Psychiatry, 139,* 1549–1557.

Duffy, C. A., & McGoldrick, A. E. (1990). Stress and the bus driver in the UK transport industry. *Work and Stress, 4,* 17–27.

Dweck, C. S., & Wortman, C. B. (1982). Learned helplessness, anxiety, and achievement motivation: Neglected parallels in cognitive, affective, and coping responses. In H. W. Krohne & L. Laux (Eds.), *Achievement, stress, and anxiety* (pp. 93–125). Washington, DC: Hemisphere.

Dyck, R. J., Bland, R. C., Newman, S. C., & Orn, H. (1988). Suicide attempts and psychiatric disorders in Edmonton. *Acta Psychiatrica Scandinavica, 77*(Suppl. 338), 64–71.

Edbril, S. D., & Rieker, P. P. (1989). The impact of testicular cancer on the work lives of survivors. *Journal of Psychological Oncology, 7,* 17–29.

Edwards, D., & Berry, N. H. (1973). Prediction for the character and behavior disorder in an occupational setting. *Journal of Clinical Psychology, 29,* 171–174.

Edwards, P., & Miltenberger, R. (1991). Burnout among staff members at community residential facilities for persons with mental retardation. *Mental Retardation, 29,* 125–128.

Effert, B. R., & Ferrari, J. R. (1989). Decisional procrastination: Examining personality correlates. *Journal of Social Behavior and Personality, 4,* 151–161.

Egli, D. (1992, August). Overview, assessment, and behavior therapy. In D. Egli (Chair), *Obsessive–compulsive disorder: Epidemiology, assessment, and comorbidity.* Symposium conducted at the meeting of the American Psychological Association, Washington, DC.

Eisenstat, R. A., & Felner, R. D. (1984). Toward a differentiated view of burnout: Personal and organizational mediators of job satisfaction and stress. *American Journal of Community Psychology, 12,* 411–430.

Ellis, A., & Knaus, W. (1977). *Overcoming procrastination*. New York: Institute for Rational Living.

Emener, W. G., Luck, R. S., & Gohs, F. X. (1982). A theoretical investigation of the construct burnout. *Journal of Rehabilitation Administration, 6,* 188–196.

Emmons, R. A. (1987). Narcissism: Theory and measurement. *Journal of Personality and Social Psychology, 52,* 11–17.

Esposito, R. P. (1977). The relationship between the motive to avoid success and vocational choice. *Journal of Vocational Behavior, 10,* 347–357.

Etzion, D. (1984). Moderating effect of social support on the stress–burnout relationship. *Journal of Applied Psychology, 69,* 615–622.

Etzion, D. (1987). Burning out in management: A comparison of women and men in matched organizational positions. *Israel Social Science Research, 5,* 147–163.

Etzion, D., & Pines, A. (1986). Sex and culture in burnout and coping among human service professionals: A social psychological perspective. *Journal of Cross Cultural Psychology, 17,* 191–209.

Evans, G. W., Palsane, M. N., & Carrere, S. (1987). Type A behavior and occupational stress: A cross-cultural study of blue-collar workers. *Journal of Personality and Social Psychology, 52,* 1002–1007.

Eysenck, H. J. (1958). A short questionnaire for the measurement of the dimensions of personality. *Journal of Applied Psychology, 42,* 14–17.

Eysenck, H. J., & Eysenck, S. B. G. (1976). *Manual of the Eysenck Personality Questionnaire*. London, England: Hodder & Stoughton.

Farber, B. A. (1984). Stress and burnout in suburban teachers. *Journal of Educational Research, 77,* 325–331.

Farber, B. A. (1985). Clinical psychologists' perceptions of psychotherapeutic work. *Clinical Psychologist, 38,* 10–13.

Farber, B. A. (1990). Burnout in psychotherapists: Incidence, types, and trends. *Psychotherapy in Private Practice, 8,* 35–44.

Farber, B. A., & Heifetz, L. J. (1982). The process and dimensions of burnout in psychotherapists. *Professional Psychology, 13,* 293–301.

Farmer, H. S. (1980). Environmental, background, and psychological variables related to optimizing achievement and career motivation for high school girls. *Journal of Vocational Behavior, 17,* 58–70.

Farnham, A. (1991). Who beats stress best—and how. *Fortune, 124,* 71-86.

Fast, I. (1975). Aspects of work style and work difficulty in borderline personalities. *International Journal of Psycho-Analysis, 56,* 397–403.

Fava, G. A., Grandi, S., Canestrari, R., & Molnar, G. (1990). Prodromal symptoms in primary major depressive disorder. *Journal of Affective Disorders, 19,* 149–152.

Feather, N. T., & Simon, J. G. (1973). Fear of success and causal attribution for outcome. *Journal of Personality, 41,* 525–542.

Fekken, G. C., & Jakubowski, I. (1990). Effects of stress on the health of Type A students. *Journal of Social Behavior and Personality, 5,* 473–480.

Felton, G. S. (1973). Use of the MMPI Underachievement scale as an aid in counseling academic low achievers in college. *Psychological Reports, 32,* 151–157.

Fenichel, O. (1945). *The psychoanalytic theory of neurosis.* Madison, CT: International Universities Press.

Fenton, W. S., & McGlashan, T. H. (1989). Risk of schizophrenia in character disordered patients. *American Journal of Psychiatry, 146,* 1280–1284.

Fimian, M. J., Lieberman, R. J., & Fastenau, P. S. (1991). Development and validation of an instrument to measure occupational stress in speech-language pathologists. *Journal of Speech and Hearing Research, 34,* 439–446.

Fine, R. (1980). Work, depression and creativity. *Psychological Reports, 46,* 1095–1121.

Fine, R. (1984). The effect of psychoanalysis on the creative individual. In H. S. Strean (Ed.), *Inhibitions in work and love: Psychoanalytic approaches to problems in creativity* (pp. 3–28). New York: Haworth.

Firth, C. J., & Hardy, G. E. (1992). Occupational stress, clinical treatment and changes in job perceptions. *Journal of Occupational and Organizational Psychology, 65,* 81–88.

Firth, H., & Britton, P. (1989). "Burnout," absence and turnover amongst British nursing staff. *Journal of Occupational Psychology, 62,* 55–59.

Firth, H., McIntee, J., McKeown, P., & Britton, P. G. (1985). Maslach Burnout Inventory: Factor structure and norms for British nursing staff. *Psychological Reports, 57,* 147–150.

Firth, H., McKeown, P., McIntee, J., & Britton, P. (1987). Professional depression, "burnout" and personality in longstay nursing. *International Journal of Nursing Studies, 24,* 227–237.

Firth, J., & Shapiro, D. A. (1986). An evaluation of psychotherapy for job-related distress. *Journal of Occupational Psychology, 59,* 111–119.

Fishbain, D. A., Goldberg, M., Labbe, E., Steele, R., & Rosomoff, H. (1988). Compensation and non-compensation chronic pain patients compared for *DSM-III* operational diagnoses. *Pain, 32,* 197–206.

Fischer, R. (1989). Psychotherapy of the narcissistic personality disorder. In J. F. Masterson & R. Klein (Eds.), *Psychotherapy of the disorders of the self: The Masterson approach* (pp. 69–89). New York: Brunner/Mazel.

Fischer, S. (1991). The focus of perssimism in performance assessments by the depressed. *British Journal of Clinical Psychology, 30,* 271–272.

Fleming, J. (1977). Predictive validity of the motive to avoid success in Black women. *Humanitas, 13,* 225–244.

Fleming, J. (1978). Fear of success, achievement-related motives and behavior in Black college women. *Journal of Personality, 46,* 694–716.

Fleming, J. (1982). Fear of success in Black female and male graduate students: A pilot study. *Psychology of Women Quarterly, 6,* 327–341.

Fletcher, B. C. (1988). The epidemiology of occupational stress. In C. L. Cooper & R. Payne (Eds.), *Causes, coping and consequences of stress at work* (pp. 3–50). New York: Wiley.

Flynn, P. M., & McMahon, R. (1984). An examination of the factor structure of the Millon Clinical Multiaxial Inventory. *Journal of Personality Assessment, 48,* 308–311.

Fogel, R., & Paludi, M. A. (1984). Fear of success and failure, or norms for achievement? *Sex Roles, 10,* 431–434.

Fogle, D. O. (1982). Toward effective treatment for music performance anxiety. *Psychotherapy Theory, Research and Practice, 19,* 368–375.

Foon, A. E. (1987). Discovery in psychotherapy: The role of the creative patient. *Psychotherapy Patient, 4,* 47–56.

Forbes, G. B., & King, S. (1983). Fear of success and sex-role: There are reliable relationships. *Psychological Reports, 53,* 735–738.

Ford, D. L., Murphy, C. J., & Edwards, K. L. (1983). Exploratory development and validation of a perceptual job burnout inventory: Comparison of corporate sector and human services professionals. *Psychological Reports, 52,* 995–1006.

Ford, M. R., & Widiger, T. A. (1989). Sex bias in the diagnosis of histrionic and antisocial personality disorders. *Journal of Consulting and Clinical Psychology, 57,* 301–305.

Frances, A., & Widiger, T. A. (1986). Methodological issues in personality disorder diagnosis. In T. Millon & G. L. Klerman (Eds.), *Contemporary directions in psychopathology: Toward the DSM–IV* (pp. 381–400). New York: Guilford Press.

Fraser, R. (1947). *The incidence of neurosis among factory workers* (Medical Research Council Health Research Board Rep. No. 90). London: Her Majesty's Stationery Office.

Freeman, A., & Leaf, R. C. (1989). Cognitive therapy applied to personality disorders. In A. Freeman, K. Simon, L. Beutler, & H. Arkowtiz (Eds.), *Comorbidity of mood and anxiety disorders* (pp. 403–433). New York: Plenum Press.

Fremouw, W. J., Gross, R., Monroe, J., & Rapp, S. (1982). Empirical subtypes of performance anxiety. *Behavioral Assessment, 4,* 179–193.

Freud, S. (1959). Those wrecked by success: Some character types met with in psychoanalytic work. In E. Jones (Ed.), *Sigmund Freud: Collected papers* (Vol. 4, pp. 318–344). New York: Basic Books. (Original work published 1915)

Freud, S. (1961). *Civilization and its discontents.* In J. Strachey (Ed. and Trans.), *The standard edition of the complete psychological works of Sigmund Freud* (Vol. 21, pp. 59–145). London: Hogarth Press. (Original work published 1930)

Freudenberger, H. J. (1983). Hazards of psychotherapeutic practice. *Psychotherapy in Private Practice, 1,* 83–89.

Freudenberger, H. J., & Richelson, G. (1980). *Burnout: The high cost of achievement.* New York: Doubleday.

Friedman, M., & Rosenman, R. H. (1974). *Type A behavior and your heart.* New York: Knopf.

Friesen, D., Prokop, C. M., & Sarros, J. C. (1988). Why teachers burn out. *Educational Research Quarterly, 12,* 9–19.

Friesen, D., & Sarros, J. C. (1989). Sources of burnout among educators. *Journal of Organizational Behavior, 10,* 179–188.

Froehle, T. C. (1989). Personal construct threat as a mediator of performance anxiety in a beginning course in counseling techniques. *Journal of College Student Development, 30,* 536–540.

Froggatt, K. L., & Cotton, J. L. (1987). The impact of Type A behavior pattern on role overload-induced stress and performance attributions. *Journal of Management, 13,* 87–98.

Frone, M. R., Russell, M., & Cooper, M. L. (1991). Relationship of work and family stressors to psychological distress: The independent moderating influence of social support, mastery, active coping, and self-focused attention. *Journal of Social Behavior and Personality, 6,* 277–250.

Frost, R. O., Lahart, C. M., Dugas, K. M., & Sher, K. J. (1988). Information processing among non-clinical compulsives. *Behaviour Research and Therapy, 26,* 275–277.

Frost, R. O., Marten, P., Lahart, C., & Rosenblate, R. (1990). The dimensions of perfectionism. *Cognitive Therapy and Research, 14,* 449–468.

Fryer, D., & Payne, R. (1986). Being unemployed: A review of the literature on the psychological experience of unemployment. In C. L. Cooper & I. Robertson (Eds.), *International review of industrial and organizational psychology 1986* (pp. 235–278). New York: Wiley.

Fuehrer, A., & McGonagle, K. (1988). Individual and situational factors as predictors of burnout among resident assistants. *Journal of College Student Development, 29,* 244–249.

Fusilier, M. R., Ganster, D. C., & Mayes, B. T. (1987). Effects of social support, role stress, and locus of control on health. *Journal of Management, 13,* 517–528.

Gabbard, G. O. (1989). Two subtypes of narcissistic personality disorder. *Bulletin of the Menninger Clinic, 53,* 527–532.

Gabbard, G. O., & Coyne, L. (1987). Predictors of response of antisocial patients to hospital treatment. *Hospital and Community Psychiatry, 38,* 1181–1185.

Gaines, J., & Jermier, J. M. (1983). Emotional exhaustion in a high stress organization. *Academy of Management Journal, 26,* 567–586.

Gallagher, J. J. (1991). Personal patterns of underachievement. *Journal for the Education of the Gifted, 14,* 221–233.

Gallant, D. M., & Simpson, G. M. (Eds.). (1976). *Depression: Behavioral, biochemical, diagnostic, and treatment concepts.* New York: Spectrum.

Ganster, D. C. (1986). Type A behavior and occupational stress. *Journal of Organizational Behavior Management, 8,* 61–84.

Ganster, D. C., & Fusilier, M. R. (1989). Control in the workplace. In C. L. Cooper & I. T. Robertson (Eds.), *International review of industrial and organizational psychology 1989* (pp. 235–280). New York: Wiley.

Ganster, D. C., Mayes, B. T., Sime, W. E., & Tharp, G. D. (1982). Managing organizational stress: A field experiment. *Journal of Applied Psychology, 67,* 533–542.

Garamoni, G. L., & Schwartz, R. M. (1986). Type A behavior and compulsive personality: Toward a psychodynamic behavioral integration. *Clinical Psychology Review, 6*, 311–336.

Garvey, M. J., & Spoden, F. (1980). Suicide attempts in antisocial personality disorder. *Comprehensive Psychiatry, 21*, 146–149.

Gastorf, J. W., & Teevan, R. C. (1980). Type A coronary-prone behavior pattern and fear of failure. *Motivation and Emotion, 4*, 71–76.

Gavin, J. F. (1975). Employee perceptions of the work environment and mental health: A suggestive study. *Journal of Vocational Behavior, 6*, 217–234.

Gedo, J. E. (1990). More on creativity and its vicissitudes. In M. A. Runco & R. S. Albert (Eds.), *Theories of creativity* (pp. 35–45). Newbury Park, CA: Sage.

Gelbort, K. R., & Winer, J. L. (1985). Fear of success and fear of failure: A multitrait–multimethod validation study. *Journal of Personality and Social Psychology, 48*, 1009–1014.

George, A., & Soloff, P. M. (1986). Schizotypal symptoms in patients with borderline personality disorders. *American Journal of Psychiatry, 143*, 212–215.

George, L. K., Hughes, D. C., & Blazer, D. G. (1986). Urban/rural differences in the prevalence of anxiety disorder. *American Journal of Social Psychiatry, 6*, 249–258.

Gerstley, L. J., Alterman, A. I., McLellan, A. T., & Woody, G. E. (1990). Antisocial personality disorder in patients with substance abuse disorders: A problematic diagnosis? *American Journal of Psychiatry, 147*, 173–178.

Gerstley, L., McLellan, A. T., Alterman, A. I., Woody, G. E., Luborsky, L., & Prout, M. (1989). Ability to form an alliance with the therapist: A possible marker of prognosis for patients with antisocial personality disorder. *American Journal of Psychiatry, 146*, 508–512.

Giannandrea, P. F. (1985).Psychodynamic approach to occupational psychiatry: Comparative case studies and review. *American Journal of Psychotherapy, 39*, 421–430.

Gibbons, P. A., & Kopelman, R. E. (1977). Maternal employment as a determinant of fear of success in females. *Psychological Reports, 40*, 1200–1202.

Gibson, D. L. (1983). The obsessive personality and the evangelical. *Journal of Psychology and Christianity, 2*, 30–35.

Gillespie, D. F., & Numerof, R. E. (1991). Burnout among health service providers. *Administration and Policy in Mental Health, 18*, 161–171.

Gilroy, F. D., Talierco, T. M., & Steinbacher, R. (1981). Impact of maternal employment on daughters' sex-role orientation and fear of success. *Psychological Reports, 49*, 963–968.

Giovacchini, P. L. (1975). Productive procrastination: Technical factors in the treatment of the adolescent. *Adolescent Psychiatry, 4*, 352–370.

Giovacchini, P. L. (1976). Ego pathology: Diagnostic and treatment implications. *Contemporary Psychoanalysis, 12*, 173–185.

Girodo, M. (1985). Health and legal issues in undercover narcotics investigations: Misrepresented evidence. *Behavioral Sciences and the Law, 3*, 299–308.

Gleick, J. (1992, September 20). Part showman, all genius. *New York Times Magazine*, pp. 39–48.

Glogow, E. (1986). Research note: Burnout and locus of control. *Public Personnel Management, 15*, 79–83.

Goh, S. C., & Mealiea, L. W. (1984). Fear of success and its relationship to the job performance, tenure, and desired job outcomes of women. *Canadian Journal of Behavioural Science, 16*, 65–75.

Gold, Y. (1984a). Burnout: A major problem for the teaching profession. *Education, 104*, 271–274.

Gold, Y. (1984b). The factorial validity of the Maslach Burnout Inventory in a sample of California elementary and junior high school classroom teachers. *Educational and Psychological Measurement, 44*, 1009–1016.

Gold, Y. (1985). The relationship of six personal and life history variables to standing on three dimensions of the Maslach Burnout Inventory in a sample of elementary and junior high school teachers. *Educational and Psychological Measurement, 45*, 377–387.

Gold, Y., Bachelor, P. A., & Michael, W. B. (1989). The dimensionality of a modified form of the Maslach Burnout Inventory for university students in a teacher-training program. *Educational and Psychological Measurement, 49*, 549–561.

Gold, Y., Roth, R. A., Wright, C. R., & Michael, W. B. (1991). The relationship of scores on the Educators Survey, a modified version of the Maslach Burnout Inventory, to three teaching-related variables for a sample of 132 beginning teachers. *Educational and Psychological Measurement, 51*, 429–438.

Goldberg, C. (1973). Some effects of fear of failure in the academic setting. *Journal of Psychology, 84*, 323–331.

Goldberg, C. (1988). Replacing moral masochism with a shame paradigm in psychoanalysis. *Dynamic Psychotherapy, 6*, 114–123.

Goldberg, N. (1988). *Writing down the bones: Freeing the writer within*. Boston: Shambhala.

Golding, J. M. (1989). Role occupancy and role-specific stress and social support as predictors of depression. *Basic and Applied Social Psychology, 10*, 173–195.

Goldstein, E. (1984). "Homo Sovieticus" in transition: Psychoanalysis and problems of social adjustment. *Journal of the American Academy of Psychoanalysis, 12*, 115–126.

Goldstein, W. N. (1985a). *DSM–III* and the narcissistic personality. *American Journal of Psychotherapy, 39*, 4–16.

Goldstein, W. N. (1985b). Obsessive–compulsive behavior, *DSM–III*, and a psychodynamic classification of psychopathology. *American Journal of Psychotherapy, 39*, 346–359.

Golembiewski, R. T., & Kim, B. (1989). Self-esteem and phases of burnout. *Organization Development Journal, 7*, 51–58.

Golembiewski, R. T., & Munzenrider, R. F. (1988). *Phases of burnout: Developments in concepts and applications*. New York: Praeger.

Golembiewski, R. T., & Munzenrider, R. F. (1991). Burnout and mental health: A pilot study. *Organization Development Journal, 9*, 51–57.

Golembiewski, R. T., Munzenrider, R., & Carter, D. (1983). Phases of progressive burnout and their work site covariants: Critical issues in OD research and praxis. *Journal of Applied Behavioral Science, 19*, 461–481.

Golembiewski, R. T., Munzenrider, R. F., & Stevenson, J. G. (1986). *Stress in organizations*. New York: Praeger.

Good, L. R., & Good, K. C. (1975). An objective measure of the motive to avoid failure. *Psychology, 12*, 11–14.

Goodwin, D. W. (1988). *Alcohol and the writer*. Kansas City, MO: Andrews & McNeel.

Goodwin, F. K., & Jamison, K. R. (1990). *Manic depressive illness*. New York: Oxford University Press.

Googins, B. K. (1991). *Work/family conflicts*. New York: Auburn House.

Gonsalves, S. V. (1983). Bibliography on fear of success in Black women: 1970-1982. *Psychological Reports, 53*, 1249–1250.

Gordon, R. E., Eisler, R. L., Gutman, E. M., & Gordon, K. K. (1991). Predicting prognosis by means of the *DSM–III* multiaxial diagnoses. *Canadian Journal of Psychiatry, 36*, 218–221.

Gorenstein, E. E., & Newman, J. P. (1980). Disinhibitory psychopathology: A new perspective and a model for research. *Psychological Review, 87*, 301–315.

Gottfredson, L. S. (1984). *The role of intelligence and education in the division of labor* (Report No. 355). Baltimore: Johns Hopkins University Center for Social Organization of Schools.

Gottfredson, L. S. (1986). Occupational Aptitude Patterns Map: Development and implications for a theory of job aptitude requirements. *Journal of Vocational Behavior, 29*, 254–291.

Gough, H. (1987). *CPI: The California Psychological Inventory administrator's guide*. Palo Alto, CA: Consulting Psychologists Press.

Gough, H. (1992). Assessment of creative potential in psychology and the development of a Creative Temperament Scale for the CPI. In J. C. Rosen & P. McReynolds (Eds.), *Advances in psychological assessment* (Vol. 8, pp. 225–257). New York: Plenum Press.

Gralnick, A. (1979). Management of character disorders in a hospital setting. *American Journal of Psychotherapy, 33*, 54–66.

Gray, A., Jackson, D. N., & Howard, J. H. (1990). Identification of a coronary-prone profile for business managers: Comparison of three approaches to Type A assessment. *Behavioral Medicine, 16*, 67–75.

Grayson, P. A. (1991). Alternative methods for solving academic problems. *Journal of College Student Psychotherapy, 5*, 47–58.

Greben, S. E. (1983). The multi-dimensional inpatient treatment of severe character disorders. *Canadian Journal of Psychiatry, 28*, 97–101.

Green, K., Fine, M. J., & Tollefson, N. (1988). Family systems characteristics and underachieving gifted adolescent males. *Gifted Child Quarterly, 32*, 267–272.

Greenberg, R. P., & Bornstein, R. F. (1988a). The dependent personality: I. Risk for physical disorders. *Journal of Personality Disorders, 2,* 126–135.

Greenberg, R. P., & Bornstein, R. F. (1988b). The dependent personality: II. Risk for psychological disorders. *Journal of Personality Disorders, 2,* 136–143.

Greene, G. (1960). *A burnt-out case.* London: Penguin Books.

Greenfeld, N., & Teevan, R. C. (1986). Fear of failure in families without fathers. *Psychological Reports, 59,* 571–574.

Greenglass, E. R. (1985). Psychological implications of sex bias in the workplace. *Academic Psychology Bulletin, 7,* 227–240.

Greenglass, E. (1988). Type A behavior and coping strategies in female and male supervisors. *Applied Psychology: An International Review, 37,* 271–288.

Greenglass, E. R. (1990). Type A behavior, career aspirations, and role conflict in professional women. *Journal of Social Behavior and Personality, 5,* 307–322.

Greenglass, E. R. (1991). Type A behavior, career aspirations, and role conflict in professional women. In M. J. Strube (Ed.), *Type A behavior* (pp. 277–292). Newbury Park, CA: Sage.

Greenglass, E. R., & Burke, R. J. (1988). Work and family precursors of burnout in teachers: Sex differences. *Sex Roles, 18,* 215–229.

Greenglass, E. R., Burke, R. J., & Ondrack, M. (1990). A gender-role perspective of coping and burnout. *Applied Psychology: An International Review, 39,* 5–27.

Greenglass, E. R., Pantony, K. L., & Burke, R. J. (1988). A gender-role perspective on role conflict, work stress and social support. *Journal of Social Behavior and Personality, 3,* 317–328.

Grey, A. L. (1987). Entitlement: An interactional defense of self esteem. *Contemporary Psychoanalysis, 23,* 255–263.

Grieff, B. S., & Munter, P. K. (1980). *Tradeoffs: Executive, family, and organizational life.* New York: New American Library.

Griffore, R. J. (1977a). Fear of success and task difficulty: Effects on graduate students' final exam performance. *Journal of Educational Psychology, 69,* 556–563.

Griffore, R. J. (1977b). Validation of three measures of fear of success. *Journal of Personality Assessment, 41,* 417–421.

Grigsby, D. W., & McKnew, M. A. (1988). Work-stress burnout among paramedics. *Psychological Reports, 63,* 55–64.

Gross, M., & Gross, E. (1985). Hypnoanalytic treatment of fear of success. *Medical Hypnoanalysis, 6,* 46–52.

Gudjonsson, G. H. (1984). Fear of "failure" and "tissue damage" in police recruits, constables, sergeants and senior officers. *Personality and Individual Differences, 5,* 233–236.

Gunderson, J. G., Ronningstam, E., & Bodkin, A. (1990). The diagnostic interview for narcissistic patients. *Archives of General Psychiatry, 47,* 676–680.

Gunderson, J. G., Ronningstam, E., & Smith, L. E. (1991). Narcissistic personality disorder: A review of data on *DSM-III-R* descriptions. *Journal of Personality Disorders, 5,* 167–177.

Gunderson, J. G., & Zanarini, M. C. (1987). Current overview of the borderline diagnosis. *Journal of Clinical Psychiatry, 48*(Suppl.), 5–11.

Gutman, S. T. (1987). Conflations in Walt Whitman's "Out of the Cradle." *American Imago, 44,* 149–157.

Guy, J. D. (1987). *The personal life of the psychotherapist.* New York: Wiley.

Hall, B. L., & Hursch, D. E. (1981–1982). An evaluation of the effects of a time management training program on work efficiency. *Journal of Organizational Behavior Management, 3,* 73–96.

Hall, E. G. (1983). Recognizing gifted underachievers. *Roeper Review, 5,* 23–25.

Halpern, H. (1964). Psychodynamic and cultural determinants of work inhibition in children and adolescents. *Psychological Review, 51,* 173–189.

Hamilton, C. A. (1987). Telecommuting. *Personnel Journal, 66,* 90–101.

Hamilton, S., Rothbart, M., & Dawes, R. M. (1986). Sex bias, diagnosis, and *DSM-III. Sex Roles, 15,* 269–274.

Hamm, R. J. (1977). Stability of self-concept and fear of failure. *Psychological Reports, 40,* 522.

Handy, J. A. (1988). Theoretical and methodological problems within occupational stress and burnout research. *Human Relations, 41,* 351–369.

Hare, R. D. (1985). Comparison of procedures for the assessment of psychopathy. *Journal of Consulting and Clinical Psychology, 53,* 7–16.

Hare, R. D., Hart, S. D., & Harpur, T. J. (1991). Psychopathy and the *DSM-IV* criteria for antisocial personality disorder. *Journal of Abnormal Psychology, 100,* 391–398.

Harenstam, A., Palm, U. B., & Theorell, T. (1988). Stress, health and the working environment of Swedish prison staff. *Work and Stress, 2,* 281–290.

Harpur, T. J., Hare, R. D., & Hakstian, A. R. (1989). Two-factor conceptualization of psychopathy: Construct validity and assessment implications. *Psychological Assessment, 1,* 6–17.

Harrell, T. W., & Harrell, M. S. (1972). The personality of MBA's who reach general management early. *Personnel Psychology, 26,* 127–134.

Harris, N. N., & Sutton, R. I. (1983). Task procrastination in organizations: A framework for research. *Human Relations, 36,* 987–995.

Harris, R. B. (1988). Reviewing nursing stress according to a proposed coping-adaption framework. *Advances in Nursing Science, 11,* 12–28.

Hartman, L. M. (1984). Cognitive components of social anxiety. *Journal of Clinical Psychology, 40,* 137–139.

Hartnett, J. J., & Barber, R. M. (1974). Fear of failure in group risk-taking. *British Journal of Social and Clinical Psychology, 13,* 125–129.

Hasin, D. S., & Grant, B. F. (1987). Psychiatric diagnosis of patients with substance abuse problems: A comparison of two procedures, the DIS and the SADS-L. *Journal of Psychiatric Research, 21,* 7–22.

Hasin, D. S., Grant, B. F., & Endicott, J. (1988). Severity of alcohol dependence and social/occupational problems: Relationship to clinical and familial history. *Alcoholism: Clinical and Experimental Research, 12,* 660–664.

Hatcher, S. W., & Underwood, J. R. (1990). Self-concept and stress: A study of a group of Southern Baptist ministers. *Counseling and Values, 34,* 187–196.

Head, S. B., Baker, J. D., & Williamson, D. A. (1991). Family environment characteristics and dependent personality disorder. *Journal of Personality Disorders, 5,* 256–263.

Heider, F. (1958). *The psychology on interpersonal relations.* New York: Wiley.

Heilbrun, A. B. (1973). Adaptation to aversive maternal control and perception of simultaneously presented evaluative cues: A further test of a developmental model of paranoid behavior. *Journal of Consulting and Clinical Psychology, 41,* 301–307.

Heim, E. (1991). Job stressors and coping in health professions. *Psychotherapy and Psychosomatics, 55,* 90–99.

Heimberg, R. G., & Barlow, D. H. (1991). New developments in cognitive–behavioral therapy for social phobia. *Journal of Clinical Psychiatry, 52,* 21–30.

Helmert, U., Herman, B., Joeckel, K. H., Greiser, E., & Madans, J. (1989). Social class and risk factors for coronary heart disease in the Federal Republic of Germany: Results of the baseline survey of the German Cardiovascular Prevention Study (GCRP). *Journal of Epidemiology and Community Health, 43,* 37–42.

Helmreich, R. L., Spence, J. T., & Pred, R. S. (1988). Making it without losing it: Type A, achievement motivation, and scientific attainment revisited. *Personality and Social Psychology Bulletin, 14,* 495–504.

Helzer, J. E., & Pryzbeck, T. R. (1988). The co-occurrence of alcoholism with other psychiatric disorders in the general population and its impact on treatment. *Journal of Studies on Alcohol, 49,* 219–224.

Hendrix, W. H., Cantrell, R. S., & Steel, R. P. (1988). Effect of social support on the stress–burnout relationship. *Journal of Business and Psychology, 3,* 67–73.

Hershman, D. J. (1988). *The key to genius: Manic-depression and the creative life.* Buffalo, NY: Prometheus.

Hetherington, C., Oliver, M. K., & Phelps, C. E. (1989). Resident assistant burnout: Factors of job and gender. *Journal of College Student Development, 30,* 266–269.

Higgins, N. C. (1986). Occupational stress and working women: The effectiveness of two stress reduction programs. *Journal of Vocational Behavior, 29,* 66–78.

Hill, M. B., Hill, D. A., Chabot, A. E., & Barrall, J. F. (1978). A survey of college faculty and student procrastination. *College Student Journal, 12,* 256–262.

Hilliard, L. J., & Riemer, J. W. (1988). Occupational stress and suicide among dentists. *Deviant Behavior, 9,* 333–346.

Hills, H., & Norvell, N. (1991). An examination of hardiness and neuroticism as potential moderators of stress outcomes. *Behavioral Medicine, 17,* 31–38.

Himle, D. P., Jayaratne, S. D., & Chess, W. A. (1983). Gender differences in work stress among clinical social workers. *Journal of Social Service Research, 10,* 41–56.

Himle, D. P., Jayaratne, S., & Thyness, P. (1991). Buffering effects of four social support types on burnout among social workers. *Social Work Research and Abstracts, 27,* 22–27.

Hirschfeld, R. M., Shea, M. T., & Weise, R. E. (1991). Dependent personality disorder: Perspectives for *DSM–IV. Journal of Personality Disorders, 5,* 135–149.

Hirschhorn, M. (1991). A bandaged secret: Emily Dickinson and incest. *Journal of Psychohistory, 18,* 251–281.

Ho, R., & Zemaitis, R. (1981). Concern over the negative consequences of success. *Australian Journal of Psychology, 33,* 19–28.

Hock, R. R. (1988). Professional burnout among public school teachers. *Public Personnel Management, 17,* 167–189.

Hodapp, V. (1989). Anxiety, fear of failure, and achievement: Two path-analytical models. *Anxiety Research, 1,* 301–312.

Hoehn-Saric, R., & Barksdale, V. C. (1983). Impulsiveness in obsessive–compulsive patients. *British Journal of Psychiatry, 143,* 177–182.

Hoffman, L. W. (1974). Fear of success in males and females: 1965 and 1971. *Journal of Consulting and Clinical Psychology, 42,* 353–358.

Hoffman, L. W. (1977). Fear of success in 1965 and 1974: A follow-up study. *Journal of Consulting and Clinical Psychology, 45,* 310–321.

Hoffman, L. W. (1982). Methodological issues in follow-up and replication studies. *Journal of Social Issues, 38,* 53–64.

Holland, J. L. (1985). *Making vocational choices* (2nd ed.). Englewood Cliffs, NJ: Prentice Hall.

Holland, J. L. (1990). *The occupational finder.* Odessa, FL: PAR.

Hollinger, C. L., & Fleming, E. S. (1984). Internal barriers to the realization of potential: Correlates and interrelationships among gifted and talented female adolescents. *Gifted Child Quarterly, 28,* 135–139.

Hollingworth, C., Matthews, G., & Hartnett, O. M. (1988). Job satisfaction and mood: An exploratory study. *Work and Stress, 2,* 225–232.

Holmes, T. H., & Rahe, R. H. (1967). The Social Readjustment Rating Scale. *Journal of Psychosomatic Research, 11,* 213–218.

Holt, R. R. (1982). Occupational stress. In L. Goldberg & S. Breznitz (Eds.), *Handbook of stress: Theoretical and clinical aspects.* New York: Free Press.

Horner, M. S. (1968). *Sex differences in achievement motivation and performance in competitive and non-competitive situations.* Unpublished doctoral dissertation, University of Michigan, Ann Arbor.

Horner, M. S. (1972). Toward an understanding of achievement-related conflicts in women. *Journal of Social Issues, 28,* 157–176.

Hornung, C. A., McCullough, B. C., & Sugimoto, T. (1981). Status relationships in marriage: Risk factors in spouse abuse. *Journal of Marriage and the Family, 43,* 675–692.

House, J. S. (1980). *Occupational stress and the mental and physical health of factory workers*. Ann Arbor, MI: Survey Research Center, Institute for Social Research.

House, J. S. (1987). Chronic stress and chronic disease in life and work: Conceptual and methodological issues. *Work and Stress, 1,* 129–134.

Houston, B. K., & Kelly, K. E. (1987). Type A behavior in housewives: Relation to work, marital adjustment, stress, tension, health, fear-of-failure and self esteem. *Journal of Psychosomatic Research, 31,* 55–61.

Howard, J. H., Cunningham, D. A., & Rechnitzer, P. A. (1977). Work patterns associated with Type A behavior: A managerial population. *Human Relations, 30,* 825–836.

Hurrell, J. J., McLaney, M. A., & Murphy, L. R. (1990). The middle years: Career stage differences. *Prevention in Human Services, 8,* 179–203.

Huse, E. F., & Cummings, T. G. (1989). *Organization development and change* (4th ed.). St. Paul, MN: West.

Hyland, M. E. (1989). There is no motive to avoid success: The compromise explanation for success-avoiding behavior. *Journal of Personality, 57,* 665–693.

Hyland, M. E., & Dann, P. L. (1988). Converging evidence that fear of success is multidimensional. *Current Psychology Research and Reviews, 7,* 199–206.

Hytten, K., Jensen, A., & Skauli, G. (1990). Stress inoculation training for smoke divers and free fall lifeboat passengers. *Aviation, Space, and Environmental Medicine, 61,* 983–988.

Ilechukwu, S. T. (1988). Sibling rivalry as an important factor in academic under-achievement: A cross-cultural contribution. *Psychiatric Journal of the University of Ottawa, 13,* 136–139.

Illfelder, J. K. (1980). Fear of success, sex role attitudes, and career salience and anxiety levels of college women. *Journal of Vocational Behavior, 16,* 7–17.

Ingram, D. H. (1982). Compulsive personality disorder. *American Journal of Psychoanalysis, 42,* 189–198.

Intons-Peterson, M. J., & Johnson, H. (1980). Sex domination of occupations and the tendencies to approach and avoid success and failure. *Psychology of Women Quarterly, 4,* 526–547.

Ireland-Galman, M. M., & Michael, W. B. (1983). The relationship of a measure of the fear of success construct to scales representing the locus of control and sex-role orientation constructs for a community college sample. *Educational and Psychological Measurement, 43,* 1217–1225.

Ishiyama, F. I. (1990). A Japanese perspective on client inaction: Removing attitudinal blocks thought Morita therapy. *Journal of Counseling and Development, 68,* 556–570.

Ivancevich, J. M., & Matteson, M. R. (1980). *Stress at work*. Glenview, IL: Scott Foresman.

Ivancevich, J. M., Matteson, M. R., Freedman, S. M., & Phillips, J. S. (1990). Worksite stress management interventions. *American Psychologist, 45,* 252–261.

Izraeli, D. N. (1988). Burning out in medicine: A comparison of husbands and wives in dual-career couples. *Journal of Social Behavior and Personality, 3,* 329–346.

Jackson, S. E., Schwab, R. L., & Schuler, R. S. (1986). Toward an understanding of the burnout phenomenon. *Journal of Applied Psychology, 71,* 630–640.

Jackson, S. E., Turner, J. A., & Brief, A. P. (1987). Correlates of burnout among public service lawyers. *Journal of Occupational Behaviour, 8,* 339–349.

Jamal, M. (1990). Relationship of job stress and Type-A behavior to employees' job satisfaction, organizational commitment, psychosomatic health problems, and turnover motivation. *Human Relations, 43,* 727–738.

James, L. R., & Jones, A. P. (1974). Organizational climate: A review of theory and research. *Psychological Bulletin, 81,* 1096-1112.

Jamison, K. R. (1989). Mood disorders and patterns of creativity in British writers and artists. *Psychiatry, 52,* 125–134.

Jamison, K. R. (1992). *Touched with fire: Manic–depressive illness and the artistic temperament.* Lexington, MA: Lexington Books.

Janda, L. H., O'Grady, K. E., & Capps, C. F. (1978). Fear of success in males and females in sex-linked occupations. *Sex Roles, 4,* 43–50.

Jastak, S., & Wilkinson, G. S. (1984). *The Wide Range Achievement Test–Revised: Administration manual.* Wilmington, DE: Jastak Associates.

Jayaratne, S., & Chess, W. A. (1984). Job satisfaction, burnout, and turnover: A national study. *Social Work, 29,* 448–453.

Jayaratne, S., & Chess, W. A. (1986). Job stress, job deficit, emotional support, and competence: Their relationship to burnout. *Journal of Applied Social Sciences, 10,* 135–155.

Jayaratne, S., Chess, W. A., & Kunkel, D. A. (1986). Burnout: Its impact on child welfare workers and their spouses. *Social Work, 31,* 53–59.

Jenike, M. A. (1990). Approaches to the patient with treatment-refractory obsessive compulsive disorder. *Journal of Clinical Psychiatry, 51,* 15–21.

Jenike, M. A., Baer, L., & Carey, R. J. (1986). Coexistent obsessive–compulsive disorder and schizotypal personality disorder: A poor prognostic indicator. *Archives of General Psychiatry, 43,* 296.

Jenkins, C. D., Rosenman, R. H., & Friedman, M. (1966). Development of an objective psychological test for determination of the coronary-prone behavior pattern in employed men. *Journal of Chronic Diseases, 19,* 599–609.

Jenkins, C. D., Zyzanski, S. J., & Rosenman, R. H. (1971). Progress toward validation of a computer scored test for Type A coronary prone behavior pattern. *Psychosomatic Medicine, 33,* 193–202.

Jenkins, S., & Calhoun, J. F. (1991). Teacher stress: Issues and intervention. *Psychology in the Schools, 28,* 60–70.

Jette, C. B., & Winnett, R. L. (1987). Late-onset paranoid disorder. *American Journal of Orthopsychiatry, 57,* 485–494.

Jones, J. (1980a). *The Staff Burnout Scale for Health Professionals.* Park Ridge, IL: London House Press.

Jones, J. (1980b). *The Staff Burnout Scale for Police and Security Personnel.* Park Ridge, IL: London House Press.

Jones, J. (1981). *The burnout syndrome.* Park Ridge, IL: London House Press.

Jones, K. V. (1985). Type A and academic performance: A negative relationship. *Psychological Reports, 56,* 260.

Jorgensen, P. (1985). Long-term course of acute reactive paranoid psychosis: A followup study. *Acta Psychiatrica Scandinavica, 71,* 30–37.

Jordan, B. K., Swartz, M. S., George, L. K., Woodbury, M. A., & Blazer, D. (1989). Antisocial and related disorders in a southern community: An application of grade of membership analysis. *Journal of Nervous and Mental Disease, 177,* 529–541.

Juran, S. (1979). A measure of stereotyping in fear-of-success cues. *Sex Roles, 5,* 287–297.

Kahill, S. (1986). Relationship of burnout among professional psychologists to professional expectations and social support. *Psychological Reports, 59,* 1043–1051.

Kahill, S. (1988). Symptoms of professional burnout: A review of the empirical evidence. *Canadian Psychology, 29,* 284–297.

Kahn, H., & Cooper, C. L. (1991). The potential contribution of information technology to the mental ill health, job dissatisfaction, and alcohol intake of money market dealers: An exploratory study. *International Journal of Human Computer Interaction, 3,* 321–338.

Kahn, S. E., & Long, B. C. (1988). Work-related stress, self-efficacy, and well-being of female clerical workers. *Counseling Psychology Quarterly, 1,* 145–153.

Kalra, J., Rosner, F., & Shapiro, S. (1987). Emotional strain on physicians caring for cancer patients. *Loss, Grief and Care, 1,* 19–24.

Kandel, D. B., Davies, M., & Raveis, V. H. (1985). The stressfulness of daily social roles for women: Marital, occupational and household roles. *Journal of Health and Social Behavior, 26,* 64–78.

Karabenick, S. A., & Marshall, J. M. (1977). Performance of females as a function of fear of success, fear of failure, type of opponent, and performance-contingent feedback. *Journal of Personality, 42,* 220–237.

Katz, D., & Kahn, R. L. (1979). *The social psychology of organizations* (2nd ed.). New York: Wiley.

Katz, J. (1984). Symptom prescription: A review of the clinical outcome literature. *Clinical Psychology Review, 4,* 703–717.

Kaufman, G. (1985). *Shame: The power of caring* (2nd ed.). Cambridge, MA: Schenkman.

Kaufman, G. (1989). *The psychology of shame: Theory and treatment of shame-based syndromes.* New York: Springer.

Kaufmann, G. M., & Beehr, T. A. (1986). Interactions between job stressors and social support: Some counterintuitive results. *Journal of Applied Psychology, 71,* 522–526.

Kaun, D. E. (1991). Writers die young: The impact of work and leisure on longevity. *Journal of Economic Psychology, 12,* 381–399.

Kavaler-Adler, S. (1991). Emily Dickinson and the subject of seclusion. *American Journal of Psychoanalysis, 51,* 21–38.

Kearney, M. (1982). Are masculine trait-factors in women a help or a hindrance in dealing with fear of success? *Psychological Reports, 51,* 558.

Kearney, M. (1984). A comparison of motivation to avoid success in males and females. *Journal of Clinical Psychology, 40,* 1005–1007.

Keita, G. P., & Jones, J. M. (1990) Reducing adverse reaction to stress in the workplace: Psychology's expanding role. *American Psychologist, 45,* 1137–1141.

Keller, L. M., Bouchard, T. J., Arvey, R. D., Segal, N. L., & Dawis, R. V. (1992). Work values: Genetic and environmental influences. *Journal of Applied Psychology, 77,* 79–88.

Kelley, H. H. (1967). *Attribution in social interaction.* Morristown, NJ: General Learning Press.

Kellner, R. (1986). Personality disorders. *Psychotherapy and Psychosomatics, 46,* 58–66.

Kendall, P. C. (1984). Cognitive processes and procedures in behavior therapy. *Annual Review of Behavior Therapy, Theory and Practice, 9,* 132–179.

Kendall, P. C., & Clarkin, J. F. (1992). Introduction to special section: Comorbidity and treatment implications. *Journal of Consulting and Clinical Psychology, 60,* 833–834.

Kendler, K. S. (1985). Diagnostic approaches to schizotypal personality disorder: A historical perspective. *Schizophrenia Bulletin, 11,* 538–553.

Kendrick, M. J., Craig, K. D., Lawson, D. M., & Davidson, P. O. (1982). Cognitive and behavioral therapy for musical-performance anxiety. *Journal of Consulting and Clinical Psychology, 50,* 353–362.

Kernberg, O. (1984). *Severe personality disorders.* New Haven, CT: Yale University Press.

Kernberg, O. F. (1989). An ego psychology object relations theory of the structure and treatment of pathologic narcissism: An overview. *Psychiatric Clinics of North America, 12,* 723–729.

Kerr, B., Shaffer, J., Chambers, C., & Hallowell, K. (1991). Substance use of creatively talented adults. *Journal of Creative Behavior, 25,* 145–153.

Kets de Vries, M. F. R., & Miller, D. (1991). Leadership styles and organizational cultures: The shaping of neurotic organizations. In M. F. R. Kets de Vries (Ed.), *Organizations on the couch* (pp. 243–263). San Francisco: Jossey-Bass.

Khanna, S., Rajendra, P. N., & Channabasavanna, S. M. (1988). Social adjustment in obsessive compulsive disorder. *International Journal of Social Psychiatry, 34,* 118–122.

Kilburg, R. R., Kaslow, F. W., & VandenBos, G. R. (1988). Professionals in distress. *Hospital and Community Psychiatry, 39,* 723–725.

Kilburg, R. R., Nathan, P. E., & Thoreson, R. W. (1986). *Professionals in distress: Issues, syndromes, and solutions in psychology.* Washington, DC: American Psychological Association.

Killinger, B. (1992). *Workaholics: The respectable addicts.* New York: Simon & Schuster.

Kimberly, J. R., Miles, R. H., & Associates. (1980). *The organizational life cycle.* San Francisco: Jossey-Bass.

Kinnuen, U. (1988). Teacher stress during an autumn term in Finland: Four types of stress processes. *Work and Stress, 2,* 333–340.

Kirkcaldy, B., Thome, E., & Thomas, W. (1989). Job satisfaction amongst psychosocial workers. *Personality and Individual Differences, 10,* 191–196.

Kirkpatrick, D. (1982). Success conflict 65 years later: Contributions and confusions. *Canadian Journal of Psychiatry, 27,* 405–409.

Kirman, J. H. (1983). Modern psychoanalysis and intimacy: Treatment of the narcissistic personality. *Modern Psychoanalysis, 8,* 17–34.

Kirmeyer, S. L. (1988). Coping with competing demands: Interruption and the Type A pattern. *Journal of Applied Psychology, 73,* 621–629.

Kirmeyer, S. L., & Biggers, K. (1988). Environmental demand and demand engendering behavior: An observational analysis of the Type A pattern. *Journal of Personality and Social Psychology, 54,* 997–1005.

Kirsch, I., Wolpin, M., & Knutson, J. L. (1975). A comparison of in vivo methods for rapid reduction of "stage-fright" in the college classroom: A field experiment. *Behavior Therapy, 6,* 165–171.

Kleinberg, J. L. (1988). Utilizing career crises to prepare patients for intensive psychotherapy. *Journal of Contemporary Psychotherapy, 18,* 240–248.

Knaus, W. J. (1973). Overcoming procrastination. *Rational Living, 8,* 2–7.

Koenigsberg, H. W., Kaplan, R. D., Gilmore, M. M., & Cooper, A. M. (1985). The relationship between syndrome and personality disorder in *DSM-III*: Experience with 2,462 patients. *American Journal of Psychiatry, 142,* 207–212.

Kofoed, L., & MacMillan, J. (1986). Alcoholism and antisocial personality: The sociobiology of an addiction. *Journal of Nervous and Mental Disease, 174,* 332–335.

Kogan, N. (1990, August). *The performing artist: Some psychological observations.* Paper presented at the 98th Annual Convention of the American Psychological Association, Boston.

Koeske, G. F., & Koeske, R. D. (1989). Construct validity of the Maslach Burnout Inventory: A critical review and reconceptualization. *Journal of Applied Behavioral Science, 25,* 131–144.

Kohut, H. (1971). *The analyses of self.* Madison, CT: International Universities Press.

Kohut, H., & Wolf, E. S. (1978). The disorders of the self and their treatment: An outline. *International Journal of Psycho-Analysis, 59,* 413–425.

Kolligan, J., Jr. (1990). Perceived fraudulence as a dimension of perceived incompetence. In R. J. Sternberg & J. Kolligan (Eds.), *Competence considered* (pp. 261–285). New Haven, CT: Yale University Press.

Kornhauser, A. (1965). *Mental health of the industrial worker: A Detroit study.* New York: Wiley.

Kottkamp, R. B., & Mansfield, J. R. (1985). Role conflict, role ambiguity, powerlessness and burnout among high school supervisors. *Journal of Research and Development in Education, 18,* 29–38.

Krakowski, A. J. (1982). Stress and the practice of medicine: II. Stressors, stresses, and strains. *Psychotherapy and Psychosomatics, 38,* 11–23.

Krakowski, A. J. (1984). Stress and the practice of medicine: III. Physicians compared with lawyers. *Psychotherapy and Psychosomatics, 42,* 143–151.

Krakowski, A. J. (1985). Medicine and physicians: Rewards and burdens. *Psychiatria Fennica, 16,* 73–83.

Kramer, W. (1990). Solid wood: A new furniture renovation project for psychiatric patients in the community. *British Journal of Occupational Therapy, 53,* 292–294.

Krantz, D. S., Contrada, R. J., Hill, D. R., & Friedler, E. (1988). Environmental stress and biobehavioral antecedents of coronary heart disease. *Journal of Consulting and Clinical Psychology, 56,* 333–341.

Kranz, P. L., & Houser, K. M. (1988). The student as director: Dealing with performance anxiety in an undergraduate psychodrama class. *Journal of Group Psychotherapy, Psychodrama and Sociometry 41,* 97–100.

Krueger, D. (1984). *Success and the fear of success in women.* New York: Free Press.

Krueger, D. (1990). Success and success inhibition. In R. J. Sternberg & J. Kolligan (Eds.), *Competence considered* (pp. 246–260). New Haven, CT: Yale University Press.

Krug, S. E. (1980). *Clinical Analysis Questionnaire manual.* Champaign, IL: Institute for Personality and Ability Testing.

Kushnir, T., & Melamed, S. (1991). Work-load, perceived control and psychological distress in Type A/B industrial workers. *Journal of Organizational Behavior, 12,* 155–168.

Kyriacou, C., & Pratt, J. (1985). Teacher stress and psychoneurotic symptoms. *British Journal of Educational Psychology, 55,* 61–64.

Lader, M. (1988). β-Adrenoceptor antagonists in neuropsychiatry: An update. *Journal of Clinical Psychiatry, 49,* 213–223.

Lake, J. H. (1988). Othello and the comforts of love. *American Imago, 45,* 327–335.

Landsbergis, P. A. (1988). Occupational stress among health care workers: A test of the job demands–control model. *Journal of Organizational Behavior, 9,* 217–239.

Lang, P. J., Levin, D. N., Miller, G. A., & Kozak, M. J. (1983). Fear behavior, fear imagery, and the psychophysiology of emotion: The problem of affective response integration. *Journal of Abnormal Psychology, 92,* 276–306.

Lang, R. J., Gilpin, J. L., & Gilpin, A. R. (1990). Stress-related symptoms among dental hygienists. *Psychological Reports, 66,* 715–722.

LaRusso, L. (1978). Sensitivity of paranoid patients to nonverbal cues. *Journal of Abnormal Psychology, 87,* 463–471.

Lasaga, J. I. (1980). Death in Jonestown: Techniques of political control by a paranoid leader. *Suicide and Life Threatening Behavior, 10,* 210–213.

Latta, R. M. (1978). Hope of success and fear of failure components of Mehrabian's scales of resultant achievement motivation. *Journal of Research in Personality, 12,* 141–151.

Lauer, J. W. (1976). The effect of tricyclic antidepressant compounds on patients with passive–dependent personality traits. *Current Therapeutic Research, 19,* 495–505.

Laux, L., & Vossel, G. (1982). Theoretical and methodological issues in achievement-related stress and anxiety research. In H. W. Krohne & L. Laux (Eds.), *Achievement, stress, and anxiety* (pp. 3–18). New York: Hemisphere.

Lawler, E. E., Hall, D. T., & Oldham, G. R. (1974). Organizational climate: Relationship to organizational structure, process, and performance. *Organizational Behavior and Human Performance, 11,* 139–155.

Lawler, K. A., & Schmied, L. A. (1987). The relationship of stress, Type A behavior and powerlessness to physiological responses in female clerical workers. *Journal of Psychosomatic Research, 31,* 555–566.

Lawner, P. (1985). Recent sociohistorical trends and the ascent of Kohutian "self-psychology." *American Journal of Psychoanalysis, 45,* 152–159.

Lawrence, J. F. (1962). The creative personality. In J. W. Haefele (Ed.), *Creativity and innovation* (pp. 115–135). New York: Reinhold.

Lay, C. H. (1986). At last, my research article on procrastination. *Journal of Research in Personality, 20,* 474–495.

Lay, C. H. (1987). A modal profile analysis of procrastinators: A search for types. *Personality and Individual Differences, 8,* 705–714.

Lay, C. H. (1988). The relationship of procrastination and optimism to judgments of time to complete an essay and anticipation of setbacks. *Journal of Social Behavior and Personality, 3,* 201–214.

Lay, C. H. (1990). Working to schedule on personal projects: An assessment of person–project characteristics and trait procrastination. *Journal of Social Behavior and Personality, 5,* 91–103.

Lazarus, R. S. (1966). *Psychological stress and the coping process.* New York: McGraw-Hill.

Lazarus, R. S. (1973). The psychology of stress and coping. In C. D. Spielberger & I. G. Sarason (Eds.), *Stress and anxiety: Vol. 10. A sourcebook of theory and research* (pp. 399–418). New York: Hemisphere.

Lazarus, R. S., & Folkman, S. (1991). The concept of coping. In A. Monat & R. S. Lazarus (Eds.), *Stress and coping: An anthology* (3rd ed., pp. 190–206). New York: Columbia University Press.

Leader, Z. (1990). *Writer's block.* Baltimore: Johns Hopkins University Press.

Lee, C., Earley, P. C., Christopher, L. A., & Hanson, L. A. (1988). Are type As better performers? *Journal of Organizational Behavior, 9,* 263–269.

Lee, C. K., Kwak, Y. S., Yamamoto, J., Rhee, H., Kim, Y. S., Hau, J. H., Choi, J. O., & Lee, Y. H. (1990). Psychiatric epidemiology in Korea: II. Urban and rural differences. *Journal of Nervous and Mental Disease, 178,* 247–252.

Lee, D. Y., Rossiter, B., Martin, J., & Uhlemann, M. R. (1990). Client cognitive responses to counselor paradoxical and nonparadoxical directives. *Journal of Clinical Psychology, 46,* 643–651.

Lee, R. T., & Ashforth, B. E. (1990). On the meaning of Maslach's three dimensions of burnout. *Journal of Applied Psychology, 75,* 743–747.

Leigh, J. H., Lucas, G. H., & Woodman, R. W. (1988). Effects of perceived organizational factors on role stress–job attitude relationships. *Journal of Management, 14,* 41–58.

Leiter, M. P. (1990). The impact of family resources, control coping, and skill utilization on the development of burnout: A longitudinal study. *Human Relations, 43,* 1067–1083.

Leiter, M. P. (1991). Coping patterns as predictors of burnout: The function of control and escapist coping patterns. *Journal of Organizational Behavior, 12,* 123–144.

Leiter, M. P., & Maslach, C. (1988). The impact of interpersonal environment on burnout and organizational commitment. *Journal of Organizational Behavior, 9,* 297–308.

Lemkau, J. P., Purdy, R. R., Rafferty, J. P., & Rudisill, J. R. (1988). Correlates of burnout among family practice residents. *Journal of Medical Education, 63,* 682–691.

Lemkau, J. P., Rafferty, J. P., Purdy, R. R., & Rudisill, J. R. (1987). Sex role stress and job burnout among family practice physicians. *Journal of Vocational Behavior, 31,* 81–90.

Leon, M. R., & Revelle, W. (1985). Effects of anxiety on analogical reasoning: A test of three theoretical models. *Journal of Personality and Social Psychology, 49,* 1302–1315.

Lerner, H. G. (1987). Work and success inhibitions in women: Family systems level interventions in psychodynamic treatment. *Bulletin of the Menninger Clinic, 51,* 338–360.

Lerner, M. P. (1982). Stress at the workplace. *Issues in Radical Therapy, 10,* 14–16.

Lester, D. (1990). An analysis of poets and novelists who completed suicide. *Activitas Nervosa Superior, 32,* 6–11.

Lester, D. (1991). Premature mortality associated with alcoholism and suicide in American writers. *Perceptual and Motor Skills, 73,* 162.

Levenkron, J. C., & Moore, L. G. (1988). The Type A behavior pattern: Issues for intervention research. *Annals of Behavioral Medicine, 10,* 78–83.

Levi, L. (1990). Occupational stress: Spice of life or kiss of death? *American Psychologist, 45,* 1142–1145.

Levine, H. G., & Langness, L. L. (1983). Context, ability, and performance: Comparison of competitive athletics among mildly mentally retarded and nonretarded adults. *American Journal of Mental Deficiency, 87,* 528–538.

Levine, R. V., Lynch, K., & Miyake, K., & Lucia, M. (1989). The Type A city: Coronary heart disease and the pace of life. *Journal of Behavioral Medicine, 12,* 509–524.

Levinson, H. (1972). *Organizational diagnosis.* Cambridge, MA: Harvard University Press.

Levinson, H. (1992). *Career mastery: Keys to taking charge of your career throughout your work life.* San Francisco: Berrett-Koehler.

Lewis, C. E., & Bucholz, K. K. (1991). Alcoholism, antisocial behavior and family history. *British Journal of Addiction, 86,* 177–194.

Lewis, F. D., Roessler, R., Greenwood, R., & Evans, T. (1985). Conversation skill training with individuals with severe emotional disabilities. *Psychosocial Rehabilitation Journal, 8,* 49–59.

Lidz, T. (1976). *The person: His and her development throughout the life cycle* (rev. ed.). New York: Basic Books.

Liebert, R. M., & Morris, L. W. (1967). Cognitive and emotional components of test anxiety: A distinction and some initial data. *Psychological Reports, 20*, 975–978.

Lilienfeld, S. O., VanValkenburg, C., Larntz, K., & Akiskal, H. S. (1986). The relationship of histrionic personality disorder to antisocial personality and somatization disorders. *American Journal of Psychiatry, 143*, 718–722.

Linehan, M. M., Hubert, A. E., Suarez, A., Douglas, A., & Heard, H. L. (1991). Cognitive–behavioral treatment of chronically parasuicidal borderline patients. *Archives of General Psychiatry, 45*, 129–137.

Lineham, K. S., Rosenthal, T. L., Kelley, J. E., & Theobald, D. E. (1977). Homogeneity and heterogeneity of problem class in modeling treatment of fears. *Behaviour Research and Therapy, 15*, 211–215.

Lion, J. R. (Ed.). (1981). *Personality disorders: Diagnosis and management (revised for DSM–III)* (2nd ed.). Baltimore: Williams & Wilkins.

Liskow, B., Powell, B. J., Nickel, E. J., & Penick, E. (1990). Diagnostic subgroups of antisocial alcoholics: Outcome at 1 year. *Comprehensive Psychiatry, 31*, 549–556.

Little, L. F., Gaffney, I. C., Rosen, K. H., & Bender, M. M. (1990). Corporate instability is related to airline pilots' stress symptoms. *Aviation, Space, and Environmental Medicine, 61*, 977–982.

Livesley, W. J., & Schroeder, M. L. (1991). Dimensions of personality disorder: The *DSM–III–R* cluster B diagnoses. *Journal of Nervous and Mental Disease, 179*, 320–328.

Livesley, W. J., & West, M. (1986). The *DSM–III* distinction between schizoid and avoidant personality disorders. *Canadian Journal of Psychiatry, 31*, 59–62.

Livesley, W. J., West, M., & Tanney, A. (1986). "Schizoid and avoidant personality disorders in *DSM–III*": Dr. Livesley and associates reply. *American Journal of Psychiatry, 143*, 1322–1323.

Lockwood, A. H. (1989). Medical problems of musicians. *New England Journal of Medicine, 320*, 221–227.

Loewenstine, H. V., & Paludi, M. A. (1982). Women's Type A/B behavior patterns and fear of success. *Perceptual and Motor Skills, 54*, 891–894.

Long, B. (1988). Stress management for school personnel: Stress-inoculation training and exercise. *Psychology in the Schools, 25*, 314–324.

Lopez, F. G., & Wambach, C. A. (1982). Effects of paradoxical and self-control directives in counseling. *Journal of Counseling Psychology, 29*, 115–124.

Lowe, G. S., & Northcott, H. C. (1988). The impact of working conditions, social roles, and personal characteristics on gender differences in distress. *Work and Occupations, 15*, 55–77.

Lowenstein, L. F. (1991). Teacher stress leading to burnout: Its prevention and cure. *Education Today, 41*, 12–16.

Lowman, R. L. (1987). Occupational choice as a moderator of psychotherapeutic approach. *Psychotherapy, 24*, 801-808.

Lowman, R. L. (1989). *Pre-employment screening for psychopathology: A guide to professional practice.* Sarasota, FL: Professional Resource Press.

Lowman, R. L. (1991a). Career assessment and job loss. *Career Development Laboratory News, 1,* 2–3.

Lowman, R. L. (1991b). *The clinical practice of career assessment: Interests, abilities, and personality.* Washington, DC: American Psychological Association.

Lowman, R. L. (1993a). The inter-domain model of career assessment. *Journal of Counseling and Development, 71,* 549–554.

Lowman, R. L. (1993b). Malpractice of what and by whom? Will the real straw theory please stand up. *Journal of Counseling and Development, 11,* 558–559.

Lowman, R. L., & Parker, D. (1988). *Symptoms of anxiety and depression in the workplace.* Unpublished manuscript.

Lowman, R. L., & Resnick, R. (1994). *The mental health professional's guide to managed mental health care.* Washington, DC: American Psychological Association.

Lowman, R. L., & Schurman, S. J. (1982). Psychometric characteristics of a Vocational Preference Inventory short form. *Educational and Psychological Measurement, 42,* 601–613.

Ludwig, A. M. (1990). Alcohol input and creative output. *British Journal of Addiction, 85,* 953–963.

Lundberg, U., Hedman, M., & Melin, B. (1989). Type A behavior in healthy males and females as related to physiological reactivity and blood lipids. *Psychosomatic Medicine, 51,* 113–122.

Lykouras, E., Ioannidis, C., Voulgarie, A., Jemos, J., & Izonou, A. (1989). Depression among general hospital patients in Greece. *Acta Psychiatrica Scandinavica, 79,* 148–152.

Lyons, N. (1992, July 26). No, no, a thousand times no. *New York Times Book Review, 1,* 20–21.

MacEvoy, B., Lambert, W. W., Karlberg, P., & Karlberg, J., Klackenberg-Larsson, I., & Klackenberg, G. (1988). Early affective antecedents of adult Type A behavior. *Journal of Personality and Social Psychology, 54,* 108–116.

Madonna, J. (1991). Countertransference issues in the treatment of borderline and narcissistic personality disorders: A retrospective on the contributions of Gerald Adler, Peter L. Giovacchini, Harold Searles, and Phyllis W. Meadow. *Modern Psychoanalysis, 16,* 37–64.

Makaremi, A. (1990). Histrionic disorder among Iranian high school and college students. *Psychological Reports, 66,* 835–838.

Malan, D. H. (1976). *The frontier of brief psychotherapy: An example of the convergence of research and clinical practice.* New York: Plenum Press.

Malanowski, J. R., & Wood, P. H. (1984). Burnout and self-actualization in public school teachers. *Journal of Psychology, 117,* 23–26.

Mallinger, A. E. (1978). Fear of success and Oedipal experience. *Journal of Psychology, 100,* 91–106.

Mallinger, A. E. (1982). Demand-sensitive obsessionals. *Journal of the American Academy of Psychoanalysis, 10,* 407–426.

Mallinger, A. E. (1984). The obsessive's myth of control. *Journal of the American Academy of Psychoanalysis, 12*, 147–165.

Manchester, R. A. (1988). Medical aspects of music development: Symposium on musical development and cognition. *Psychomusicology, 7*, 147–152.

Mandel, H. P., & Marcus, S. I. (1988). *The psychology of underachievement: Differential diagnosis and differential treatment.* New York: Wiley.

Mandes, E., & Gessner, T. (1986). Prediction of vocational success among emotionally impaired and learning-disabled persons. *Journal of Employment Counseling, 23*, 163–166.

Manganello, J. L., Carlson, T. K., Zarrillo, D. L., & Teevan, R. C. (1985). Relationship between hypnotic susceptibility, fear of failure and need for achievement. *Psychological Reports, 56*, 239–242.

Manning, M. R., Williams, R. F., & Wolfe, D. M. (1988). Hardiness and the relationship between stressors and outcomes. *Work and Stress, 2*, 205–216.

Marohn, R. C. (1987). John Wesley Hardin, adolescent killer: The emergence of a narcissistic behavior disorder. *Adolescent Psychiatry, 14*, 271–296.

Marsden, C. D. (1986). Hysteria: A neurologist's view. *Psychological Medicine, 16*, 277–288.

Marshall, J. M., & Karabenick, S. A. (1977). Validity of an empirically derived projective measure of fear of success. *Journal of Consulting and Clinical Psychology, 45*, 564–574.

Martin, P. A. (1981). Defining normal values in marriage. *International Journal of Family Psychiatry, 2*, 105–114.

Martin, R. A., Kuiper, N. A, & Westra, H. A. (1989). *Personality and Individual Differences, 10*, 771–784.

Martin, R. L., Cloninger, C. R., Guze, S. B., & Clayton, P. J. (1985). Mortality in a follow-up of 500 psychiatric outpatients: I. Total mortality. *Archives of General Psychiatry, 42*, 47–54.

Martindale, C. (1989). Personality, situation, and creativity. In J. A. Glover, R. R. Ronning, & C. R. Reynolds (Eds.), *Handbook of creativity* (pp. 211–232). New York: Plenum Press.

Martocchio, J. J., & O'Leary, A. M. (1989). Sex differences in occupational stress: A meta-analytic review. *Journal of Applied Psychology, 74*, 495–501.

Maslach, C. (1982). *Burnout—The cost of caring.* Englewood Cliffs, NJ: Prentice Hall.

Maslach, C., & Florian, V. (1988). Burnout, job setting, and self-evaluation among rehabilitation counselors. *Rehabilitation Psychology, 33*, 85–93.

Maslach, C., & Jackson, S. E. (1981). *Maslach Burnout Inventory: Research Edition.* Palo Alto, CA: Consulting Psychologists Press.

Maslach, C., & Jackson, S. E. (1984). Burnout in organizational settings. *Applied Social Psychology Annual, 5*, 133–153.

Maslach, C., & Jackson, S. E. (1985). The role of sex and family variables in burnout. *Sex Roles, 12*, 837–851.

Massel, H. K., Liberman, R. P., Mintz, J., Jacobs, H. E., Rush, T. V., Gianni, C. A., & Zarate, R. (1990). Evaluating the capacity to work of the mentally ill. *Psychiatry, 53*, 31–43.

Masterson, J. F. (1988). *The search for the real self: Unmasking the personality disorders of our age.* New York: Free Press.

Masterson, J. F. (1990). Psychotherapy of borderline and narcissistic disorders: Establishing a therapeutic alliance (A developmental, self, and object relations approach). *Journal of Personality Disorders, 4,* 182–191.

Masterson-Allen, A. S., Mor, V., Laliberte, L., & Monteiro, L. (1985). Staff burnout in a hospice setting. *Hospice Journal, 1,* 1–15.

Masterson-Allen, A. S., Mor, V., & Laliberte, L. (1987). Turnover in national hospice study sites: A reflection of organizational growth. *Hospice Journal, 3,* 147–164.

Mather, D. B. (1987). The role of antisocial personality in alcohol rehabilitation treatment effectiveness. *Military Medicine, 152,* 516–518.

Matteson, M. T., & Ivancevich, J. M. (1987). *Controlling work stress: Effective human resource and management strategies.* San Francisco: Jossey-Bass.

Matteson, M. T., Ivancevich, J. M., & Smith, S. V. (1984). Relation of Type A behavior to performance and satisfaction among sales personnel. *Journal of Vocational Behavior, 25,* 203–214.

Matthews, D. B. (1990). A comparison of burnout in selected occupational fields. *Career Development Quarterly, 38,* 230–239.

Matthews, K. A., Rosenman, R. H., Dembroski, T. M., Harris, E. L., & MacDougall, J. M. (1984). Familial resemblance in components of the Type A behavior pattern: A reanalysis of the California Type A Twin Study. *Psychosomatic Medicine, 46,* 512–522.

Mattick, R. P., & Newman, C. R. (1991). Social phobia and avoidant personality disorder. *International Review of Psychiatry, 3,* 163–173.

Mavissakalian, M., Hamann, M. S., & Jones, B. (1990). Correlates of *DSM–III* personality disorder in obsessive–compulsive disorder. *Comprehensive Psychiatry, 31,* 481–489.

Mavissakalian, M., & Michelson, L. (1983). Tricyclic antidepressants in obsessive–compulsive disorder: Antiobsessional or antidepressant agents? *Journal of Nervous and Mental Disease, 171,* 301–306.

May, H. J., & Revicki, D. A. (1985). Professional stress among family physicians. *Journal of Family Practice, 20,* 165–171.

Mayes, B. T., Sime, W. E., & Ganster, D. C. (1984). Convergent validity of Type A behavior patterns scales and their ability to predict physiological responsiveness in a sample of female public employees. *Journal of Behavioral Medicine, 7,* 83–108.

Maynard, I. W., & Howe, B. L. (1987). Interrelations of trait and state anxiety with game performance of rugby players *Perceptual and Motor Skills, 64,* 599–602.

Mazur, P. J., & Lynch, M. D. (1989). Differential impact of administrative, organizational, and personality factors on teacher burnout. *Teaching and Teacher Education, 5,* 337–353.

McCann, B. S., & Matthews, K. A. (1988). Antecedents of the coronary-prone behavior pattern. In M. F. Tiffany, P. M. McCabe, & N. Schneiderman

(Eds.), *Stress and coping across development* (pp. 71–88). Hillsdale, NJ: Erlbaum.

McCann, J. T. (1988). Passive–aggressive personality disorder: A review. *Journal of Personality Disorders, 2,* 170–179.

McCown, W., Carise, D., & Johnson, J. (1991). Trait procrastination in self-described adult children of excessive drinkers: An exploratory study. *Journal of Social Behavior and Personality, 6,* 147–151.

McCown, W., Johnson, J. L., & Petzel, T. (1989). Procrastination, a principal components analysis. *Personality and Individual Differences, 10,* 197–202.

McCown, W., Petzel, T., & Rupert, P. (1987). An experimental study of some hypothesized behaviors and personality variables of college student procrastinators. *Personality and Individual Differences, 8,* 781–786.

McCranie, E. W., & Brandsma, J. M. (1988). Personality antecedents of burnout among middle-aged physicians. *Behavioral Medicine, 14,* 30–36.

McCrank, E., & Rabheru, K. (1989). Four cases of progressive supranuclear palsy in patients exposed to organic solvents. *Canadian Journal of Psychiatry, 34,* 934–936.

McDermott, D. (1984). Professional burnout and its relation to job characteristics, satisfaction, and control. *Journal of Human Stress, 10,* 79–85.

McElroy, M. A., & Willis, J. D. (1979). Women and the achievement conflict in sport: A preliminary study. *Journal of Sport Psychology, 1,* 241–247.

McGee, R. A. (1989). Burnout and professional decision making: An analogue study. *Journal of Counseling Psychology, 36,* 345–351.

McGrath, A., Houghton, D., & Reid, N. (1989). Occupational stress, and teachers in Northern Ireland. *Work and Stress, 3,* 359–368.

McGrath, A., Reid, N., & Boore, J. (1989). Occupational stress in nursing. *International Journal of Nursing Studies, 26,* 343–358.

McIntyre, T. C. (1984). The relationship between locus of control and teacher burnout. *British Journal of Educational Psychology, 54,* 235–238.

McMichael, A. J. (1978). Personality, behavioural, and situational modifiers of work stressors. In C. L. Cooper & R. Payne (Eds.), *Stress at work* (pp. 127–147). New York: Wiley.

McReynolds, P. (1973). Changing conceptions of anxiety: A historical review and a proposed integration. In C. D. Spielberger & I. G. Sarason (Eds.), *Stress and anxiety: Vol. 10. A sourcebook of theory and research* (pp. 131–158). New York: Hemisphere.

Mehrabian, A. (1989–1990). Effects of affective and informational characteristics of work environments on worker satisfaction. *Imagination, Cognition and Personality, 9,* 293–301.

Meier, S. T. (1984). The construct validity of burnout. *Journal of Occupational Psychology, 57,* 211–219.

Meier, S. T. (1991). Tests of the construct validity of occupational stress measures with college students: Failure to support discriminant validity. *Journal of Counseling Psychology, 38,* 91–97.

Meir, E. I., Melamed, S., & Abu-Freha, A. (1990). Vocational, avocational, and skill utilization congruences and their relationship with well-being in two cultures. *Journal of Vocational Behavior, 36,* 153–165.

Meissner, W. W. (1979). Narcissism and paranoia: A comment on "paranoid psychodynamics." *Contemporary Psychoanalysis, 15,* 527–538.

Meissner, W. W. (1982–1983). Notes on countertransference in borderline conditions. *International Journal of Psychoanalytic Psychotherapy, 9,* 89–124.

Melamed, S., Kushnir, T., & Meir, E. I. (1991). Attenuating the impact of job demands: Additive and interactive effects of perceived control and social support. *Journal of Vocational Behavior, 39,* 40–53.

Meloy, J. R. (1986). Narcissistic psychopathology and the clergy. *Pastoral Psychology, 35,* 50–55.

Meltzer, H. Y. (1982). What is schizophrenia? *Schizophrenia Bulletin, 8,* 433–434.

Merskey, H., & Trimble, M. (1979). Personality, sexual adjustment, and brain lesions in patients with conversion symptoms. *American Journal of Psychiatry, 136,* 179–182.

Messer, A. A. (1976). Narcissistic people. *Medical Aspects of Human Sexuality, 19,* 169–184.

Mezzich, J. E., Fabrega, H., & Coffman, G. A. (1987). Multiaxial characterization of depressive patients. *Journal of Nervous and Mental Disease, 175,* 339–346.

Michener, J. A. (1991). *The novel.* New York: Random House.

Mickleburgh, W. E. (1986). Occupational mental health: A neglected service. *British Journal of Psychiatry, 148,* 426–434.

Midgley, N., & Abrams, M. S. (1974). Fear of success and locus of control in young women. *Journal of Consulting and Clinical Psychology, 42,* 737.

Milgram, N. A. (1988). Procrastination in daily living. *Psychological Reports, 63,* 752–754.

Milgram, N. A., Sroloff, B., & Rosenbaum, M. (1988). The procrastination of everyday life. *Journal of Research in Personality, 22,* 197–212.

Millar, J. D. (1990). Mental health and the workplace: An interchangeable partnership. *American Psychologist, 45,* 1165–1166.

Miller, A. (1986). Brief reconstructive hypnotherapy for anxiety reactions: Three case reports. *American Journal of Clinical Hypnosis, 28,* 138–146.

Miller, J. R. (1980). Relationship of fear of success to perceived parental attitudes toward success and autonomy in men and women. *Psychological Reports, 47,* 79–86.

Miller, L. S. (1991). The relationship between social support and burnout: Clarification and simplification. *Social Work Research and Abstracts, 27,* 34–37.

Miller, M. J., Smith, T. S., Wilkinson, L., Tobacyk, J. J. (1987). Narcissism and social interest among counselors-in-training. *Psychological Reports, 60,* 765–766.

Millon, T. (1981). *Disorders of personality: DSM–III. Axis II.* New York: Wiley.

Millon, T. (1986). Schizoid and avoidant personality disorders in DSM-III. *American Journal of Psychiatry, 143,* 1321–1322.

Millon, T. (1990). The disorders of personality. In L. A. Previn (Ed.), *Handbook of personality: Theory and research* (pp. 339–370). New York: Guilford Press.

Millon, T., & Klerman, G. L. (1986). *Contemporary directions in psychopathology: Toward the DSM–IV*. New York: Guilford Press.

Mirowsky, J., & Ross, C. E. (1983). Paranoia and the structure of powerlessness. *American Sociological Review, 48*, 228–239.

Mitchell, G. (1990). Living and dying for the ideal: A study of Willy Loman's narcissism. *Psychoanalytic Review, 77*, 391–407.

Mitchell, G. (1991). The great narcissist: A study of Fitzgerald's Jay Gatsby. *American Journal of Psychoanalysis, 51*, 387–396.

Mohler, S. R. (1983). The human element in air traffic control: Aeromedical aspects, problems, and prescriptions. *Aviation, Space, and Environmental Medicine, 54*, 511–516.

Molestrangler, R. S. (1975). The curse of over-achievement. *AEP Association of Educational Psychologists Journal, 3*, 33–35.

Mollinger, R. N. (1980). Antitheses and the obsessive–compulsive. *Psychoanalytic Review, 67*, 465–477.

Moloney, D. P., Bouchard, T. J., & Segal, N. L. (1991). A genetic and environmental analysis of the vocational interests of monozygotic and dizygotic twins reared apart. *Journal of Vocational Behavior, 39*, 76–109.

Moot, S. A., Teevan, R. C., & Greenfeld, N. (1988). Fear of failure and the Zeigarnik effect. *Psychological Reports, 63*, 459–464.

Moreland, J. R., & Liss-Levinson, L. N. (1977). Interrater agreement of experts' fear of success imagery scoring. *Applied Psychological Measurement, 1*, 153–154.

Morrison, A. P. (1983). Shame, ideal self, and narcissism. *Contemporary Psychoanalysis, 19*, 295–318.

Morrison, J. (1989). Histrionic personality disorder in women with somatization disorder. *Psychosomatics, 30*, 433–437.

Morse, L. A. (1987). Working with young procrastinators: Elementary school students who do not complete school assignments. *Elementary School Guidance and Counseling, 21*, 221–228.

Moses, N. C. (1989). Coping with the fear of failure: The case of Justin. *Career Development Quarterly, 37*, 302–305.

Motley, M. T. (1990). Public speaking anxiety qua performance anxiety: A revised model and an alternative therapy. *Journal of Social Behavior and Personality, 5*, 85–104.

Motowidlo, S. J., Packard, J. S., & Manning, M. R. (1986). Occupational stress: Its causes and consequences for job performance. *Journal of Applied Psychology, 71*, 618–629.

Moulton, R. (1985). The effect of the mother on the success of the daughter. *Contemporary Psychoanalysis, 21*, 266–283.

Mulig, J. C., Haggerty, M. E., Carballosa, A. B., Cinnick, W. J., & Madden, J. M. (1985). Relationships among fear of success, fear of failure, and androgyny. *Psychology of Women Quarterly, 9*, 284–287.

Mullins, L. S., & Kopelman, R. E. (1988). Toward an assessment of the construct validity of four measures of narcissism. *Journal of Personality Assessment, 52*, 610–625.

Mumford, M. D., & Gustafson, S. B. (1988). Creativity syndrome: Integration, application, and innovation. *Psychological Bulletin, 103,* 27–43.

Murphy, L. R., & Schoenborn, T. F. (Eds.). (1989). *Stress management in work settings.* New York: Praeger.

Murray, H. (1943). *Thematic Apperception Test manual.* Cambridge, MA: Harvard University Press.

Murray, H. (1965). Uses of the Thematic Apperception Test. In B. I. Murstein (Ed.), *Handbook of projective techniques* (pp. 425–432). New York: Basic Books.

Murray, S. R., & Mednick, M. T. (1977). Black women's achievement orientation: Motivation and cognitive factors. *Psychology of Women Quarterly, 1,* 247–259.

Myers, I. B., & McCaulley, M. H. (1985). *A guide to the development and use of the Myers–Briggs Type Indicator.* Palo Alto, CA: Consulting Psychologists Press.

Nagel, J. J., Himle, D. P., & Papsdorf, J. D. (1989). Cognitive behavioural treatment of musical performance anxiety. *Psychology of Music, 17,* 12–21.

Nagy, S. (1985). Burnout and selected variables as components of occupational stress. *Psychological Reports, 56,* 195–200.

Nagy, S., & Davis, L. G. (1985). Burnout: A comparative analysis of personality and environmental variables. *Psychological Reports, 57,* 1319–1326.

Naughton, T. J. (1987). A conceptual view of workaholism and implications for career counseling and research. *Career Development Quarterly, 35,* 180–187.

Neff, W. S. (1968). *Work and human behavior.* New York: Anthem.

Neiss, R. (1988a). Reconceptualizing arousal: Psychobiological states in motor performance. *Psychological Bulletin, 103,* 345–366.

Neiss, R. (1988b). Reconceptualizing relaxation treatments: Psychobiological states in sports. *Clinical Psychology Review, 8,* 139–159.

Nelson, D. F. (1988). Hermann Hesse: Narcissism and mother-complex. *Psychohistory Review, 16,* 237–257.

Nelson, D. L., & Kletke, M. G. (1990). Individual adjustment during technological innovation: A research framework. *Behaviour and Information Technology, 9,* 257–271.

Nelson, R. R., & Condrin, J. L. (1987). Avocational readiness and independent living skills program for psychiatrically impaired adolescents. *Occupational Therapy in Mental Health, 7,* 23–38.

Nestadt, G., Romanoski, A. J., Brown, C. H., Chahal, R., Merchant, A., Folstein, M. F., Gruenberg, E. M., & McHugh, P. R. (1991). DSM–III compulsive personality disorder: An epidemiological survey. *Psychological Medicine, 21,* 461–471.

Nestadt, G., Romanoski, A. J., Chahal, R., Merchant, A., Folstein, M. F., Gruenberg, E. M., & McHugh, P. R. (1990). An epidemiological study of histrionic personality disorder. *Psychological Medicine, 20,* 413–422.

Newton, T. J. (1989). Occupational stress and coping with stress: A critique. *Human Relations, 42,* 441–461.

Newton, T. J., & Keenan, T. (1990). The moderating effect of the Type A behavior pattern and locus of control upon the relationship between change in job demands and change in psychological strain. *Human Relations, 43,* 1229–1255.

Ng, T. P., Ong, S. G., Lam, W. K., & Jones, G. M. (1990). Neurobehavioral effects of industrial mixed solvent exposure in the Chinese printing and paint worker. *Neurotoxicology and Teratology, 12,* 661–664.

Nicholson, P. J., & Goh, S. C. (1983). The relationship of organization structure and interpersonal attitudes to role conflict and ambiguity in different work environments. *Academy of Management Journal, 26,* 148–155.

Nowack, K. M. (1986). Type A, hardiness, and psychological distress. *Journal of Behavioral Medicine, 9,* 537–548.

Nowack, K. M. (1987). Health habits, type A behaviour and job burnout. *Work and Stress, 1,* 135–142.

Nurmi, J. E. (1991). The effect of others' influence, effort, and ability attributions on emotions in achievement and affiliative situations. *Journal of Social Psychology, 131,* 703–715.

Oates, J. C. (1991, April 14). The man who detested the sea [Review of *Joseph Conrad: A Biography*]. *The New York Times Book Review,* pp. 15–16.

O'Connell, A. N., & Perez, S. (1982). Fear of success and causal attributions of success and failure in high school and college students. *Journal of Psychology, 111,* 141–151.

O'Driscoll, M. P., & Schubert, T. (1988). Organizational climate and burnout in a New Zealand social service agency. *Work and Stress, 2,* 199–204.

Ogus, E. D., Greenglass, E. R., & Burke, R. J. (1990). Gender-role differences, work stress and depersonalization. *Journal of Social Behavior and Personality, 5,* 387–398.

Oldham, J. M. (1988). Brief treatment of narcissistic personality disorder. *Journal of Personality Disorders, 2,* 88–90.

O'Leary, J., & Wright, F. (1986). Shame and gender issues in pathological narcissism. *Psychoanalytic Psychology, 3,* 327–339.

O'Leary, V. E. (1974). Some attitudinal barriers to occupational aspirations in women. *Psychological Bulletin, 81,* 809–826.

Olson, D. H., & Claiborn, C. D. (1990). Interpretation and arousal in the counseling process. *Journal of Counseling Psychology, 37,* 131–137.

O'Neill, C. P., & Zeichner, A. (1985). Working women: A study of relationships between stress, coping and health. *Journal of Psychosomatic Obstetrics and Gynecology, 4,* 105–116.

Orland, R. M., Orland, F. J., & Orland, P. T. (1990). Psychiatric assessment of Cleopatra: A challenging evaluation. *Psychopathology, 23,* 169–175.

Orpen, C. (1989). Predictors of fear of academic success among university students. *Psychological Reports, 65,* 439–442.

Orth-Gomer, K., & Unden, A. L. (1990). Type A behavior, social support, and coronary risk: Interaction and significance for mortality in cardiac patients. *Psychosomatic Medicine, 52,* 59–72.

Osipow, S. H., & Spokane, A. R. (1984). Measuring occupational stress, strain, and coping. *Applied Social Psychology Annual, 5,* 67–86.

Ottenberg, P. (1975). The physician's disease: Success and work addiction. *Psychiatric Opinion, 12,* 6–11.

Overholser, J. C. (1989). Differentiation between schizoid and avoidant personalities: An empirical test. *Canadian Journal of Psychiatry, 34,* 785–790.

Overholser, J. C. (1992). Interpersonal dependency and social loss. *Personality and Individual Differences, 13,* 17–23.

Paine, W. S. (1984). Professional burnout: Some major costs. *Family and Community Health, 6,* 1–11.

Palazzoli, M. S. (1986). The organization plays a game of its own. In M. S. Palazzoli, L. Anolli, P. DiBlasio, C. Ricci, M. Sacchi, & V. Ugazio (Eds.), *The hidden games of organizations* (pp. 113–124). New York: Pantheon Books.

Palinkas, L. A., & Coben, P. (1988). Psychiatric casualties among U.S. Marines in Vietnam. *Military Medicine, 153,* 521–526.

Paludi, M. A. (1979). Horner revisited: How successful must Anne and John be before fear of success sets in? *Psychological Reports, 44,* 1319–1322.

Paludi, M. A. (1984). Psychometric properties and underlying assumptions of four objective measures of fear of success. *Sex Roles, 10,* 765–781.

Pappo, M. (1983). Fear of success: The construction and validation of a measuring instrument. *Journal of Personality Assessment, 47,* 36–41.

Paykel, E. S., Klerman, G. L., & Prusoff, B. A. (1976). Personality and symptom pattern in depression. *British Journal of Psychiatry, 129,* 327–334.

Payne, R. (1988). Individual differences in the study of occupational stress. In C. L. Cooper & R. Payne (Eds.), *Causes, coping and consequences of stress at work* (pp. 209–232). New York: Wiley.

Pelletier, K. R., & Lutz, R. (1989). Mindbody goes to work: A critical review of stress management programs in the workplace. *Advances, 6,* 28–34.

Pelletier, K. R., & Lutz, R. (1991). Healthy people—healthy business: A critical review of stress management programs in the workplace. In A. Monat & R. S. Lazarus (Eds.), *Stress and coping: An anthology* (3rd ed., pp. 483–498). New York: Columbia University Press.

Pendleton, M., Stotland, E., Spiers, P., & Kirsch, E. (1989). Stress and strain among police, firefighters, and government workers: A comparative analysis. *Criminal Justice and Behavior, 16,* 196–210.

Penn, M., Romano, J. L., & Foat, D. (1988). The relationship between job satisfaction and burnout: A study of human service professionals. *Administration in Mental Health, 15,* 157–165.

Perlman, B., & Harman, E. A. (1982). Burnout: Summary and future research. *Human Relations, 35,* 283–305.

Perrewe, P. L., & Anthony, W. P. (1990). Stress in a steel pipe mill: The impact of job demands, personal control, and employee age on somatic complaints. *Journal of Social Behavior and Personality, 5,* 77–90.

Perrewe, P. L., & Ganster, D. C. (1989). The impact of job demands and behavioral control on experienced job stress. *Journal of Organizational Behavior, 10,* 213–229.

Perry, J. C. (1986). Borderline personality disorders: Research issues and new empirical findings. *Journal of the American Psychoanalytic Association, 34,* 179–192.

Perry, J. C., & Flannery, R. B. (1982). Passive–aggressive personality disorder: Treatment implications of a clinical typology. *Journal of Nervous and Mental Disease, 170,* 164–173.

Perry, J. C., Lavori, P. W., Cooper, S. H., Hoke, L., & O'Connell, M. E. (1987). The Diagnostic Interview Schedule and *DSM–III* antisocial personality disorder. *Journal of Personality Disorders, 1,* 121–131.

Perry, J. C., O'Connell, M. E., & Drake, R. (1984). An assessment of the Schedule for Schizotypal Personalities and the *DSM–III* criteria for diagnosing schizotypal personality disorder. *Journal of Nervous and Mental Disease, 172,* 674–680.

Person, E. S. (1982). Women working: Fears of failure, deviance and success. *Journal of the American Academy of Psychoanalysis, 10,* 67–84.

Peters, C. P. (1990). Critical issues in the evaluation and treatment of the borderline patient: I. *Occupational Therapy in Mental Health, 10,* 79–84.

Pfohl, B. (1991). Histrionic personality disorder: A review of available data and recommendations for *DSM–IV. Journal of Personality Disorders, 5,* 150–166.

Pfost, K. S., & Fiore, M. (1990). Pursuit of nontraditional occupations: Fear of success or fear of not being chosen? *Sex Roles, 23,* 15–24.

Pfouts, J. H. (1980). Birth order, age-spacing, IQ differences, and family relation. *Journal of Marriage and the Family, 42,* 517–531.

Phelan, J., Schwartz, J. E., Bromet, E. J., Dew, M. A., Parkinson, D. K., Schulberg, H. C., Dunn, L. O., Blane, H., & Curtis, E. C. (1991). Work stress, family stress, and depression in professional and managerial employees. *Psychological Medicine, 21,* 99–102.

Philipson, I. (1985). Gender and narcissism. *Psychology of Women Quarterly, 9,* 213–228.

Piedmont, R. L. (1988). An interactional model of achievement motivation and fear of success. *Sex Roles, 19,* 467–490.

Pierce, C. M., & Molloy, G. N. (1990a). The construct validity of the Maslach Burnout Inventory: Some data from Down Under. *Psychological Reports, 65,* 1340–1342.

Pierce, C. M., & Molloy, G. N. (1990b). Psychological and biographical differences between secondary school teachers experiencing high and low levels of burnout. *British Journal of Educational Psychology, 60,* 37–51.

Pierloot, R. A., & Ngoma, M. (1988). Hysterical manifestations in Africa and Europe: A comparative study. *British Journal of Psychiatry, 152,* 112–115.

Pierson, H. D., & Archambault, F. X. (1987). Role stress and perceived intensity of burnout among school psychologists. *Psychology in the Schools, 24,* 244–253.

Pietropinto, A. (1986). The workaholic spouse. *Medical Aspects of Human Sexuality, 20,* 89–96.

Pillemer, K., & Bachman-Prehn, R. (1991). Helping and hurting: Predictors of maltreatment of patients in nursing homes. *Research on Aging, 13,* 74–95.

Pines, A. M., & Aronson, E. (1983). Combatting burnout. *Children and Youth Services Review, 5,* 263–275.

Pines, A., Aronson, E., & Kafry, D. (1981). *Burnout: From tedium to personal growth.* New York: Free Press.

Pines, A., & Maslach, C. (1978). Characteristics of staff burnout in mental health settings. *Hospital and Community Psychiatry, 29,* 233–237.

Piotrowski, C. S. (1979). *Work and the family system: A naturalistic study of working class and lower-middle-class families.* New York: Free Press.

Pirot, M. (1986). The pathological thought and dynamics of the perfectionist. *Individual Psychology Journal of Adlerian Theory, Research and Practice, 42,* 51–58.

Pitman, R. K., & Jenike, M. A. (1989). Normal and disordered compulsivity: Evidence against a continuum. *Journal of Clinical Psychiatry, 50,* 450–452.

Plakun, E. M. (1987). Distinguishing narcissistic and borderline personality disorders using *DSM-III* criteria. *Comprehensive Psychiatry, 28,* 437–443.

Pollak, J. M. (1979). Obsessive–compulsive personality: A review. *Psychological Bulletin, 86,* 225–241.

Pollak, J. M. (1987). Obsessive–compulsive personality: Theoretical and clinical perspectives and recent research findings. *Journal of Personality Disorders, 1,* 248–262.

Popp, G. E., & Muhs, W. F. (1982). Fear of success and women employees. *Human Relations, 35,* 511–519.

Post, J. M. (1986). Narcissism and the charismatic leader–follower relationship. *Political Psychology, 7,* 675–688.

Powell, L. H., & Thoreson, C. E. (1987). Modifying the Type A behavior pattern. In J. A. Blumenthal & D. C. McKee (Eds.), *Applications in behavioral medicine and health psychology: A clinician's sourcebook* (pp. 171–207). Sarasota, FL: Professional Resource Exchange.

Prentky, R. (1989). Creativity and psychopathology: Gamboling at the seat of madness. In J. A. Glover, R. R. Ronning, & C. R. Reynolds (Eds.), *Handbook of creativity* (pp. 243–269). New York: Plenum Press.

Price, V. A. (1982). *Type A behavior pattern: A model for research and practice.* San Diego, CA: Academic Press.

Price, V. A. (1988). Research and clinical issues in treating Type A behavior. In B. K. Houston & C. R. Snyder (Eds.), *Type A behavior pattern: Research, theory, and intervention* (pp. 275–311). New York: Wiley.

Puryear, G. R., & Mednick, M. S. (1974). Black militancy, affective attachment, and the fear of success in black college women. *Journal of Consulting and Clinical Psychology, 42,* 263–266.

Quick, J. C., Bhagat, R. S., Dalton, J. E., & Quick, J. D. (Eds.). (1987). *Work stress: Health care systems in the workplace.* New York: Praeger.

Quick, J. C., & Quick, J. D. (1984). *Organizational stress and preventive management.* New York: McGraw-Hill.

Rachel Hecker, Artist. (1991, July 18). *Houston Press,* p. 6.

Rafferty, J. P., Lemkau, J. P., Purdy, R. R., & Rudisill, J. R. (1986). Validity of the Maslach Burnout Inventory for family practice physicians. *Journal of Clinical Psychology, 42,* 488–492.

Rahe, R. H. (1975). Stress and strain in coronary heart disease. *Journal of the South Carolina Medical Association, 72,* 7–14.

Rajendran, R., & Kaliappan, K. V. (1990). Efficacy of behavioural programme in managing the academic stress and improving academic performance. *Journal of Personality and Clinical Studies, 6,* 193–196.

Rand, A. (1968). *The fountainhead: 25th anniversary edition with special introduction by the author.* New York: Bobbs-Merrill. (Original work published 1943)

Raquepaw, J. M., & Miller, R. S. (1989). Psychotherapist burnout: A componential analysis. *Professional Psychology: Research and Practice, 20,* 32–36.

Raskin, R., & Novacek, J. (1989). An MMPI description of the narcissistic personality. *Journal of Personality Assessment, 53,* 66–80.

Raskin, R., Novacek, J., & Hogan, R. (1991). Narcissistic self-esteem management. *Journal of Personality and Social Psychology, 60,* 911–918.

Raskin, R., & Shaw, R. (1988). Narcissism and the use of personal pronouns. *Journal of Personality, 56,* 393–404.

Raskin, R., & Terry, H. (1988). A principal-components analysis of the Narcissistic Personality Inventory and further evidence of its construct validity. *Journal of Personality and Social Psychology, 54,* 890–902.

Raven, J. C., Court, J. H., & Raven, J. (1977). *Manual for Raven's Progressive Matrices and Vocabulary Scales: Section 3. Standard Progressive Matrices.* London: H. K. Lewis.

Rayburn, C. A. (1991). Counseling depressed female religious professionals: Nuns and clergywomen. *Counseling and Values, 35,* 136–148.

Razin, A. M., Swencionis, C., & Zohman, L. R. (1986–1987). Reduction of physiological, behavioral, and self-report responses in Type A behavior: A preliminary report. *International Journal of Psychiatry in Medicine, 16,* 31–47.

Reed, G. F. (1977). The obsessional–compulsive experience: A phenomenological reemphasis. *Philosophy and Phenomenological Research, 37,* 381–385.

Regier, D. A., Burke, J. D., & Burke, K. C. (1990). Comorbidity of affective and anxiety disorders in the NIMH Epidemiologic Catchment Area Program. In J. D. Maser & C. R. Cloniger (Eds.), *Comorbidity of mood and anxiety disorders* (pp. 113–122). Washington, DC: American Psychiatric Press.

Reich, J. (1985). The relationship between antisocial behavior and affective illness. *Comprehensive Psychiatry, 26,* 296–303.

Reich, J. (1987). Sex distribution of *DSM–III* personality disorders in psychiatric outpatients. *American Journal of Psychiatry, 144,* 485–488.

Reich, J. H. (1990a). Comparisons of males and females with *DSM–III* dependent personality disorder. *Psychiatry Research, 33,* 207–214.

Reich, J. H. (1990b). Relationship between *DSM–III* avoidant and dependent personality disorders. *Psychiatry Research, 34,* 281–292.

Reich, J. H., & Green, A. I. (1991). Effect of personality disorders on outcome of treatment. *Journal of Nervous and Mental Disease, 179,* 74–82.

Reich, J., Noyes, R., & Troughton, E. (1987). Dependent personality disorder associated with phobic avoidance in patients with panic disorder. *American Journal of Psychiatry, 144,* 323–326.

Reich, J., Noyes, R., & Yates, W. (1989). Alprazolam treatment of avoidant personality traits in social phobic patients. *Journal of Clinical Psychiatry, 50,* 91–95.

Reich, J., & Yates, W. (1988). A pilot study of treatment of social phobia with alprazolam. *American Journal of Psychiatry, 145,* 590–594.

Reis, S. M. (1987). We can't change what we don't recognize: Understanding the special needs of gifted females. *Gifted Child Quarterly, 31,* 83–89.

Reiser, M., & Geiger, S. P. (1984). Police officer as victim. *Professional Psychology: Research and Practice, 15,* 315–323.

Renneberg, B., Goldstein, A. J., Phillips, D., & Chambless, D. L. (1990). Intensive behavioral group treatment of avoidant personality disorder. *Behavior Therapy, 21,* 363–377.

Repetti, R. L. (1987). Individual and common components of the social environment at work and psychological well-being. *Journal of Personality and Social Psychology, 52,* 710–720.

Revicki, D. A., & May, H. J. (1985). Occupational stress, social support, and depression. *Health Psychology, 4,* 61–77.

Reviere, R., & Posey, T. B. (1978). Correlates of two measures of fear of success in women. *Psychological Reports, 42,* 609–610.

Rhoads, J. M. (1977). Overwork. *Journal of the American Medical Association, 237,* 2615–2618.

Rhodewalt, F., & Fairfield, M. (1991). An alternative approach to Type A behavior and health: Psychological reactance and medical noncompliance. In M. J. Strube (Ed.), *Type A behavior* (pp. 293–312). Newbury Park, CA: Sage.

Richardson, M., & West, P. (1982). Motivational management: Coping with burnout. *Hospital and Community Psychiatry, 33,* 837–840.

Richardson, P. A., Jackson, A., & Albury, K. W. (1984). Measurement of fear of failure using the Self-Deprecation and Insecurity Scale. *Journal of Sport Behavior, 7,* 115–119.

Richman, J. A., & Flaherty, J. A. (1988). "Tragic man" and "tragic woman": Gender differences in narcissistic styles. *Psychiatry, 51,* 368–377.

Rider, M. S. (1987). Music therapy: Therapy for debilitated musicians. *Music Therapy Perspectives, 4,* 40–43.

Riggar, T. F., Garner, W. E., & Hafer, M. D. (1984). Rehabilitation personnel burnout: Organizational cures. *Journal of Rehabilitation Administration, 8,* 94–104.

Rimpela, A. (1989). Death amongst doctors. *Stress Medicine, 5,* 73–75.

Rippetoe, P. A., Alarcon, R. D., & Walter-Ryan, W. G. (1986). Interactions between depression and borderline personality disorder: A pilot study. *Psychopathology, 19,* 340–346.

Ris, M. D., & Woods, D. J. (1983). Learned helplessness and "fear of success" in college women. *Sex Roles, 9,* 1067–1072.

Robbins, A. (1988). The interface of the real and transference relationships in the treatment of schizoid phenomena. *Psychoanalytic Review, 75,* 393–417.

Robinson, B. E. (1989). *Work addiction: Hidden legacies of adult children.* Deerfield Beach, FL: Health Communications.

Rohrlich, J. B. (1980). *Work and love: The crucial balance.* New York: Summit Books.

Rohrlich, J. B. (1981). The dynamics of work addiction. *Israel Journal of Psychiatry and Related Sciences, 18,* 147–156.

Romine, P. G., & Crowell, O. C. (1981). Personality correlates of under- and overachievement at the university level. *Psychological Reports, 48,* 787–792.

Romney, D. M. (1987). A simplex model of the paranoid process: Implications for diagnosis and prognosis. *Acta Psychiatrica Scandinavica, 75,* 651–655.

Ronningstam, E., & Gunderson, J. (1988). Narcissistic traits in psychiatric patients. *Comprehensive Psychiatry, 29,* 545–549.

Ronningstam, E., & Gunderson, J. (1989). Descriptive studies on narcissistic personality disorder. *Psychiatric Clinics of North America, 12,* 585–601.

Ronningstam, E., & Gunderson, J. G. (1990). Identifying criteria for narcissistic personality disorder. *American Journal of Psychiatry, 147,* 918–922.

Ronningstam, E., & Gunderson, J. (1991). Differentiating borderline personality disorder from narcissistic personality disorder. *Journal of Personality Disorders, 5,* 225–232.

Rorer, L. G. (1983). "Deep" RET: A reformulation of some psychodynamic explanations of procrastination. *Cognitive Therapy and Research, 7,* 1–10.

Rose, M. (1984). *Writer's block: The cognitive dimension.* Carbondale, IL: Southern Illinois University Press.

Rosenberg, M. S. (1987). Characteristics of the passive aggressive personality disorder: Males. *Journal of Training and Practice in Professional Psychology, 1,* 29–42.

Rosenman, R. H. (1990). Health consequences of anger and implications for treatment. *Activitas Nervosa Superior, 28,* 1–23.

Rosenman, R. H., Brand, R. J., Sholtz, R. I., & Friedman, M. (1976). Multivariate predication of coronary heart disease during 8.5 year follow-up in the Western Collaborative Group Study. *American Journal of Cardiology, 37,* 903–910.

Rosenman, R. H., & Friedman, M. (1959). Association of specific behavior patterns with blood and cardiovascular findings: Blood cholesterol level, clotting time, incidence of arcus senilis, and clinical coronary artery disease. *Journal of the American Medical Association, 169,* 1286–1325.

Rosenman, R. H., Friedman, M., Wurm, M., Jenkins, C. D., Messinger, H. B., & Strauss, R. (1966). Coronary heart disease in the Western Collaborative Group Study. *Journal of the American Medical Association, 189,* 15–22.

Rosenthal, R. J. (1986). The pathological gambler's system for self-deception. *Journal of Gambling Behavior, 2,* 108–120.

Roskies, E. (1987). *Stress management for the healthy Type A: Theory and practice.* New York: Guilford Press.

Roskies, E. (1990). Type A intervention: Where do we go from here? *Journal of Social Behavior and Personality, 5,* 419–438.

Roskies, E., Seraganian, P., Oseasohn, R., Hanley, J. A., Collu, R., Martin, N., & Smilga, C. (1986). The Montreal Type A Intervention Project: Major findings. *Health Psychology, 5,* 45–69.

Ross, H. E., Glaser, F. B., & Stiasny, S. (1988). Sex differences in the prevalence of psychiatric disorders in patients with alcohol and drug problems. *British Journal of Addiction, 83,* 1179–1192.

Ross, R. R., Altmaier, E. M., & Russell, D. W. (1989). Job stress, social support, and burnout among counseling center staff. *Journal of Counseling Psychology, 36,* 464–470.

Rotella, R. J., Hanson, T., & Coop, R. H. (1991). Burnout in youth sports. *Elementary School Journal, 91,* 421–428.

Rothblum, E. D., Solomon, L. J., & Murakami, J. (1986). Affective, cognitive, and behavioral differences between high and low procrastinators. *Journal of Counseling Psychology, 33,* 387–394.

Rothenberg, A. (1987). To err is human: The role of error in creativity and psychotherapy. In D. P. Schwarts, J. L. Sacksteder, & Y. Akabane (Eds.), *Attachment and the therapeutic process: Essays in honor of Otto Allen Will, Jr., M.D.* (pp. 155–181). Madison, CT: International Universities Press.

Rothenberg, A. (1990a). *Creativity and madness: New findings and old stereotypes.* Baltimore: Johns Hopkins University Press.

Rothenberg, A. (1990b). Creativity, mental health, and alcoholism. *Creativity Research Journal, 3,* 179–201.

Rush, A. J. (1982). *Short-term psychotherapies for depression: Behavioral, interpersonal, cognitive, and psychodynamic approaches.* New York: Guilford Press.

Russell, D. W., Altmaier, E., & Van-Velzen, D. (1987). Job-related stress, social support, and burnout among classroom teachers. *Journal of Applied Psychology, 72,* 269–274.

Ryan, S. (1980). Petain and Vichy: Abandonment, guilt, "love of harlot," and repetition compulsion. *Journal of Psychohistory, 8,* 149–158.

Saab, P. G., Dembroski, T. M., & Schneiderman, N. (1990). Coronary-prone behaviors: Intervention issues. In K. D. Craig & S. M. Weiss (Eds.), *Health enhancement, disease prevention, and early intervention: Biobehavioral perspectives* (pp. 233–268). New York: Springer.

Sadd, S., Lenauer, M., Shaver, P., & Dunivant, N. (1978). Objective measurement of fear of success and fear of failure: A factor analytic approach. *Journal of Consulting and Clinical Psychology, 46,* 405–416.

Sadd, S., Miller, F. D., & Zeitz, B. (1979). Sex roles and achievement conflicts. *Personality and Social Psychology Bulletin, 5,* 352–355.

Saltoun, J. (1980). Fear of failure in career development. *Vocational Guidance Quarterly, 29,* 35–41.

Salz, C. (1983). A theoretical approach to the treatment of work difficulties in borderline personalities. *Occupational Therapy in Mental Health, 3,* 33–46.

Salzman, L. (1979). Psychotherapy of the obsessional. *American Journal of Psychotherapy, 33,* 32–40.

Salzman, L., & Thaler, F. H. (1981). Obsessive–compulsive disorders: A review of the literature. *American Journal of Psychiatry, 138,* 286–296.

Sancho, A. M., & Hewitt, J. (1990). Questioning fear of success. *Psychological Reports, 67,* 803–806.

Sandblom, P. (1989). *Creativity and disease: How illness affects literature, art and music.* Philadelphia: Lippincott.

Sassen, G. (1980). Success anxiety in women: A constructivist interpretation of its social significance. *Harvard Educational Review, 50,* 13–24.

Satow, R. (1988). Psychic functions of failure. *Psychoanalytic Review, 75,* 443–457.

Sauter, S. L., Murphy, L. R., & Hurrell, J. J. (1990). Prevention of work-related psychological disorders: A national strategy proposed by the National Institute for Occupational Safety and Health (NIOSH). *American Psychologist, 45,* 1146–1158.

Savage, J. E., & Stearns, A. D. (1979). Relationship of internal–external locus of control, self-concept, and masculinity–femininity to fear of success in Black freshmen and senior college women. *Sex Roles, 5,* 373–383.

Savickas, M. L. (1991). The meaning of work and love: Career issues and interventions. *Career Development Quarterly, 39,* 315–324.

Savicki, V., & Cooley, E. (1987). The relationship of work environment and client contact to burnout in mental health professionals. *Journal of Counseling and Development, 65,* 249–252.

Schaubroeck, J., Cotton, J. L., & Jennings, K. R. (1989). Antecedents and consequences of role stress: A covariance structure analysis. *Journal of Organizational Behavior, 10,* 35–58.

Schecter, D. E. (1979). Fear of success in women: A psychodynamic reconstruction. *Journal of the American Academy of Psychoanalysis, 7,* 33–43.

Scherwitz, L., & Brand, R. (1990). Interviewer behaviors during structured interviews to assess Type A/B behavior in the Western Collaborative Group Study and the Multiple Risk Factor Intervention Trial. *Journal of Psychopathology and Behavioral Assessment, 12,* 27–47.

Scherwitz, L., Graham, L. E., Grandits, G., & Billings, J. (1990). Speech characteristics and coronary heart disease incidence in the Multiple Risk Factor Intervention Trial. *Journal of Behavioral Medicine, 13,* 75–91.

Schiff, S. (1992, December/1993, January). The shadows of William Trevor. *The New Yorker,* pp. 158–163.

Schloss, P. J., Sedlak, R. A., Wiggins, E. D., & Ramsey, D. (1983). Stress reduction for professionals working with aggressive adolescents. *Exceptional Children, 49,* 349–354.

Schneider, B. (1972). Organizational climate: Individual preferences and organizational realities. *Journal of Applied Psychology, 56,* 211-217.

Schneider, B. (1987). The people make the place. *Personnel Psychology, 40,* 437–453.

Schneider, B., & Schmitt, N. (1986). *Staffing organizations* (2nd ed.). Glenview, IL: Scott Foresman.

Schonfeld, I. S. (1990). Psychological distress in a sample of teachers. *Journal of Psychology, 124,* 321–338.

Schonfeld, I. S., & Ruan, D. (1991). Occupational stress and preemployment measures of depressive symptoms: The case of teachers. *Journal of Social Behavior and Personality, 6,* 95–114.

Schroeder, M. L., Schroeder, K. G., & Hare, R. D. (1983). Generalizability of a checklist for assessment of psychopathy. *Journal of Consulting and Clinical Psychology, 51,* 511–516.

Schubert, D. S., Wolf, A. W., Patterson, M. B., Grande, T. P., & Pendleton, L. (1988). A statistical evaluation of the literature regarding the associations among alcoholism, drug abuse, and antisocial personality disorder. *International Journal of the Addictions, 23,* 797–808.

Schwab, R. L., Jackson, S. E., & Schuler, R. S. (1986). Educator burnout: Sources and consequences. *Educational Research Quarterly, 10,* 14–30.

Seidman, S. A., & Zager, J. (1986–1987). The Teacher Burnout Scale. *Educational Research Quarterly, 11,* 26–33.

Seligman, M. E. P. (1975). *Helplessness: On depression, development, and death.* San Francisco: Freeman.

Sepie, A. C., & Keeling, B. (1978). The relationship between types of anxiety and under-achievement in mathematics. *Journal of Educational Research, 72,* 15–19.

Seraganian, P., Roskies, E., Hanley, J. A., Oseasohn, R., & Collu, R. (1987). Failure to alter psychophysiological reactivity in Type A men with physical exercise or stress management programs. *Psychology and Health, 1,* 195–213.

Serban, G., & Siegel, S. (1984). Response of borderline and schizotypal patients to small doses of thiothixene and haloperidol. *American Journal of Psychiatry, 14,* 1455–1458.

Shankar, J., & Famuyiwa, O. O. (1991). Stress among factory workers in a developing country. *Journal of Psychosomatic Research, 35,* 163–171.

Shapiro, J. P. (1979). "Fear of success" imagery as a reaction to sex-role inappropriate behavior. *Journal of Personality Assessment, 43,* 33–38.

Sharma, S., & Acharya, T. (1990). Coping strategies and job anxiety. *Psychological Studies, 36,* 112–117.

Shea, M. T., Pilkonis, P. A., Beckham, E., Collins, J. F., Elkin, I., Sotsky, S. M., & Docherty, J. P. (1990). Personality disorders and treatment outcome in the NIMH Treatment of Depression Collaborative Research Program. *American Journal of Psychiatry, 147,* 711–718.

Shea, M. T., Widiger, T. A., & Klein, M. H. (1992). Comorbidity of personality disorders and depression: Implications for treatment. *Journal of Consulting and Clinical Psychology, 60,* 857–868.

Shepperson, V. L. (1982). Differences in assertion and aggression between normal and neurotic family triads. *Journal of Personality Assessment, 46,* 409–414.

Sherman, J. A. (1987). Achievement related fears: Gender roles and individual dynamics. *Women and Therapy, 6,* 97–105.

Shinn, M., Rosario, M., Morch, H., & Chestnut, D. E. (1984). Coping with job stress and burnout in the human services. *Journal of Personality and Social Psychology, 46,* 864–876.

Shirom, A. (1986). On the cross-environment generality of the relational view of stress. *Journal of Environmental Psychology, 6,* 121–134.

Shoham-Salomon, V., Avner, R., & Neeman, R. (1989). You're changed if you do and changed if you don't: Mechanisms underlying paradoxical interventions. *Journal of Consulting and Clinical Psychology, 57,* 590–598.

Shulman, D. G., & Ferguson, G. R. (1988). Two methods of assessing narcissism: Comparison of the Narcissism–Projective (N-P) and the Narcissistic Personality Inventory (NPI). *Journal of Clinical Psychology, 44,* 857–866.

Shulman, D. G., McCarthy, E. C., & Ferguson, G. R. (1988). The projective assessment of narcissism: Development, reliability, and validity of the N-P. *Psychoanalytic Psychology, 5,* 285–297.

Siegel, R. G., Galassi, J. P., & Ware, W. B. (1985). A comparison of two models for predicting mathematics performance: Social learning versus math aptitude-anxiety. *Journal of Counseling Psychology, 32,* 531–538.

Silva, J. M. (1982). An evaluation of fear of success in female and male athletes and nonathletes. *Journal of Sport Psychology, 4,* 92–96.

Silver, M., & Sabini, J. (1981). Procrastinating. *Journal of the Theory of Social Behavior, 11,* 207–221.

Simonton, D. K. (1988). Age and outstanding achievement: What do we know after a century of research? *Psychological Bulletin, 104,* 251–267.

Simonton, D. K. (1989). Age and creative productivity: Nonlinear estimation of an information-processing model. *International Journal of Aging and Human Development, 29,* 23–37.

Simonton, D. K. (1990). Creativity and wisdom in aging. In J. E. Birren & K. W. Schaie (Eds.), *Handbook of the psychology of aging* (3rd ed., pp. 320–329). San Diego, CA: Academic Press.

Singer, R. N., Grove, J. R., Cauraugh, J., & Rudisill, M. (1985). Consequences of attributing failure on a gross motor task to lack of effort or ineffective strategy. *Perceptual and Motor Skills, 61,* 299–306.

Singer, R., & Scott, N. E. (1987). Progression of neuropsychological deficits following toluene diisocyanate exposure. *Archives of Clinical Neuropsychology, 2,* 135–144.

Singh, I. L. (1989). Personality correlates and perceptual detectability of locomotive drivers. *Personality and Individual Differences, 10,* 1049–1054.

Skeen, D. R., & Zacchera, W. (1974). Relation of academic achievement to scales of Famous Sayings Test. *Psychological Reports, 34,* 433–434.

Slavney, P. R. (1984). Histrionic personality and antisocial personality: Caricatures of stereotypes? *Comprehensive Psychiatry, 25,* 129–141.

Slavney, P. R., Teitelbaum, M. L., & Chase, G. A. (1985). Referral for medically unexplained somatic complaints: The role of histrionic traits. *Psychosomatics, 26,* 103–109.

Smart, J. C., Elton, C. F., & McLaughlin, G. W. (1986). Person–environment congruence and job satisfaction. *Journal of Vocational Behavior, 29,* 216–225.

Smith, H. E. (1982). Doctors and society: A Northern Thailand study. *Social Science and Medicine, 16,* 516–526.

Smith, J. J. (1987). The effectiveness of a computerized self-help stress coping program with adult males. *Computers in Human Services, 2,* 37–49.

Smith, K. J. (1990). Occupational stress in accountancy: A review. *Journal of Business and Psychology, 4,* 511–524.

Smith, S. S., & Newman, J. P. (1990). Alcohol and drug abuse–dependence disorders in psychopathic and nonpsychopathic criminal offenders. *Journal of Abnormal Psychology, 99,* 430–439.

Snapp, M. B. (1992). Occupational stress, social support, and depression among Black and White professional–managerial women. *Women and Health, 18,* 41–79.

Snyder, S., Pitts, W. M., & Pokorny, A. D. (1986). Selected behavioral features of patients with borderline personality traits. *Suicide and Life Threatening Behavior, 16,* 28–39.

Solomon, L. J., & Rothblum, E. D. (1984). Academic procrastination: Frequency and cognitive–behavioral correlates. *Journal of Counseling Psychology, 31,* 503–509.

Solyom, L., Ledwidge, B., & Solyom, C. (1986). Obsessiveness and adjustment. *Comprehensive Psychiatry, 27,* 234–240.

Sommer, R. (1973). The burnt-out chairman. *American Psychologist, 28,* 536–537.

Sorensen, G., Jacobs, D. R., Pirie, P., Folsom, A., Luepker, R., & Gillum, R. (1987). Relationships among Type A behavior, employment experiences, and gender: The Minnesota Heart Survey. *Journal of Behavioral Medicine, 10,* 323–336.

Sorotzkin, B. (1985). The quest for perfection: Avoiding guilt or avoiding shame? *Psychotherapy, 22,* 564–571.

Sorrentino, R. M., & Short, J. A. C. (1977). The case of the mysterious moderates: Why motives sometimes fail to predict behavior. *Journal of Personality and Social Psychology, 35,* 478–484.

Sothmann, M. S., Ismail, A. H., & Chodepko-Zapjiko, W. (1984). Influence of catecholamine activity on the hierarchical relationships among physical fitness condition and selected personality characteristics. *Journal of Clinical Psychology, 40,* 1308–1317.

Sparr, L. F., Boehnlein, J. K., & Cooney, T. G. 1986). The medical management of the paranoid patient. *General Hospital Psychiatry, 8,* 49–55.

Spearman, C. (1930). *Creative mind.* London: Nisbet.

Spector, P. E. (1987). Interactive effects of perceived control and job stressors on affective reactions and health outcomes for clerical workers. *Work and Stress, 1,* 155–162.

Spector, P. E., & Jex, S. M. (1991). Relations of job characteristics from multiple data sources with employee affect, absence, turnover intentions, and health. *Journal of Applied Psychology, 76,* 46–53.

Spence, J. T., Helmreich, R. L., & Pred, R. S. (1987). Impatience versus achievement strivings in the Type A behavior pattern: Differential effects on students' health and academic achievement. *Journal of Applied Psychology, 72,* 522–528.

Spicuzza, F. J., & deVoe, M. W. (1982). Burnout in the helping professions: Mutual aid groups as self-help. *Personnel and Guidance Journal, 61,* 95–99.

Spielberger, C. D. (1975). Anxiety: State-trait process. In C. D. Spielberger & I. G. Sarason (Eds.), *Stress and anxiety* (vol. 1, pp. 115–143). New York: Hemisphere.

Spillane, R. (1983). Fighting fear of failure with rational–emotive therapy. *International Journal of Eclectic Psychotherapy, 2,* 1–13.

Spitzer, J. (1990). On treating patients diagnosed with narcissistic personality disorder: The induction phase. *Issues in Ego Psychology, 13,* 54–65.

Spokane, A. R. (1993). Are career counselors really guilty of malpractice? A critique of the inter-domain theory. *Journal of Counseling and Development, 71,* 556–557.

Srivastava, A. K. (1989). Moderating effect of n-self actualization on the relationship of role stress with job anxiety. *Psychological Studies, 34,* 106–109.

Stabenau, J. R. (1990). Additive independent factors that predict risk for alcoholism. *Journal of Studies on Alcohol, 51,* 164–174.

Standage, K., Bilsbury, C., Jain, S., & Smith, D. (1984). An investigation of role-taking in histrionic personalities. *Canadian Journal of Psychiatry, 29,* 407–411.

Stangler, R. S., & Printz, A. M. (1980). *DSM-III:* Psychiatric diagnosis in a university population. *American Journal of Psychiatry, 137,* 937–940.

Stanley, M. A., Turner, S. M., & Borden, J. W. (1990). Schizotypal features in obsessive–compulsive disorder. *Comprehensive Psychiatry, 31,* 511–518.

Starcevic, V. (1990). Relationship between hypochondriasis and obsessive–compulsive personality disorder: Close relatives separated by nosological schemes? *American Journal of Psychotherapy, 44,* 340–347.

Stark, M. I. (1989). Work inhibition: A self-psychological perspective. *Contemporary Psychoanalysis, 25,* 135–138.

Statham, A., & Bravo, E. (1990). The introduction of new technology: Health implications for workers. *Women and Health, 16,* 105–129.

Stavosky, J. M., & Borkovec, T. D. (1987). The phenomenon of worry: Theory, research, treatment and its implications for women. *Women and Therapy, 6,* 77–95.

Steffy, B. D., Jones, J. W., Murphy, L. R., & Kunz, L. (1986). A demonstration of the impact of stress abatement programs on reducing employees' accidents and their costs. *American Journal of Health Promotion, 1,* 25–32.

Steffy, B. D., Jones, J. W., & Noe, A. W. (1990). The impact of health habits and life-style on the stressor–strain relationship: An evaluation of three industries. *Journal of Occupational Psychology, 63,* 217–229.

Stein, A. H., & Bailey, M. M. (1973). The socialization of achievement orientation in females. *Psychological Bulletin, 80,* 345–366.

Stein, D. J., Hollander, E., DeCaria, C. M., & Trungold, S. (1991). OCD: A disorder with anxiety, aggression, impulsivity, and depressed mood. *Psychiatry Research, 36,* 237–239.

Steinberg, J. A. (1986). Clinical interventions with women experiencing the impostor phenomenon. *Women and Therapy, 5,* 19–26.

Steinberg, L. (1988). Stability (and instability) of Type A behavior from childhood to young adulthood. In S. Chess, A. Thomas, & M. Hertzig (Eds.), *Annual progress in child psychiatry and child development, 1987* (pp. 162–186). New York: Brunner/Mazel.

Steketee, G. (1990). Personality traits and disorders in obsessive–compulsives. *Journal of Anxiety Disorders, 4,* 351–364.

Steketee, G., & Cleere, L. (1990). Obsessional–compulsive disorders. In A. S. Bellack, M. Hersen, & A. E. Kazdin (Eds.), *International handbook of behavior modification and therapy* (2nd ed., pp. 307–332). New York: Plenum Press.

Steketee, G., Grayson, J. B., & Foa, E. B. (1987). A comparison of characteristics of obsessive–compulsive disorder and other anxiety disorders. *Journal of Anxiety Disorders, 1,* 325–335.

Steptoe, A. (1989). Stress, coping and stage fright in professional musicians. *Psychology of Music, 17,* 3–11.

Steptoe, A., & Fidler, H. (1987). Stage fright in orchestral musicians: A study of cognitive and behavioural strategies in performance anxiety. *British Journal of Psychology, 78,* 241–249.

Stevenson, B. (1964). *The home book of quotations: Classical and modern.* New York: Dodd Mead.

Stone, M. H. (1983). Conflict resolution in schizotypal vs. affective borderlines. *Journal of the American Academy of Psychoanalysis, 11,* 377–389.

Stone, M. (1985). Schizotypal personality: Psychotherapeutic aspects. *Schizophrenia Bulletin, 11,* 576–589.

Stoneman, Z., & Crapps, J. M. (1988). Correlates of stress, perceived competence, and depression among family care providers. *American Journal on Mental Retardation, 93,* 166–173.

Stout, J. K., & Williams, J. M. (1983). Comparison of two measures of burnout. *Psychological Reports, 53,* 283–289.

Stravynski, A., & Greenberg, D. (1985a). Patients who complain of social dysfunction as their main problem: I. Clinical and demographic features. *Canadian Journal of Psychiatry, 30,* 206–211.

Stravynski, A., & Greenberg, D. (1985b). Patients who complain of social dysfunction as their main problem: II. Comparison with other outpatients seen for behavior therapy. *Canadian Journal of Psychiatry, 30,* 212–216.

Stravynski, A., Grey, S., & Elie, R. (1987). Outline of the therapeutic process in social skills training with socially dysfunctional patients. *Journal of Consulting and Clinical Psychology, 55,* 224–228.

Stravynski, A., Lesage, A., Marcouiller, M., & Elie, R. (1989). A test of the therapeutic mechanism in social skills training with avoidant personality disorder. *Journal of Nervous and Mental Disease, 177,* 739–744.

Strelau, J. (1989). Individual differences in tolerance to stress: The role of reactivity. In C. D. Spielberger & I. G. Sarason (Eds.), *Stress and anxiety* (Vol. 12, pp. 155–166). New York: Hemisphere.

Stricker, G., & Gold, J. R. (1988). A psychodynamic approach to the personality disorders. *Journal of Personality Disorders, 2,* 350–359.

Strong, S. R. (1984). Experimental studies in explicitly paradoxical interventions: Results and implications. *Journal of Behavior Therapy and Experimental Psychiatry, 15,* 189–194.

Strong, S. R., Wambach, C. A., Lopez, F. G., & Cooper, R. K. (1979). Motivational and equipping functions of interpretation in counseling. *Journal of Counseling Psychology, 26,* 98–107.

Strub, R. L. (1989). Frontal lobe syndrome in a patient with bilateral globus pallidus lesions. *Archives of Neurology, 46,* 1024–1027.

Strube, M. J. (Ed.). (1991). *Type A behavior.* Newbury Park, CA: Sage.

Strube, M. J., Berry, J. M., & Moergen, S. (1985). Relinquishment of control and the Type A behavior pattern: The role of performance evaluation. *Journal of Personality and Social Psychology, 49,* 831–842.

Strube, M. J., Deichmann, A. K., & Kickham, T. (1989). Time urgency and the Type A behavior pattern: Time investment as a function of cue salience. *Journal of Research in Personality, 23,* 287–301.

St. Yves, A., Freeston, M. H., Godbout, F., Poulin, L., St. Amand, C., & Verret, M. (1989). Externality and burnout among dentists. *Psychological Reports, 65,* 755–758.

Suinn, R. M. (1982). Interventions with Type A behaviors. *Journal of Consulting and Clinical Psychology, 50,* 933–949.

Sutherland, E. (1978). Fear of success and the need for power. *Psychological Reports, 43,* 763–766.

Sutherland, V. J., & Cooper, C. L. (1991). Personality, stress and accident involvement in the offshore oil and gas industry. *Personality and Individual Differences, 12,* 195–204.

Sutherland, V., & Davidson, M. J. (1989). Stress among construction site managers: A preliminary study. *Stress Medicine, 5,* 221–235.

Sutker, P. B., DeSanto, N. A., & Allain, A. N. (1985). Adjective self-descriptions in antisocial men and women. *Journal of Psychopathology and Behavioral Assessment, 7,* 175–181.

Swan, G. E., Carmelli, D., & Rosenman, R. H. (1991). Cook and Medley Hostility and the Type A behavior pattern: Psychological correlates of two coronary-prone behaviors. In M. J. Strube (Ed.), *Type A behavior* (pp. 89–106). Newbury Park, CA: Sage.

Swearingen, C. (1990). The impaired psychiatrist. *Psychiatric Clinics of North America, 13,* 1–11.

Sweeney, G. A., & Horan, J. J. (1982). Separate and combined effects of cue-controlled relaxation and cognitive restructuring in the treatment of musical performance anxiety. *Journal of Counseling Psychology, 29,* 486–497.

Syme, S. L. (1990). Control and health: An epidemiological perspective. In J. Rodin, C. Schooler, & K. W. Schaie (Eds.), *Self-directedness: Cause and effects throughout the life course* (pp. 213–229). Hillsdale, NJ: Erlbaum.

Symonds, A. (1976). Neurotic dependency in successful women. *Journal of the American Academy of Psychoanalysis, 4,* 95–103.

Tang, T. L. (1986). Effects of Type A personality and task labels (work vs. leisure) on task preference. *Journal of Leisure Research, 18,* 1–11.

Tang, T. L., & Liu, H. (1989). Effects of Type A behavior and task label on goal setting. *Journal of Psychology, 123,* 79–89.

Tannenbaum, A. S. (1968). *Control in organizations.* New York: McGraw-Hill.

Tannenbaum, A. S. (1974). *Hierarchy in organizations.* San Francisco: Jossey-Bass.

Taylor, K. M. (1982). An investigation of vocational indecision in college students: Correlates and moderators. *Journal of Vocational Behavior, 21,* 318–329.

Taylor, M. S., Locke, E. A., Lee, C., & Gist, M. E. (1984). Type A behavior and faculty research productivity: What are the mechanisms? *Organizational Behavior and Human Performance, 34,* 402–418.

Tesser, A., & Blusiewicz, C. O. (1987). Dependency conflict and underachievement. *Journal of Social and Clinical Psychology, 5,* 378–390.

Teevan, R. C. (1983). Childhood development of fear of failure motivation: A replication. *Psychological Reports, 53,* 506.

Teevan, R. C., & Fischer, R. I. (1974). Hostile press and internal versus external standards of success and failure. *Psychological Reports, 34,* 855–858.

Teevan, R. C., & Greenfeld, N. (1985). Note on fear of failure in golfers. *Perceptual and Motor Skills, 60,* 910.

Teevan, R. C., & Smith, B. D. (1975). Relationships of fear-of-failure and need achievement motivation to a confirming-interval measure of aspirational levels. *Psychological Reports, 36,* 967–976.

Teevan, R. C., & Yalof, J. (1979). Fear of failure in athletes and in non-athletes. *Psychological Reports, 44,* 798.

Teevan, R. C., Zarrillo, D., & Greenfeld, N. (1983). Relationship of fear of failure to amount of time spent in a final examination. *Psychological Reports, 53,* 343–346.

Theroux, P. (1991, April 21). An Edwardian on the Concorde: Graham Greene as I knew him. *The New York Times Book Review,* p. 3.

Thompson, E. H., Grisanti, C., & Pleck, J. H. (1987). Attitudes toward the male role and their correlates. *Sex Roles, 13,* 413–427.

Thompson-Pope, S. K., & Turkat, I. D. (1988). Reactions to ambiguous stimuli among paranoid personalities. *Journal of Psychopathology and Behavioral Assessment, 10,* 21–32.

Thoren, P., Asberg, M., Cronholm, B., Lennart, J., & Traskman, L. (1980). Clomipramine treatment of obsessive–compulsive disorder: I. A controlled clinical trial. *Archives of General Psychiatry, 37,* 1289–1294.

Thorneloe, W. F., & Crews, E. L. (1981). Manic depressive illness concomitant with antisocial personality disorder: Six case reports and review of the literature. *Journal of Clinical Psychiatry, 42,* 5–9.

Tick, E. (1987). Creativity and loneliness. *Psychotherapy Patient, 4,* 131–137.

Tobacyk, J. J., & Downs, A. (1986). Personal construct threat and irrational beliefs as cognitive predictors of increases in musical performance anxiety. *Journal of Personality and Social Psychology, 51,* 779–782.

Topf, M. (1989). Personality hardiness, occupational stress, and burnout in critical care nurses. *Research in Nursing and Health, 12*, 179–186.

Tout, L. R., & Shama, D. D. (1990). A burnout instrument for hospice. *Hospice Journal, 6*, 31–38.

Tracy, L., & Johnson, T. W. (1981). What do the role conflict and role ambiguity scales measure? *Journal of Applied Psychology, 66*, 464–469.

Tresemer, D. (1976). Do women fear success? *Signs, 1*, 863–874

Trillin, C. (1993). *Remembering Denny*. New York: Farrar, Straus & Giroux.

Trull, T. J., Widiger, T. A., & Frances, A. (1987). Covariation of criteria sets for avoidant, schizoid, and dependent personality disorders. *American Journal of Psychiatry, 144*, 767–771.

Turkat, I. D., & Banks, D. S. (1987). Paranoid personality and its disorder. *Journal of Psychopathology and Behavioral Assessment, 9*, 295–304.

Turkat, I. D., Keane, S. P., & Thompson-Pope, S. K. (1990). Social processing errors among paranoid personalities. *Journal of Psychopathology and Behavioral Assessment, 12*, 263–269.

Turner, S. M., Beidel, D. C., Borden, J. W., Stanley, M. A., & Jacob, R. G. (1991). Social phobia: Axis I and II correlates. *Journal of Abnormal Psychology, 100*, 102–106.

Turner, S. M., Beidel, D. C., Dancu, C. V., & Keys, D. J. (1986). Psychopathology of social phobia and comparison to avoidant personality disorder. *Journal of Abnormal Psychology, 95*, 389–394.

Ulrich, D. N., & Dunne, H. P., Jr. (1986). *To love and work: A systematic interlocking of family, workplace, and career*. New York: Brunner/Mazel.

Ursprung, A. W. (1986). Burnout in the human services: A review of the literature. *Rehabilitation Counseling Bulletin, 29*, 190–199.

Vaillant, G. E. (1984). A debate on *DSM-III*: The disadvantages of DSM-III outweigh its advantages. *American Journal of Psychiatry, 141*, 542–545.

Vaillant, G. E., & Vaillant, C. O. (1982). Natural history of male psychological health: X. Work as a predictor of positive mental health. *Annual Progress and Child Psychiatry and Child Development*, 602–619.

Vaitenas, R., & Wiener, Y. (1977). Developmental, emotional, and interest factors in voluntary mid-career change. *Journal of Vocational Behavior, 11*, 291–304.

Van der Kolk, B. A. (1986). Uses of lithium in patients without major affective illness. *Hospital and Community Psychiatry, 37*, 675, 684.

Van Egeren, L. F. (1991). A "success trap" theory of Type A behavior: Historical background. In M. J. Strube (Ed.), *Type A behavior* (pp. 45–58). Newbury Park, CA: Sage.

Vanvaria, K., Agrawal, R., & Singh, S. (1981). Some characteristics of fantasy-based measure of fear of success among males and females. *Indian Journal of Clinical Psychology, 8*, 95–100.

Vaughan, M. (1976). The relationships between obsessional personality obsessions in depression and symptoms of depression. *British Journal of Psychiatry, 129*, 36–39.

Vealey, R. S. (1990). Advancements in competitive anxiety research: Use of the Sport Competition Anxiety Test and the Competitive State Anxiety Inventory–2. *Anxiety Research, 2,* 243–261.

Victor, G. (1987). Basic compulsivity and human nature. *Journal of Human Behavior and Learning, 4,* 33–42.

Virkkunen, M., & Luukkonen, P. (1977). WAIS performances in antisocial personality (disorder). *Acta Psychiatrica Scandinavica, 55,* 220–224.

Vollmer, F., & Almas, R. (1974). Sex differences in achievement motivation. *Scandinavian Journal of Psychology, 15,* 310–313.

Vollmer, F., & Kaufmann, G. (1975). Achievement motivation and problem solving. *Scandinavian Journal of Psychology, 16,* 323–326.

von der Lippe, A., & Torgersen, S. (1984). Character and defense: Relationships between oral, obsessive and hysterical character traits and defense mechanisms. *Scandinavian Journal of Psychology, 25,* 258–264.

Wallace, J. E., & Brinkeroff, M. B. (1991). The measurement of burnout revisited. *Journal of Social Service Research, 14,* 85–111.

Wallace, P. A., Roberg, R. R., & Allen, H. E. (1985). Job burnout among narcotics investigators: An exploratory study. *Journal of Criminal Justice, 13,* 549–559.

Walsh, J. (1990). Assessment and treatment of the schizotypal personality disorder. *Journal of Independent Social Work, 4,* 41–59.

Wang, T. H., & Creedon, C. F. (1989). Sex role orientations, attributions for achievement, and personal goals of Chinese youth. *Sex Roles, 20,* 473–486.

Ward, C. (1978). Is there a motive to avoid success in women? *Human Relations, 31,* 1055–1067.

Warr, P. (1987). *Work, unemployment, & mental health.* London: Oxford University Press.

Warr, P. (1990). The measurement of well-being and other aspects of mental health. *Journal of Occupational Psychology, 63,* 193–210.

Warr, P. (1992). Age and occupational well-being. *Psychology and Aging, 7,* 37–45.

Warring, D. F. (1991). Attributions and the implications of strategy in the attribution model. *Journal of Instructional Psychology, 18,* 179–186.

Wasylenki, D. A. (1984). Psychodynamic aspects of occupational stress. *Canadian Journal of Psychiatry, 29,* 295–301.

Watkins, C. E. (1983). Combatting student burnout: A structured group approach. *Journal for Specialists in Group Work, 8,* 218–225.

Watson, G., & Glaser, M. (1980). *Watson–Glaser Critical Thinking Appraisal: Manual.* San Antonio, TX: Psychological Corporation.

Watson, P. J., Taylor, D., & Morris, R. J. (1987). Narcissism, sex roles, and self-functioning. *Sex Roles, 16,* 335–350.

Weber, B. (1993, January 4). An actor's quest: From audition to audition to . . . *New York Times,* pp. B1, B3.

Wechsler, D. (1981). *WAIS-R manual.* San Antonio, TX: Psychological Corporation.

Weeda, M., Winny, L., & Drop, M. J. (1985). The discriminative value of psychological characteristics in anorexia nervosa: Clinical and psychometric comparison between anorexia nervosa patients, ballet dancers and controls. *Journal of Psychiatric Research, 19,* 285–290.

Weerts, T. C., & Lang, P. C. (1978). Psychophysiology of fear imagery: Differences between focal phobia and social performance anxiety. *Journal of Consulting and Clinical Psychology, 46,* 1157–1159.

Weinberg, R. S. (1990). Anxiety and motor performance: Where to from here? *Anxiety Research, 2,* 227–242.

Weiner, B. (1982). An attribution theory of motivation and emotion. In H. W. Krohne & L. Laux (Eds.), *Achievement, stress, and anxiety* (pp. 223–245). New York: McGraw-Hill.

Weinreich-Haste, H. (1978). Sex differences in fear of success among British students. *British Journal of Social and Clinical Psychology, 17,* 37–42.

Weiss, R. S. (1990). *Staying the course: The emotional and social lives of men who do well at work.* New York: Free Press.

Weissman, M. M., Leaf, P. J., Tischler, G. L., Blazer, D. G., Karno, M., Bruce, M. L., & Florio, L. P. (1988). Affective disorders in five United States communities. *Psychological Medicine, 18,* 141–153.

Wells, M. C., Glickauf-Hughes, C., & Buzzell, V. (1990). Treating obsessive-compulsive personalities in psychodynamic/interpersonal group therapy. *Psychotherapy, 27,* 366–379.

Wesner, R. B., Noyes, R., & Davis, T. L. (1990). The occurrence of performance anxiety among musicians. *Journal of Affective Disorders, 18,* 177–185.

Wesp, R. (1986). Reducing procrastination through required course involvement. *Teaching of Psychology, 13,* 128–130.

White, D. J. (1988). Taming the critic: The use of imagery with clients who procrastinate. *Journal of Mental Imagery, 12,* 125–133.

White, J. W., Lawrence, P. S., Biggerstaff, C., & Grubb, T. D. (1985). Factors of stress among police officers. *Criminal Justice and Behavior, 12,* 111–128.

Whitehead, J. T. (1986). Job burnout and job satisfaction among probation managers. *Journal of Criminal Justice, 14,* 25–35.

Widiger, T. A., Frances, A., Warner, L., & Bluhm, C. (1986). Diagnostic criteria for the borderline and schizotypal personality disorders. *Journal of Abnormal Psychology, 95,* 43–51.

Widiger, T. A., Freiman, K., & Bailey, B. (1990). Convergent and discriminant validity of personality disorder prototypic acts. *Psychological Assessment, 2,* 107–113.

Widiger, T. A., & Shea, T. (1991). Differentiation of Axis I and Axis II disorders. *Journal of Abnormal Psychology, 100,* 399–406,

Widiger, T. A., & Trull, T. J. (1991). Diagnosis and clinical utility. *Annual Review of Psychology, 42,* 109–133.

Wilke, H. J. (1977). The authority complex and the authoritarian personality. *Journal of Analytical Psychology, 22,* 243–249.

Williams, R. B., Jr. (1989). Psychological factors in coronary artery disease: Epidemiologic evidence. In L. L. Carstensen & J. M. Neale (Eds.), *Mech-*

anisms of psychological influence on physical health: With special attention to the elderly (pp. 145–159). New York: Plenum Press.

Williams, R. B., Jr., & Anderson, N. B. (1987). Hostility and coronary heart disease. In J. W. Elias & P. H. Marshall (Eds.), *Cardiovascular disease and behavior* (pp. 17–37). Washington, DC: Hemisphere.

Williams, R. B., Jr., & Barefoot, J. C. (1988). Coronary-prone behavior: The emerging role of the hostility complex. In B. K. Houston & C. R. Snyder (Eds.), *Type A behavior pattern: Research, theory, and intervention* (pp. 189–211). New York: Wiley.

Williams, S. L., & Zane, G. (1989). Guided mastery and stimulus exposure treatments for severe performance anxiety in agoraphobics. *Behaviour Research and Therapy, 27,* 237–245.

Wilson, A. (1989). Levels of adaptation and narcissistic psychopathology. *Psychiatry, 52,* 218–236.

Wilson, D., & Mutero, C. (1989). Personality concomitants of teacher stress in Zimbabwe. *Personality and Individual Differences, 10,* 1195–1198.

Wine, J. D. (1982). Evaluation anxiety: A cognitive–attentional construct. In H. W. Krohne & L. Laux (Eds.), *Achievement, stress, and anxiety* (pp. 207–219). New York: McGraw-Hill.

Wink, P., & Gough, H. G. (1990). New narcissism scales for the California Psychological Inventory and MMPI. *Journal of Personality Assessment, 54,* 446–462.

Winnubst, J. A. M. (1985). Type A behavior patterns and the anal-obsessive time attitude. In W. D. Gentry, H. Benson, & C. J. deWolff (Eds.), *Behavioral medicine: Works, stress, and health* (pp. 141–156). Dordecht, The Netherlands: Nijhoff.

Wixen, B. N. (1973). *Children of the rich.* New York: Crown.

Wolf, E. S., & Wolf, I. (1979). We perished, each alone: A psychoanalytic commentary on Virginia Woolf's *To The Lighthouse. International Review of Psycho-Analysis, 6,* 37–47.

Wolfe, T. (1929). *Look homeward, angel: A story of the buried life.* New York: Modern Library.

Wolpin, J., Burke, R. J., & Greenglass, E. R. (1991). Is job satisfaction an antecedent or a consequence of psychology burnout? *Human Relations, 44,* 193–209.

Wood, M. M., & Greenfeld, S. (1979). Fear of success in high achieving male and female managers in private industry vs. the public sector. *Journal of Psychology, 103,* 289–297.

Woodham, R. L. (1987). A self-psychological consideration in cocaine addiction. *Alcoholism Treatment Quarterly, 4,* 41–46.

Woods, P. J. (1987). Reductions in Type A behavior, anxiety, anger, and physical illness as related to changes in irrational beliefs: Results of a demonstration project in industry. *Journal of Rational Emotive Therapy, 5,* 213–237.

Workers' compensation: Mental impairments. (1986). *Mental and Physical Disability Law Reporter, 10,* 375–376.

Wright, F. (1987). Men, shame and antisocial behavior: A psychodynamic perspective. *Group, 11*, 238–246.

Wright, F., O'Leary, J., & Balkin, J. (1989). Shame, guilt, narcissism, and depression: Correlates and sex differences. *Psychoanalytic Psychology, 6*, 217–230.

Wulach, J. S. (1983). Diagnosing the DSM-III antisocial personality disorder. *Professional Psychology: Research and Practice, 14*, 330–340.

Yamauchi, H. (1982). Sex differences in motive to avoid success on competitive or cooperative action. *Psychological Reports, 50*, 55–61.

Yarnold, P. R., Mueser, K. T., & Lyons, J. S. (1988). Type A behavior, accountability, and work rate in small groups. *Journal of Research in Personality, 22*, 353–360.

Yates, W. R., Petty, F., & Brown, K. (1988). Alcoholism in males with antisocial personality disorder. *International Journal of the Addictions, 23*, 999–1010.

Yates, W. R., Sieleni, B., Reich, J., & Brass, C. (1989). Comorbidity of bulimia nervosa and personality disorder. *Journal of Clinical Psychiatry, 50*, 57–59.

Yoder, L. (1987). Modifying the Type A behavior pattern. *Journal of Religion and Health, 26*, 57–72.

Yogev, S. (1983). Judging the professional woman: Changing research, changing values. *Psychology of Women Quarterly 7*, 219–234.

Yuen, L. M., & Depper, D. S. (1987). Fear of failure in women. *Women and Therapy, 6*, 21–39.

Yuen, S. A., & Kuiper, N. A. (1991). Cognitive and affective components of the Type A hostility dimension. *Personality and Individual Differences, 12*, 173–182.

Zappert, L. T., & Weinstein, H. N. (1985). Sex differences in the impact of work on physical and psychological health. *American Journal of Psychiatry, 142*, 1174–1178.

Zastrow, C. (1984). Understanding and preventing burn-out. *British Journal of Social Work, 14*, 141–155.

Zedeck, S. (1992). *Work, families, and organizations.* San Francisco: Jossey-Bass.

Zedeck, S., Maslach, C., Mosier, K., & Skitka, L. (1988). Affective response to work and quality of family life: Employee and spouse perspectives. *Journal of Social Behavior and Personality, 3*, 135–157.

Ziestat, H. A., Rosenthal, T. L., & White, G. M. (1978). Behavioral self-control in treating procrastination. *Psychological Reports, 42*, 59–69.

Zuckerman, M., & Allison, S. N. (1976). An objective measure of fear of success: Construction and validation. *Journal of Personality Assessment, 40*, 422–430.

Zuckerman, M., Larrance, D. T., Porac, J. F. A., & Blanck, P. D. (1980). Effects of fear of success on intrinsic motivation, causal attribution, and choice behavior. *Journal of Personality and Social Psychology, 39*, 503–513.

Zuckerman, M., & Wheeler, L. (1975). To dispel fantasies about the fantasy-based measure of fear of success. *Psychological Bulletin, 82*, 932–946.

Index

Ability
  achievement and, 73
  overcommitment patterns and, 110
  performance anxiety and, 150–151, 157
  Type A behavior and, 120
Ability testing
  achievement patterns and, 73
  career choice and, 236
Absenteeism, 129–130
Accomplishment
  burnout and, 124–125
  narcissistic personality disorder and, 203, 205
  paranoid personality and, 207
  See also Achievement
Acedia, 166. *See also* Depression
Achievement
  academic, 89
  anxiety and, 144–146
  borderline personality disorders and, 200
  conflict and, 65, 72
  fear of success and, 77
  motivation and, 104–105
  personality factors and, 71–72
  procrastination and, 84, 89
  underachievement treatment and, 104
  undercommitment patterns and, 71–72, 74
Achievement-oriented behavior, 71–72
Achievement patterns, 71–72, 73
Ackerley, G. D., 128
Adjustment disorder with work, 39 n.2

Adjustment reaction with depressed mood, 162
Adolescents
  Type A behavior and, 117
  work role and, 16–17
Adrenaline levels, overachievement and, 71
Affective disorders
  antisocial personality disorder and, 196
  creative individuals and, 220
  creativity and, 223
Age
  achievement patterns and, 73
  anxiety and, 144
  burnout and, 125
  depression and, 162, 167 n.4
Akerstedt, T., 166
Alcohol abuse, 221. *See also* Substance abuse
Alfredsson, L., 166
Alienation, 136
Allen, H. E., 128
Anger
  overcommitment patterns and, 136, 138, 140–141
  personality disorders and, 197, 200, 202
  procrastination and, 91–92, 97
  undercommitment patterns and, 66
Antidepressant medication, 191
Antisocial personality disorder, 178 n.2, 194–199
Anxiety, 144–161
  burnout and, 127
  case studies of, 158–161

About the Author

Rodney L. Lowman is founder and CEO of The Development Laboratories, Houston, Texas, which offers psychological assessment and counseling on career, work, and mental health issues. He is an adjunct professor of psychology at Rice University and also has served on the faculties of Duke University Medical Center's occupational medicine and medical psychology divisions and the faculties of other major universities. Lowman has written widely on mental health in the workplace and occupational and career issues and serves as a consultant to national media. He has served on the American Psychological Association's Ethics Committee, on the Committee on Psychological Tests and Assessments, and as chair of the Board of Professional Affairs. He has also held the office of president of the Society of Psychologists in Management.